Colección Támesis

SERIE A: MONOGRAFÍAS, 384

LIMINALITY IN CUBA'S TWENTIETH-CENTURY IDENTITY

STEPHEN M. FAY

LIMINALITY IN CUBA'S
TWENTIETH-CENTURY IDENTITY

RITES OF PASSAGE AND REVOLUTIONS

TAMESIS

First published 2019
Tamesis, Woodbridge

ISBN 978 1 85566 334 3

Tamesis is an imprint of Boydell & Brewer Ltd
PO Box 9, Woodbridge, Suffolk IP12 3DF, UK
and of Boydell & Brewer Inc.
668 Mt. Hope Avenue, Rochester, NY 14620-2731, USA
website: www.boydellandbrewer.com

The publisher has no responsibility for the continued existence or accuracy of
URLs for external or third-party internet websites referred to in this book, and
does not guarantee that any content on such websites is, or will remain, accurate
or appropriate

A CIP record for this title is available
from the British Library

This publication is printed on acid-free paper

Contents

Acknowledgements

Primary thanks go to Antoni Kapcia and Mark Millington. Even before I met Tony, his landmark books on Cuba had guided me in my initial explorations of the island's identity and culture. From our first meeting in 2008, when I took a half-baked research idea up to him in Nottingham, Tony always offered the perfect combination of encouragement and *exigencia*. The former restored energies and instilled confidence; the latter was never far behind and helped improve this book no end. Mark's reading of my research was steadfastly insightful: while helping me towards greater clarity in my writing, he also often revealed the enormous investigative potential of what I had left unwritten. I am very grateful to both.

I had the rare good fortune of attending the regular postgraduate Cuban seminar series, tirelessly organised by Tony at the University of Nottingham, and I thank Chris Hull, Christabelle Peters, Luis Pérez, Fabienne Viala, Anna Clayfield and Rosie Smith for making those *ciclones cerebrales* so stirring, and so much fun. Particular thanks go to my pal Jorge Catalá whose animation and integrity I have always admired and sought to emulate.

I light a devoted candle to Jerome, the patron saint of librarians and archivists. Without the forbearance and good humour of the staff at the Centro de Estudios Martianos, at the Archivo Nacional de Cuba and at the Instituto de Literatura y Lingüística in Havana (who satisfied my every unreasonable request for books, documents and obscure trails of paper), my research would simply have been impossible. I also thank José Carlos Vázquez López and the staff at the Facultad de Historia of the Universidad de La Habana who hosted me and pointed me in the right direction during my research trips. I sincerely thank Nancy Martínez at the University's Departamento de Relaciones Internacionales who bravely fought for a way through the bureaucratic labyrinth in which my fieldwork was almost lost.

I will always be grateful to my neighbours and friends in Cuba, Guillermo, Tony and Barbarita, Maily and Ariel, Mónica and Tomás, who breathed life into bibliographic exploration and taught me the *historias* the libraries hadn't even heard of.

I was very fortunate to receive the support of the Arts and Humanities Research Council for my work in Havana and in the UK. I sincerely thank Goodenough College in London, an inimitable home that sheltered my family whilst we raised a son, wrote a couple of theses, and made friends for a lifetime. I'd particularly like to thank Yuval, Laura, Edward, Vicki and Jason for our scholarly brainstormers in the Goodenough basement. I'd also like to pay homage to the Mecklenburgh Square garden which kept my ethereal academic feet rooted in one of the most beautiful patches of London clay.

I would like to thank my mum, dad and *suegra*. My parents set me on the path towards this book when they put me on the school bus all those years ago, and I hope they think that the miles and the years have been fruitfully spent. My *suegra* has been the maternal and grandmaternal rock upon which we have built several homes and all their endeavours on both sides of the Atlantic. I'd like to thank my brother Andrew and his family for generous and cherished escapes from the city and its cloistered thoughts, and my sister Rebecca for being consistently close and unwaveringly in touch.

I thank Marisol, Joseph and Antonio, *sin más*.

Introduction

On a street corner in Old Havana, two women stand talking against the white wall. Above their heads is a slogan. It's as well known to them as to everyone else on the island; they've heard it at work, and at school, and in marches on the most notable days of the patriotic calendar; they hear it most days on the radio, read it in the newspaper, see it on billboards and walls everywhere:

¡Hasta la victoria siempre!

Underneath the slogan, the women go on chatting:

'¿Y tú cómo etá, mi'jita?', says one.[1]
'Aquí mami, en la luchita', replies the other with a shrug.

In a (somewhat simplistic) sense, these phrases spotted and overheard on a Havana street corner synthesise the different (and often antagonistic) approaches to Cuban national identity in the twentieth century that will be traced in this study. Up on the wall, the slogan exhorts the retort *¡Venceremos!* and so accomplishes a collective sense and sensibility that is supremely self-assured, wholly confident of Cuba's manifest *destino* (as both future fate and next destination), teleological in tenor and intent. The slogan points to and rushes towards a proximate victory in which all setbacks will have been left behind, trials overcome, failures forgotten, enemies overthrown; it looks toward a perfect future in which destiny will become reality and *venceremos* will make way for the future perfect *habremos vencido*. This teleological reading of the past and the present as precursors, as sites of necessary but temporary struggles towards future peace, as the beginnings and middles to the story's inevitably happy ending, is at the epistemological epicentre of

---

[1] Spoken Spanish in Cuba can have a number of phonetic peculiarities: loss of intermediate and final s (as in *etá* for *estás*), universal use of *b* for 'v' and 'b' sounds, assimilation of 'r' into following consonant and duplication of this, compression of vowel sounds in adjacent words (as in *mi'jita* for *mi hijita*), etc.

some of the perceptions and projections of Cuban national identity that will be examined here.

The *luchita* of the two friends also speaks of struggle, but with little teleological inflection. In their mouths, the perfect future is swapped for an undecided, uncomfortable and pugnacious present. In that shrug, the future perfect becomes a speculative, even subjunctive, present tense where the mood is of 'maybe', setbacks are here to stay, and future victory is only a tenuous *quizás*. Nevertheless, this uncertainty has not extinguished all optimism: there remains an oblique, even playful resilience where fortitude comes not from rising heroically to life's challenges, but from undermining their gravity, where the *lucha* is brought down a peg to a mere *luchita*, ineluctable and potentially painful, but not the end of the world after all. This ambivalent, ludic and inconclusive ethos is at the heart of the other approaches to Cuban collective identity that shall be explored here.

This book will trace the ideological confrontation between *venceremos* and *luchita* across a broad bibliography of political, literary, journalistic, propagandistic and even lexicographic texts within and between two critical periods in Cuba's twentieth century: 1923–33 and 1953–65. Whilst acknowledging that debates around collective identity were prevalent throughout Cuba's first century as an independent country,[2] this book will dwell on particular moments when historical, social and cultural circumstance made these reflections particularly acute; on years in which Cuba seemed to reach what could be described as historical turning points. Some of these turning points are undisputed (and have been extensively explored): 1933, when brutal President Gerardo Machado was finally overthrown; or 1959, when the ragged rebel army led by Fidel Castro drove the dictator of the day, Fulgencio Batista, into exile. Others are less obvious (and will be exposed to cultural studies scrutiny for the first time here): 1927, when the antagonism between the vanguard and the old guard reached a particularly virulent peak; 1957, when collective faith in future victory seemed about to fade altogether; 1965, when the Revolutionary[3] government took structural steps to assert ideological unity in the new Cuba. At all turning points, this study will suggest, the combination of Cuba's relatively recent inauguration as an independent country, the significant, often transcendental, events taking place at those times and the intense public attention consistently focused on the question of collective identity, all come together to suggest a new and insightful mode of analysis: the book will

2   Spanish colonialism on the island came to an end in 1898, but four years of US military occupation followed before the Cuban Republic was declared on 20 May 1902.

3   The capital R is used here as a shorthand method of indicating the transformation of 'revolution', as an episode or phase, into *Revolución* as a socio-civic and ideological state of being.

explore national identity debates in these periods as part of a post-colonial 'rite of passage'. Deploying conceptual methods suggested by anthropology, we will trace this rite of passage as a socio-cultural process marked by an initial 'separation' from established structures, followed by a middle, or liminal, phase in which identity is recalibrated, and a consummating phase of re-entry into social structures, or what Arnold van Gennep called 'incorporation' (1965: 210) and Victor Turner called 'reaggregation' (1974: 232).[4] This book seeks to show that during seven twentieth-century turning points, which led up to and then moved on from the revolutions of 1933 and 1959, the key socio-cultural, psychological and discursive characteristics of the rite of passage were evident in Cuba and in the public debate that took place about the island's history, its sense of ideal (even idealised) citizenship and its attitudes towards the particular destiny envisaged for the young Republic. Evidence will be presented, therefore, to demonstrate that during all turning points, collective dissatisfaction with the established social structures (and the ethos they had engendered) led to moments of critical introspection in which, as Turner would say, 'the cognitive schemata that give sense to everyday life no longer apply, but are, as it were, suspended' (1982: 84). From within this conceptual construct, the most intense debate around national identity will be shown to take place in Cuba's own twentieth-century 'limens'.

Here, as in the anthropological studies of van Gennep and Turner (and of others), the limen can be a spatial threshold cut off from the core,[5] or more spatially integrated but ethically peripheral, sites.[6] But the limen can also be a metaphysical turning point, both in terms of separation from the normal spheres, routines and schemata of everyday life, and in terms of eliding normal chronological order and entering a 'time that is not a time' (Turner 1974: 239). In this sense, the limen is an extraordinary self-reflective hiatus within which identity 'becomes ambiguous, neither here nor there, betwixt and between all fixed points of classification' (Turner 1974: 232). The limen is also a potentially cathartic margin where past debilities and fallibilities can be addressed as the 'neophytes' make their way towards social reintegration.

---

4   If van Gennep established the fundamental conceptual coordinates of liminality, Turner charted its full socio-cultural topography in essays and books such as 'Three Symbols of Passage in Ndembu Circumcision Ritual: An Interpretation' (1962), *The Ritual Process: Structure and Anti-Structure* (1969), *The Forest of Symbols: Aspects of Ndembu Ritual* (1970), *Dramas, Fields and Metaphors: Symbolic Action in Human Society* (1974), *From Ritual to Theatre: The Human Seriousness of Play* (1982). We will return to Turner's understanding of liminality often.

5   Such as the specially cleared sites on the edge of the Ndembu villages in southern Zambia, the subject of Turner's first fieldwork ('Three Symbols of Passage in Ndembu Circumcision Ritual: An Interpretation').

6   Such as monasteries, prisons or even airports (see Turner, in Alexander 1991).

And so in this study the *venceremos* or *luchita* approaches to Cuban national identity become competing ideologies in the island's liminal phases of intense collective introspection. Whilst recognising, therefore, that the Cuban thinkers who populate this analysis didn't express themselves in terms directly drawn from the writings of anthropologists such as Turner or van Gennep (although words and phrases such as 'umbral', 'margen', 'entre dos aguas', 'estar en la cerca' and other such liminal lexis will be heard throughout), the limen and liminality are used here as an illuminating shorthand for a wide range of discursive dichotomies around understandings of the relationship between past, present and future, about teleological momentum as a social ideal (or a social ill), around notions of psycho-social 'purity' and around notions of selfhood and otherness, as we shall see.

This is not the first cultural hermeneutics to make use of the investigative potential of the rite of passage and its pivotal limen. Hence, whereas van Gennep was convinced of the tripartite structure of this rite and insisted that 'one should always remember that the threshold is only part of the door and that most of these rites should be understood as direct and physical rites of entrance, of waiting, and of departure' (1965: 25), literary scholars have challenged this inevitability and have suggested that the liminal 'phase' can actually become a permanent 'state'. Reading texts they see as on the borders between literature and folklore, for example, Aguirre, Quance and Sutton question the equation of transitional and temporary, suggesting instead that

> It is part of the nature of the liminal that it be 'transitional' without being unstable or provisional. If it lacks order, this does not mean that it is merely chaotic [...]; if it is in constant flux, this only means that flux is in the nature of the liminal (2000: 68).

In this, these authors actually draw alongside the later writings of Turner. Although his earlier and African fieldwork-based work certainly pointed to the implacable momentum of the rites he recorded, one of his principal conceptual contributions to understandings of socio-cultural transitions was to accept that liminality could become a perennial state: 'It has become clear to us that liminality is not only transition but also potentiality' (1978: 3). Gustavo Pérez Firmat's 1986 exploration of liminality in Hispanic literature (from José Zorrilla's *Don Juan Tenorio* to Luis Martín-Santos's *Tiempo de silencio*)[7] finds its own theoretical interstice between Turner and van Gennep.

---

7   Pérez Firmat, *Literature and Liminality: Festive Readings in the Hispanic Tradition.*

While supplementing the processual for the positional, Pérez Firmat recovers a certain processual perspective by displacing spatial fixity and suggesting that out-on-a-limb liminality 'consistently threatens to collapse the center-periphery distinction' (xvii). In *The Cuban Condition* (1989) he builds on this notion of unfixity to propose that the 'essence' of identity in the literary works he explores here (from Nicolás Guillén's *Sóngoro cosongo* to Carlos Loveira's *Juan Criollo*) is actually an 'effervescence' governed by what Mayz-Vallenilla describes as the 'no-ser-*siempre*-todavía' complex of Latin American identity (in Pérez Firmat 1989: 25).

This examination of the debates about Cuban national identity during a twentieth-century rite of passage, marked by limens of acute collective intro-spection, follows these analytical antecedents, and then goes further. From one ideological flank, we will meet thinkers who (like Aguirre et al., Pérez Firmat and the later Turner) were unconvinced by teleology, unpersuaded by the possibility (even the desirability) of a psycho-social catharsis, and rather more prepared to linger on an ambivalent, undecided and subjunctive threshold, not as a temporary transition, but as a constant condition. These are the 'liminalists' of this study who see an ongoing *luchita* at the heart of Cuban identity. But we will demonstrate that this was only half the story of Cuban selfhood in the period studied (and beyond). For we will also come across thinkers who (like van Gennep) did indeed interpret the turning points and their inherent introspection as a mere momentary arrest of forward and progressive momentum, as a necessary but necessarily temporary and cathartic exposure to flux that would ensure the durability of future regen-erated order, as a time to examine the collective 'conscience' in order to expunge all 'sin'. For these thinkers, the betwixt-and-between subjectivity of the interstice would eventually make way for the elaboration of a definitive Cuban archetype. These are the committed 'reaggregationists' of this study, the *venceremos* brigade of twentieth-century articulations of Cuban national identity. The space given over to these thinkers is not just in the interests of analytical balance; the inclusion of the reaggregationists is critical in a thorough analysis of the identity debate in Cuba because it was they who would assail the hermeneutic high ground after the Revolutionary victory of 1959, as we shall also see.

Given the epicentrality of the limen to this new reading of the debate, it will be explored in its every manifestation: as both phase and/or state, but also as place and psycho-geographic space. In this latter application, liminality corresponds closely to an important spatial trope of Cuban identity: insularity. In communication with critics such as Antonio Benítez Rojo, for whom the coastline of Cuba became the crucible of 'lo criollo' and the island's 'cultura supersincrética' in the eighteenth century (1989: 71), but also in dialogue with those who rather see the coast as a perfidious edge that diluted Cuba's telluric essence with offshore cultural imports, this study will shed new light on debates on Cuba's insular or 'archipelagic' identity.

As suggested by Pérez Firmat, Benítez-Rojo and others, the spatial margin will be shown here to be mobile, to be able to move in from the margins to colonise the core. This mobility will be explored both as an innnervating loosening of core structures, but also, and perhaps principally, as something much less positive: as a liminal flexibility that becomes the total dissolution of all structures and a descent in chaos. In this, we will move away from Benítez-Rojo and others to join Paul Giles, who takes both Turner and other liminal scholars to task for their idealisation of the limen, seeking rather to 'demythologize' liminality and 'restore to the term some of its surreptitiously aberrant quality' (2000: 43). In this sense, we will here seek to 'disorder' what Turner called the 'dérèglement ordonnée [sic] de tous les sens' he saw as typical of the limen (1974: 264); we will turn from merely possible perversions to face the aberrant limen full on, and explore turning points as producing pain but no catharsis and placing Cuban society on a permanently perilous ethical edge. Thus, the concept of liminality will be used here to encapsulate some of the most important (and most fiercely contested) tropes within collective identity debates during momentous turning points of the Republican and early Revolutionary years; the limens therein will be charted to enable us to offer radically new readings of the twentieth-century Cuban national narrative.

The terms 'collective identity' and 'national narrative' are clearly at the heart of this analysis and so call for some initial introduction (even justification). The assertion that a heterogeneous and multi-million-strong group of people can 'identify' with each other in any meaningful and communicable way has as many naysayers as advocates. Given this study's geographic focus on Cuba and temporal focus on a period from the 1920s to the 1960s, however, these debates are informative, but not instrumental. In Cuba at that time argument clearly raged around the sense and sensibililty of ideal collective identity, but very few thinkers questioned the validity, currency and immanence of the concept itself. In fact, from the first flickers of impetus towards independence, reflection on the contours of collective identity has constituted one of Cuba's most durable national pastimes – what Antoni Kapcia calls a 'constant, evolving and almost obsessive theme' (2005: 5). This evolution, and these obsessions, are the principal objects of study here, but initial mention of some particularly Cuban contributions to the overarching discussion on identity may be useful at this stage.

The sense of national identity as a social covenant towards collective cohesion and willing submission to certain structures and rules, or what Cicero called *civitas*,[8] was expressed in the early twentieth-century Cuban context as what Fernando Ortiz called *cubanidad* or Cubanness: 'la condición genérica de cubano' (1940b: 172).[9] Both *cubanidad* and its distant Roman cousin *civitas* have interpretative merit for this study. For Cicero, the common bond that brought the people (or *civis*) together was the law, its consensual sway ensured citizens saw civic obedience in their own best interests and collective cohesion as fortifying rather than stultifying. Common understandings of civic structures and strictures and a common goal of consensual social harmony will be seen as both fundamental, and fundamentally challenged, in all the turning points studied here. Perhaps more suggestively still, in this analysis a slight etymological twist turns Cicero's law, or *lex*, into lexis. In other words, the vital organ of the Cuban *civis* is not law at all but shared story, and collective identity becomes truly immanent when written up in a common narrative (and we will return to the credibility of the relationship between and experience and text shortly).

Ortiz actually brought up the term *cubanidad* only to knock it immediately back down again, only wrote of the Cuban 'manera de ser' as a rather lifeless foil to his more vital 'cubanía', or 'cubanidad plena, sentida, consciente y deseada; cubanidad responsable, cubanidad con las tres virtudes, dichas teologales, de fe, esperanza y amor' (1940b: 172). Ortiz's articulation of national identity as *cubanía* would be unavoidable here, even if he wasn't one of the prime 'protagonists' of this study, because it points to the profound emotional commitment to collective cohesion, alongside the more pragmatic aspects of socio-civic participation. In this sense, it charges collective identity with psycho-social power, makes it a potent meta-myth that elicits a devotional as well as a democratic response, makes it something to believe in (and obsess about) even when its outlines are blurred. *Cubanía* also has the great merit of being a Cuban (to wit, an Ortizian) invention.[10] In this it is a primary example of the kind of neologistic liberty that the nascent nation allowed itself to describe itself, and hence transports us to the core of debates around the civic structures of *lex* versus the creative flexibility of lexis, to insular idiosyncrasies versus more mainland conformity, to orthodoxy versus heterodoxy within the national narrative. *Cubanía* also has great currency here because of its widespread use by many of the critics with which this book

---

8   A term originally coined by Cicero (106–43 BC) to describe the equilibrium between civic rights and responsibilities at the heart of the late Roman Republic. These rights were guaranteed both by law, and by common consent (or *concilium*). See Cowell's introduction to *Cicero and the Roman Republic* (1973).

9   In his essay 'Los factores humanos de la cubanidad', originally delivered as a lecture at the University of Havana in 1939.

10   Ortiz took his neologistic lead from Miguel de Unamuno's coining of the term *hombría*.

opens dialogue.[11] As has already been indicated, an important interlocutor amongst these is Gustavo Pérez Firmat, who seems to delight in lexical flair as much as Ortiz did. To *cubanía*, Pérez Firmat brings 'the Cuban condition', which has descriptive force for this study because of its echo with one of the principal rite-of-passage discourses already mentioned: the representation of Cubanness as either frail or hale, as sickly and needing a radical remedy, or as fundamentally well despite (or perhaps because of) its latent (and perhaps inevitable) malaise.

Alongside these terminological contributions (and preferred as the most apposite expression for this study) is the interpretation of Cuban national identity as 'national sensibility', which Louis Pérez Jr sees as 'a more inclusive and less reified framework in which to explore [...] culturally fashioned responses to life' (2005: 10 & 11). Identity will therefore be explored here as collective *sensibilidad*, and for two reasons. First, the inclu-siveness that Pérez Jr points to resonates with the comprehensiveness of this analysis, that will introduce and interrogate very diverse representations of collective identity from many different authors occupying alternative (often antagonistic) ideological positions, and writing in many distinct genres (from absurdist short stories to newspaper editorials, from political manifestoes to vernacular dictionaries). Second, *sensibilidad* is also adopted as the primary investigative term because of its suggestiveness across both languages of this study, in which it will aid analysis of the 'sensible', practical, and level-headed traits of *cubanidad* and of the *sensibles*, impassioned and very un-level-headed obsessiveness of *cubanía*. In this, the term shuttles between objective distance and subjective proximity in a translational twist and also, and crucially, speaks both to the narrated 'sense' of identity that is at the heart of this analysis, and to the more corporeal, visceral and embodied 'sensibility' of selfhood suggested by the word's far-off but keenly felt roots in *sensus*, *sensitivus* and *sentire*. In short, *sensibilidad* is a term that thinks and feels at the same time and speaks simultaneously of the *lex* of *civitas* and the *corpus* of *cubanía*. And it is to initial consideration of the possibility of encapsulating selfhood in narrative at all, and of being both an objective analyst and a subjective author of Cuban collective identity, that we now turn.

Can identity be articulated through text, and if so, who has the right (the author-ity, one could say) to produce such a collective narrative? For some critics the answer is immediately clear: in the 'grind of text and countertext', some claim that the phenomenological facets of life are crushed, that the

---

[11] Antoni Kapcia, for example, traces the development of different *cubanía* codes on the island (from *cubanía anexionista* to *cubanía rebelde* to *cubanía revolucionaria*) in *Cuba Island of Dreams* (2000).

'indelibly corporeal nature of human being, knowledge, experience and perception' is blithely ignored (Thrift 2008: 121; Wylie 2007: 147). Narrative, from this perspective, is a mere facsimile of real life; text can achieve only a partial (in the senses both of 'incomplete' and of 'partisan') representation of reality. And in terms of the authority of authorship, some critics are equally forthright, with César Graña suggesting that in the Spanish American context from the nineteenth century, intellectuals' contribution to national identity debates was in fact a 'self-legitimating device' through which they attempted to crack a code of nationhood that they themselves had invented in order to hold on to 'an otherwise untenable position as mediators between the state and the masses' (in Miller 1999: 2). In the terms proposed by Ángel Rama, these intellectuals are a zealous intellectual elite jealously guarding the gates to the *ciudad letrada* (the title of Rama's seminal text) against intrusion by any who could menace their predominance, whether this was the illiterate indigenous people of the colonial period (who were not subjugated by the sword, Rama suggests, but by potent bureaucratic pens that brought their own version of reality into existence in impenetrable edicts which only 'enlightened' administrators in colonial courts on both sides of the Atlantic could decipher, but to which everyone was subjected), or even the *criollo* intelligentsia whose attempts at independent cultural self-expression (until at least the mid-nineteenth century) were partially hamstrung by the metropolitan authority of the 'mother tongue'.[12]

Other critics disagree, and are equally adamant about the epicentral importance of text for the inscription, and the experience, of subjectivity. For these, narratives are not dispassionate lexical artefacts against which to measure the non-narrative universe, but constitutive contributions to the collective psyche and sense of belonging. For Paul Ricouer (one of the high priests of narrative identity), one of the principal products of narrative 'is to allow us to construct a narrative identity – both at the level of history (e.g. the identity of a nation), and at the level of the individual life' (in Wood 1991: 4). For Benedict Anderson, national identity is not an immutable expression of timeless subjectivity, but rather an 'imagined' experience of communion amongst compatriots that transcends isolation, difference and disaggregation. Narrative, for Anderson, lies at the heart of this imagined coherence; nation and national identity are both 'cultural artefects' that can be created, narrated and read in accordance with the prevalent historical and ideological tides of the time (1983: 4). Anderson goes on to examine the national press as a potent evangelist for this 'imagined community', whereby newspapers are at the hub

---

12 See chapters 1–3 of *La ciudad letrada* (1984).

of a ritualised mass ceremony of belonging in which distant but homologous readers across the country simultaneously 'consume' accounts of the most salient events of the national yesterday and are reassured that their imagined world and everyday life are one and the same. Thus, 'fiction seeps quietly and continuously into reality, creating the remarkable confidence of community in anonymity which is the hallmark of modern nations' (ibid.: 36).

This book seeks to deploy the insights of these defenders of narrativised identity and go on to make a particularly Cuban (but also distinctly universal) contribution to the debate. We aim to demonstrate that in the context of a nascent nation's first century, suggestions that text suffers from an irremediable two-dimensionality that distances it from daily life are misplaced. We will show that the Cuban thinkers whose *letras* will be examined here did not retreat behind the exclusive walls of an elitist lettered city, nor ensconce themselves in self-defensive ivory towers, but rather eroded all walls between their object of study and their own intimate and subjective experience of it. The case for the immanence of Cuban national narratives will be built gradually as we go along, of course, but it might be useful to make some initial statements here. In the first instance, the cultural studies disciplinary foundations underlying this analysis allow for a bibliographic breadth that other more exclusively literary studies rarely reach. Thus, while some of the contributions to the national narrative studied here are conspicuously literary and even self-consciously distant from the real world (Virgilio Piñera's stories are notoriously fantastical and only obliquely glance towards Cuban times and spaces[13]), others can hardly be chided for their lack of proximity to the phenomenological complexity of life on the island at the time of their writing. Many of the texts presented here come from 'writers' who were only faintly acquainted with the 'lettered city' as Rama understands it. To Piñera's surreal stories, we add Carlos Montenegro's 1933 prison diaries, Fidel Castro's 1953 self-defence speech before a Santiago court,[14] Faure Chomón's autobiographical account of the 1957 assault on the presidential palace in which thirty-five of his comrades 'embodied' the national narrative of heroic struggle and didn't survive to tell their own tales.

Beyond these obvious activists, even the more bookish intellectuals included here are no bureaucrats keen to wield the power of the exclusive word as a way of subjugating others' subjectivities. Many of the thinkers in

---

[13] Discernible Cuban territory is usually invisible in Piñera's stories and plays: his heroes are Greeks or stateless souls inhabiting washed out landscapes or featureless cells.

[14] On July 26 1953, in the eastern city of Santiago de Cuba, Fidel Castro and more than a hundred comrades tried to topple then President Fulgencio Batista's government by storming the important Moncada barracks. The attack failed, seventy-one rebels were killed, and Castro and most of the other surviving assailants were captured and imprisoned.

this study were inhabitants of the elitist and exclusive *ciudad letrada* in its prime, and of that same *ciudad* as it slid towards decline in the late nineteenth and early twentieth centuries. For Rama this decline was provoked both by external assault (the arrival from the end of the nineteenth century of millions of non-Spanish-speaking migrants fleeing the impoverished Old World for the rapidly industrialising New), and by internal dissent from a new generation of *letrados* whose promotion of public education and popular (even vernacular) literature became the Trojan horses that brought the walls of *ciudades letradas* from Buenos Aires to Havana crumbling precipitously down.[15] So whilst Fernando Ortiz, for example, was a bureaucrat and supposed guardian of the prelapsarian *civitas* of the lettered city (he was a lawyer, university professor and member of the Cuban Senate), he was also a rebellious Trojan *letrado*, an ethnographer and lexicographer who listened to and narrated the sounds of Afro-Cuban culture he saw as the 'corazón de ébano' of Cuban cultural identity (Ortiz 1923d: viii). In our opening chapter, we will explore the very direct contribution Ortiz made to Cuban *letras* in his 1923 dictionary of 'cubanismos' that, far from being a 'self-legitimating device' or tool with which to safeguard his fellow *letrados'* incantatory control over language, was rather a lexicographic battering ram to break down the doors of peninsular Spanish's predominance on the island. Many other Cuban thinkers will be shown to join Ortiz in this democratic, vulgar and vernacular attack on cultural and narrative elitism.

In further potent contrast to Graña's suggestion of intellectuals' elitist self-justification, we will instead come across the kind of personal commitment that makes the *letrados* in this study thoroughly active, both in text and in body. This is the kind of subjectivity, or *embullo*, that Pérez Firmat points to in Ortiz and that leads him to conclude that the ethnographer was 'never a very good scientist' because he simply couldn't keep his distance (1989: 17).[16] The present study takes its lead from Pérez Firmat's analysis to show that many other Cuban intellectuals were actually able to shuttle between objective distance and up-close *embullo*; commented on, and yet were unable to unpick themselves from, the oftentimes tangled fabric of everyday life on the island. In fact, we will suggest that this shuttling is what made them truly perspicacious observers of Cuba's psycho-social phenomena in which, as Lévi-Strauss suggested elsewhere, 'the observer himself is a part of his observation'

---

15 Their vanguard text, Fernández de Lizardi's *El periquillo sarniento*, was published periodically and sporadically between 1816 and 1831 because of harrying from the censors.

16 Pérez Firmat goes on to point out this lack of objectivity heightens, rather than limits, Ortiz's creative contribution to what he calls 'critical criollism' (see chapter 1 of *The Cuban Condition*).

(in Bhabha 2010: 215). To Pérez Firmat's reading of 'Mister Cuba',[17] we add the reflections of a saint. Pondering the conundrum of whether it was actually necessary to confess to a omniscient God, St Augustine of Hippo came to a conclusion which in effect unites the individual and the collective through the medium of text. Instead of merely speaking his confession in private, Augustine wanted to 'do the truth' (*veritatem facere*); but the essence of this activism is actually textual testimony before many witnesses: 'in stilo autem meo coram multis testibus' (in Derrida 1995: 39). In this, the textual enactment of individual experience transforms unique subjectivity into collective identity, written confession makes intimate experience communal, soliloquy becomes collective discourse; from personal autobiography a national narrative emerges. In the specific case of many of the thinkers studied here, St Augustine's declaration also echoes with their particular approach to Cuban *sensibilidad*, particularly in the sense of this equating to what some of them refer to as Cuba's *conciencia colectiva*. Just like Augustine, these writers do not point their fingers in blame at others for the troubles faced by (or 'sins' committed in) Cuba, nor retreat to the self-defensive distance of the second or the third persons; instead, many include themselves intimately in the confession and call for an act of contrition in the collective first-person for the '*culpa cubana*' (Ortiz 1923a: 11–12). In this, of course, we come again to the descriptive power of *sensibilidad*, collective identity examined with objective intelligence and felt with subjective force, a national narrative that is read and simultaneously written.

If this wasn't enough to soothe the phenomenologists' ire, it will also be shown that many of the authors studied here were experts in what would nowadays be known as 'outreach'; that their texts were rooted in what they'd experienced in life and then returned to the world with 'impact'. Again, in some cases this is immediately apparent. Fidel Castro's 1953 self-defence speech became the foundational manifesto of his 26 July Movement and then went on to inform historiography, political philosophy and cultural politics for the next half-century. But Castro was not the only one. Whereas few would argue that Ortiz's 1911 *La reconquista de América: Reflexiones sobre el panhispanismo* (actually published in Paris) had a huge impact on common comprehensions of the island's fraught cultural intercourse with Spain, the Institución Hispanocubana de Cultura (which Ortiz founded in 1926) brought some of the most important Spanish intellectuals of the early twentieth century

---

[17] Ortiz was actually so closely identified with Cuba that he became metonymic of his nation but, as Pérez Firmat points out, simultaneously undermined any sense of exceptionalism on an island of which he is the paramount *señor* through the jocund translation of his personal title (see *The Cuban Condition*: 16–17).

to give conferences in Havana that were attended by hundreds of curious Cubans.[18] Similarly, whereas another important intellectual in this study, Jorge Mañach, presented his 1925 essay 'La crisis de la alta cultura' before the claustrum of the Sociedad Económica de Amigos del País,[19] and prescribed the predominance of an intellectual elite as an antidote to national decline, his three decades of commentary on Cuban culture was published in some of the most widely circulated periodicals in Latin America (*Bohemia*, *Diario de la Marina*, *Carteles*, etc.). Mañach took his engagement with the broadest possible public even further in his Universidad del Aire radio lecture series that, from 1932 to 1933 and 1949 to 1952, broadcast accessible analysis of themes ranging from the evolution of Cuban culture to new horizons in Cuban cinema.[20]

This marriage of commentary on and contribution to the national narrative is actually one of the principal traits that unifies almost all the Cuban thinkers included in this analysis. Whereas Fidel Castro was an ardent activist with an extraordinary ability to deploy rhetorical force to capture the popular mood, Jorge Mañach was an owlish man of letters who nevertheless co-penned the manifesto of one of the most effective anti-dictatorial terrorist organisations on the island in the 1930s.[21] Hence, to the phenomenologists' dessicated intellectuals and Rama's rarefied inhabitants of a glittering and exclusive lettered city, this book brings a pantheon of *letrados activos* and *activistas letrados*. Given this revelation, a new term is therefore proposed for the thinkers examined here, which recognises the fundamental challenge they pose to binaries of text/phenomenon, representation/reality, elite/masses, letters/life. Such is these thinkers' contribution to, as well as commentary on, the inscription of Cuba's collective story of selfhood, they will henceforth be referred to as the 'analyst-authors' of the national narrative. And it shall be seen that the relationship between life and *letras*, activism and analysis, and the one-time harmonious interaction between *letrados activos* and *activistas letrados* will not remain stable. An important corollary in this study is its monitoring of the tectonic shifts under the *ciudad letrada cubana* and its analyst-author inhabitants as the Republic made way for the Revolution.

Analyst-authors who may seem absent from this analysis (at least at first) are women and black Cubans. The absence of a distinctly female narrative

18 Gregorio Marañón, Juan Ramón Jiménez, Fernando de los Ríos, María Zambrano and Federico García Lorca, amongst others, were assiduous *conferencistas*.

19 An elitist mercantile and intellectual association (of which Ortiz was then president) that drew its members almost exclusively from the upper classes.

20 See Norma Díaz Acosta's excellent compilation and analysis of the lectures, *Universidad del Aire (conferencias y cursos)* (2001) for more information.

21 A political and terrorist organisation known as the ABC, which we will analyse in depth in Chapter 3.

from this study is in many ways a reflection of women's relative exclusion from the socio-cultural centre stage in both periods and following both revolutions. By as late as the mid-1980s, for example, by which time gender roles and relations had been fundamentally recalibrated on the island,[22] women's structural liberation had not translated into full female participation in the articulation of identity, nor automatically transformed female intellectuals into analyst-authors of the national narrative. By then, some critics were pointing to a bitter paradox in which dramatic social change in almost every sphere had brought about limited change to the narrative silence of, and about, Cuban women, with Luisa Campuzano suggesting that: 'de acuerdo con lo que se leía en los textos de narradores cubanos de ambos sexos, entre 1959 y 1984 en la Isla no había pasado nada notable, contable, novelable, en la vida de las mujeres' (1988: 25). Of course, the absence of *autoras* of the national narrative during the turning points studied here does not lead inexorably towards unisexual articulations of identity (as we shall see). Nevertheless, the fact remains (and must be recognised) that narrative interpretations of Cuba's sense of self during a significant portion of the twentieth century were distinctly male, and distinctly white.

The end of slavery in Cuba in 1886 and the transition from colony to Republic after 1898 brought relatively few improvements to the limited life opportunities of the vast majority of black Cubans.[23] Although making up 32% of the population in 1899 and contributing, by some accounts, up to 85% of the ranks of the *Ejército Libertador* in the anti-colonial wars, the end of

[22] Article 27 of the 1975 Código de la Familia famously enshrines housework equality into law: 'Los cónyuges están obligados a contribuir a la satisfacción de las necesidades de la familia que han creado con su matrimonio, cada uno según sus facultades y capacidad económica. No obstante, si alguno de ellos sólo contribuyere a esa subsistencia con su trabajo en el hogar y en el cuidado de los hijos, el otro cónyuge deberá contribuir por sí solo a la expresada subsistencia, sin perjuicio del deber de cooperar a dichos trabajo y cuidado' (see the 'Código de la familia', under 'Del matrimonio')

[23] A thought-provoking earlier example of the very ambiguous 'liberation' of manumission can be seen in the case of Juan Francisco Manzano whose *Autobiografía de un esclavo* (1840) is often read as a proto-contribution to the enunciation of a black aesthetic and black experience within the early national narrative. Manzano's text is actually more illustrative of this black experience when closer attention is paid to its omissions, to the elusiveness of the author, and to his safeguarding of his own subjectivity. Hence, whereas the *Autobiografía* is a mediated text on nearly every level (originally commissioned and propagandistically translated by ardent abolitionists), Manzano surreptititously saved the 'true' story of his life for himself: 'Al momento que vi lo que en ella me pide su merced, me he preparado para haceros una parte de la historia de mi vida, reservando los más interesantes sucesos de ella, para si algún día me hallo sentado en un rincón de mi patria, tranquilo, asegurada mi suerte y subsistencia, escribir una novela propiamente cubana' (in a 19 September 1835 letter to Domingo del Monte [in Manzano 2007: 126]. See William Luis's introduction and notes in the 2007 edition of the *Autobiografía* and Sylvia Molloy's *At Face Value* [1991] for further reading).

the conflict saw many black Cubans returned to positions of marginality and exclusion: by 1907 there were only four black lawyers and nine black doctors in the entire country (Thomas 2001: 308).[24] In the same year, black liberal activist Evaristo Estenoz launched the Partido Independiente de Color to create 'an egalitarian, sovereign and independent republic, without racial divisions or social antagonisms' (Estenoz, in Chomsky et al. 2003: 163) The government of the day (under President José Miguel Gómez) first banned all parties formed on a colour basis and then in 1912, in response to agitation amongst the black population in the east of the island, launched a terror campaign that killed 3,000 (including Estenoz). Although such concerted state violence against the Afro-Cuban community was not repeated, many white civic and intellectual figures remained extremely anxious about the demographic balance between black and white Cubans and about the Afro-Cuban contribution to the national narrative. The literary-aesthetic *negrismo* movement that came to prominence on the island in the early 1920s (inspired by the *négritude* movement that was flourishing in Paris and the Francophone Caribbean at the time) offered only ambiguously Afro-Cuban cultural inflections, given that many of its principal exponents were actually white.[25] A notable exception is Nicolás Guillén. In *Motivos de son* (1930), Guillén intones the Afro-Cuban *vox populis* with all its vernacular inflections intact:

> ¡Ay, negra,
> si tú supiera!
> Anoche te bi pasá
> y no quise que me biera.
> A é tú le hará como a mí,
> que cuando no tube plata
> te corrite de bachata,
> sin acoddadte de mí. (Guillén 1985: 104)[26]

24 See chapter 1 of Aline Helg's *Our Rightful Share: The Afro-Cuban Struggle for Equality, 1886–1912* for a comprehensive survey of the anticlimactic post-slavery period in nineteenth-century Cuba.

25 Two of the three canonical *negrismo* texts of the first half of the twentieth-century cited by Pérez Firmat, for example, were written by white men: Alejo Carpentier's *Ecue-Yamba-O!* (1933) and Emilio Ballagas's *Cuaderno de poesía negra* (1934). Another contribution to this aesthetic is José Z. Tallet's poem 'Rumba' (1928).

26 See *The Cuban Condition* for an insightful reading of the transition between the vernacular voice of *Motivos* and the more syncretic and subversive *poesis* of *Sóngoro cosongo* (1931) in which Pérez Firmat sees Guillén translating the Petrarchan sonnet and its *donna angelicata* into a syncopated Cuban *son* with a very *nueva* and *negra* woman as its muse ('Mujer nueva' is one of the poems in the collection; see Pérez Firmat 1989: 67–94).

Of course, although the majority of analyst-authors studied here are white, this does not exclude *lo afrocubano* from our analysis. The primary consideration given to the works of Fernando Ortiz is important, and will guarantee that the contribution to archetypal identity of the 'corazón de ébano' of Afro-Cuban culture will be duly dissected (Ortiz 1923d: viii). Although his first book, *Los Negros Brujos* (1906) was influenced by Italian positivist criminology and regurgitated much of the racist discourse imported from Europe at the beginning of the twentieth century, Ortiz underwent a progressive graphic epiphany, becoming the magnum scholar of Afro-Cuban culture and its axiomatic role within the island's sense of self. Our explorations of this selfhood will begin with Ortiz's insistence (in *Un catauro de cubanismos*, 1923) on the African accents of the vernacular *voz* and draw to a close with his scathing attack on attempts to exorcise alterity of any kind (in *Una pelea cubana contra los demonios*, 1965).

The revolution of 1959 had unquestionably profound effects on the socioeconomic situation of the majority of the Cuban population, whatever their ethnicity, but the ardent calls of the early Revolutionary years for one united (and colourless) nation in many senses stifled the imaginative space for a distinctly Afro-Cuban identity. An early and vociferous critic of Revolutionary monochromacy was Walterio Carbonell whose *Cómo surgió la cultural nacional* (1961) lamented the fact that the new regime had done little to revise the old master-narrative of *cubanidad* in which a small group of white (and in many cases slave-owning) intellectuals were elevated as the undisputed founding fathers of the independent Cuban nation and its narrative.[27] In short, even beyond the momentous turning point of 1959, the black contribution to Cuba's *sensibilidad* was somewhat marginalised.

In some sense, therefore, the absence of female and black analyst-authors from this study is symptomatic of the socio-cultural exclusion of these communities and their analyses of (and contributions to) the national narrative during the periods of study. One possible caveat is that the constitutive 'other' against which archetypal identity was calibrated during several of the turning points was not race- or gender-based at all. Instead, we will often come across what could be called 'temporal alterity': otherness not from elsewhere but from 'elsewhen'.

---

[27] See Carbonell 1961. In 1968 Carbonell was briefly imprisoned, and then faded from public view and consciousness until *Cómo surgió la cultural nacional* was republished and reappraised in 2005. Critic Alejandro de la Fuente agrees with Carbonell, claiming that the discourse of absolute Revolutionary unity 'delegitimized racially defined forms of political mobilization as racist and antinational' (2001: 335).

This book will trace the inscriptions and analyses of the Cuban national narrative and the *sensibilidad colectiva* therein during seven important turning points, analysed here as part of a twentieth-century post-colonial rite of passage within which the liminal moment of acute collective introspection becomes paramount. This book aims to expand the breadth and depth of existing scholarship in several interlacing ways. First, it will expose often overlooked moments of Cuba's history to intense scrutiny in order to contribute new evidence to existing debate about Cuban identity formation and bring new thinking to issues previously identified as central to this debate, such as insularity, generational conflict, violence and heroism, history and historiography, and the fundamental question of the nexus between analysis and praxis (in other words, between *los letrados* and *los activistas*). Thus, in Chapter 2 we will explore the under-studied turning point of 1927, presenting ample evidence of the generational antagonism that many critics identify at other moments of the Republic and early Revolutionary periods.[28] Nevertheless, this chapter will also present new evidence that challenges this antagonism and shows that some members of the vanguard and the old guard actually came together in a kind of age-blind and liminal harmony. Similarly, in 1957, where others read the struggle between Fidel Castro's *guerrilleros* and the dictatorial government of Fulgencio Batista as leading to a military and a collective psychological impasse, we will instead, in Chapter 5, point to a radical turning point in the very ontology of identity on the island. Whilst some analyst-authors will be seen indeed to have been weighed down by the 'ausencia de mitos fundadores', as Rafael Rojas suggests (2006: 51), seeking to infill that absence by re-enacting what they saw as the most salient lessons from the mythical past, others will be brought to the fore who actually embraced *ausencia* as a paradoxical *presencia* and set all historiography aside in their contrapuntal celebration of the bearable lightness of Cuban being.

Second, this study also aims to open new perspectives in the analysis of more widely recognised moments of great historical signficance in Cuba. So to readings of 1933 as a frustrated revolution that 'se fue a bolina', that was 'traicionada, vendida, mixtificada, calumniada y exprimida' by partisan politics and retrograde self-interest (Roa 1969: 184),[29] this study (in Chapter 3) will rather explore the stubborn liminality of this turning point in which a *dérèglement de tous les sens* spread from the island's physical

---

[28] Jorge Ibarra, for example, suggests that a 'youthocracy' often came to the fore in Cuba's twentieth century and sought to impose its version of Cuban *civitas* over its elders' interpretations (1998: 159).

[29] The nautical *cubanismo* 'irse a bolina' could perhaps be translated as the more terrestrial 'to go to the dogs'.

and psychological margins to colonise the core and which, crucially, was not arrested at all by the flight of the dictator of the day or the sanguinary purge of his followers (Turner 1974: 264). The year 1953 is often cited as an undisputed turning point in Cuba's twentieth-century trajectory, as that which saw the launch of Fidel Castro's revolutionary campaign with an assault on the main eastern barracks of the Cuban army. But in Chapter 4 we will turn from transcendental history to fiercely disputed historiography through new readings of the commemorations of the centenary of Cuba's most emblematic patriot, José Martí. Whilst recognising, as others do, that for Cuban thinkers at the time fidelity to the meta-myth of *historia* (through reverence for the so-called 'Apostle' Martí) was perceived as the lodestone of authentic patriotism,[30] we will also bring out alternative, sometimes subversive or even iconoclastic, readings of Martí, of Cuban history, and of the mythography of the nation and its collective *sensibilidad*.

And so to 1959, the most apparently transcendental turning point of all, in which many critics record a sense of irrevocable schism between the Republican *antes* and the Revolutionary *después*. For Nicola Miller, for example, the new Revolutionary government quickly instigated practical measures and pedagogical campaigns to ensure the popular apprehension of Fidel Castro and his followers as the 'culmination of Cuban history', to thus draw an indelible frontier across Cuba's twentieth century with 'history' becoming 'what took place before the revolution, or *antes*, as it is popularly known', and all post-1959 events being thenceforth referred to simply as 'the Revolution' (2003: 148 & 149). Whilst acknowledging the nihilistic impulse during this turning point, Chapter 6 will also present evidence that points to the resilient and liminal continuity across the historical divide, both because a margin was specifically (if temporarily) left open for some percolation of the Republic into the Revolution, but also (and mostly) because of those we will describe as Cuban 'Rip van Winkles',[31] who woke on the leeside of the transcendental episode to fundamentally challenge the *nihil admirari* ethos of the new regime.

Critically, an important innovation in this book is to bring the two Cuban revolutions together in comparative analysis, but not out of a desire to prove partisan points about either the 'failure' of 1933 (which is presented in stark

---

30 Kapcia sees the conjunction of the 'counter-myths' of the Platt Amendment, generational change and Martí coming together as a 'complex and powerful myth-set that explicitly extolled the redemptive power of *historia*' (2000: 170).

31 In echo of Washington Irving's famous somnambulist who fell asleep in the Catskill Mountains of New York State and only woke twenty years later when the Revolutionary War had been won and George Washington had replaced George III as the North American figurehead.

contrast to the 'triumph' of 1959),[32] or about its democratic 'authenticity' (in comparison to the perceived dictatorial tendencies of 1959 onwards).[33] Instead we will offer evidence of the striking ideological, imaginative, discursive and liminal similarities between the two revolutions. Thus, the second period under analysis here (1953–65) will be shown to return to key debates from the first (1923–33), whether around Martí's axiomatic example to the nation, the role of heroic action within collective *sensibilidad*, the rural or urban psychogeographic coordinates of ideal identity; or between opposing historiographies and teleologies; between conflicting ideas about the best cure, most effective act of contrition and most potent exorcism for the ills, sins and devils of the Cuban national narrative. In essence, this book seeks to liminalise some of the fundamental debates around Cuban history, culture and collective *sensibilidad*. And it will experiment with the theoretical insights of this liminal perspective in the first period in order to approach the second with greater clarity. In this, it will offer a radical re-charting of the build-up to, 'triumph' and consolidation of the 1959 revolution that moves away from the ideological fault lines between the political right and left, the temporal schism between *antes* and *después*, and the cultural divide between 'committed' and 'passive' intellectuals, to rather reveal, in distinction from what has been identified previously, the persistence of very similar ideological terrain, chronological flux and analyst-author equilibrium.

Thus, this analysis reaches its conclusion in 1965, examining evidence for its being the year of a determined turn towards ideological unity, a self-assured elaboration of the *sensibilidad* of Cuba's new men and women, the placing of a Revolutionary full-stop at the end of nearly a hundred years of independent national narrative. But from the surreptitious margins of public debate and cultural endeavour, this final and conclusive reaggregation of national identity will once again be challenged, both by the liminalists who will inhabit this study from the outset, but also, and more unexpectedly, by younger, nearly-new analyst-authors writing texts that have hitherto been included within the Revolutionary (and reaggregationist) canon. At the end of the book as at the beginning, therefore, *venceremos* and *la luchita* will meet across the pages of Cuba's national narrative.

---

[32] This is the fundamental argument of much post-1959 insular Cuban historiography (see Raúl Roa's *La Revolución del 30 se fue a bolina*, Lionel Soto's *La Revolución del 33*, José A Tabares del Real's *La Revolución del 30: sus dos últimos años*, and Luis E. Aguilar's *Cuba 1933: Prologue to Revolution*, for example).

[33] See Domínguez 1978 & 2007 and Masó 1976, for example.

Historical Prologue

To approach the first turning point of this study (1923) with clarity, some prior historical context is called for. Compared to most other Latin American countries, Cuba came late to independence. Throughout the first half of the nineteenth century, white Cubans' fear of a Saint Domingue-style slave-led revolution[34] stultified anti-colonial aspirations on the island as the agricultural and commercial elite opted for the Spanish military-guaranteed status quo rather than risk an independence in which their own prosperity (and personal safety) could be in jeopardy. Thus, while Spain had been forced off the Latin American mainland by the early 1830s,[35] Cuba remained *siempre,* and stubbornly, *fiel.*[36] Ideological and commercial factors combined with this paranoia regarding an upset to the racial and social (im)balance to temper inclinations towards independence: while the success of the slave revolt on the neighbouring island brought fear to some Cubans, for example, the resultant collapse of the Haitian sugar industry opened a lucrative hole in the world market that Cuban planters rushed to fill, becoming ever-more zealous defenders of the socio-economic status quo on the island in the process.

By the mid-nineteenth century, however, as demographics began to calm jangled and racist *criollo* nerves (the census of 1860–61 showed that the majority of the island's population was in fact still white), this status quo had become more irksome. It found its voice in the eastern city of Bayamo in 1868, when local landowner (and slave owner) Carlos Manuel de Céspedes effectively declared war on Spanish imperialism with his *grito de Yara.*[37] The resultant *Guerra de los diez años* pitted white and black *independentistas* against the Spanish army and those still loyal to the Empire.[38] After ten gruelling years,

---

[34] In 1804 the French colony of Saint Domingue became the second American republic (after the United States) when its majority slave population rose against the white minority and declared independence. The price of independence was high, however, with France claiming reparations of 150 million francs, a debt that independent Haiti was not to pay off until 1947.

[35] By 1830 there were eleven inchoate Latin American countries: Mexico, Haiti, the United Provinces of Central America, Gran Colombia, Peru, Bolivia, Chile, Paraguay, Uruguay, the United Provinces of La Plata and Brazil.

[36] 'Cuba siempre fiel' was a popular slogan in Spain after the loss of the majority of her other American colonies. Although uprisings and anti-colonial rebellions did take place (the Morales uprising of 1795, the masonic rebellion of 1810, José Antonio Aponte's conspiracy of 1812, the Soles y Rayos de Bolívar plot of the 1820s and the *Escalera* conspiracy of 1843–44), all were quickly, and often brutally, extinguished (see Gott 2004: 44–70).

[37] An echo of the *gritos* that had launched earlier independence movements on the Latin American mainland.

[38] Of particular importance were the all-white and decidedly racist *voluntario* brigades that were formed of (often recently arrived) *peninsulares* and which came to be 'an essential bulwark of the Spanish state' (Gott 2004: 48).

in which in-fighting between the *independentistas* about the status of former slaves in the Cuba-to-be and about the ideal future relationship with the United States (which had only recently emerged from its own civil war with slavery at its heart) badly dented the united front against the Spanish, the Cuban generals finally agreed to a truce (known as the Pacto de Zanjón) in February 1878. Over the next seventeen years, small-scale and *staccato* uprisings on the island were easily put down, but Cuba's independence movement was gathering momentum offshore under a new leader, the journalist, political theorist, poet and polymath José Martí. Martí was revolutionary in many ways. Although he was always an advocate of complete independence for Cuba and soundly rejected either a form of autonomy within the Spanish empire or any kind of annexation by the United States, his attitude towards Cuba's northern neighbour struck a balance between admiration and caution. In his landmark 1891 essay 'Nuestra América', Martí saves all his best rhetorical barbs for Spain, seeing the US as a potent and successful country against whom confident self-cognizance by Latin American republics was the very best defence:

> El desdén del vecino formidable, que no la conoce, es el peligro mayor de nuestra América; y urge, porque el día de la visita está próximo, que el vecino la conozca, la conozca pronto, para que no la desdeñe. Por ignorancia llegaría, tal vez, a poner en ella la codicia. Por el respeto, luego que la conociese, sacaría de ella las manos (Martí 2001: 22).[39]

In this sense, Martí's oft-quoted characterisation of the United States as a 'monstruo' (with whose 'entrañas' he was more than familiar)[40] overlooks and seeks to silence the admiration he had expressed for the country previously.[41] Martí also had an innovative approach to the question of race in the constitution of an independent Cuba, seeing the archetypal future *cubanos* (and all future citizens of 'nuestra' America) as those, regardless of their ethnic origin, who had cultivated intimate knowledge of the country, its people and

[39] The fourteen years Martí spent in the US gave him good insight into the *sensibilidad*, and geopolitical ambitions, of that country.

[40] Martí made the comment ('Viví en el monstruo, y le conozco las entrañas') in an unfinished letter to his friend Manuel Mercado that he began the day before his death (1895/2001: 168).

[41] In 1880, for example, Martí looked (somewhat cautiously) towards the United States as an example of successful decolonisation: 'The vision of this new country rising from the ruin of old nations, awakens the attention of thinking men who, in the last century, had begun to build the foundations for a new era of humanity. This could be, this ought to be, the significance of the United States' (in López 2014: 213–14).

its culture. For Martí, this intimate knowledge (almost a sublime gnosis) was an essential precursor to closer communication and cooperation between Latin American countries prior to individual and collective projection towards the rest of the world: 'Los pueblos que no se conocen han de darse prisa para conocerse, como quienes van a pelear juntos' (1891/2001: 15). Martí did not see his philosophy come to fruition: he was killed during a skirmish near Dos Ríos in the east of the island on 19 May 1895.

Three years after Martí's death, and after two wars over thirty years had killed a tenth of the island's population, the military victory over Spain was snatched from Cuban forces by the eleventh-hour and twenty-six-day intervention of the United States. In December 1898, Spain and the US made peace at the Treaty of Paris (to which the Cubans were only invited as observers) and on 1 January 1899 the US Governor-General replaced the Spanish Capitan-General as overlord of the island. Cuba's long fight for freedom had come to an anticlimatic end. The United States went on to occupy the island for the next four years and so the rite of passage from colony to independent country entered an interstice within which the demise of the former and the coalescence of the latter remained incomplete. Whereas other Latin American countries had moved directly, if turbulently, from colony to revolution to republic, in Emilio Roig de Leuchsenring's opinion, 'entre nosotros ocurre una brusca y trascendental interrupción: la ocupación americana' (1961b: 7). Down to her last able and willing soldiers and with the colonial coffers nearly empty, Spain, Roig de Leuchsenring claims, made a desperate last-minute pact to preserve at least some of the material benefits, if none of the geopolitical prestige, of a presence in the so-called *Perla de las Antillas*: 'se agarró desesperadamente a esa áncora de salvación que le tendía la ocupación militar americana en Cuba, e hizo causa común con gobernantes y negociantes yanquis' (1961b: 10). Many aspects of colonial infrastructure and many ex-colonialists were indeed relatively unaffected by the transition to formal independence. Roig bitterly laments, for example, the fact that *independentista* heroes were obliged to form the first Cuban government with their old antagonists: 'guerrilleros, voluntarios y autonomistas' (1961b: 87). Demographically, independence was certainly ambivalent, with the established Spanish-born *peninsulares* being joined by 200,000 new Iberian arrivals between 1902 and 1910: more, in fact, than had arrived in the previous two hundred years of colonial control (Thomas 2001: 295). Although perhaps initially employed in lowly posts, many of these *gallegos*[42] came to own large tracts of the Cuban

---

[42] Due to the predominance of immigrants from the then-impoverished north-eastern region of Galicia, Spaniards in Cuba were (and sometimes still are) metonymically referred to as *gallegos*.

countryside and to dominate areas of the mercantile sector.[43] And although it appeared at times that the United States' four-year occupation was merely a prelude to formal annexation of the island, the solitary Cuban star was ultimately not added to the federal flag, due largely to the fact that the US realised that indirect control over Cuba would be politically and economically less burdensome, but no less rewarding.[44] Thus, as the hard fought-for distance from *Madre España* was truncated, so the stultifying new proximity to Uncle Sam made itself felt.

The legislative axis of the United States' neo-colonisation of Cuba was the so-called Platt Amendment, proposed first to the 1901 US Army Appropriations Act, but subsequently annexed to Cuba's new constitution in 1902. The Amendment gave the United States the right to intervene in Cuban affairs and on Cuban soil for 'the maintenance of a government adequate for the protection of life, property and individual liberty'; it prohibited the signing of treaties with foreign powers (other than the US) which would 'impair or tend to impair the independence of Cuba', thus granting the US a virtual veto over Cuban foreign policy; and through the lease of 'lands necessary for coaling or naval stations', it ensured that there would always be a corner of Cuba (the Guantánamo Bay naval station) that was actually part of the United States (Congress of the United States of America 1901: under 'Provided further'). When the Republic was formally inaugurated on 20 May 1902, therefore, the flag of full independence really only made it half way up the pole; *Cuba Libre* seemed as far off as ever.

Alongside Cuba's stymied political autonomy, the island's economic independence was also hamstrung. While the devastation of the Wars of Independence had laid the foundations for US economic infiltration on the island, this was only a prelude to the mass expropriation of Cuban resources provoked by the so-called *danza de los millones* in 1920. World sugar prices had begun to inflate when the outbreak of the First World War took countless men and fertile acres away from European beet production. When demand after the 1918 armistice outstripped sluggish post-war beet production, sugarcane prices rose to unimaginable heights (by May 1920 they were at 22.5¢ per pound from a 1914 high of 1.93¢). Bewitched by the chance of

---

[43] Fidel Castro's father, Ángel Castro y Argiz, for example, began his immigrant's life in Cuba in 1899 as a United Fruit Company labourer. By 1920, he was the owner of a 25,000-acre estate in the east of the island (Castro 2007: 28). Of the 32,000 people who described themselves as salesmen in 1910, more than 60% were Spaniards (Thomas 2001: 297).

[44] The second Governor-General, Leonard Woolf, allegedly told then-president Theodore Roosevelt that 'es bien evidente que Cuba está en nuestras manos [...]. La Isla se norteamericanizará gradualmente y a su debido tiempo, contaremos con unas de las más ricas y deseables posesiones que haya en el mundo' (in Fernández Valledor 1993: 53).

(further) immense wealth, the Cuban saccharocracy (and the banks that financed it) tore down vast hardwood forests to make space for more cane and took on huge debts to modernise their production processes. But just as the *danza* reached its crescendo, the music stopped. When beet tops emerged once more over Flanders fields and demobbed soldiers turned their hands to the harvest, Cuba's bubble of saccharine prosperity burst: by the end of 1920 prices had plummeted by almost 85%, goods ordered at the height of the boom piled up uncollected in Havana harbour, banks that had overstretched themselves collapsed and sugar barons across the island went bankrupt. The end of the *danza* was not a disaster for everyone, however. Whilst Cuban banks closed their doors, the more stable US houses weathered the storm and reaped opportunistically the benefits of their competitors' demise: in 1920, foreign banks held only 20% of Cuban cash deposits, but by 1923 this had risen to 76% (Aguilar 1972: 43), and it was to the now predominantly US-owned banks that many Cuban and Spanish sugar mill owners handed over the deeds to their *centrales* in lieu of impossible-to-pay debts.[45] For Fernández Valledor, the *danza* debacle quite simply signified the beginning of 'el control norteamericano de la economía nacional' (1993: 57). The toxic combination of the Platt Amendment and the *danza de los millones* meant that by the early 1920s Cuba's political and economic destinies were being decided offshore.

Beyond the infrastructural implications of what could be called the Plattist paradigm, the early anticlimatic experience of independence had a more insidious effect: the neo-colonisation of independent Cuba's *sensibilidad*. Whilst recognising the Amendment's detrimental effects on Cuba's constitutional autonomy, Roig de Leuchsenring's 1923 *Análisis y consecuencias de la intervención norteamericana en los asuntos interiores de Cuba* focuses instead on the United States' ideological conquest of Cuban history and Cuban sensibility. Through the popularisation of the legend of Teddy Roosevelt's Rough Riders charging to Cuba's rescue up San Juan Hill near Santiago, the second *Guerra de Independencia* was translated into the 'Spanish–American War' and the island was encumbered with an eternal debt of gratitude: 'realmente es una duda eterna, porque siempre la estamos pagando' (Roig de Leuchsenring 1923: 7). Apparently unable to defeat the Spanish in wartime or resist the incursions of the United States in peace, Cuban self-confidence shrivelled in a cold neo-colonial shadow: 'en lugar de fortalecerse la personalidad política, la confianza en el propio esfuerzo, el sentimiento de la soberanía, se fueron debilitando más y más todos estos principios tan indispensables para la vida de una nación' (ibid: 9). Moreover, deprived of ultimate authority, and therefore

---

45 By the early 1920s, one fifth of Cuba's territory and 70% of its sugar industry was owned by US corporations (Manzoni 2001: 43).

of ultimate responsibility for the (mal)administration of Cuban affairs, this debilitated *sensibilidad* was unable to shake off the bad colonial-era habits of 'el peculado, el monopolio, el contrabando, el juego, la ausencia de educación y cultura' (Roig de Leuchsenring 1961b: 9). This asphyxiation of the *Cuba Libre* dream for which so much had been sacrificed led to a potent double complex of inferiority and licence: civic probity and collective self-confidence gave way to venality and the sneaking suspicion that Cuba was incapable of self-rule.[46]

What made this suspicion even more uncomfortable was the frustrating fact that some of those who had fought so fervently against the Spanish did not now display a similar hostility to United States neo-colonialism. In the perennial tussle between Cuban liberals and conservatives for top political office, US backing was often critical for electoral success. The scramble for executive power was perhaps inevitable: with intra-national commerce monopolised by Spaniards, and the sugar industry, utilities and banks in the hands of the North Americans, members of the Cuban elite used politics to corner the only sectors left open to them: corruption, graft and lucrative control of the national lottery. The lottery epitomises the corrupt and self-serving politics of the early Republic. Divided amongst the director-general of the lottery, senators and representatives, each able to sell their allotment of tickets at up to 600% profit, the lottery became the 'most efficient method of illegal enrichment, and above all for buying the silence or support of the legislature or press' (Thomas 2001: 513). Installed and enriched by US patronage, Cuban political protégés expressed their gratitude through the dispensation of concessions, franchises and licences to US corporations, being rewarded in turn with lucrative boardroom sinecures: President José Miguel Gómez (1909–13) was a director of the Cuban Cane Sugar Corporation, President Mario García Menocal (1913–21) was on the board of the Cuban-American Sugar Company and President Gerardo Machado (1925–33) was vice-president of the Cuban Electric Company (Pérez Jr 1986: 229). Though the synergies were often complex, the result was quite clear: by the early 1920s it was almost impossible to determine where exogenous interference ended and endogenous malfeasance began. Influential discursive tendencies (that will be traced throughout our two periods) began to coalesce and public debate turned to obsessive reflections on how to live up to the *independentistas*' legacy, how

---

46 In the past, Cuba's alleged incapacity for independence had been insisted upon both by the Spanish and by those Cubans (the *criollos* of the 1820s and most of the *anexionistas* and *autonomistas* of the 1840s onwards) who predicted that full freedom would lead inevitably to race riots or social revolution, each anathema to their positions of privilege within the colonial structure.

to turn the formal structural components of *cubanidad* into *cubanía* 'plena, sentida, consciente y […] responsable (Ortiz 1940b: 172), about what to do with the 'original sin' of the Platt Amendment and the shameful sovereignty it entailed, about who to include and who to exclude from the national narrative, about whether the country could and should strive 'ever onwards to victory' or linger in a less conclusive *luchita*. The stage was set for the turning point of 1923 and the first acute examination of Cuba's *conciencia colectiva*.

PART I

1923–1933

1923: *Annus mirabilis*

The liminal epiphany of 1923

Despite the fact that by 1923 the sugar industry had clambered to its feet after the catastrophic *danza* (with a bumper crop to be sold at the highest prices since independence, bar the extraordinary summer of 1920), the persistent political self-interest, economic subservience and ethical collapse ensured that the gloomy mood of neo-colonial impotence lingered. Taunted by a stubborn Spanish economic influence, bullied by an overbearing United States and undermined by a cynical Cuban political elite, the task of constructing the *civitas* of an independent nation and the *sensibilidad* to match seemed doomed to failure. But just as Cuba's 'vitalidad como nación' (Ortiz 1923d: 87) seemed about to expire, a spark of stubborn resistance was ignited: 'reform was in the air, and it was a presence that offered the prospect of nothing less than a total regeneration of the republic' (Pérez Jr 2006: 236). 1923 was an *annus mirabilis* for the Cuban Republic, a turning point in which the *sensibilidad* of the age shifted suddenly from lassitude and bitter frustration to the kind of 'heightened pitch of self-consciousness' that Turner describes as typical in liminal transitions (1969: 167). A series of financial scandals involving the widely disliked (and sexagenarian) president coincided with the coming of age of a new generation of analyst-authors of the national narrative. Whilst recognising and analysing this generational clash, this chapter will rather suggest that the prime discursive confrontation in 1923 was not based on age at all. Instead, the reflection on identity typical of the liminal phase of the rite of passage took place on the spatial plane, around very different interpretations of Cuban insularity and its implications for nationhood, and on the ethical plane, around very different attitudes towards the 'sins' and 'sicknesses' afflicting Cuban *sensibilidad* and the possibility (even desirability) of a collective pardon or cure.

Fuelled by an intolerance of neo-colonial corruption and by an appetite for collective catharsis, the so-called *Generación del '23* was undoubtedly in the vanguard of this anguished introspection:

En los años del gobierno de Alfredo Zayas, llegan a la madurez los cubanos
nacidos entre 1895 y 1902, esto es, una nueva generación que ni tiene
complicidad con el deterioro creciente de la República intervenida ni está
comprometida, como sucedía con la masa de los libertadores, a seguir deter-
minados cabecillas, caudillos o líderes. (Le Riverend 2001: 198)[1]

The agitation for change began at the University of Havana where impatience
with sinecure-installed pseudo-professors erupted in January 1923 with the
formation of the Federación de Estudiantes Universitarios (FEU) under firebrand
Julio Antonio Mella. This university-based genesis was understandable:
thousands of young people from relatively diverse social backgrounds were
brought together for up to eight years in what Ibarra calls a 'mass concentration'
comparable to the fraternity of the factory and resulting in the same kind of
socialisation and collective agitation (1998: 157). This youthful solidarity had
produced radical results just five years earlier in the student reform movement
in Córdoba, Argentina.[2] Calling for university reform that would be a catalyst
'para que se reorganice la Patria Cubana', the FEU's youthful crusade soon
spilled out from the classrooms into the city beyond (Mella 1975: 45). On 18
March, a group of fifteen intellectuals (led by twenty-three year old poet and
propagandist Rubén Martínez Villena) walked out of an event at the Academia
de Ciencias as Justice Minister Erasmo Regüeiferos, who was implicated in
one of the Zayas government's most public financial scandals, was about to
speak.[3] Thirteen of the intellectuals later signed the landmark 'Protesta de los
Trece' bluntly declaring that the time had come to 'reaccionar vigorosamente y
de castigar de alguna manera a los gobernantes delincuentes' (Martínez Villena
et al.: under 'Quinto').[4] This was transcendentalism write large, a turning point

[1]   Cira Alonso (in Novás Calvo 2003: 31) puts Alejo Carpentier, Jorge Mañach, Juan
Marinello and Nicolás Guillén amongst this *Generación del '23*. I would add Rubén Martínez
Villena and Emilio Roig de Leuchsenring.
[2]   Interestingly, this reform movement, which began in March 1918, had its textual
expression in the so-called *Manifiesto liminar*. Although meeting severe resistance from both
the government and the Catholic church, the movement did achieve moderate reforms, including
increased university autonomy and some student participation in the university executive. José
Arce, who had been closely involved with the Córdoba movement before becoming rector of the
University of Buenos Aires, visited Havana in 1922.
[3]   The sale and then re-purchase at a grossly inflated price of the Convento de Santa Clara,
which caused widespread public outcry.
[4]   Many of those thirteen *protestantes* would go on to form part of the so-called 'Grupo
minorista', a loosely articulated network of young intellectuals determined to 'influir honrada-
mente en el desarrollo de nuestra vida pública, dando una fórmula de sanción social y actividad
revolucionaria a los intelectuales cubanos' (*La Declaración del Grupo Minorista* 1927, under
'Aquel acto [...]').

that few could ignore, with Ramiro Guerra claiming that from the 'Protesta de los Trece' onwards Cuba experienced

> otra medida llena de audacia y de juvenil insolencia y, al mismo tiempo, de elevada rectitud moral; después de aquella tarde nadie se sintió seguro en la posesión de una reputación legítima, cada hombre debía ser capaz de resistir los recios martillazos de la verdad. (in Kuchilán 1975: 12)

Despite their obvious delight in zealous attacks on the structures of established order, the ethos of some members of the *Generación del '23* was distinctly reaggregationist. If they sought a radical catharsis for Cuba, they were determined that this should be temporary and serve to turn the tide irrevocably away from the unsatisfactory recent past and towards a future over which they would preside. If they slighted government grandees with a disrespectful departure, they reserved their most virulent attacks for the kind of 'ambivalence and unset definition' of liminality (Dening 1997: 2). If they were peripatetic in their protests, they nevertheless looked towards myths of spatial fixity and unambiguous insularity for Cuba, with some even advocating a kind radical physical and cultural exclusion of the Other reminiscent of the most elitist *letrado* of Ángel Rama's *ciudad*. In contrast (and in forceful challenge to the apparent generational divide that some critics see as paramount in this period), here we will read some of the Cuban 'old guard' contributing indubitable 'audacia' and 'juvenil insolencia' to the pages of the national narrative. Our investigations in this chapter, therefore, will keep generational schisms in mind, but rather suggest that collective self-reflection in 1923 began with otherness.

The Others

In countries fighting for cultural decolonisation as an essential, but by no means inevitable, corollary to formal independence, alterity often looms large. For Homi Bhabha, an immanent and cohesive sense of national identity is often fomented as a response to 'the threat of cultural difference' from other people (Bhabha 2010: 214); the cognitive frontiers of nationhood are fortified with what Freud called a psychology of enmity through which 'it is always possible to bind together a considerable number of people in love, so long as there are other people left to receive the manifestation of their aggressiveness' (ibid.: 215). And for Aída Beaupied, the 'mito integracionista' she perceives at the discursive core of early manifestations of Cuban identity (and which she hears synthesised in Martí's maxim 'con todos y para el bien de todos') is exclusive as well as inclusive, depends upon the ability to integrate, but also to excoriate, 'sacrificar aquello que se percibe separado, distinto, Otro' (2010: 10). This Cuban encounter with otherness in 1923 can be traced both through myths of collective identity and more tangibly along the island's coastal frontier.

Decolonising countries reclaiming the right to act, speak and imagine for themselves often undertake a re-examination, re-authorisation or even invention of foundational myths of national becoming. In an attempt to shed years of imposed subalternity and demonstrate that they are more than just 'ex-colonies', newly independent nations often seek to reconnect with what Bhabha calls their 'constituted historical origin', not as a distant and irrelevant antecedent, but as an unfulfilled prophecy of proto-nationhood to be pursued in the post-colonial era (Bhabha 2010: 208). For Rafael Rojas, as we have seen, the absence of 'mitos fundadores' led to a pervasive discourse of Cuba as 'una cultura ingrávida, sin tradición firme ni legado discernible' and a concomitant compulsion amongst Cuban intellectuals of the early twentieth century to seek the 'restitución' of those myths in their writings (2006: 51). Here we will suggest that this was certainly the case, but only for one side of the discursive divide in 1923.

The discovery of an ancient and strangely shaped skeleton in a cave in Sancti Spíritus in 1914 provided a potent early catalyst for feverish debate on the ethnogenesis of Cuban identity (Rojas 2010: 249–50). In *Cuatro años en la Ciénaga de Zapata*, Juan Antonio Cosculluela suggested that the skeleton's unusual dimensions demonstrated that the indigenous people of Cuba had not arrived in the Americas from Asia after an epic trek over the frozen Behring Straits, but had always and forever inhabited their tropical island redoubt In a remarkably imaginative interweaving of archaeology and nationalism, the fossil was fleshed out into a self-defensive mythology of insularity in which authentic identity was rooted in Cuba's originary distance and difference from the rest of the world. Although even the most credulous academics probably recognised that the genetic and cultural legacy of the pre-Columbian peoples was all but lost, this did not diminish the propagandistic force of insularity within articulations of early Republican identity. In response to uncomfortable echoes from the colonial past and the apparently effortless neo-colonial conquest of contemporary Cuba, belligerent insularity and the fixing of indelible frontiers between *dentro* and *fuera* and their allegedly incompatible inhabitants became a forceful anti-colonial ideology. Determined to demonstrate that the island was very much more than a mere splinter of a more significant mainland, whether Spain or the United States, these archaeo-nationalists insisted that *homo cubensis* was a true child of insular Cuban *tierra* threatened by debilitating offshore alterity (ibid.). This myth of autochthonous distinctiveness also played an insidious role, however. In 1923, as panic about economic disaster ceded to more far-reaching reflections on the state of the nation, this insistence on an insular and exclusive identity was sometimes inflected into crude ethnocentrism in which *homo cubensis* became not an indigenous forefather at all, but a distinctly Europeanised mythological defender of the realm against incoming Afro-otherness.

The intellectual history of racism in Cuba is as long and complex as anywhere else in the New or Old Worlds, with some of the most fêted champions of Cuban independence often displaying an almost hysterical preoccupation with the future colour of *Cuba Libre*. In an anti-slavery pamphlet written in Paris in 1845, for example, José Antonio Saco (one of Cuba's most influential early ideologues) condemned the trans-Atlantic trade in Africans, not for its inhumanity, but for the threat it posed to the bright-white future that he and many of his contemporaries advocated for the Republic-to-be: 'Cerrando las puertas a nuevas introducciones de negros, quedan abiertas para los blancos; y con ellos, al paso que aumentaremos el número de nuestros amigos, disminuiremos el de nuestros enemigos' (in Le Roy 1929: 9). As we saw earlier, entrenched race inequality on the island (only exacerbated by the importation of segregationist policies and practices during the first US occupation)[5] led to an even more acute sense of post-independence anticlimax amongst Afro-Cubans, who had fought for *Cuba Libre* only to see their own freedom curtailed because of the colour of their skin. And as we also saw earlier, these frustrations led not to dialogue, compromise and change, but to internecine and inter-racial bloodshed. The race question in the early Republic stubbornly resisted attempts at answer, and remained an enigma in 1923. Writing in the March–April edition of the *Revista Bimestre Cubana*, Carlos Trelles found much to praise in the intolerance of black immigration during the first US occupation, only lamentably overturned as the shortage of cheap labour in the east of the island during pre-*danza* sugar expansion opened the borders to Caribbean *braceros* (a word terribly evocative of their indefatigable and almost disembodied cane-cutting arms). In Mario García Menocal's two presidential terms (1913–17 and 1917–21), 81,000 Haitians and 75,000 Jamaicans arrived on the island in what Trelles condemned as 'un verdadero salto en las tinieblas, que amenaza con destruir la civilización de Cuba y el predominio de la raza caucásica' (1923: 361). In *Inmigración anti-sanitaria*, Jorge Le Roy focused on the physiological dangers brought in by the foreign bodies entering the island: 'nos han introducido enfermedades que habíamos borrado de nuestros cuadros nosológicos, como son las viruelas' (1929: 5).

---

5   The Guardia Rural, for example, which was re-established by the US authorities in 1900 in lieu of a standing army, operated overtly segregationist policies with almost no black officers (see Gott 2004: 104–10).

Nevertheless, this notionally medical survey of the Cuban condition soon reveals its true colour bias in a call for the defence of white Cuba's psycho-cultural superiority menaced by the 'vicio' of the new arrivals from the black Caribbean. Although seemingly willing to include 'los morenos cubanos' within the eugenicist island frontiers, Le Roy demonstrates his latent anxiety about the possibility of 'contaminación' between offshore and onshore blacks producing 'un atávico salto atrás' (19) that would reduce the Republic to 'un grado de inferioridad respeto a las naciones civilizadas que nos obligue a avergonzarnos de ostentar la ciudadanía que tan caro nos ha costado obtener' (5).

Despite the ill fit of this racist insularity in ethnically diverse Cuba, the ideological appeal of unambiguous borders enclosing an unapologetically idiosyncratic national community remained potent, even among the young. Although Trelles and Le Roy were by then both in their late fifties (Trelles was born in 1866, Le Roy in 1867), Alberto Lamar Schweyer, author of *La crisis del patriotismo: Una teoría de las inmigraciones*, was only twenty-one and one of the signatories of the 'Protesta de los Trece'. Lamar Schweyer's contri-butions to the re-cognisance of Cuban identity is a virulent anti-immigration tract in which he blames Cuba's 'bajo nivel patriótico' on enervating ethnic and cultural diffusion caused by an excessive 'influencia marítima' (1923: 44) For Lamar Schweyer, the threat of 'una total desaparición de la cubanidad' (152) was not only based in race: for this member of the *Generacion del '23*, all offshore contributions to the *sensibilidad cubana* were to be repulsed: immigrants from Haiti and Jamaica, but also from Spain, were all to be repelled by an immutable insular frontier. We will return to the question of racial otherness later in this chapter, in the 1923 contribution to the national narrative of an analyst-author more than twenty years' Lamar Schweyer's senior, Fernando Ortiz.

Unambiguous Identity

Within re-interpretations of Cuban identity in 1923 a particularly acute intolerance was reserved, not for the alterity of nationality or race, but for any and all ambiguity between selfhood and otherness. Whilst many of the younger generation of analyst-authors in 1923 are seen to revel in the rebellion against the 'rutinaria artificialidad de todas las asociaciones clásicas' (Roig de Leuchsenring 1961a: 8) and make a policy out of disrespect and dissolution of hierarchical structure, many paradoxically perceived the 'ambivalence and unset definition' of this period as one of the principal problems of Cuba's inchoate identity (Dening 1997: 2). For some of the *Generación del '23*, the examination of the *conciencia colectiva* actually provoked anxiety about Cuba's perceived lack of substance, with Rubén Martínez Villena, for example, complaining that 'en Cuba apenas queda de cubano, más que el símbolo ridículo de una ficticia soberanía, el himno y la bandera' (1978: 170). The possibilities Turner saw in the 'potentially unlimited series of alternative social arrangements' that came to the fore during the liminal transition were experienced by some as much less of a liberation (1974: 13–14). In the neo-colonial context of exogenous interference and endogenous vice, an adherence to ambiguous identity and ethics could in fact be blamed for placing the destiny of the young Republic in the hands of those least qualified to safeguard it.

The personality and political trajectory of the fourth President of the Republic, Alfredo Zayas y Alonso, seem soaked in the potentially pernicious ambivalence of the historical period he presided over. Whereas his predecessor, Menocal, was blatantly attuned to the United States' (and his own) interests at the expense of Cuban economic and political sovereignty, and whereas his successor Machado was unquestionably a tyrant, Zayas was rather betwixt and between benevolence and malevolence. Originally an *autonomista*, he joined the *independentistas* late in the anti-colonial campaign but quickly took refuge in the United States (Le Riverend 2001: 182). Returning to Cuba in 1898, he made his way up the ranks of the Liberal Party, becoming vice-president to Gómez in 1908. But when Gómez won the race for the Liberal presidential ticket in the 1920 elections, a disgruntled Zayas formed his own Partido Popular Cubano before entering a political tryst with Conservative Menocal to form the ideologically ambivalent Liga Nacional. After years of clambering towards top political office as a liberal, therefore, Zayas eventually became president with arch-conservative support. By the time he assumed the executive mandate on 20 May 1921, however, the US president's special representative General Enoch H. Crowder had arrived in Havana, charged (in an increasingly intrusive interpretation of Article II of the Platt Amendment) with supervising the expenditure of J. P. Morgan's recent $50million loan in a climate of apparently incurable Cuban economic incompetence.[6] Crowder's 'purposefully ominous' presence aboard the *USS Minnesota* (whose guns pointed not out into the harbour but at the heart of Havana) suggested that ultimate authority resided on the US warship, not at the Cuban Presidential Palace (Pérez Jr 1986: 190). Although apparently

---

6   Article II declares: 'The Government of Cuba shall not assume or contract any public debt to pay the interest upon which, and to make reasonable sinking-fund provision for the ultimate discharge of which, the ordinary revenues of the Island of Cuba, after defraying the current expenses of the Government, shall be inadequate' (Congress of the United States of America 1901).

resigned to this usurpation (a 1922 *Política Cómica* caricature shows Crowder holding Zayas's hand as he signs his first edicts [in Thomas 2001: 333]), in April 1923 the previously pliable president performed a sudden *volte face*, sacked the so-called 'gabinete de la honestidad' (effectively appointed by Crowder) and stirred the press against US 'intervencionismo' (Le Riverend 2001: 188). This rallying behind the nationalist cause became just another self-serving ploy, however, as the newly appointed cabinet soon abandoned their anti-neo-colonial stance to concentrate on restoring the habitual disorder of sinecures, graft and the national lottery racket to Cuban civic life. What most enraged many in 1923 was Zayas's assault on the binary divide between good and bad, legality and vice, rectitude and rakishness. Whilst committing and permitting crimes against the public purse and the public person, Zayas simultaneously made such liberal use of amnesty laws and the presidential pardon that it became impossible to distinguish fair from foul, especially amongst those in high political office, with claims that in the 1920 elections 'más de la quinta parte de la totalidad de los candidatos postulados tenían antecedents penales' (Ortiz 1923d: 94). Liberal or conservative, *mano dura* or presidential pushover, malleable stooge or wily nationalist, Zayas was defined by his lack of definition and inspired the ire of many.

What Turner lauds as the manifold psycho-cultural possibilities of the limen, therefore, came to be seen by some of the youngest Cuban analyst-authors as dangerous obstacles to a coherent and cohesive national identity. After initially celebrating the cathartic exposure to ambiguity and flux, many now called for a drive to define Cuban citizenship and the *sensibilidad* that would inspire it. And in a significant discursive development, many now wrote of the need for a potent act of contrition for the 'sins' of this new nation, looked to draw clear frontiers between innocence and guilt, and began to dedicate themselves in earnest to the teleological pursuit of a future perfect Cuba.

Although not all agreed on the detailed psycho-civic contours of this future collective self, significant consensus is evident amongst some analyst-authors' faith in the inherent moral purity of the long-suffering Cuban people and its axiomatic role within archetypal Cuban identity. Whilst most concurred that the Republic had 'errado el camino', therefore, the *venceremos* prophets of a reaggregated Cuba believed that the innocent Cuban *pueblo*'s integrity would ensure that this was a temporary and rectifiable deviation, not Cuba's denouement as a nation (Varona 1922: 91). This recovery of a bi-focal faith in *el pueblo* and *la patria* as an antidote to debilitating ambiguity and self-doubt is one of the most significant aspects of the national narrative in the *annus mirabilis* of 1923.

Sin and cathartic contrition hence become predominant themes for Roig de Leuchsenring and Martínez Villena. In the opening pages of his diagnosis of the *Males y vicios* that had plagued the Republic, Roig de Leuchsenring makes it clear that he exonerated *el pueblo* from all guilt: 'Hay que decir bien alto, en el umbral de este libro – de los males y vicios que en esta obra se examinan y condenan no es culpable, en ningún caso, nuestro magnífico pueblo cubano' (1961b: 14). Similarly, Martínez Villena claims that it was not the unrest of an intellectual elite that had inspired what he calls 'la Revolución del 1923', but the 'innegable virtud del pueblo cubano' (1923: 26). Both writers attempt to reassert the binary divide between benevolence and malevolence within Cuban *sensibilidad*, between the 'angels' and 'devils' they perceived to be at war within the *conciencia colectiva*. Roig de Leuchsenring, for example, presents a rogues' gallery of wrongdoers straddling the decolonisation divide, from the 'voluntario español' to the 'negociantes yanquis', from the colonial 'cleri-galla' to the 'politiqueros y desgobernantes' that came after (1961b: 271). For Martínez Villena, the cardinal sinners were 'los gobernantes obcecados' who must be forced to search their souls and make sincere and contrite amends:

> Cuenta a cuenta, hay que rezar ese rosario de rectificación. Así creará el pueblo en el arrepentimiento de los malos [...]. Y nada de subterfugios y saltos, y rezar avemarías de pensiones, pasando por alto padrenuestros de Tarafa y Lotería. Medidas radicales que beneficien al mayor número posible de ciudadanos y extirpen de una vez los malos mayores, éso queremos. (1978: 19)

For both writers, the *pueblo* is pure, its only sin being an excess of integrity and good faith: 'Ha sido traicionado, una y otra vez, en su afán, que bien merece llamarse patético, de honestidad, que lo ha impulsado [...] a apoyar en la lucha por el poder a quien enarbolase la consigna de la honradez' (Roig de Leuchsenring 1961b: 14). This hyperbole is not accidental; Roig de Leuchsenring and Martínez Villena are actively elaborating a *pueblo puro* myth that is almost as fantastical as Cosculluela's *homo cubensis*. If identity in the limen incorporates manifold and often contradictory experiences and expressions of reality, this understanding of Cuban *sensibilidad* rather sought coherence in the suppression of flux and enunciated ethical uniformity and psychological homogeneity as a defence against what these analyst-authors saw as the debilitating ambivalence of a Zayas-type archetype. Whereas the dissolution of structures is welcomed in the liminal phase, this teleological reading of the national narrative urged the reassertion of order and progress. If the limen halts historical momentum in a 'moment in and out of time', Roig de Leuchsenring and Martínez Villena reasserted the dominance of *chronos* over *logos* and pushed Cuba's story of self towards conclusion (Turner 1969: 96). Whereas the archaeo-nationalists sought to overcome the empirical limitations of *homo cubensis* with an ideological appeal to insularity, these *pueblo puro* myth-makers looked to a leap of faith in the future Cuban nation as a counterpoint to the disappointments and frustrations of 1923. Despite the fact that twenty-one years of formal independence had brought Cuba no closer to meaningful freedom and that stubborn ambivalence in every sphere had stymied the country's ability to decide its own destiny, these analyst-authors retained a fervent belief in the morality of the Cuban people and the noble manifest destiny of their nation. For Martínez Villena and Roig de Leuchsenring, this bi-focal faith became the key coordinate along the frontier between Cuban selfhood and otherness. On the maleficent side of the divide, the inveterate doubters lingered in an ambivalent limen of ideological oscil-lation and archipelagic flux between colonial and neo-colonial poles. Just as Martí had vilified those he called 'hombres de siete meses' because of their under-developed 'fe en su pueblo' (in Roig de Leuchsenring 1961b: 9), so Martínez Villena reserved special spite for the 'ciudadanos pesimistas' who stunted the wholesome growth of the Cuban Republic with indecision and self-doubt (1923: 20). Facing them across the faith divide, the inherently pure Cuban *pueblo* (formerly given to guileless trust in the hero of the day but chastened by the experience of national near-disaster) placed its faith not in individuals but in an epistemology: a temporary turning point overcome by the 'national discourse of the teleology of progress' (Bhabha 2010: 216), uncertain self-cognisance making way for the pursuit of a definitive, irrevocable and unambiguous identity. For the prophets of this luminous Cuban *porvenir* populated by a *pueblo puro*, the liminal middle of the rite of passage, therefore, was only a temporary heuristic exposure to fallibility and flux that served to inoculate the archetypes of the future against psycho-social malady and make the regenerated order more unassailable. The trajectory from this perspective was clear: from sickness and sin through catharsis to post-rite of passage purity, always inspired by the *imago* of a true *Cuba Libre* liberated from exogenous interference and endogenous vice. Although this future still seemed distant in 1923, for Martínez Villena and Roig de Leuchsenring its arrival was guaranteed: 'según las causas señaladas, hay obligación y la necesidad de triunfar; según los factores comparados, hay la probabilidad, acaso la seguridad de ese triunfo' (Martínez Villena 1923: 30). In short: *venceremos*.

The Cuban Language Community

Not all examinations of the *conciencia colectiva* in 1923 were driven by such fervid faith in a perfectible future. If Roig de Leuchsenring and Martínez Villena preached about the pure thoughts and deeds of *el pueblo* to come, Ortiz's vernacular dictionary, *Un catauro de cubanismos* (1923), insisted that 'Cuba tiene el lenguaje sucio de su mala vida' and proudly laid claim to appropriately dirty words for every aspect of this inexorably hard life (Ortiz 1923d: 10).

Language and identity are of course irrevocably enmeshed; from within the infinitely complex quotidian chaos, language distils, performs and expresses experience. For Roy Harris, language-making is the 'essential process by which men construct a cultural identity for themselves, and for the communities to which they see themselves as belonging' (1980: Preface). Through exploration of the lexicographic landmarks of a 'language community', therefore, it is possible to map the topography of its collective consciousness and apprehend and analyse what Wittgenstein calls the 'limits of [its] world' (1955: 149). Ortiz's *Catauro* is just such an attempt to map Cuba's cultural territory through exploration of its lexicographic distance and difference from both the metropolitan mother tongue and all other linguistic shores. In this, it is a critical text in the decolonisation of Cuban *sensibilidad* and makes an influential contribution to the *lex* and lexis of Cuban *civitas* in 1923.

The extrication of distinct *cubanismos* from within peninsular Spanish was complex and contested. Although ardent Cuban anti-neo-colonialists may have sought ideological support in myths of pre-colonial national genesis, their assertions of idiosyncrasy were discomforted by the fact that those myths were inevitably conceived and communicated in *el castellano*: 'Somos a través de un idioma que es nuestro siendo extranjero', bemoaned Juan Marinello in his *Americanismo y cubanismo literario* (1977: 48–9). And since 1713, the Real Academia de la Lengua Española had used its *Diccionario* to fight any erosion of idiomatic empire by charting inflexible frontiers of Castilian orthodoxy. Three hundred years on, independence struggles in Hispanic America had forced the edges of imperial influence back, but the Academy persevered in its lexicographic and ideological endeavours. The fourteenth edition of the *Diccionario* was published in 1914 and soon provoked a flurry of *suplementos* from Latin American lexicographers determined to win recognition for the peculiarities of their own vernacular voices. One of the most notable Cuban supplements was Constantino Suárez's *Vocabulario cubano* (1921). The author (who actually wrote under the pseudonym 'El Españolito') sought not to undermine the official lexicon's 'autoridad suprema', but rather to make a Cuban contribution to the Academy's efforts *limpiar, fijar y dar esplendor* to the Spanish language everywhere (Suárez 1921: viii).[7] Ortiz's *Catauro de cubanismos* is more boldly heterodox, more charged with the 'audacia' and 'insolencia' that some critics see as the preserve of the young (Guerra, in

---

[7] The official motto of the Real Academia Española. The Academia Cubana de la Lengua was not established until 1926.

Kuchilán 1975: 12). Unlike Suárez, Ortiz did not offer a supplement to the Academy's authoritative lexicography nor a re-reading of the Americanisms at the edge; the *Catauro* contains a fundamental re-articulation of the Spanish language within audaciously independent idiomatic frontiers by an author intimately attuned to the island's *mala vida*.

Although a dictionary might seem an unlikely medium through which to deliver a manifesto for expressive autonomy, even the most seemingly dispassionate lexicons, as Raymond Williams suggests, may have occult agendas:

> The air of massive impersonality which the Oxford Dictionary communicates is not so impersonal, so purely scholarly, or so free of active social and political values as might be supposed from its occasional use. Indeed, to work closely in it is at times to get a fascinating insight into what can be called the ideology of its editors. (1976: 16)

Despite Ortiz's self-effacing assertion that the *Catauro* recorded nothing more than 'algunos frutos de la tierra, que habíamos recogido cruzando la selva del lenguaje criollo', it is hardly necessary to read between its lines to reveal an unapologetically subjective approach to identity and identity's idiomatic articulation (1923d: vii). With the title alone Ortiz made it clear that his dictionary was designed to put carefully chosen and infinitely *criollo* words into the collective Cuban mouth. Instead of an encyclopaedia or lexicon, Ortiz wrote a *Catauro* (or woven basket for collecting food), an Americanism redolent of aromatic tropical exuberance. A step further into this idiomatic undergrowth and we are told that the *Catauro* is a catalogue, not of *voces*, *frases* or *refranes* (as in Suárez), but 'un mamotreto de "cubicherías" lexicográficas' (Ortiz 1923d: 17). From the opening pages, therefore, it is clear that the *Catauro* offers a most enigmatic map through 'la selva del lenguaje criollo' for those not already familiar with the expressive Cuban terrain.[8]

Ortiz's definition of one of the most emblematic of Cuban fruits (both culturally and agriculturally) is a neat synthesis of the *Catauro*'s tone and purpose:

> *Guayabo* – el árbol que produce la *guayaba*, dice el diccionario de la Academia. ¿Pero por qué añade: 'En francés: *goyavier*'? ¿Quiere decir con ésto que es un galicismo? ¿Sí? Pues no es verdad: como no lo es *guayaba*, tampoco lo es *guayabo*. ¿No? Pues que, ¿acaso en cada otra papeleta del Diccionario se trae a colación la traducción francesa de cada vocablo?

---

[8]   The fact that the first edition of *Un catauro de cubanismos* was not ordered alphabetically but rather presented in 'su forma deshilvanada' would not have helped (Ortiz 1923d: vii).

¡Fuera, pues, el *goyavier*! Esa etimología, si se propone como tal, no vale una *guayaba*, para decirlo en criollo. Recuérdese, en cambio, algunas de las veintidós acepciones y derivados de *guayaba*, traidas por Suárez, que, como *guayabal*, *guayabera*, *guayabito*, harían mejor papel en el diccionario castellano que esta inexplicable etimología gabacha. ¡Que no nos vengan la Academia con *guayabas*!, y consignemos así, de paso, otro cubanismo. (43)

Although this contemptuous assault on the Academy smacks of militant linguistic nationalism, in Ortiz's defence of Cuban definitions for the fruits of Cuban soil lies the kernel of what could be called his liminality. As one of the magnum Cuban scholars of the twentieth century, and one of its most active analyst-authors (as we shall see), Ortiz (up)rooted his epistemology in a constant oscillation between critical distance and impassioned proximity. Although shunning the imaginative liberty of literary expression for the apparent objective constraints of criminology, anthropology, lexicography and ethnography, many of Ortiz's texts often read more like ardent manifestoes than scientific tracts, with Pérez Firmat arguing, as we have seen, that Ortiz's prose was less scientific and more 'exuberant, tendentious, and even fruity' (1989: 18). I rather see the importance of Ortiz's contribution to the analysis and concomitant inscription of the Cuban national narrative in precisely that oscillation between measured academic endeavour and flights of illuminated imagination, in both the objective sense and subjective sensibility of his narrative. It would be difficult to deny, for example, the investigative achievement of his six-hundred page dissertation on the socio-economic history of tobacco and sugar on the island, yet it remains indubitable that the most evocative insights of the *Contrapunteo cubano del tabaco y el azúcar* (1940) are born of the metaphoric meta-narrative of the bittersweet *contrapunteo* (both a dialectic encounter and an intimate dance) between Don Tabaco and Doña Azúcar. Ortiz's imaginative energy makes him no less scientific, only more liminal. Turner would agree. Although he admires intellectuals' patient construction of objective theoretical systems, it is in the 'scattered ideas [and] flashes of insight taken out of systemic context' that Turner perceives true liminal percipience (1969: 23). Hence, although the *Catauro* appears to be driven by a desire to wrest descriptive authority from the distant Academy and its insular acolytes and 'decirlo en *criollo*', a close reading reveals what I would call the latent liminality of this manifesto for Cuba's linguistic and imaginative decolonisation. Whilst it certainly reflects on the foundational myths of nationhood, traces the linguistic evidence of Cuba's insularity, undertakes a radical review of racial and cultural identity and seeks to forge a vernacular voice from within 'the matrix of the mother tongue' (Pérez Firmat 1989: 27), whilst simultaneously parrying the bombastic linguistic expansion of 'the Americans' (who had metonymically conquered both continents in anticipation of a more physical presence south of the Rio Grande, with the Spanish 'e' silenced), Ortiz's epistemology and the conclusions it leads toward are quite different to those of Le Roy, Lamar Schweyer, Roig de Leuchsenring or Martínez Villena.

Liminal Ortiz

Archaeology was one of Ortiz's earliest passions. In *Historia de la arqueología indocubana* (1923), he contributed to the debate on *homo cubensis* by parrying the arch-insularists' thesis with a defence of Columbus's stubborn insistence that he had discovered the westward passage to Cipango, given that the Taínos and Ciboneyes the Admiral encountered in Cuba were, in their ethnogenetic origins, actually Chinese.[9] This sarcastic swipe at the kind of *siboneyismo*[10] purveyed by Cosculluela persists into the *Catauro*, in which Ortiz adds lexicographic to his archaeological impatience with the notion of an autochthonous proto-*hombre* founding an original Cuban *sensibilidad* to which all subsequent offshore contributions are undesirable appendages. Interrogating the etymology of the *voces* in the dictionaries of Suárez and others, Ortiz is scathing of their ingenuousness:

> El siboneyismo [...] ha llevado en Cuba al prurito de catalogar como voces autóctonas todas las palabras de origen dudoso y, aún, a muchas de reconocida derivación castellana, catalana, gallega, andaluza, vascuence, africana or gitana [...]. A menudo a un bastardo de inglés o americano nos lo convierten en siboney o caribe, como a cualquier pelagatos o mataperros achinado en descendiente directo de Amadís de Gaula, *por los cuatro costados*. (1923d: 9 & 12)

Whilst other lexicographers turned eager ears to echoes of indigenous etymologies in contemporary *cubanismos* to thus buttress romantic mythologies with linguistic fact, Ortiz counters with evidence of Cuba's place in a linguistic archipelago that extended well beyond the Caribbean basin. Scorning what he saw as Suárez's autochthonous myopia in claiming that a word such as *jaba*,

---

9   See Rojas 2008b: 250.

10   *Siboneyismo* was originally a movement born in the literary *tertulias* of Domingo del Monte in the 1840s in an attempt to 'Cubanise' the Spanish poetic form of *el romance* and thus 'propagate a tentative and derivative sense of their Cuban identity' (Kapcia 2005: 52). The emblematic text of the movement is José Fornaris's *Cantos del Siboney*, which made an oblique critique of the social stratification of colonial Cuba and evoked a utopian age of noble indigenous savagery.

or 'cesta, cuya mayor dimensión es la altura', was a 'voz Caribe', for example, Ortiz insists instead that 'fueron los marinos y conquistadores andaluces los que le aplicaron la voz comunísima arabe, *al-chaba*, que aún conserva el diccionario de la Academia para significar la larga cesta para flechas, *aljaba*' (ibid.: 39). To other lexicons' insistence on etymological immobility, Ortiz brings the immense complexity of living languages colliding and colluding over centuries of migration into and out of the island:

> *Guafe* – pequeño muelle o tablado sobre el mar. Añade Zayas, dándola como indiana: "probablemente la letra F, se ha introducido en este vocablo sustituyendo erróneamente a otra." Nada de eso. Cuervo, varios lustros antes de escribir Zayas, ya había dicho que procede del inglés *wharf*, y … *pax Christi*, no fueron siboneyes, taínos ni caribes los que nos la legaron, sino piratas o filibusteros de muy distinto linaje. (134)

By refusing to accept contemporary Cuba's genealogical and cultural debt to *homo cubensis* and the *siboneyismos* he allegedly spoke, Ortiz eschews any attempt to find or found a mythical and autarkic language community, positioning himself instead in the limen between origin and invention, between endogenous immobility and exogenous flux, from where to best appreciate and give authority to the multivalent voices that he hears articulating Cuba's insular idiosyncrasy.

Although challenging the inexorable bonds between island frontiers and the homogeneous nation within, however, Ortiz does not altogether abandon 'the recurrent metaphor of landscape as the inscape of national identity' (Bhabha 2010: 205). Many of Ortiz's *cubanismos* emerge from a fundamentally spatial praxis and are suggestive of a national narrative inspired by the physical milieu within which it is inscribed. In the *Catauro*, flora, fauna and even climatic conditions all acquire metaphorical significance in the Cuban vernacular *voz*. The *seboruco*, for example, is a 'piedra roquiza, porosa y erizada, que se encuentra a flor de tierra, particularmente en las costas', but is also a hard-headed, 'bruto, ignorante' person who stubbornly resists the tides of others' opinions (1923d: 126). *Sabina*, 'árbol indígena y silvestre de hojas aplanadas', is applied with metaphorical malice to 'el curioso o dado a enterarse de lo que no le importa' (Ortiz 1985: 439). The *bijirita* is 'un pájaro emigrante […] que pasa en Cuba el otoño y el invierno', but is also a Cuban *criollo* born of a Spanish father with seasonal affiliations to both shores (ibid.: 64). The hurricanes that torment the island during the autumn months have been at the heart of insular mythology since well before *el castellano* conquered Cuba. Once more on the liminal threshold, Ortiz judiciously defends the Antillean origins of the word *juracán*, lamenting that the word 'haya caído aquí en desuso, sustituida por un cultismo helenista, como es ciclón, importado por los ingleses' (1923d: 52).

Domestic, as well as savage, spaces have taken their place within the national consciousness through the kind of metaphorical osmosis in which Ortiz delights. In analysing the exclamatory expression *cierrapuertas*, he distances the *cubanismo* from the antiquated Spanish war cry *¡cierra españa!* used in the wars of re-conquest against the North Africans, describing instead

> el ruido y acción de cerrar precipitádamente las puertas de las casas por alarma de algún alboroto o peligro, *se armó un cierrapuertas*, se dice. Sí tiene relaciones, por composición y prudencia, con el otro cubanismo *salpa-fuera*; solo que con éste se procura que salgan y con aquél que no entren. En uno y otro caso suele *armarse* un *correcorre* en una y otra dirección. (ibid.: 31)

In the first expression the domestic haven is secured against external menace, whereas the second produces a chaotic *correcorre* to escape the enemy within. In whichever direction the metaphoric travel takes us, the *leitmotif* is the idiomatic innervation of mobility and flux. As a metaphor for the sanctity and sanctuary of the island redoubt, *cierrapuertas* and *salpafuera* eloquently encapsulate the liminal indecision between resolute insularity and archipelagic interaction. Cuba, it seems, is caught in a perennial *correcorre* between the two.

Although Ortiz's claims to have composed his *Catauro* 'cruzando la selva del lenguaje criollo' (Ortiz 1923d: vii), the land-life-language association is at its most intense when he emerges from the forest and reaches the sea. The *Catauro* is peppered with 'expresiones náuticas' and 'acepciones marítimas' that are clear proof of the 'secular contacto con gente marinesca' (21 & 23). What for the Real Academia's dictionary were mere states of the sea became for Ortiz profound states of the soul. *Calmachicha*, which in the peninsular *Diccionario* described maritime tranquillity, becomes in the vernacular *voz* a 'calmudo, flemático' Cuban (21). *Escarceo* in Spain was 'un movimiento en la superficie del mar', but even intimate and interpersonal relations on *la isla* seem ruled by the humours of the sea with the word being applied, 'elegante y apropiadamente [...], a los incidentes orales que como pequeñas olas suelen levantarse en los debates [...]. Tuvo un escarceo con su suegra' (51). The word *aguada*, originally used to describe the coastal wells from where the Spanish colonial fleet replenished its drinking water, has formed a beachhead, 'como otras muchas compañeras tan saladas o salobres', and conquered the entire Cuban language community: 'hoy la usamos, en general, para decir el sitio donde bebe el ganado' (31–2).

The *Catauro*'s cataloguing of this oceanic irrigation of land-locked language in even the most intractable inland terrain erodes more than lexicographic frontiers. The insular coastline, which for other analyst-authors offered a clear geopolitical and ideological border from where to resist colonial and neo-colonial incursions or stand fast against epidemics of otherness, becomes a liminal space where collusion overcomes collision, dialogue subverts diatribe and insiders leaking out cross paths with outsiders wandering in. The collective cohesion that other analyst-authors attempted to foment with evocations of an insular archetype always and forever isolated from the rest of the world is battered by Ortiz's insistence on the fluid anti-essence of oceanic subjectivity. To the telluric rootedness of endogenous origins, Ortiz brings an 'anoriginal ontology' that 'erodes the sedentary *habitus* of the modern subject' (Dubow 2004: 219). To the Siboneyistas' *homo cubensis*, Ortiz counters *homo maritimus*, baptised in the liquid epiphany of an immigrant's epic voyage and unable to forget the saltwater idioms of his beginnings. Far from marking the 'the boundary that secures the cohesive limits of the Western nation', the insular edge in Ortiz becomes what Bhabha calls 'a contentious *internal* liminality providing a place from which to speak both of, and as, the minority, the exilic, the marginal and the emergent' (2010: 213–14). Just as the island's seemingly secure physical and metaphysical edge is worn away, so the frontier between identity and alterity is equally exposed to Ortiz's corrosive liminality.

Ortiz opens with the Afro-Cuban other, and is as scathing of other lexicons' colour-blindness as he is of their deafness to non-indigenous etymologies. Although his book *Los negros brujos* (1906) was fundamentally racist in tenor, by 1923 Ortiz was the leading scholar of Afro-Cuban culture and its axiomatic role in the island's heterogeneity. One of the *Catauro*'s most virulent criticisms of Suárez's *Vocabulario*, for example, refers to its utter failure to recognise and accredit the African etymologies of many *cubanismos*: 'como si la gran población africana que vino a nuestro país no hubiera importado junto con sus cuerpos doblados por la servidumbre, su alma, su cultura, su religión, sus lenguajes' (Ortiz 1923d: 12). Just as Ortiz replies to the Siboneyistas' romantic mythology of autochthonous peculiarity with evidence of ethnographic and linguistic imports from everywhere, so to the eugenicists' horror of a descent into black *barbarie* he retorts by dissecting the collective *corpus* and exposing 'el corazón de ébano' that the slave trade had transplanted from the coast of Africa (viii). In many ways, the *Catauro* is an indispensable guide to Ortiz's later explorations of Afro-Cuban culture. Alongside the *indigenismos* exposed as *andalucismos*, many of the most significant imports in Ortiz's lexicon come from the west coast of Africa. Citing words such as *bilongo*, *cocorioco*, *cumbancha*, *fufú*, *guarapo* and *sirimbo*, Ortiz claims that the original stimulus of the *Catauro* was his intention to bring to light the 'raíces y flores traídas y arrojadas al azar por los esclavos africanos, mientras tumbaban monte en nuestra isla para siembra de cañas y cafetos' (ibid.: Prologue).[11]

But I read Ortiz as driven by more than a desire to acknowledge the ethnic and linguistic complexity of multi-coloured Cuba. The *Catauro* effectively deconstructs the epistemology of identity that relies for its understanding of 'I' on an antagonistic counterpoint with 'You'. Ortiz's understanding of identity rather resembles Derrida's 'negative theology', in which self emerges, not by recoiling from other, but by accepting the presence of alterity at the heart of identity. Ortizean, like Derridian, identity turns simultaneously inwards and outwards, towards the familiar and the alien, the ancient and the recently arrived. But this celebration of the ambiguity of apostrophic identity does not diminish the *Catauro*'s significance as a determined manifesto for the Cuban language community. Although tossing the Real Academia's *goyaviers* back in its face, Ortiz nevertheless acknowledges that more *cubanismos* were born in the mouths of Andalucians than of Arawaks; whilst insisting that Cuba must rebel against 'la autoridad del real diccionario', the *Catauro* takes Spain's side in numerous examples of excessive dogmatism on the part of insular lexicographers (Ortiz 1923d: 68–9). Beyond the *Catauro*, Ortiz's engagement with Spanish cultural influence in Cuba followed a similarly ambiguous trajectory. In *La reconquista de América: Reflexiones sobre el panhispanismo* (1911), he had reacted ferociously against what he described as the 'neoimperialismo manso' of Rafael Altamira y Crevea's proposal of pan-Hispanic consolidation under the banner of common cultural heritage (Ortiz 1911: 9). In 1926, however, as already indicated, Ortiz founded the Institución Hispanocubana de Cultura to foment intellectual collaboration between Cuba and Spain through conferences and cultural exchange. Ortiz's attitude towards US neo-colonialism was equally complex. In 'La decadencia cubana', a 1924 diagnosis of Cuba's parlous economic and cultural condition, he seemed to concur with Fernández Valledor's opinion that the *danza de los millones* had rung the death-knell for Cuba's endogenous productive capacity:

> Y las minas son extranjeras. Y los ferrocarriles son extranjeros, aún los mas pomposamente exhibidos como de compañías cubanas, y los teléfonos. Y los muelles y, sobre todo, los bancos, ya que bien pocos de los que había hispano-cubanos, han logrado resistir el sacudimiento de 1920. (Ortiz 1973b[1924]: 26)

---

[11] Ortiz's analysis of the Afro-Cuban contribution to the vernacular voice was stated more explicitly in his 1924 *Glosario de afronegrismos*.

And yet the *Catauro* does not replicate this sentiment in lexicographic anti-imperialism, with Ortiz fully acknowledging the linguistic invasion from the north in words such as '*Bordin* – casa de huéspedes o "boarding" ', '*Florimbó'* – madera para entablar. Del inglés "floaring [sic] board" ' and '*Lonchar* – merendar. Comer fiambres. Del inglés "to lunch" ' (Ortiz 1923/1985: 45). In *Reconquista*, Ortiz even seemed to commit the cardinal sin of anti-patriotism by suggesting that closer proximity to the US could be beneficial for the adolescent Republic: 'Civilización mundial, sólo civilización. Hemos de beberla pronto y mucha, donde más cerca la encontremos, aunque sea rodilla en tierra e inclinándonos sobre la fuente norteamericana' (1911: 34–5). Far from a Renan-like exhortation of innervating conquest by a foreign force,[12] I rather read Ortiz's ambivalence not as a cession of Cuba's *destino* to foreign powers, nor as the pursuit of purity through externally-imposed catharsis, but as a bold declaration of confidence in the power of plurality: 'Si todos los cubanos, además del castellano, hablásemos el inglés, estaríamos más lejos de una absorción política que en la actualidad, porque el poliglotismo es cultura, la cultura es fuerza y la fuerza es independencia' (ibid.: 54). In this ideological equation of multiplicity, identity and liberty, Ortiz rejects the pursuit of collective strength through the homogenisation of *el pueblo* and eschews the discursive frontiers of socio-cultural homogeneity, displaying instead a virulent allergy to over-simplification. Hence, in unearthing the Anglo-Saxon roots of words others claimed as part of a mythological indigenous legacy, Ortiz demonstrates that the encounter between exogenous and endogenous accents is 'supersincrética', as Benítez Rojo suggests (1989: 71). Anglicisms may have been unloaded onto the Cuban *guafe* but they are not passively and aculturally accepted, but creatively mauled and masticated, even acquiring a dubious indigenous genealogy along the way, which Ortiz mocked, but may well have admired as the height of syncretic irreverence and lexicographic inventiveness.

In 1923, therefore, in response to the perceived menace of persistent cultural neo-colonialism and the potential erosive force of otherness (whether racial or [up]rooted in a lack of definition), Ortiz neither retreats onto an insular bulwark nor resigns himself to a cultural eclipse from the north, launching instead a remarkable lexicographic counter-colonialism. To defend Cuba's vernacular voice he projects it far beyond the island's shores. To the Academia's entry for *plátano*, for example, which suggested that the fruit is

---

[12] As Paris was squeezed in the 1871 Prussian siege, Renan allegedly welcomed the defeat of the decadent French by the vigorous Teutons with the exclamation: '¡Que nos conquisten!' (in Unamuno 1996: 52).

eaten either raw or in preserves, Ortiz responds by pointing to Cuban flavours
and inflections at the geo-cultural heart of Castilian orthodoxy:

> Y frito, tambien, señores académicos, frito de varias maneras, y salcochado.
> Y conste que el autor de este mamotreto ha comido plátanos fritos en
> Madrid, fritos por manos cubanas. Prueben los venerables académicos y, a
> buen seguro, que en la próxima edición de su diccionario darán cabida a los
> platanitos fritos. (Ortiz 1923d: 81)

Far from welcoming foreign influences in order to purge Cuba and
cubanismos of their impurities, as Renan histrionically hoped of the Prussians,
Ortiz proudly advocates the exportation of the lexicographic products of
Cuba's dirty mouth and hard life. This is because, unlike Martínez Villena,
Roig de Leuchsenring and others, Ortiz is simply not convinced by either the
congenital innocence of the Cuban people or the merit of pursuing perfection
as a national ideal. In his 1923 presidential address to the Sociedad Económica
de Amigos del País, Ortiz bemoans the same 'momentos muy sómbrios'
identified by others, but does not attempt any moral taxonomy of 'angels'
and 'devils', calling instead for collective recognition that the catastrophic
state of the Republic: 'no es culpa de un sólo gobernante, no es culpa de
un sólo partido. Es algo más doloroso; es culpa de todos, es *culpa cubana*'
(1923d: 11–12). Ortiz therefore, like St Augustine, sees blame beginning with
nosotros, not *ellos*. Nevertheless, he doesn't rush to recommend an act of
national contrition to atone for and expunge these sins. Rather than pious faith
in the purity of today leading to the perfection of tomorrow, Ortiz advocates
pragmatic recognition of ethical, alongside linguistic, fallibility. He points not
to the future victory but to the here-and-now *luchita*. In giving voice to the
island's 'mala vida', he stubbornly resists both offshore attempts to 'clean' *el
castellano* and the onshore purge of Cuba's collective *sensibilidad*. Defending
the indecorous term *sinvergüenza*, for example, which had been excised both
from the peninsular *Diccionario* and insular *suplementos*, Ortiz is adamant:

> Si la supresión del vocablo fuera indicio de supresión de la especie, a fe que
> pudiera la Academia y todos los gramáticos darse por muy contentos; más
> parece que no ha sucedido así, y esto lo comprueba la existencia de algunos
> magníficos ejemplares que todavía pululan por estos mundos bien rollizos y
> satisfechos. (Ortiz 1923d: 10)

But this is not the kind of pessimistic resignation to human debility that
outraged Martínez Villena. Ortiz is rather elaborating a subversive counter-
faith which exchanges perfectibility for a celebration of congenital flaws,

which eschews the pursuit of purity in favour of a candid acceptance of fallibility as fecund for human consciousness. In this, Ortiz closely resembles his near-contemporary Miguel de Unamuno (in *Del Sentimiento Trágico de la Vida*) who turned to the history of medicine to demonstrate that a healthy organism was not necessarily one that was free from disease:

> No consiste tanto el progreso en expulsar de nosotros los gérmenes de las enfermedades, o más bien las enfermedades mismas, cuanto en acomodarlas a nuestro organismo, enriqueciéndolo tal vez, en macerarlas en nuestra sangre [...]. Podríamos decir que un hombre perfectamente sano no sería ya un hombre, sino un animal irracional [...] por falta de enfermedad alguna que encendiera su razón. (1931: 27)

This acceptance of psycho-social sickness and sin as integral elements of collective well-being further distances Ortiz's understanding of identity from the dialectic antagonism of self and other. Like Emmanuel Lévinas four decades later, Ortiz is reluctant to ascribe to an epistemology of identity that seeks either to expel alterity beyond impermeable metaphysical frontiers or to assimilate it forcefully within the overly-simplistic discursive *pueblo*. Instead of this 'ethico-political violence', both the French philosopher and the Cuban ethnographer posit an understanding of identity that undermines the pursuit of (post-liminal) progress and order with the counter-metaphor of dialogue (Lévinas, in Young 2004: 44). Instead of a teleological pursuit of reconciliation and conclusion, this dialogue proposes an acceptance of asymmetry and the promotion of intercourse without ever dissolving the fundamental irreconcilability of opposites. This notion of a dialogic *sensibilidad* is manifest in the *Catauro* in two ways. First, the author insists on the open-endedness of his lexicon. With disarming humility amidst others' strident diagnoses of Cuba's malaise and prescriptions for an all-inclusive cure, the *Catauro* is presented as a stroll along one, but by no means the only, path through the 'selva del lenguaje criollo' (Ortiz 1923d: vii):

> Hemos de insistir en que nuestras apuntaciones sólo son tales; acopio de material para que el artifice pueda construir su obra. Ni agotan los cubanismos, que aún faltarán, sin duda, por registrar; ni las definiciones pueden estimarse como definitivas, ni la etimologías como inconmutables. (18)

Second, the *Catauro* welcomes contestation and contradiction, seeking coherence within, not dogmatic cohesion to its enunciation of the vernacular *voz*. In defining the colloquial *pararse*, for 'ponerse de pie', for example,

'El Españolito' Suárez's dictionary sought to distance 'cuantos gustan de hablar bien' from both the Cuban *vulgos* and the Academy's tolerance of their linguistic barbarity (1921: 400). Ortiz rounds on Suárez's attempt to cling to a purity of expression that even the Academy had abandoned, and instead proposes a fertile and fluid dialogue between the Academy, the insular elite and the mass of Cubans more intimately familiar with the island's hard life *luchitas*:

> En defensa del americanismo, ¿con qué derecho se nos puede exigir que aquí renovemos el lenguaje al compás de España? Acaso por conservar ciertos vocablos castellanos, muy propios y muy legítimamente adquiridos, ¿no venimos a ser en ello más puristas que los españoles? Que resistuyan los españoles su circulación al vocablo, que ningún delito cometió contra las leyes del lenguaje para vivir desterrado de su patria, bien que aquí le vaya tan guapamente, que puede decirse que se ha parado. (Ortiz 1923d: 9 & 58)

Ortiz sees this exchange as ongoing and doesn't pretend that his catalogue of *cubanismos* is conclusive; it is enough that the vernacular voice has clambered to its feet: *se ha parado*.

In this acceptance of flux lies the principal counterpoint between Ortiz's *Catauro* and others' 1923 examinations of Cuba's *conciencia colectiva*. Whereas Trelles, Le Roy and Lamar Schweyer posited impermeable insular frontiers to repel all others (and their alterities) and safeguard the racial and cultural purity within, Ortiz's identity ideal is a *bijirita*, an archipelagic archetype in constant migratory movement. Whereas Roig de Leuchsenring and Martínez Villena perceived ambiguity and ill-definition as a canker at the core of resolute *cubanía*, Ortiz gave voice to the indefinite uncertainty and perennial flux of the Cuban language community and the life it enunciated. Whereas those younger analyst-authors looked towards a teleological and optimistic future, driven by a forward-looking historiography of constant dialectical progression, Ortiz was reluctant to make a leap of faith towards a conclusive vernacular voice in the mouth of a pure and fully accomplished *pueblo*. In my interpretation, this epistemological distance is the result of fundamentally different approaches to the collective rite of passage and the liminal interstice therein. As already suggested, the prophets of a Cuban *pueblo puro* saw sustained ambiguity and flux as potentially catastrophic, and advocated their subjugation through resolute faith in a perfect future in which coherent and wholly cohesive identity *vencerá*. For Ortiz, this teleological pursuit of perfection was quixotic, the liminal and subjunctive mood of 'may-be, might-be, as-if, fantasy, hypothesis' was not a temporary disturbance but a congenital Cuban state, not a temporary evil but the permanent presence of ambiguity and hesitation (Turner, in Alexander 1991: 30). The *imago* of identity, from this perspective, is not a definitive metamorphosis into a perpetual archetype, but a constant transformation; catharsis becomes a Unamunean acceptance of infirmity as integral to long-term human health, contrition becomes a dialogic encounter between the angels and devils within the *conciencia colectiva*. The goal of Ortiz's *Catauro*, therefore, was not to move beyond mutability towards a conclusive Cuban *sensibilidad*, but to come to terms with ongoing ambivalence, irresolution and guilt as integral elements of the Cuban condition.

Un catauro de cubanismos offered no conclusions; the liminal moment that inspired it did not ask for any. 1923 was an *annus mirabilis* in Cuba's self-cognisance that called not for idiomatic answers, but for an uninhibited exploration of all cultural and linguistic possibilities, opening the frontiers to the most awkward Anglicism one minute and drawing in the next towards the archaic eye of the indigenous *juracán*. The *Catauro* subverted metropolitan metaphors for life on the edge of the Hispanic world, challenged precon-ceived archetypes emerging from the romantic fog of insular *indigenismo*, and impugned the pure codes of *cubanía* purveyed by ardent prophets of a future Cuban utopia. In this chapter we have seen that the *Catauro*'s most influential contribution to the articulation of Cuban national identity was to embrace the poetics of perennial uncertainty and applaud the contingency of manifold re-tellings of the national narrative. For Ortiz, as for the deconstructionist Derrida, 'the final *Beschluß* is not the conclusion of a demonstration, but the farewell of an envoi' (Derrida 1995: 42).

2

1927: *Nihil admirari*?

As the 1920s progressed, Ortiz's suspicion of a teleological pursuit of integrated national identity seemed well founded. The venal President Zayas made way in 1925 for the soon-to-be much worse Machado and future victory for the embattled *pueblo* seemed as far away as ever. In 1927, a year often considered a mere 'preamble, footnote or epilogue' to the national narrative (Wright 1988: 109), the twenty-fifth anniversary of independence marked another turning point in in Cuba's twentieth-century trajectory and provoked renewed reflection on the Republic's past, present and future: '¿Qué hemos hecho en estos veinte y cinco años de cruento aprendizaje cívico?', asked the editors of vanguard magazine *revista de avance*,[1] which first appeared in March 1927 (1:4: 97). This chapter examines some of the answers offered by analyst-authors of Cuba's collective identity. It will show that the 'liminalists' once again faced the 'reaggregationists' over the pages of the national narrative, but will point to a significant discursive shift in this confrontation. From 1923's concentration on spatial, racial or cultural otherness, we will now see the debate displaced towards the notion of temporal alterity; in 1927 the Other comes not from elsewhere, but from 'elsewhen'. This chapter examines the Cuban vanguard's assault on the old guard's aesthetic, ideological and discursive dominance on the island at a watershed moment, a moment Celina Manzoni describes as 'la confluencia [...] de una conciencia estética y de una conciencia social capaces de constituir una cultura nueva a partir de la ruptura de la tradición' (2001: 21). This chapter will suggest, however, that this 'ruptura' was only half the collective story. We will see examine evidence of definite attempts to elucidate a 'nihilistic'[2] collective *sensibilidad* wholly unencumbered by the past, but we will also uncover counter-narratives that point to psycho-cultural continuity across any schismatic divide.

---

[1] The magazine's name was always in lower case.

[2] The terms 'nihilism' and 'nihilistic' are used here to describe a type of generational conflict, a kind of historical nihilism in the sense of a 'total rejection of current [...] principles', rather than in the sense of 'an extreme form of scepticism, involving the denial of all existence' (*OED* 1989).

Old guard *vs* vanguard

Although their endeavours in the Wars of Independence had transformed the *veteranos* into almost unimpeachable national heroes in 1898, the United States' usurpation of the laurels of victory, the ratification of the despised Platt Amendment and the self-serving peacetime behaviour of some of the campaign's most senior commanders cast a gloomy pall over the heroic legacy of the *independentista* struggle. With José Martí, Antonio Maceo, Calixto García and Máximo Gómez all dead by 1905, the veteran generals who were left oscillated between venerability and vice with a be-medalled chest being no guarantee of reputable Republican conduct. In the early 1920s, however, the desire for a nihilistic rupture with the perceived venalities of the past was only inchoate. The Movimiento Nacional de Veteranos y Patriotas (founded in August 1923), for example, was the result of collaboration between some of Cuba's most venerable elder statesmen and its most radical youngsters. Led by General Carlos García Velez (Calixto García's son), but ideologically guided by Martínez Villena, the Movimiento was a mercurial mix of martial tradition-alism and iconoclastic revolt. In many senses it captured the popular desire for harmony between these two forces and was on the cusp of becoming a signif-icant challenge to the Liberal–Conservative political monopoly when Zayas's government realised the threat and sought to snuff the Movimiento out. An indecisive uprising led by General Laredo Brú followed, but the ideological friction between the younger participants and those Le Riverend calls 'los elementos más conservadores' saw the rebellion and then the Movimiento itself fade quickly away (2001: 198). Whilst frustratingly anticlimactic for its supporters, others saw this denouement as irrefutable proof that the surviving senior *independentistas* had become pariahs in the Republic and that radical regeneration was the only option for a future Free Cuba.

This regeneration, at least in the highest political office, was not quick to come. As Zayas stepped down in a last frantic flurry of self-enrichment, the choices before the jaded Cuban people were limited. In the 1925 presi-dential campaign the ever-buoyant Menocal (whose record was already blemished by his dubious performance in two previous presidential terms) faced another 'hero' of 1898, General Gerardo Machado. Although some already muttered about Machado's past acts of 'heroism' (Thomas reports that he misspent his youth rustling cattle with his father [2001: 34]), the ex-butcher's pledge to use a merciless *mano dura* to clean up Cuban civic and political life appealed to many. In this, the beginnings of a shift from the lexis of *civitas* towards the strong-arm and sword-wielding *lex* of what would become the *machadato* was perhaps clear from the outset. Faced with a choice between Menocal and Machado, many opted for the devil they did not yet know: 'hubo una gran votación espontánea a favor de Machado por razón de la demagogia de sus manifestaciones y como repulsa nacional al candidato conservador' (Le Riverend 2001: 230). The first two years of Machado's presidency were marked by relative calm before the sanguinary storm to come. Bumper sugar crops came in (although at low prices), gambling and prostitution dens were closed, the promised public works programmes got underway (including a *carretera central* to join Havana and Santiago de Cuba) and General Crowder (who would remain US ambassador until mid-1927) told Secretary of State Kellogg that 'most Cubans favoured a second term for Machado' (in Thomas 2001: 355). But beneath the surface, sinister violence seethed. Whilst critical journalists were mysteriously murdered and student leaders menaced, the fiercest blows from Machado's *mano dura* were reserved for workers protesting against deteriorating labour conditions. In the autumn of 1925, a strike by the Sindicato de la Industria Fábrica was broken up by wildly firing police. Later in the year Julio Antonio Mella was arrested and then nearly perished in an eighteen-day hunger strike. In early 1926, the Confederación Nacional Obrera de Cuba's (CNOC) secretary-general, Alfredo López, was thrown to the sharks in Havana harbour (Thomas 2001: 347–52). In April 1927, when the Cuban Congress began to discuss constitutional reform that would allow the president and all senators and representatives to serve an extra two years without re-election, many Cubans' (and particularly young Cubans') illusions about Machado 'el bueno' began to evaporate.

Once again, those charged with piloting Cuba through the uncertain waters of early independence seemed determined to dash the Republic against the rocks of malfeasance, thuggery and theft. After twenty-five years of bitter disappointment, many Cubans looked not to reform or repair through electoral renovation, but to a radical schism from the perceived perniciousness of the past.[3] Writing in the 15 May 1927 issue of *avance*, for example, Francisco Ichaso called for a nihilistic catharsis, regardless of the potentially ruinous consequences for established structures:

> Una de las características, tal vez la esencial, de estas épocas insumisas, es el afán de revisar valores [...]. No importa que, para ello, sea preciso derribar ruinosos edificios que se habían mantenido como monumentos nacionales en virtud de ese espejismo histórico-sentimental que retrotrae al primer plano de visión cosas pretéritas. (1927b: 113)

---

[3] The so-called political *cooperativismo* instigated in 1926 ensured almost seamless cohesion between Machado and his political ex-adversaries.

Although undoubtedly responding to the calamitous conditions in Cuba in the mid-1920s, much of the intellectual vanguard's early ire was directed exclusively at cultural traditions: their forward-looking 'esfuerzo renovador y militante, preñado de promesas para el futuro' was circumscribed within an appeal for aesthetic, not socio-political rejuvenation (Casanovas 1927b: 100). Even as the situation deteriorated under an ever more despotic Machado, *revista de avance* (as a paragon example of vanguard publications in Cuba) was determined to keep its distance from the political pell-mell: 'No extrañe nadie el silencio de "1927" sobre los asuntos de política inmediata. Su comentario no cae dentro del sector de esta revista que va mar afuera, a la contemplación de horizontes y firmamentos nuevos' (1:3: 41). Although this apparent apolitical instinct was a source of embarrassment in later years to some of the magazine's editors, it was in fact a defining characteristic of many vanguardist critiques of the perceived expressive and ethical crisis of the first decades of the twentieth century.[4] A young Cuban intellectual like Ichaso and a magazine like *avance* were not alone in their call for cultural regeneration, of course. The slaughter of the First World War seemed to point to the moral bankruptcy of the Western liberal model, and many thinkers began to argue for a radical rupture in the collective consciousness to set the modern present in irremediable contradistinction to the traditional past. *revista de avance*, and Cuban vanguardism in general, was part of an expressive and ideological trajectory stretching all the way back to the Impressionist explosion of kaleidoscopic colour in *fin de siècle* Parisian salons, to Nietzsche's insistence on the metaphoric, metonymic and anthropomorphic elusiveness of truth, or even Karl Marx's assertion that 'the tradition of all the dead generations weighs like a nightmare on the brain of the living' (in Lewis 2007: 20). Particularly influential within early Cuban vanguardism was the Futurism of F. T. Marinetti, which reached Havana through an article ('El futurismo') in *El Fígaro* only six weeks after the Italian poet published his manifesto in Paris in 1909.[5] Although European Futurism remained a popular topic (particularly in *El Fígaro*) for the next two decades, many Cuban intellectuals rejected Marinetti's fascistoid tendencies and turned instead to modernist influences from the rest of the Americas.[6] *avance* was just one of a panoply of

4   In a 1977 interview, Juan Marinello (who would play a leading role in Cuban socialist parties from the 1920s and would become a member of the Central Committee of the Cuban Communist Party in 1965) lamented 'lo absurdo de su apoliticismo', which he saw leading ultimately to *avance*'s demise (Marinello 1989: 141).

5   In her illuminating account of Cuban *vanguardismo*, Manzoni argues that this early critical reception of Futurism on the island belies the common portrayal of Cuban modernism as a sluggish provincial cousin of the more energetic European movement (in particular, see pp. 34–40 of *Un dilema cubano*).

6   Marinetti was an ardent supporter of Benito Mussolini's National Fascist Party and

vanguardist Latin American magazines and movements in the 1920s. Oswald de Andrade's *Manifesto Antropófago*, Joaquín García Monge's *Repertorio Americano*, Jorge Luis Borges's *Proa* and others all heralded the dawn of a new age guided by a regenerated moral and imaginative compass:

> Jamás ha sido tan justo titular una nueva generación como en la hora presente [...]. Y es tan palpable la diferencia que caracteriza a los que velamos por la conservación del fuego sagrado, con las que vivieron las horas 'felices' de la civilización que moría, que es inutil confrontar dos mentalidades cuya lucha se descubre en el último matiz de la vida cotidiana. (Borges et al. 1924, in Schwartz 1991: 230)

But this quest to to 'get rid of the weight of dead men's thoughts'[7] was not cultural alone. In the case of Cuba's *avance*, the editorial insistence on political neutrality came from the belief that the intellectuals' efforts to encapsulate and simultaneously stimulate a fitting collective *sensibilidad* was struggle enough; that taking the textual and expressive *lex* of *civitas* into their own hands was the true calling of *letrados* who were at the same time *activistas*. Fifty years before lamenting *avance*'s political indifference, Marinello had stoutly defended the disassociation of pen and sword:

> La labor del escritor, del pintor, del escultor y del músico – se declara – sólo tienen razón de existencia por su inmediata utilidad, por el apoyo que den al anhelo de una nueva realidad social [...]. Quien niegue que toda labor de seria cultura – seria en su propósito y en su anhelo, al menos – no trae como fatal secuela, a la postre, hondas mutaciones sociales, está cegado o quiere estarlo [...]. ¿Podría exigirse, con justicia, a un Julián del Casal que fuera al verso encendido de gérmenes revolucionarios y de inquietudes libertarias? ¿No se obtendría, con ello, el arquetipo del mal poeta y el ejemplo del agitador comprometedor del triunfo de su credo? (1928: 5–7)

Although declaring wilful disinterest in 'los asuntos de política inmediata', therefore, the *avance* editors' compromise with the socio-cultural panorama of

---

proclaimed large-scale war as 'the only health giver of the world' (in the *Initial Manifesto of Futurism* 1912: 4). Although many *vanguardistas* turned from Futurism, Alberto Lamar Schweyer, the Iscariot of the *minorista* movement, applauded Marinetti's manifesto in an *El Fígaro* article of his own ('Los fundamentos lógicos del futurismo', Oct. 1921). Lamar Schweyer went on to write the notorious *apologia* for dictatorship *Biología de la democracia (ensayo de sociología americana)* in 1927 and became one of Machado's most loyal ideologues.

7   Nathaniel Hawthorne's hope for another corner of the Americas at another revolutionary juncture (in 'Earth's Holocaust', cited in Lewis 1965: 13–14).

the mid-1920s was unquestionable, their commitment to be both *poetas* and *agitadores* quite clear. Whether all editors of the magazine agreed with the kind of cathartic nihilism that Ichaso advocated is another question. In its title, *avance* certainly seemed to advocate relentless forward motion. Moreover, this uncompromising call for future-orientation was in fact only a subtitle; the magazine actually began life as *1927*, and then changed its title every year (to *1928*, *1929* and *1930*) for its four-year lifetime. In this, *avance* appears committed to the drawing of an impermeable frontier between 'before' and 'after' in Cuba's cultural panorama as an attempt to negate 'the power of the past over the present' through 'future-oriented memory' (Habermas 1991: 69). In what appears to be a determined application of the *nihil admirari* maxim, *avance* even liberated itself from the burden of duty to its own annual legacy:

> Una explicación importante: hemos escrito en la proa ese nombre, ese número:
>
> 1927
>
> No que creamos que 1927 signifique nada, sin embargo, el año que viene, si aún seguímos navegando, pondremos en la proa '1928'; y al otro, '1929'; y así … ¡Queremos movimiento, cambio, avance, hasta en el nombre! (1:1: 1)

One of the striking features of vanguardist projects in Latin America was the degree of resonance around what Manzoni describes as the 'la valoración de la juventud como un valor en sí mismo' (2001: 97). For many, the unity of youth ameliorated any friction caused by differences in political outlook. In the *Proa* editorial cited above, for example, Borges recognised that its editors (himself, Alfredo Brandán Caraffa, Ricardo Guiraldes and Pablo Rojas Paz) were 'formados en distintos ambientes', but emphasised their 'perfecta coincidencia de sensibilidad y de anhelos' emanating from the common bond of youth (in Schwartz 1991: 225, n1). In Cuba, however, some observers of (and even some participants in) *avance* portray the young editors of the magazine as riven by ideological schisms.[8] Writing in the late 1960s, Marinello described a doctrinal 'discrepancia central' between those editors who 'entendieron, cada día con mas claridad, que la verdad estaba en organizar y realizar un cambio de estructura social regido por el marxismo-leninismo' (and he indicates himself, Martí Casanovas, Alejo Carpentier and José Z. Tallet) and those he labelled 'típicos representantes de la pequeña burguesía isleña' (Mañach, Ichaso and Félix Lizaso), whose initial leftism withered in the face of the political choices that arose as the *machadato* dictatorship developed. Rojas criticises

---

8   Of the more permanent editors (Mañach, Marinello, Ichaso, Lizaso and Tallet), Lizaso was the oldest (thirty-six) and Ichaso was the youngest (twenty-seven) in 1927.

Marinello's retrospective (and Revolutionary) interpretation of *avance* for understating (or deliberately diminishing) the fecund intellectual exchange the editors sustained during the lifetime of the magazine and well beyond. To Marinello's ideological schism, Rojas posits 'el nexo intelectual propio de un pacto republicano, en el que diferentes ideologías y estilos respetan ciertas normas de convivencia dentro del campo literario' (2006: 102). Alongside, or perhaps in between Marinello and Rojas' readings, *avance* can actually be interpreted as an example of intellectual and ideological liminality. Whilst not wholly subscribing to the notion that Latin American *vanguardismo* in general, and the Cuban magazine in particular, were governed by a seamlessly coherent synthesis, the cracks in the 'pacto' that are of interest here were not provoked by differences of political opinion between communists and conservatives, but rather by alternative diagnoses of the Republic's ongoing psycho-social malaise and different prescriptions for its cure. In this sense, *avance* is presented here as a forum for an antithetical encounter between nihilists and liminalists; between those who called for 'la liquidación del pasado' (Casanovas 1927a: 156) to enable the genesis of a novel *sensibilidad* from a socio-cultural *tabula rasa*, and those who advocated a distinctly 'betwixt and between' approach to tradition and innovation within Cuba's national narrative.

Nihilism and primitivism

To return to the aesthetic revolution proposed by the Cuban vanguard, some of the most strident calls for a nihilistic new beginning were made with reference to the visual arts. Just as the Semana de Arte Moderna in Brazil in 1922 marked 'el año clave de la eclosión vanguardista', so the May 1927 'Arte Nuevo' exhibition (organised by *avance*) was an uncompromising declaration that Cuban artistic representation would never be the same again (Shwartz 1991: 23). In 'Nuevos Rumbos: La Exposición de *1927*', for example, Casanovas condemned the 'mañoso' art of the previous 'siglo estúpido' and declared that 'todo el esfuerzo y la máxima aspiración de los artistas jóvenes, es olvidar que todo aquello ha existido' (Casanovas 1927b: 99). This notion of an artistic vanguard that was wholly scornful of the aesthetic conventions of the past was developed further in a rare textual contribution by one of *avance*'s most frequent artistic collaborators, *minorista* Eduardo Abela. Whereas Mañach's conference 'La Nueva Estética' (delivered as part of the Arte Nuevo event) defended the merit of a rigorous historical and technical education for young Cuban artists to ensure the future 'encauzamiento del desbordamiento presente', in 'El Futuro Artista', Abela responded to Mañach by celebrating what he called 1927's 'revolución de las revoluciones', not only in terms of artistic technique, but in the very *sensibilidad* of Cuban artists-to-be. In keeping with the temporal tenor of his title, although of a particular nihilistic stripe, Abela saw salvation from the contemporary degradation of the Cuban aesthetic spirit not in a leap forwards towards a perfect future, but in a paradoxical return to the instinctive sensibility of a much more distant past: 'El goce que sintió el primer hombre al trazar sobre la piedra la primera forma, jamás fue superado' (1927: 104). Although Abela advocated the nihilistic eradication of all recent artistic conventions in an almost biblical cataclysm in which 'el dique que contenía el caudal' would burst, and previously marginalised art forms and artists would be revived by 'la bienhechora humedad de la obra de Dios', his archetypal 'futuro artista' drew little inspiration from a Marinetti-type Futurism, being much closer instead to earlier enunciations of a Cuban *pueblo puro* rooted in the primitive ideals of the island's pre-colonial and almost pre-historic past (ibid.). To Cosculluela's *homo cubensis*, who promised to arrest archipelagic dissipation with ancient and unambiguous insularity, Abela brought *homo artibus*, a primitive yet percipient spirit in perfect communion with the vestal paradise he inhabited. Again, this passion for artistic primitivism was something of a cultural import. Picasso's self-declared search for his own aesthetic innocence lost, for example, is well documented, with Pericles Lewis reporting his starry-eyed comments after attending an exhibition of children's art in Paris: 'When I was a child I drew like Rafael. I have been trying to draw like these children ever since' (in Lewis 2007: 71). Perhaps inspired by Picasso (whom he cites twice in his article), Abela saw future Cuban artists as either children or preternatural peasants. In counterpoint to the grown-up and grand 'industria artística [...], hoy en franca quiebra', Abela offered the unassailable innocence of the child, 'con su imaginación ingenua, abierta y maravillada ante el espectáculo inefable de la virginidad del mundo' (1927: 104). To break through the stratification of artistic expression between 'una casta de hombres especializados' and 'el común de los hombres', Abela proposed a radical recalibration of the very understanding of artistry and an assault on the division of labour that set artists apart from the common man and his daily toil (ibid.). Although ostensibly elaborating an archetype for artists alone, Abela actually portrayed a legion of simple citizens all driven by the same artistic *sensibilidad*: 'El futuro artista será el hombre que después de ganar su sustento, regresará por la tarde a su hogar, y para satisfacer una necesidad de su espíritu, se recreará pintado las emociones del día' (105).

This contribution to the discourse of identity at the 1927 turning point echoes certain strains from 1923 and introduces some new notes. For Abela, as for Roig de Leuchsenring and Martínez Villena, the average Cuban citizen was fundamentally 'pure' and willing to cast off contemporary socio-cultural structures to reconnect with a more fundamental ethos of subjectivity and self-expression (and was hence engaged in a liminal recalibration of the cognitive schemata of life). But for Abela, the tension between tradition and innovation was resolved by eschewing all complex interaction with the recent past in favour of a retreat into the mists of mythological and fantastical history. His 'futuro artista' would not glorify the 'polyphonic surf of revolutions in modern capital cities' nor 'the nocturnal vibrations of arsenals and workshops beneath violent electric moons' (as in Marinetti's manifesto [4]), nor incorporate primitive artifice into arresting modern arrangements (as in Picasso's paintings), but rather (like Cosculluela and the Siboneyistas before him) make an imaginative leap backwards from the present and all those who inhabit it: 'el hombre sensible, vuelve la espalda a los hombres [...] y vuelve a la virginidad pura de la primera emoción' (105). For Abela, therefore, the solution to Cuba's 1927 malaise lay 'elsewhen', in a prelapsarian past that was informed more by science fiction than by science fact. In this, even the historical past of trials and errors, successes and defeats, is colonised by a perfection- and purity-obsessed future tense marching onwards (by marching far backwards) to victory.

Mella the Hero

Although joining Abela in lambasting the political and expressive sensibility of bourgeois 'hombres especializados', Julio Antonio Mella's contribution to the 1927 identity debate is different. An archetypal angry young man and one of the most important ideologues of the day, Mella often seemed determined to alter the disappointing course of Cuban history by deploying fierce nihilism against the edifice of the island's past and any in the present who dared defend it:

> Existe entre muchos jóvenes un acendrado amor al pasado [...] imposibilitándonos para la acción fecunda y necesaria en el momento actual. Unos creen que al morir Martí terminó la historia cubana, que todas las epopeyas gloriosas terminaron, se agotaron, en el pasado siglo de las revoluciones emancipadoras. (1975: 77)

But a careful reading of this nihilism reveals novel inflections. Despite the obliquely iconoclastic reference to Martí already cited, Mella seems unable to liberate himself fully from 'the power of the past' stored within the ideological legacy of the so-called Apostle Martí. In this, Mella's pioneering critical review, *Glosando los pensamientos de José Martí* (1926),[9] is a suggestive text within

---

[9] Published at the end of 1926, but coming particularly to the public's attention after its review in the 15 May 1927 edition of *avance*.

which to study what Manzoni calls 'la tensión entre la necesidad política, ideológica y estética de construir una tradición nacional y la de desplegar una ruptura modernizadora' (2001: 97), or what could be called his attempt in a moment of liminal flux to anchor the young Republic upon the rock of a heroic tradition whilst simultaneously sloughing off the perceived ignobility of the past, thus to stimulate a revitalisation of Cuba and its *sensibilidad*.

Mella certainly seems to relish the kind of 'ruptura modernizadora' that Manzoni describes. In *Glosando*, he is merciless with the 'estériles emuladores de la mujer de Lot' for whom 'las tumbas de las generaciones pasadas pesan sobre sus espaldas como el cadaver del equilibrista sobre la de Zaratustra' (1975: 268). Caught between rupture and tradition, however, Mella seems unable to tolerate the nihilistic notion of a Cuban nation completely cut off from its history, no matter how unsatisfactory, and was equally severe with those who 'ignoran, o pretenden ignorar todo el pasado' (ibid.). Whilst influenced to an extent by this past–present tension, Mella is by no means resigned to temporal or ideological ambivalence. For him there is a solution, and it lies in the accurate analysis of the legacy of Martí and a faithful emulation of the heroism he perceives at its epicentre.

Mella's interaction with Martí initially seems marked by the effusive adulation that was common within the so-called *culto martiano*[10] from the 1920s onwards: 'Cuando hablo de José Martí, siento la misma emoción, el mismo temor, que se siente ante las cosas sobrenaturales' (1975: 267). But *Glosando* is no wistful elegy to a fallen hero. Mella insists that the homage paid Martí must consist of audacious actions as well as flamboyant words; for him, hermeneutics and heroism are inseparable. Lambasting 'tanto adulón, tanto hipócrita' who paid facile lip service to the historical figure whilst ignoring the relevance of his legacy in contemporary times, Mella claims that only a man of action (like himself) was properly qualified to interpret the Apostle's *oeuvre* (ibid.). The resultant seminal *martiano* text (for which *Glosando* is proposed as a prelude) would be Mella's masterpiece, although he suggests that it would necessarily be written in the sporadic 'idle' moments of a life of unrelenting activism: 'Lo hará esta pluma en una prisión, sobre el puente de un barco, en el vagón de tercera de un ferrocarríl, o en la cama de un hospital, convaleciente de cualquier enfermedad' (267–8). For Mella, activism will always precede analysis.

Despite his hyperbolic description of a supernatural Martí, the kind of hermeneutic that Mella proposes is actually grounded in historiographic and dialectic practice. Mella approaches the Apostle's *ideario*, not as an inviolable

10 We will come back to this *culto* in 1953 and in Chapter 4.

creed to be afforded almost religious reverence, but as a secular ideology be examined 'a la luz de los hechos de hoy' and exposed to a rigorous dialectic that situates its author 'en el momento histórico en que actuó' (1975: 269). Unlike in Abela's prelapsarian and science fiction fable of *cubanía*, here the past is read from within the context of the present. Nevertheless, the *hechos* and *momentos* are interpreted in *Glosando* according to Mella's own political and ideological inclinations And as a founding member of the Partido Comunista Cubano (established in August 1925), Mella's interpretation of Cuba's socio-cultural panorama was inevitably coloured by a doctrinal adherence to the notion of social progress beyond the denouement of colonial and neo-colonial capitalism towards a more just socio-economic system. To a present-tense contextual interpretation of the past, therefore, Mella brings faith in a better, even perfect, future, or what he calls 'ese gran paraíso del socialismo internacional' (272). Although initially seeming to balance between past, present and future, Mella remains convinced that forward momentum can be restored to tempestuous contemporary times through the dialectical application of Martí's teachings. All that was needed were the most qualified dialecticians, and Mella is in no doubt where to find them:

> Es imprescindible que una voz de la nueva generación, libre de prejuicios y compenetrada con la clase revolucionaria, escriba ese libro. Es necesario dar un alto, y si no quieren obedecer, un bofetón a tanto canalla, tanto mercachifle, tanto patriota, tanto adulón, tanto hipócrita ... que escribe o habla sobre José Martí. (268)

Mella effectively claims supreme exegetical authority over Martí's intellectual legacy for himself and his 'hermanos en ideales' from 'la nueva generación' (267). From this position, he seeks not to historically contextualise the intellectual inheritance of the past, but rather to re-articulate *martiano* thought in an attempt to discover therein the teleological seeds of subsequent and inevitable progress towards collective emancipation through socialism. In essence, Mella tries retrospectively to convert Martí to Marxism and in doing so make him a prophet of its conviction of the resolution of contemporary socio-political shortcomings through dialectical progression.[11] He builds his case gradually. First, he asks a hypothetically resurrected Martí questions about the predominant socio-political themes of the mid-1920s: '¿Qué hubiera dicho y hecho ante el avance del imperialismo, ante el control de la vida política y económica por el imperialismo, ante las maniobras de éste entre los nacionales para

---

[11] This philosophy is perhaps most clearly expressed in Friedrich Engels's *The Part Played by Labour in the Transition from Ape to Man* (1895).

salvaguardar sus intereses?' (269) For Mella, the response that the 'orgánica-
mente revolucionario' *Apóstol* would have given is unquestionable: Martí
was a proven internationalist whose solidarity with other American nations
overcame any ideological myopia typical of his social class:

> Fue, como decía Lenin de Sun Yat Sen, representante de una democrática
> burguesía capaz de hacer mucho, porque aún no había cumplido su misión
> histórica. Luchaba por Cuba porque era el último pedazo de tierra del conti-
> nente que esperaba la revolución. Pero jamás ignoró el carácter internacional
> de la lucha revolucionaria. (271)

By the end of the book, the dialectic that Mella proposes between Martí's
'momento histórico' and the 'hechos de hoy' has ceded to a more partial interpretation of the Apostle's ideological legacy. From his initial description of
Martí as an enlightened member of a decadent class, Mella has transformed
him into a committed precursor of the Cuban Marxist tradition: 'Si la envidia
de los roedores del genio no lo hubiese llevado a inmolarse prematuramente
en Dos Ríos, el habría estado al lado de Diego Vicente Tejera en 1899 cuando
fundó el Partido Socialista de Cuba' (272–3). Although Mella's text is seen
initially to be caught in the liminal middle between construction and rupture,
Glosando los pensamientos de José Martí ultimately attempts to resolve that
tension and break the power of the past over the present by inscribing the
martiano tradition within a teleological meta-narrative that leads inexorably
towards future-oriented memories of a socialist paradise to come.

Beyond its ideological tenor, Mella's reading is of great interest for its
reflection on and emulation of the heroism of José Martí. Whereas Martí is
often presented as an extraordinary poet transformed into a dogged fighter by
the strategic demands of the independence campaign's *realpolitik*, Mella the
'Homeric hero' was different, and seems barely able to contain his instinctive
bellicosity (Thomas 2001: 341). In a January 1923 speech to University
of Havana students, for example, Mella's rhetoric becomes charged with
melodrama: 'Vengo a dejar que salgan las palabras por la boca como brota
la sangre por la herida, porque sangre son mis palabras y herida está mi alma
al contemplar la Universidad como está hoy' (1975: 41). This should not be
read as purposeless histrionics; for Mella, antagonism and outright conflict
were fundamental facets of his political commitment, whether spilling blood
for university reform or aiming an uncompromising *bofetón* at the *canallas*
he saw ruining Cuba. And so although he recognised that his generation was
pulled taut between the need to edify a national tradition and the need to
eradicate antecedent sins, this angry young man was determined to fight his
way out of the dilemma. Whereas Abela retreated from the mechanisation of

life and art and the contradictions of modern Cuba, Mella readies himself for acts of self-conscious sacrifice and derring-do.[12] In this, it is perhaps Mella who comes closest to Marinetti's archetype for the future in which 'aggressive movement, feverish insomnia, the double quick step, the somersault, the box on the ear, the fisticuff' were to be extolled as high virtues (Marinetti 1912: 3). In this, Mella's reference to Zarathustra (in Nietzsche's re-imagining) is perhaps not accidental. Whereas a Christian hero 'is meek and possesses, above all virtues, charity', Mella rather seems to emulate the 'Heroic Vitalist' of the (Nietzschean) Zarathustran creed, who 'possesses above all virtues, courage [...]; if he is generous, it is not through compassion but magnanimity' (Bentley 1969: 95). This Zarathustran and Futuristic re-reading of the lessons of *el maestro* is made perfectly clear on the final line of Mella's glossary:

> "Trincheras de ideas valen tanto como trincheras de piedras." ¡Que tus palabras se cumplan! ¡Aunque serían mejor ambas trincheras a la vez! (Mella 1975: 274)

revista de avance and liminality

At times, *revista de avance*'s inaugural editorial, 'Al levar el ancla' seems simultaneously to be infused with Mella-type derring-do and to exhort an Abela-type cathartic distance from an irredeemably spoiled past as the key to national recovery:

> Zarpa esta embarcación con cierto brío heroico, dispuesta a hundirse, como tantas otras, si le soplase viento adverso; pero negada de antemano a todo patético remolque. Al fin y al cabo, su tripulación es escasa y todos, mal que bien, sabemos nadar [...]. Por ahora sólo nos tienta la diáfana pureza que se goza mar afuera, lejos de la playa sucia, mil veces hollada, donde se secan, ante la mirada irónica del mar, los barcos inservibles o que ya hicieron su jornada. (1:1: 1)

But *avance*'s collective editorial voice is more nuanced than Mella's Zarathustran roar of self-determination, eschews the simplicity of a nihilistic turning away from 'las tumbas de las generaciones pasadas' towards a perfect future, and instead seems to be prepared for a more prolongued *luchita* (Mella 1975: 268). This is immediately apparent. Although 'Al levar el ancla' seems

---

[12] Tina Modotti's iconic images of assassin-slain Mella on a Mexican street in 1929 only seem to confirm his preordained destiny as a heroic martyr.

proud of its self-declared heroism and convinced of the moral and imaginative purity to be found offshore, any strident determinism is undercut by a subtle, self-effacing irony: 'Vamos hacia un puerto – ¿mítico? ¿incierto? – ideal de plenitud; hacia un espejismo tal vez de mejor ciudadanía, de hombría mas cabal. Pero no nos hacemos demasiadas ilusiones' (1:1: 1). All Mella-type bombast or Abela-type mythological puritanism are reflected back in their histrionic excesses by this candid self-criticism in which integral *cubanía* is but a mirage. And although *avance*'s transient title and persistent use of maritime metaphors to suggest invigorating distance from the 'barcos inservibles' of the past point to the magazine as a manifesto of teleological momentum, it can equally be perceived in an ambiguous interstice between past and present. Despite its annual titular regeneration, for example, *avance* claimed for itself 'una independencia absoluta – hasta del tiempo' to enable the orientation of memories towards the future whilst at the same time harnessing, rather than neutralising, 'the power of the past' (Habermas 1991: 69). In this, some echo of Mella's dialectic engagement with *martianismo* could be discerned. Unlike Mella, however, the magazine, and particularly Mañach's 1927 articles therein, appears fuelled by a determined resistance to dialectical synthesis and by a stubborn reluctance to pursue the word-perfect (and future perfect) translation of the past 'a la luz de los hechos de hoy' (Mella 1975: 269).

One of the principal discursive axes around which the tradition–innovation tension pivots in *avance* is the notion of 'el respeto'. In 'La crisis del respeto', Ichaso seizes upon disrespect as the most potent weapon in the youthful revolution of the mid-1920s: 'Esta época joven, desenfadada, rebelde, por imperativo de sus años, ha hallado en la irrespetuosidad la palanca de Arquimedes para remover los cimientos del mundo' (1927a: 276). After this nihilistic beginning, however, Ichaso actually charts a complex bilateral crisis in which the old guard belittle the appetites and inclinations of the vanguard, who in turn respond in disrespectful kind: ' "¡Bah! – dicen – estamos en época de crisis", y al decirlo se les llena la boca de suficiencia pontifical' (1927a: 275). Whereas Ortiz charted the lexicographic landmarks of the Cuban language community in 1923, this laconic and confrontational '¡Bah!' becomes 'la marca fonética' of the conservative *ancien régime* in 1927, an antagonistic barrier behind which they refuse to entertain either linguistic or ideological compromise with *los nuevos* (Ichaso 1927a: 276). The youthful retaliation comes in the form of an 'actitud provocativa, burlona, insolente, pugnaz' against the venerable elders and all their endeavours: 'No se siente respeto por las figuras del pasado' (ibid.). Ichaso's initial conclusion, therefore, is gloomy: there is no hope of reconciliation between the past and the present; the truculence of the former has sealed its fate. Whereas 1923 saw attempts to distance Cuban selfhood from racial, spatial and cultural otherness, the constitutive other against which identity was asserted in Ichaso's article comes not from foreign lands, but from other times; the irremediable anachronism of the forebears becomes the psycho-cultural canker to be eliminated with disinfecting disrespect: '¿Irrespetuosidad? No; digamos necesidad. Había que higienizar el mundo y ¿qué mejor desinfectante que la risa?' (ibid.).

A reading of this 'crisis del respeto' as an irreparable generational divide cutting across the national narrative is myopic, however. Despite his obvious *vanguardista* ardour, Ichaso recognised that the binary divide between old and young was perforated by subtlety and nuance. Although raging against the reactionary arrogance of his elders, he admitted that it was not the antecedent *obras* themselves that warranted disrespectful dismissal, but only attempts to preserve eternally those past endeavours within sacrosanct canons: 'no siempre se asume la actitud irrespetuosa contra el esfuerzo de ayer, sino contra el esfuerzo anacrónico de quienes pretenden que perdure' (1927a: 276).

On the basis of this oblique admission of a possible parley between the old guard and the vanguard, Mañach goes on to elaborate what could be called a liminal solution to the tradition–rupture dilemma within the Cuban national narrative. Like Ichaso, Mañach posits 'el respeto' as the *leitmotif* of what is undoubtedly a moment of significant socio-cultural transition: 'Estamos atravesando [...] una crisis del respeto. Cundan vientos de revolución política, social, cultural sobre la haz del mundo; y toda revolución es, genéricamente, una acumulada falta de respeto que toma la ofensiva' (Mañach 1927c: 42). But this is where Mañach's analysis begins to differ from his *avance* co-editor's. Examining the 'suficiencia pontifical' that so enraged Ichaso, Mañach rather points to an understandable, if cynical, self-defensive reaction from elders witnessing the undermining of their life's work by the iconoclasm of *los nuevos*: 'Lo que les lastima no es tanto la urgencia innovadora del más juvenil ejército, cuanto las negaciones y desprecios absolutos que esgrime contra ellos' (ibid.). Far from an Archimedean lever with which to split Republican society down its generational middle, Mañach rather posits 'el respeto' as a communicative axon between two calcified poles, as a tool not for collision, but for collusion. Hence, although the old guard's desperate cry of '¿Qué cosa es ser nuevo?' appeared worthy of youthful contempt, Mañach defends its respectability and, balanced objectively on the fulcrum between recalcitrant tradition and dogmatic nihilism, is equally critical of the the myopia of his intransigent contemporaries: 'En su furor nihilista, tachan de huera o falsa toda la obra del pasado. Repudian hasta a los mismos dioses' (ibid.).[13] The subtly expressed

---

[13] In reference, perhaps, to Nietzsche's most famous maxim, 'Gott ist tot' (which first appeared in 1882 in *The Gay Science* although it is more commonly associated with *Thus Spake Zarathustra*, 1883–85).

caution in the *avance* editorial about a vanguard quest for a *tabula rasa* upon which to sow exclusively 'future-oriented memories' (Habermas 1991: 69), becomes in Mañach an outright condemnation of nihilistic extremism: 'Hay que decir bien claro, pues, que ser nuevo no es – ni para ser nuevo se exige – la negación o menosprecio de toda la obra prestigiada por el elogio de los siglos' (1927c: 43). Far from celebrating 1927 as a transcendental turning point in the Republic's quarter-century, or applauding the introspective turn as a definitive 'revolución de las revoluciones' (Abela 1927: 104), Mañach rather sees temporal, moral and cultural continuity eroding the frontier between the supposedly malignant past and the utopian future, between ossified tradition and blithe innovation: 'resulta indudable que toda revolución no es sino el clímax dramático de una larga evolución' (1927c: 43). Despite lambasting both the traditionalists and the nihilists, Mañach was no bombastic rhetorical warrior in the style of Mella. Instead of a *bofetón* to those he saw as in the wrong on both sides of the tense generational divide, Mañach advocates mutual comprehension and collaboration. Far from condemning the 'acento patético' of the elders or the 'furor nihilista' of the youngsters, he proposes bringing them together in dialogue.

Mañach on the margin between tradition and revolution

Although Marinello would in later life accuse his former *avance* co-editor of having 'entraña conservadora' (1989: 140), Mañach can rather be read as being inspired by the kind of creative ambivalence and equilibrium typical of the limen, seeking not to entrench Cuban culture and Cuban identity in the preterite forms he obviously admired, but neither hoping to shelter tradition from the 'huracán de modernidad' that blew across the island and many other parts of the world in the first three decades of the twentieth century (Manzoni 2001: 33). From this perspective, Mañach's collection of Havana vignettes, *Estampas de San Cristóbal*, can be read as a bi-vocal tale of betwixt-and-between *habaneros* living out their ambivalent lives in an interstitial city.[14] From one perspective, the book is simply a *criollista* account of the idiosyncracies of the Cuban capital: each vignette follows the narrator, Mañach, and his friend and ageing *procurador*, Luján, as they stroll through the old city from 'El Morro' to 'El muro del Malecón', crossing paths as they do so with the 'Muchachas ventaneras', 'El niño del silbato' and 'La madre pordiosera'

---

[14] Although *Estampas* was published at the end of 1926, most reviews date from mid-1927 (the review in the *Diario de la Marina*'s literary supplement appeared at the end of June 1927, for example), suggesting that the lag between publication and widespread purchase may have been lengthy.

(all chapters in *Estampas*) that inhabit its theatrical streets. A more attentive reading, however, discovers *Estampas* as both an elegy and a birthsong for the animated capital suddenly suspended in a liminal limbo between two times and what Mañach called two 'fisonomías':

> Una Habana pintoresca, noblemente tradicional, que es muy antigua a la vez que muy moderna y por tanto muy absurda y muy lógica, muy de lo extinto y de lo que vendrá, imagen calidoscópica del ayer, visión radial del futuro [...]. Nuestra absorbente y tentadora capital, ayer villa de San Cristóbal, hoy febricitante Ciudad de La Habana. (1926: 88–9)

In this Mañach shuns nostalgia for the preterite and blind faith in the future for the subjunctive mood of the limen. This was not true of all of his reflections on Cuba's *sensibilidad*. Through landmark analyses of Cuban history and identity (*Indagación del choteo* [1928], *Martí el Apóstol* [1933], *Historia y el estilo* [1940]), Mañach won a reputation as a dispassionately objective observer able to examine the ills and euphorias of the collective *corpus* with 'una suerte de positivismo de laboratorio: con la fría prosopopeya del investigador analítico que no se entusiasma, que no se deprime, que desconoce igualmente la oratoria de los himnos y la de los responsos, que examina las cosas como son' (Mañach 1999: 7). But in *Estampas*, the distanced and clinical scholar approaches his native city with intimacy; the *ellos* of other studies becomes the *nosotros* of this text. The subjectivity on display in *Estampas*, however, is actually more complex. Through a remarkably postmodern narrative conceit, Mañach splits himself into both object and subject: in *Estampas*, Mañach is both himself and Luján and examines Havana as both a dispassionate 'investigador analítico' and a visceral participant on the street. Critically for us, Mañach's authorial voice speaks from both sides of the generational divide, splitting his critical vision between that of a clear-sighted and impetuous biblical Benjamin and a sage Jacob in the twilight of his life:

> él es viejo y yo soy joven; él ama sobre todo la tradición; yo, el progreso; él es irónico y caudaloso; yo, directo y sobrio; él en ninguna hechura de los hombres se ilusiona ya, y yo todo lo tomo en serio (1926: 12).

But these differences do not translate into discrepancies; for Mañach, the old guard and the vanguard could avoid antagonism by surrendering themselves to a betwixt-and-between ateleological way of being: 'En el caminar, como en el charlar, discurrimos entonces a la buena de Dios [...] por las calles y sobre los temas menos transitados. Casi nunca estamos de acuerdo más que en ese suave y antojadizo dejarnos ir' (ibid.). In this writing and in these flâneuresque wanderings, Mañach and Luján seem to occupy a different tense altogether, a progressive imperfect with no clear end (either physical or philosophical) in sight. And far from seeking to accommodate the past into the present through dialectical contemporisation, as Mella proposed, Mañach posits an inconclusive dialogue that seeks a percipient distance from, rather than the assimilation of, temporal otherness, and which accepts asymmetry and the promotion of mutually respectful intercourse without ever dissolving the fundamental irreconcilability of opposites, whether ideological or generational.

Mañach's approach to the tension between tradition and rupture can be intercalated amidst geographically distant (but epistemologically congruent) narratives of continuity and schism at times of transcendental socio-cultural change. In one literary articulation from the earliest experience of decolonisation in the Americas, Washington Irving's famous somnambulist Rip van Winkle falls asleep in bucolic colonial Pennsylvania and only awakens twenty years later, after the American Revolutionary War is over. All that was familiar has become uncanny for Rip: his fellow Tarrytowners are 'strange and incomprehensible', the 'George III' tavern has been renamed the 'George Washington' and everyone talks in a 'perfectly Babylonish jargon' about 'rights' and 'citizens' and 'liberty'. When asked how he will vote, Rip stuns the townsfolk into a horrified hush by declaring that he is a 'loyal subject of the king, God bless him' (Irving 1883: 62–4). Tarrytown's memory of its past self has been erased from the narratives of its present and Rip and his former fellows are estranged on opposite sides of the temporal schism. As a present, if puzzled, protagonist of the revolutionary transition, Rip's identity enters what Giles calls a liminal state of confusion: 'Caught in the hinge between pre-Revolutionary and post-Revolutionary America, Rip van Winkle experiences a sense of "bewilderment" as his understanding of selfhood becomes fractured and doubled' (2000: 40). But this confusion does not lead to alienation, nor does Irving attempt to contemporise his character in a Mella-like act of revisionism. Instead, as Pease suggests, Rip is presented as an example of the potential for cathartic dialogue across a schismatic socio-cultural divide:

> As a figure in transition from a town life before the war, Rip enabled the townspeople to elaborate upon the changes the war made in their lives. When he appeared from out of the 'nowhere' that once was Tarrytown, he made it necessary for the rest of the townspeople to do what the Revolutionary pundits claimed they should never do: that is, remember the conditions, cultural attitudes, and characters in village life before the war [...]. Because it took place while he slept and thus never happened as an event in his life, the Revolution made no drastic change in Rip's life. He enabled the rest of the village to drop it out of their lives as well, and recover relation to the

town's past, their personal pasts, and the locale's history [...], he enabled the
villagers to give up their need for an exclusive attachment to one historical
period and make it continuous with others. (1987: 15)

The Mañach-Luján amalgamation in *Estampas* can be read as the Rip van
Winkle of the 1927 Cuban condition, the old guard that awakes amongst and
within the vanguard and can speak of and for both. And from this liminal
perspective, Mañach's text can be seen to recalibrate the coordinates of the
generational clash, stimulate a re-cognisance of the tropes of respect, heroism,
salvation, and a recasting of the links between past, present and future.

In 'Cañones de la Punta', for example, Mañach places his meditations
on the 'crisis del respeto' into the mouths of his protagonists. Observing the
monolithic fortress that juts out into the sea at the mouth of Havana harbour,
both Luján and the narrator are initially embarrassed by the anachronistic
bellicosity of the cannons that impart 'un aspecto tonto de batería' to the
coastline, wholly at odds with the fun-loving contemporary spirit of 'nuestra
plácida ciudad' (Mañach 1926: 22). But Luján insists that their anachronism
makes them no less worthy of respect and laments their degrading transformation into seaside rubbish receptacles: 'Y estos pobres cañones, estos tristes
cañones veteranos, valetudinarios, inservibles ya, que apuntan hacia el blanco
blanquísimo del pasado como si quisieran dispararle su innoble contenido de
residuos plebeyos' (21). The cannons' ire at this ignobility seems aimed, not at
the disrespectful passers-by, but at the 'blanco' of the past, as if railing against
the abandonment to which the inexorable passage of time has condemned
them. They have quite simply outlived their historical context, a time when
'España todavía pensaba en filibusteros y el Cid' and these weapons were
in the front line of the 'defensa de la villa' (the reference to 'la villa' rather
than 'la ciudad' only emphasising the anachronism) (21–2). But any drawing
of indelible chronological frontiers between past and present is riddled with
ambivalence in *Estampas*. The divide between a bellicose past and 'plácida'
present, for example, is approached with considerable irony: although 'la
villa' of yesteryear may have been menaced from overseas and lined its
promenades with monumental weapons of war, it never lost its devotion to 'el
romanticismo' and 'la retórica' (21). By the same token, the cannons' ill-fit in
modern times may be little to do with contemporary pacifism, but rather with
the modern-day technological perfection of slaughter that has left their bulk
far behind: 'su descomunalidad resulta irrisoria en estos tiempos de síntesis y
de perfección, cuando el más grande estragón se encierra en armas mínimas'
(ibid.).

Far from seeking to erase the recent past from Cuba's collective memory
by either making an imaginative leap backwards to a prelapsarian age of

expressive authenticity or by doggedly dragging selected antecedent episodes and individuals towards teleological conclusion in the future, Mañach, like Washington Irving, is simply content to present the unsettled and unsettling confusion of yesterday and today and their supposedly differentiated 'fisonomías'. From his vantage point betwixt *ayer* and *hoy*, Mañach reports nostalgia amongst the youngsters and an elderly appetite for dispassionate progress: whilst army recruits gave the cannons a tender 'palmadita protectora', Luján the ageing *procurador*, who 'ama sobre todo la tradición', welcomes the cannons' inexorable obsolescence and warns against sheltering them behind a protective fence: 'Sin verja mejor. Eso les haría parecer aún más infelices, que nada agrava tanto lo ridículo como hacerlo venerado' (ibid.: 22).

One figure from the past for whom Mañach reserves unmitigated respect is Luján himself. In many respects, the *procurador* can be read as a critical counterpoint to the bombastic archetype proposed and incarnated by Mella, as a 1927 inspirational anti-hero of Cuba's liminal national narrative. In contrast to Mella's 'Homeric hero' caught in noble profile as he gazed sternly towards a future that had to be fought for, Luján is a humorous, almost ridiculous figure with 'su verruga jocunda en el entrecejo, con su bigote caedizo y quemado' and with his worn-out shoes as a sublime symbol of humble but indefatigable optimism as they point to the sky in 'un esfuerzo de lo pedestre hacia lo ideal' (ibid.: 11). In distinction from Mella's hyperbolic assessment of the trials and triumphs of life, in which constant *activismo* would inevitably keep him from paying proper analytical homage to Martí until illness or imprisonment provided him with time, Luján offers a more reflexive and mundane interpretation of suffering, a more democratic, if less melodramatic, portrayal of common lives spent between 'alguna alegría limpia y humilde' and 'algún vago dolor disimulado' (11 & 12). Consequently, whilst Abela and to some extent Mella (like Roig de Leuchsenring and Martínez Villena before them) had no difficulty in describing an indelible frontier between virtue and vice, between the peasant and urban worker angels and bourgeois devils of the national narrative, Mañach (like Ortiz in *Un catauro de cubanismos*) rather sees every member of the *pueblo* contaminated by the 'pugnacidades' and 'enredos' of Cuba's *mala vida* (12). And although a *procurador* and so professionally obliged to aid others *desenredarse*, Luján is only a reluctant saviour. Far from magnanimous Zarathustran redemption through derring-do, Luján offers only an empathetic demonstration of common humanity, a heartfelt but inconclusive condolence for the inescapable pain of the human condition: 'Luján se detiene, se muerde o pellizca el bigote, se le encandilan o se le aguan los ojillos' (ibid.). Not that Mañach claims saviour status for his anti-heroic alter ego. Instead, Luján's fellow *habaneros* recognise his ambiguity and marginality and duly condemn him to the physical and metaphysical edge:

'las demás gentes transeuntes tropiezan con él, apártanle sin delicadeza hacia el amago de los "fotingos" en el arroyo' (ibid.). But this marginality does not condemn Luján to either alienation or ignorance; rather this 'arroyo', a liminal space at the side of the road, offers a privileged perspective from which to observe the urban micro-histories that make up Havana's idiosyncratic contribution to the Cuban national narrative: 'otros ojos no lo ven. Luján sí' (ibid.).

If Mella's heroic archetype saw its destiny in the life of a pugnacious warrior spilling sacrificial blood for the sake of a better future, the anti-heroic Luján is much less dramatic. If 'el azar del sexo, la tradición familiar y la contingencia' had not made of Luján a clerk, he would have found perfect identification with the generous existence of the wetnurse: 'el más generoso y natural de los oficios lucrativos, el que más da de sí, el más saturado de aquella "leche de la bondad humana" ' (ibid.: 11). Rejecting the Spartan heroism that tears infants from their mothers and that heard Mella declaiming before his fellow students that 'sangre son mis palabras y herida está mi alma' (1975: 41), Luján's anti-heroism is rather rooted in the kinds of 'buenos humores' that align him more closely with Ortiz's tongue-in-cheek mockery of the Real Academica than with Abela's nihilistic primitivism or Mella's Heroic Vitalism. Balanced in the liminal middle until the end, Mañach's avatar is neither a magnanimous father nor a mythological mother, but a humble *nodriza*, offering Cuba the sustenance it needs at a time of crisis, without the over-protection or over-expectation of a parent. Salvation, for Mañach, comes not through the promise of a prelapsarian or socialist paradise where all trials would be forever overcome, but rather through 'un consuelo, un chiste o una limosna', mere momentary relief from a fellow sufferer (Mañach 1926: 12).

Confronting the generational clash of 1927 and the tension between recalcitrant tradition and the nihilistic desire to move irreversibly on, Abela sought to eliminate the stratification of modern art and modern life through the resurrection a mythological past when Cuba was governed by a primitive *sensibilidad campesina* and authentic peasant artists 'libaron todos los ritmos esenciales de la vida' (1927: 104). Mella combined the nihilist's desire for destruction with an ideologically motivated re-reading of *martianismo*, to thus accommodate the past within the present and move teleologically towards a socio-politically conclusive future. Mañach, on the other hand, offers no simple solutions. In 'La "cuadra" niña', he initially seems to agree with elements of both approaches and portrays the Luján-Mañach old guard-vanguard odd couple as resigned to their irredeemable differences: 'Yo no soy tan tradicionalista como usted, Luján. Pienso que al pasado – según enseña cierto nuevo filósofo de España – hay que amarlo como tal pasado y no deseando que fuese todavía presente' (Mañach 1926: 36). But even the slightest suggestion of a simple binary divide between the generations is undermined by the duplicity of Mañach's exposition. Whereas Luján was resigned to the silent obsolence of the past in 'Los cañones de la Punta', Mañach unabashedly admits nostalgia for his own *cuadra niña*, for the 'callejón' where he grew up. Exclusively future-oriented memories will always perish, Mañach suggests, when even *vanguardistas* were determined to save their own tender micro-histories from the flames of the nihilistic pyre: 'uno no puede menos que exceptuar de ese criterio el pasado personal, el propio tiempo niño' (ibid.).

On the twenty-fifth anniversary of the Republic, the tension between dogged memory and nihilistic momentum remained unresolved, and the national narrative lingered in the liminal middle. For Mañach, however, this indecision is no crisis at all. The *avance* editor proposes, not a solution rooted in arch-conservatism, as Marinello would suggest, but a radical prescription for socio-cultural health; he rejects attempts to soothe temporal tensions simply or administer utopian palliatives to resolve the 'crisis del respeto'. Just as Martí had advised leaving ailing nations 'sudar su propia calentura' (in *Denuncia*, 1 February 1933: 1), just as Unamuno had warned that the purification of the social *corpus* could lead to certain death and just as Ortiz had advocated the embrace of Cuba's collective *mala vida*, so Mañach sees great potential for socio-cultural stimulation in the tension and crisis of 1927:

> Este drama tan evidente, esta guerra civil de las épocas, es el hervor que las salva de estancamiento, la oscilación que les mantiene su ritmo e impide tanto la precipitación como la inercia estériles. (1927b: 18)

Just as Rip van Winkle had stood on the threshold between the old world of George III and the new world of George Washington, Mañach (and Luján) celebrate the ongoing inscription of, not the definitive end to, the Cuban national narrative, both engaged in the old guard–vanguard collision and collusion from the perspicacious side of the road.

But this ardent adherence to the kind of betwixt-and-between balance so typical of the limen could wield its own oppressive tyranny; the 'no-ser-*siempre*-todavía' complex could fall foul of its own inconclusion (Mayz Vallenilla, in Pérez Firmat 1989: 25). The next chapter will explore the degeneration of Cuba's political, cultural and imaginative situation under the brutal regime of Gerardo Machado in the early 1930s, exploring the physical and metaphysical space of the penal colony on the Isle of Pines as a 'surreptitiously aberrant' limen (Giles 2000: 43).

3

1933: *Un dérèglement de tous les sens*

We now come to one of the most volatile periods of twentieth-century Cuban history: the island's first revolution. In this chapter we will return to the notion of liminality, but from a very different perspective. We have examined the cases put forward by Roig de Leuchsenring and Martínez Villena, Abela and Mella for historical turning points and the introspection they stimulate as moments of temporary catharsis to right wrongs, cure ills and save the collective soul with a leap backward to a prelapsarian past, or a vital and heroic leap forward towards social (and socialist) perfection. In these approaches we have seen a van Gennep-type approach to liminality, and have heard the teleological tones of the *venceremos* contribution to the national narrative. We have contrasted these approaches with Ortiz, Ichaso and Mañach's arguments for the congenital ambivalence and flux they perceived at the heart of Cuban identity and the unresolved *luchita* they saw running through the national narrative. In these approaches we have seen parallels with Turner's portrayal of the limen as a potentially beneficial threshold upon which societies can achieve greater integrity by welcoming the dissolution and innovative re-articulation of the schemata of everyday life. We will now turn aside from both approaches to 'demythologize' the limen and 'restore to the term some of its surreptitiously aberrant quality' (Giles 2000: 43). We will first uncover the epitome of this aberrant liminality in the Isla de Pinos's prison (the Presidio Modelo), a notorious penal facility on Cuba's territorial edge. We will see physical and metaphysical marginality coming together and present evidence of what Turner (citing Rimbaud) calls 'un dérèglement ordonnée [*sic*] de tous les sens' (1974: 264). Critically, however, we will argue that this liminal riot of the senses was not ordered, but deranged, leading not to a positive recalibration of identity, but to the dissolution of all social structures and a nefarious descent into savagery. In further contradistinction to the anthropologists, this chapter will suggest that, unlike in the ritual transitions they describe, the liminal *dérèglement* of the early 1930s in Cuba was neither spatially nor temporally restricted. In the second half of the chapter we will see aberrant liminality spreading from the spatial margins towards the core of the Cuban capital.[1] And whereas the anthropologists pointed to the prophylactic benefit of exposure to extremes (even extreme violence) to prepare neophytes for post-liminal reaggregation, this chapter will present evidence of a stubborn persistence of aberrant liminal traits in the post-*machadato* period and suggest that the national narrative and *sensibilidad* therein remained under the potent sway of a destructive 'acumulación de tánatos' for some time (Cabrera Infante 1992: 182).

At the same time, this chapter will shed new light on the relatively incognito Cuban revolution of the early 1930s (always the understudy to the 1959 event). In dialogue with the limited historiography of the so-called 'revolución del '33', this chapter's exploration of the liminality before, during and after Machado's fall will bring a new perspective on the chronological confusion surrounding this revolutionary episode, both at the time and subsequently. In this sense, where Raúl Roa (followed by Tabares del Real and most other socialist historians after 1934[2]) sees the revolution commencing with the murder of student leader Rafael Trejo on 30 September 1930 and fizzling out with the failure of the general strike and assassination of former interior minister Antonio Guiteras in March 1935, and where Le Riverend[3] (followed by Soto)[4] rather sees the revolution commencing with Machado's flight on 12 August 1933 and coming to a desultory close with Fulgencio Batista's coup of 15 January 1934 against the mercurial 'gobierno de los cien días' (presided over by Ramón Grau San Martín), this chapter rather proposes a more long-sighted analysis of the aberrant *sensibilidad* of this period that led up to, was prevalent during, and lasted long after Machado's downfall in the summer of 1933. Hence, the 'Revolution of 1933' in this analysis is seen to start with Machado's laying of the foundation stone for the Presidio Modelo in February 1927 and continue until the election of a Cuban Constitutional Assembly in November 1939. We will also suggest here that the lack of historiographic consensus is not simply the result of ideological or analytical differences, but rather that the transitions from dictatorship to revolution and revolution to the restoration of order were so riddled with ambiguity and indeterminateness as to represent no kind of turning points at all. And although agreeing that a prevalent sense of frustration marked the post-Machado period, this chapter will point to very different causes than those suggested by Roa and Tabares, Le Riverend and Soto.

---

[1]   Pérez Firmat also recognises this potential mobility of the margins (which 'occupy the periphery only transitorily, while maintaining the centre under constant siege') in his 'festive' analysis of Hispanic literature (1986: xviii).

[2]   See Tabares del Real 1975.

[3]   In particular, see Le Riverend 2001[1966].

[4]   See Soto 1977.

Presidio Modelo: Cuba's aberrant limen

In some of his later examinations of the theoretical coordinates of the limen, Turner actually makes his own contribution to the de-mythologisation of the trope. Although he initially perceived the Rimbaudian *dérèglement* as positive, enabling neophytes to use this heightened if chaotic cognition to re-imagine the world and their place in it, he later recognises that in liminal seclusion, 'degradation occurs as well as elevation' (1974: 232). This sense of degradation is at the core of aberrant liminality, a rite of passage that does not lead neophytes towards re-integration into social structure 'at a higher status level', but rather drags them back towards a state of chaos, an unstructured limbo where visceral instincts rule, a moment when 'much that the depth psychologists insist has been repressed into the unconscious tends to appear' (256–7). This aberrant limen is a double challenge to the inscription of a national narrative, by either reaggregationists or liminalists: it stalls the kind of social (and socialist) reintegration postulated by Martínez Villena, Mella and others, but also defies the positive not-*ever*-yet perennial flux celebrated by Ortiz and Mañach, bringing instead the dissolution of all structures and a turn towards a much more pessimistic not-ever ethos of collective identity. This is the liminality of the Presidio Modelo.

In many ways, the entire Isla de Pinos has always been on Cuba's psycho-geographic edge.[5] The island is actually the seventh largest in the Caribbean archipelago (larger than Barbados, Dominica and St Lucia, for example) and has thus always seemed capable of gravitating away from the Cuban mainland. This was certainly the case at the culmination of the Wars of Independence in 1898, when the Treaty of Paris almost wilfully infused the Isla de Pinos's status with ambiguity. For the Cubans, the island was clearly within the new nation's sovereign borders and only temporarily occupied by the United States. For others, and particularly for the several thousand US settlers who had bought parcels of land there, it was clearly intended that the Isla be included amongst those 'other islands now under Spanish sovereignty in the West Indies' that were ceded to the US as war reparations (Treaty of Paris 1898, under 'Article II'). The Platt Amendment did little to dispel the doubt, with Article VI specifically omitting the island from the proposed 'constitutional boundaries of Cuba, the title thereto being left to future adjustment by treaty' (Congress of the United States of America 1901). In 1902, a treaty was duly drawn up to relinquish US control over the island, but it did not reach the floor

---

5   Given the context within which the island will be examined, it seems appropriate to retain its historical nomenclature; it was renamed Isla de la Juventud in 1978 to better evoke its new role as an educational centre for young people from all over the developing world.

of the Senate with sufficient time to be ratified before the stipulated proce-
dural deadline expired. In 1904, a more concerted effort was made to resolve
the matter in the Hay-Quesada Treaty. This provoked such ire amongst the
US settlers that civil strife was only avoided when fresh water supply of the
principal town (Nueva Gerona) was interrupted, forcing both the rebels and
the Cuban Rural Guard to slake their thirst with rum, with McManus claiming
that, 'Before the hour set for the declaration of war, Cubans and Americans
had reached a state of sentimental good humour' (2000: 22). The island's
geopolitical position was finally fixed not by a diplomatic pen or a rebel sword,
but by tax law. When Edward J. Pearcy claimed an exemption from duty on
his Isle of Pines cigar imports into New York because they did not come from
a foreign country, the United States' Internal Revenue Service jumped in and
decided (in *Pearcy v. Stranahan*, Apr. 1907) that Cuba 'historically and politically, included the Isle of Pines' (McManus 2000: 24). But after tipsy civil
unrest and cigar smuggling, the history of the Isla de Pinos took a turn for
the sinister when Gerardo Machado laid the foundation stone of the Presidio
Modelo in February 1927.

The prison was a liminal institution on a liminal isle. Many of the
characteristics so typical of ritualised seclusion described by Turner in other
scenarios are all present in the Presidio, but in aberrant form. And ample
evidence of this aberration comes to the fore in an account of the Presidio
by one of the most extraordinary Cuban analyst-authors of the early 1930s.
Carlos Montenegro arrived in Havana from an impoverished Galician village
in 1907. In a drunken altercation in 1919, Montenegro killed his adversary
and was condemned to twelve years in prison. He began his sentence in
Havana's municipal prison, but was transferred to the Isla de Pinos at the
end of the 1920s. In the Presidio he discovered his literary gift, and his short-
story collection *El Renuevo, y otros cuentos* was published by the enthusiastic
revista de avance editors in 1929. The stories that we will explore (and of
which no previous analysis exists) come from his serialised account of life
in the Presidio Modelo, 'Suicidados, fugados y enterrados vivos: Una serie
sobre los horrores de «Cambray»', published in *Carteles* magazine between
December 1933 and January 1934.

Whereas for van Gennep the limen is merely a 'waiting' phase in the rite of
passage before an inevitable 'departure' (1965: 25), for Turner, an outstanding
liminal feature is a sense of timelessness. For him it is a space that elides
normal chronological rules, a state to which the 'structural view of time is
not applicable', where 'every day is, in a sense, the same day, writ large or
repeated', and where neophytes are led to intense and fruitful introspection
by the absence of external variation (Turner 1974: 238 & 239). Montenegro's
account challenges both anthropologists' interpretations; there the limen

certainly becomes a state, not a phase, but the relentless routine is one of the most unbearable aspects of prison life, the senses are starved and idle minds are led not to beneficial introspection, but towards inexorable decay: 'ya harto de los mismos rincones pobres de sol y aire, ansioso de un cambio cualquiera que éste fuese, agobiado por los días semejantes y la vida sin sucesos' (Montenegro 17 Dec. 1933: 66). The first story in the series describes one such 'cambio' for those prisoners transferred from Havana to the Isla de Pinos to build and then become the first inhabitants of the Presidio Modelo. The change of scenery seems to promise at least fleeting liberation from ferrous routine, an infusion of new colours and novel experiences to be savoured later in the suspended animation of their cell-bound lives:

> Se prometían gozar del buen paseo; saldrían – ¡por fin! – de allí, verían la calle que pisarían fuertemente y después vendría el mar que atravesarían plenos de júbilo […]. Tal vez pensaron que aquel viaje dejaría en sus ánimos deleite para mucho tiempo; que no terminaría en lo que va del toque de silencio al de diana. (ibid.)

The liminality here is multifaceted and cruelly inescapable: the prisoners are excited to leave the spatial (and social) margin of the urban prison and cross the threshold of the sea to a place that is at least different and new; they hope to infuse the monochromatic tedium of their present lives with novel sensations; they hope time will be on their sides once more and night-time a moment for retrospective and pleasurable reflection. They are proved wrong on all counts. The subjunctive and *tal vez* possibilities of the limen welcomed by analyst-authors previously has here become the negation of all sense and *sensibilidad*. Quite simply, what the prisoners who volunteered to build the Presidio and serve out their sentences there did not realise was that this fleeting escape would lead them ever closer to an absolute loss of liberty, or even loss of life, under a merciless routine in which they could not count on any form of structural protection.[6] In the Presidio Modelo, even the truth was incarcerated and unable to leave the island: 'La verdad está enterrada, muerta y enterrada' (24 Dec. 1933: 54). In Havana, the prisoners had been socially invisible, stigmatised by their alleged or actual crimes and by 'el prejuicio arraigado tan profundamente en nuestra sociedad de que un presidiario no pasa de ser un número' (17 Dec. 1933: 66). This invisibility is a common liminal theme, with Turner suggesting that the neophyte is 'structurally if not physically invisible

---

6 The 'ley de fuga' was often used as a pretext for the murder of troublesome prisoners: the first death at the new prison was a convict who was shot in the head for refusing to work in the prison's marble mines but reported as executed during a failed escape attempt.

in terms of his culture's standard definitions and classifications' (1974: 232). In the Presidio Modelo, the recently transferred prisoners exchanged symbolic for absolute invisibility in a place on the very fringes of Cuban territory and Cuba's collective consciousness. Despite the fact that most prison sentences and the social exclusion they entail are finite, Montenegro's description is not of a temporary isolation at all: to be sent to the Presidio Modelo was to run the risk of disappearing forever:

> Amanecerían en el destierro – muchos ya para siempre – lejos, tan lejos que ya sus gritos no podrían oírse, ¡que ya ni los podrían lanzar! No pensaron que serían ya en lo sucesivo como extranjeros del mundo entero, ya de hecho sin patria, cuando por derecho lo eran desde sus condenas. (17 Dec. 1933: 66)

Incarceration on the Isle of Pines, therefore, meant endless and inescapable aberrant liminality. The *lex* of *civitas* has lost its sway over these incarcerated citizens and their link to the nation itself is in doubt. Whereas Ortiz had lauded the fecund margin between psycho-linguistic purity and the *mala vida*, and Mañach had sought to balance himself and his generation between canonical deference and nihilistic disrespect, the 'place that is not a place and a time that is not a time' described by Montenegro is an interstice of anomie and despair (Turner 1974: 239). When Turner wrote that liminars are 'betwixt and between the positions assigned and arrayed by law, custom, convention', he could not have imagined the utter lawlessness of the Presidio Modelo (1969: 81). On this timeless and semi-invisible edge, the laws, customs and conventions are dictated by one person alone – prison governor Pedro Abraham Castells:

> Decir el Presidio Modelo es decir el comandante Castells. Está hecho a su imagen y semejanza. Éste le ha dado al Presidio su cuerpo y su alma y todos sus actos, aún los más íntimos e insignificantes, corroboran esta entrega absoluta […]. Hace más de seis años que el Presidio piensa con el cerebro de Castells, sanciona con su concepto bárbaro de la justicia, medra en relación a su capacidad de organización […] Si no fuera por su absoluto desprecio a la vida humana, sería el funcionario ideal. (24 Dec. 1933: 50)

It is in this absolute despotism that the difference between the anthropologists' and Montenegro's descriptions of the limen is most marked. Turner, for example, observes that in times of ritual transition, hierarchy and social stratification are amongst those structures which tend to be softened, if not completely set aside, in favour of a 'generalized social bond' that he calls 'communitas': 'an unstructured or rudimentarily structured and relatively undifferentiated *comitatus*, community, or even communion of equal individuals' (1969: 96). Communitas is governed by spontaneous solidarity and the replacement of formal structures with the informal and more instinctive organisation said to suddenly govern during moments of acute crisis or change. In ritualised rites of passage, this spirit sees the logic of human interaction freed from competitive pressures and hierarchical vertigo: liminars are able to return to more equitable human interchange, 'flowing from *I* to *Thou*' or towards the collective strength and solidarity of 'We' (Turner 1969: 127). In the aberrant limen on Cuba's edge, on the other hand, even though numbers have replaced names and all prisoners were theoretically cut off from any prior claims to social superiority, a perverse hierarchy soon became central to the prison's idiosyncratic structure. And this hierarchy was not based on the distinctions between common and political prisoners,[7] between prisoners and prison guards or between the guards and the commandant; all standard structural separations had been subverted by the aberrant logic of this anti-communitas and its despotic director. Montenegro describes Castells making a histrionic speech in response to an accusation made against him by a prisoner:

> "¡Que sea éste mi Waterloo si tal acusación es cierta! Me someto a vuestra justicia. Quiero que me juzguéis, ¡lo impongo!" Cuando el amo habla así a los esclavos, de antemano se gana su veredicto. Se pidió a gritos la muerte del murmurador; los más indignos fueron los más indignados; los más injustos ofrecieron sus propias manos para hacer justicia; los más insensibles lloraron rechazando la investigación *impuesta* [...]. Los propios presos se encargarían de hacer justicia y los escoltas se limitarían a cuidar exteriormente el Penal. (31 Dec. 1933: 30)

Dissonant echoes can be heard here between this high-walled prison colony and the lettered city. To Rama's bureaucratic *letrados* Montenegro brings an oratorical *funcionario*, swapping text for spoken lexis but still laying down the law in irresistible rhetoric that makes his interpretation of this self-contained world all there is for this truly perverse language community.[8] And far from the fraternity of the limen described by Turner, the *sensibilidad* of the prisoners on the Isla de Pinos is ruled by egotism and mutual mistrust; Castells's perverse moral order has made 'de cada preso [...] un delator, de

---

7　The Presidio Modelo was the favoured place to marginalise internal opposition in the first half of the twentieth century: in the early 1930s, Marinello, Pablo de la Torriente Brau, Roa and future president Grau San Martín were all imprisoned there; Fidel Castro followed them in 1953.

8　Although the subsequent publication of Montenegro's *letras* of course reasserts some of the authority of the written word.

cada sentimiento un ojo en acecho, de cada instinto una lengua mentirosa' (24 Dec. 1933: 50). But this move away from 'We' toward a terrified and self-defensive 'I' did not lead only to *desconfianza* and *delación*; every aspect of communitas was defiled as the so-called *sargentos mayores* (prisoners granted privileges in exchange for their participation in the brutal regime) guarded, punished and even executed their fellow inmates. Montenegro describes the death of 'Changuito', for example, garrotted by a *sargento mayor* as all the other prisoners looked on in silence:

> En esa tragedia no tomó parte ningún empleado. Ningún uniforme, con la execpción del nuestro, envilecido, apareció en escena. Preso la víctima, presos los verdugos, presos los espectadores ... Es la gran obra de Castells, el triunfo de su régimen. (7 Jan. 1934: 55)

In this internecine execution we see another challenge to those analyst-authors for whom the pure Cuban *pueblo*'s only sin had been an excess of faith in the abusive 'gobernantes obcecados' (Martínez Villena 1978: 19). Here instead is a *pueblo corrupto*, far from any of the meaning or morals of ideal collective *sensibilidad* and well beyond all absolution or cure. Similarly, in this stratification of Presidio society can be read an aberrant example of bi-polar liminal identity to bring alongside Mañach's positive response to generational change in *Estampas*. Whereas Mañach described the pacific equilibrium that could be achieved between the ironic traditionalist and the dogmatic progressive, in Montenegro's story binary opposites come together in a nefarious accord between 'el funcionario ideal' and the most mercenary *sargento mayor* of all, Gregorio Santiesteban:

> Castells es una fuerza ciega a la que Santiesteban ha puesto ojos bizcos utilizándola en su provecho y satisfacción. Para Castells la ley es la disciplina; para Santiesteban la ley no existe: la ha violado formal e infor-malmente. El primero pudo ser un hombre *honrado*; el segundo no: nació delincuente de derecho común. (31 Dec. 1933: 30)

The Manichean division between pure and perfidious, hale and frail that Roig, Martínez Villena, Abela and others saw being resolved for the good during collective turning points is made impossible in the psycho-spatial margin of the Presidio. By the same token, the Janus-like double vision that Ortiz and Mañach saw as integral to authentic Cuban identity, able to hold the potentially antagonistic forces of high culture and *mala vida*, tradition and innovation in subtle and stimulating balance, has now become the perfect algorithm for savagery. And the Presidio Modelo was just the beginning.

The limen unbound

In Montenegro's account of Cuba's physical and moral margin in the early 1930s we have observed that (as Turner suggested for other secluded limina) 'the cognitive schemata that give sense to everyday life no longer apply, but are, as it were, suspended' (1982: 84). On the Isla de Pinos, however, this led not to a critical re-calibration of social structures and the collective *sensibilidad*, either towards ultimate victory or an ongoing and innervating *luchita*, but to a subversion of all structures and the predominance of the bestial whims of a bi-polar and two-headed tyrant. For both van Gennep and Turner a critical facet of liminality, even whilst recognising that it can involve the irruption of base instincts, is that these are closely contained within proscribed times and spaces. In Cuba in the early 1930s, however, the extreme violence that blossomed on the geographic and imaginative edge of the Republic was matched by equally macabre events on the mainland, and particularly in the Cuban capital. If we take the laying of the foundation stone for the Presidio Modelo as the catalyst for the degeneration of the *machadato* that would ultimately lead to a revolutionary response, it is in 1933 that the supposedly delimited *dérèglement* of the senses became axiomatic in Cuba. We will examine this colonisation of the core by aberrant periphery in one fictionalised account, and a number of editorials from 1933 editions of *Bohemia* magazine.

Alfonso Hernández Catá's *Cementerio en las Antillas* is a collection of seven short stories written clandestinely whilst the author was the Cuban Consul to Spain. (He was removed from his post when his son was imprisoned on the Isla de Pinos for anti-Machado activities). 'Por Él' is a story in which place, time and identity all hover in an uneasy interstice between visibility and invisibility, day and night, the human and the demonic. The story describes a young anti-*machadista* who has fallen into the hands of the *porra*[9] and is being interrogated in an underground cell in the capital. Just as in the Presidio, physical and moral status and standing are all confused in this story as the 'criminal' refuses to obey the policemen, insisting that 'los que están fuera de la ley son ustedes, no yo' (Hernández Catá 1933: 111). As the thugs lead their victim towards absolute invisibility in 'otra mazmorra más profunda', all borders blur as the young man realises he is approaching the ultimate threshold between reality and aberrant sub-reality, between life and death:

En el umbral de la mazmorra había quedado, no sólo la esperanza, como en la puerta dantesca, sino la piedad. No era un hombre entre la cólera de otros

[9] Machado's infamous unofficial police force that spread terror throughout Cuba in the early 1930s.

hombres: era un hombre entre demonios insensibles a ninguno de los signos por los cuales los semejantes se reconocen entre si. (114)

As on the Isla de Pinos, this 'umbral' or margin is no place to rethink and re-chart selfhood; instead *sensibilidad* has been de-sensitised (losing both feelings and morals) and the innocent and the guilty come together in perverse communitas in which the former has no hope and the latter have no pity. After being viciously beaten, the definitive end of death seems finally to spare the prisoner any more torment, but Hernández Catá eliminates all hope that this macabre limbo will ever come to an end; the future tense in this story marks only a terrible defeat:

– No muere, no. Resiste.
– Mejor. En cuanto se pueda, otro interrogatorio. ¡Hablará! (116)

Just as between the prison and the city, the island and the mainland, here the barrier containing aberrant excesses to the almost invisible margin, and preserving the self-conscious decorum of the core, is punctured. After the torture is over, the *porra* captain ascends from the obscure dungeon and stands before his window to admire 'un cielo de purísimo azul y un aire vibrante' (118). At first the aberrant underworld appears completely concealed: 'nadie hubiese dicho al verlo, entre la sonrisa matinal de todas las cosas, que subía del más horrendo subsuelo y del más abominable pasado'; but alongside the window is a portrait of 'Él', the smugly smiling president. The luminous upper world, like the aberrant netherworld, is watched over and ruled by the ultimate architect of all that subterranean horror; the bicephalous Castells-Santiesteban monster is replicated: '*Él* era un hombre, una trágica apariencia de hombre nada más, igual que las fieras que servían su poder inhumano' (117 & 118).

In Hernández Catá's stories, as in reality, the Cuban capital was not the only place to suffer the sanguinary crimes of the early 1930s. One of Machado's most notorious thugs was Arsenio Ortiz, a murderous police chief and so-called 'Chacal de Oriente' who was only relieved of his duties in Santiago de Cuba after being implicated in forty-four homicides, but would go on to receive a presidential pardon and reappear in the central city of Santa Clara in 1933. 'El pagaré', in which a swaggering police superintendent menaces a farmer into lending him a large sum of money, only to 'pay off' the debt by murdering the creditor, is clearly based on *el Chacal*'s brutal exploits in the Cuban heartland. Once again, the story unfolds on an uneasy margin where aberrant ambiguity rules. Herminio the farmer feels out of place in the city, where 'las calles, las casas, hasta el modo de hablar de la población, lo oprimían', but also shuns the increasingly lawless *campo* where never before have 'los rifles, los machetes y las sogas' made their appearance 'con menos respeto a la ley' (Hernández Catá 1933: 202). He thus seeks safety for his family in the liminal space of a humble *bohío*, 'confluencia de ciudad y monte', on the very outskirts of town, 'en el límite de los dos elementos' (198 & 202). But the spatial ambiguity and psycho-social flux of this margin offer little solace, the penumbra of the *bohío* is menaced by unwelcome illumination from both sides: 'miraba, indeciso, a un lado el fresco silencio del manigual surcado a veces por la tenue fosfores-cencia de los cocuyos, y, en la negrura opuesta, el enjambre artificial de las luces de la población' (202). The superintendent has brought the *dérèglement* of the senses out of the peripheral penal colony and the urban dungeon and into the most central of Cuban cities and the most archetypal of Cuban domestic spaces:

> Ya hacía un mes que estaba en la ciudad, y la muerte no había tenido ni un día de reposo. Nunca jamás, ni en los días peores de la guerra de emanci-pación, habían caído tantos hombres a fuego y a hierro. Era una epidemia de homicidios, una especie de *amok* occidental, un barbarismo tan refinado, tan inconcebible, que el estupor paralizaba las reacciones viriles de la ira. (209)

In contrast both to the autarkic Cuban identity that Cosculluela saw being born in a cave in the rural heartland, and to the *homo maritimus* that Ortiz saw importing vitality into Cuban *letras* and life, here insular identity is under concerted attack by an inside-outside savage, by the exotic 'amoks' turned native, by an alien invader who is simultaneously one of Cuba's own. And so the reaction to this insidious internal-external menace is perhaps understandable. Far from galvanising the combined strength of solidarity typical during the trials of ritual transition, whether in the form of a heroic Mella-type *bofetazo* or a more understated and Luján-type act of charity, citizens on both sides of the urban–rural divide have been 'paralizados' into complicit indecision, mutual suspicion and fear. Just as in the Presidio Modelo described by Montenegro, the extreme violence of the aberrant limen in Hernández Catá's stories has not provoked a move towards liminal commu-nitas, nor the development of sensibilities better equipped for the challenges of post-transition life, but led rather to a degradation into cowardly inactivity. Although the farmer's neighbour perceives the menace drawing close, he fails to act:

> Era uno de esos seres de talento y sapiencia a quienes la cobardía y el egoísmo esterilizan. Si se hubiera atrevido habría aconsejado a Hermino que emprendiera hacia el interior uno de aquellos viajes que duraban un par de

meses [...]. Sin embargo, puso al impulso los frenos de la egolatría y apretó la boca. (205–6)

Violence and counter-violence: the ABC

Not all remained passive before 'the crime of Cuba'.[10] In Havana once more, an outstanding example of a *bofetazo* that was both bellicose and ideological was being meted out by the anti-Machado group the ABC. The ABC was founded at the end of 1931 by young lawyers Carlos Saládrigas and Joaquín Martínez Sáenz as 'una organización que aspira a efectuar una renovación integral de la vida pública cubana' (ABC manifesto, in Padrón Larrazábal 1975: 119). There was nothing new in this call for moral regeneration, of course. From Ortiz's Junta Cubana de Renovación Nacional to the thirteen-strong 'protesta' in the Academia de Ciencias, the promotion of integral and law-abiding *civitas* as a remedy for the Republic's parlous moral health had been at the core of collective identity debates since independence. What made the ABC's contribution to the debate so remarkable was not so much the ideology they put forward, as the tactics they deployed. Whereas Ortiz's Junta had lobbied in the Cuban Congress and Martínez Villena's *Protestantes* had organised debates in Havana cafés, the ABC planted bombs in government offices, murdered policemen and *porristas* and even shot the Speaker of the Senate, Clemente Vásquez Bello, as he strolled through the doors of his beachfront club. The ABC was both a political party and a terrorist cell.[11] The outlandish violence of the ABC was marked by the same *dérèglement* of the senses that made their enemies so *insensibles*: the notorious commander of the Atarés fortress, Miguel Calvo, was riddled with bullets as he rode along the seafront promenade, the politician Carlos García Sierra was blown up in his own study, and the assassination of Vázquez Bello was only the first part of an audacious plan to wipe out Machado's entire cabinet by booby-trapping the mausoleum where the ABC believed the *machadista* mourners would gather for such a notable funeral.[12] As in the 'model' prison and Havana dungeon, the appetite for destructive violence seemed insatiable and practically indiscriminate. The ABC's clandestine paper *Denuncia* had a regular section called 'Galería de Apapipios' in which suspected Machado sympathisers were identified (with details of their addresses and any nearby police posts) and readers exhorted

---

10 The title of Carleton Beals's influential 1930 book, illustrated with photographs by Walker Evans.

11 Whose cell A, cell B, cell C, etc. members were ignorant of the identity, actions or whereabouts of *abecedarios* from other cells, thus frustrating the government's intelligence-gathering efforts, despite the macabre methods often employed.

12 When the family decided to bury the late Speaker in Santa Clara instead of the capital city,

to mercilessly hunt them down: 'Ya lo saben, compañeros, ¡a buscarlo! ¡A cogerlo, compañeros! (*Denuncia*, 26 Apr. 1933: 7). When read alongside the ABC's manifesto, which dismisses the *porrista* as 'un ser irresponsable' and rather identifies 'el gran criminal de esta hora' as 'el hombre de cierta posición social y cierto desahogo económico, que se limita a defender sus intereses', the potential for large-scale slaughter becomes clear (Padrón Larrazábal 1975: 144). Quite simply, the nocturnal world of police brutality and the diurnal world of cowardly self-serving citizens were indistinguishable to the ABC. On both sides of this civil strife the law of Cuban *civitas* was suspended and violent actions were supplanting all debate.

This liminal blurring of temporal, legal and moral boundaries is the key narrative fulcrum in Hernández Catá's story 'Estudiantina', clearly inspired by the activities of ABC terror cells. In an Old Havana safe-house, two young terrorists are carefully constructing a bomb. Their youth is significant. Although grown into adult responsibilities, these bombers are only adolescents, on their own interstice between the levity of youth and the premature gravity of maturity that circumstances have forced upon them. In this story, the *machadato* is a wholly unwelcome rite of passage that other precocious adults-in-waiting will soon be obliged to face: 'si caían todos los que ahora conspiraban, cada mes, cada hora, mientras más extremaba la tiranía su ferocidad, héroes precoces dejaban el ámbito seguro de la niñez para entrar con la sonrisa en la boca en las encrucijadas del exterminio' (1933: 161). But at this crossroads the clear frontier between life and death is eroded by ambiguity. The young terrorists seem to be fighting, not for a new life, but because the morbid omnipresence of death has left them little choice: 'a morir estaban dispuestos desde el principio: se consideraban muertos ya' (158). And yet in this liminal 'borde trágico que separa la vida de la muerte' evidence of an upsurge of the spontaneous solidarity celebrated by Turner is scant (159). Between the terrorists and their targets the only common bond is a desire for mutual annihilation. Even amongst the intra-cellular co-conspirators, communitas seems fallible. Whereas the two men building the bomb have trusted each other 'desde el primer día', both are suspicious of the bomb planter, Chucho: 'He tenido ya tres veces malos pensamientos. Sospechas, sí ... ¡Hay tanto *apapipio*, tanto vendido! ¿desde cuándo lo conoces tú?' (153). In this tense and irresolute world every border is menaced: day and night mean nothing in the twilight world of the safe-house, and even the innocent sound of a child whistling outside the front door could be a harbinger of imminent doom:

the explosives were eventually stumbled upon by the Havana cemetery gardener (Thomas 2001: 364).

Los verdugos se servían de todo [...], podían utilizar a niños en su espio-
najes. ¿No los utilizaban también los patriotas para poner petardos, para
llevar recados, para observar entre juego y juego los vaivenes de los policías
y los *porristas*? Lo mismo que se habían borrado las lindes entre la seguridad
y el peligro, se habían borrado las de las edades. (157–8)

Here space and psycho-geographic place are fundamentally disturbed. Whereas
Ortiz had celebrated the jocular *correcorre* that kept all the island's doors open
and ensured danger could be averted by simply never standing still, here the
vaivenes of seemingly innocent children are heavy with menace.

Mañach on the aberrant edge

Although the aberrant liminality of the prison colony, secret police dungeon
and terrorist safe-house seemed omnipresent in 1933, analyst-authors nevertheless looked to chart its particular topography and thus plan a collective
escape. For some, the fundamental faultlines remained the same as in 1923
and 1927: ambiguity and flux versus the resolution of radicalism: what Roa
called 'un duelo abierto, sin concesiones ni reservas' between indecision
and the determined forging of 'un mundo nuevo' (1969: 26). Although the
rhetoric is similar, however, the ultimate aim in 1933 was much more limited
than in the previous rites of passage. Although making almost obligatory
reference to a near-perfect future Cuba-to-come, which had been at the
forefront of Martínez Villena, Roig and Mella's analysis of and contributions
to the national narrative, the teleological discourse of 1933 did not share
its predecessor's long-sightedness: the 'end' pointed towards was not full
reaggregation in a post-rite of passage reality, but a much more proximate and
bloody denouement beyond which everything remained uncertain. And some
advocates of this near-future resolution are surprising.

By the early 1930s, Mañach's position as a champion of ideological and
generational equilibrium was under concerted attack. In October 1930, the final
edition of *revista de avance* was published. From its initially confident declaration that political commentary simply did not fall 'dentro del sector de esta
revista', Machado's increasingly thuggish tactics saw some of the magazine's
editors opt for more overt involvement in the political fight against the dictator
(*revista de avance* 1927: 1). When Marinello was imprisoned on the Isla de
Pinos in 1930 for his involvement in the outlawed Directorio Estudiantil
Universitario (DEU), the magazine declared that to avoid censorship and
government-decreed closure, publication would be suspended 'hasta que
el pensamiento pueda emitirse libremente' (*revista de avance* 1930: 2).
Whilst Marinello struggled to survive in the Presidio, Mañach faced his own

calvary back in Havana. Whereas his friend had been incarcerated for anti-government activism, Mañach was attacked for his apparent lack of action in the deteriorating situation. In a letter of November 1931, Roa (who was to become Mañach's ideological arch-enemy over the next thirty years) vilified Mañach as an 'alma desencantada' who refused to involve himself in the bloody business of political opposition. Mañach's cardinal crime, in Roa's eyes, was that he lacked the mettle for the bloody fight against Machado because of his apparent 'incapacidad temperamental – más de una vez confesada por tí, con sinceridad plausible – para enrolarte en una lucha que exige fe combativa y denuendo heroico hasta el garrote' (1969: 27). Roa and his radical *compañeros* in the early 1930s had as little truck with Mañach the in-betweener as they did with Machado the despot. The divide on both sides was irreconcilable: 'tu lenguaje y tu ideario reflejan tu posición contemplativa y cauta, así nuestro ideario y nuestro lenguaje reflejan la nuestra, beligerante, afirmativa, revolucionaria, incompatible, por eso, con la ambigüedad, el oportunismo, el *flirt* y el criollísimo nadar entre dos aguas' (ibid.). The bond between authorship and analysis that had remained mostly harmonious at the two previous turning points, now came under intense pressure; the sense that the sword was far superior to the pen was rehearsed (it will be an idea that we will return to consistently); for some, Cuba's *letrados* and *activistas* were not collaborative twins, but irreconcilable twains never fully to meet. Somewhat notoriously, Mañach never replied to Roa's challenge, but his shifting *letrado activista* identity perhaps went some way towards answering his harshest critic. Finding himself and his *ideario* suddenly out of step with the belligerent *fisonomía* of the early 1930s, the author of articles that had lauded psycho-social equilibrium and of stories that had proposed a wetnurse as the archetypal Cuban, Mañach joined forces with Saládrigas and Martínez Sáenz and was responsible (in 1931) for writing large parts of the ABC manifesto that reserved, as we have already seen (and in clear echo of Roa's impatience with indecision), its most bilious attacks not for *machadista* murderers but for the timid and ambivalent spectators of these crimes: 'Permanecer indiferente, significa traicionar al pueblo. No sublevarse, en la medida de sus fuerzas, contra la barbarie machadista, equivale a tener alma de esclavo' (in Padrón Larrazábal 1975: 144). By 1932, Mañach's conversion to the cause of radical action seemed complete. In a 26 May letter to Lino Novás Calvo, he appeared infused with Roa-type dogmatic resolution: 'Ya no es posible seguir viviendo en esta barbarie sin encanallarse. Yo he optado por la guerra de guerrilla, para salvarme del encanallamiento' (in Cairo 1993: 55).

The cyclical and outlandish violence of the aberrant limen is evident in this interpretation of salvation. If Cuba was ruled by a *bestia*, then setting aside *civitas* and *sensibilidad* to become violent beasts themselves was the only way many Cuban thinkers saw of saving themselves and their country. This sense of liminal excess is actually in keeping with the anthropologists' under-standings of psychological momentum within the rite of passage. Examples of extreme violence deployed as a socio-cultural prophylactic are common in Turner's writings: amongst the Ndembu people, for example, the chief-elect undergoes his own liminal rites in which he is divested of all symbols of authority, dressed 'just like a slave', and physically abused by lowly members of society (Turner 1969: 88). This cathartic release of normally suppressed urges enables the abusers to succumb subsequently to inflexible hierarchy and instructs the chief-elect in the supreme self-control that will be essential thereafter 'in face of the temptations of power' (ibid.). In oblique disagreement with Turner, however, Hernández Catá's fictional account of ABC terrorists suggested that violence in Cuba in the early 1930s had become the common sense and *sensibilidad*, and so catharsis would prove elusive: 'Cuando ésto acabe vamos a quedar inservibles, peor que muertos', says one of the terrorists, 'y no vamos a acostumbrarnos a vivir como personas' (1933: 159). It is to this potential for emergence from the aberrant limen that we now turn.

Life after Machado: escape from the aberrant limen?

At 9.30 on the morning of 12 August 1933, Machado descended from his office in the presidential palace and calmly left the scene of his crimes against Cuba. The tense crowd outside allowed his car to pass in silence. For the moment, cautious expectation ruled on the streets of Havana. Some hours later, three of Machado's close collaborators, Orestes Ferrara (Secretary of State), Ramiro Guerra (Presidential Secretary) and the propagandist and ex-*minorista* Alberto Lamar Schweyer also fled the palace, just as the storm of pent-up rage broke over the city: 'Seeing these men, enraged, sweating, hoarse from shouting, eyes bulging from their sockets, thirsty for vengeance, and waving their green flag like Mahomet's, we knew we were lost' (Guerra, in Thomas 2001: 381). The first reprisals against *machadistas* were impulsive and chaotic. Known *porristas* were hunted down and lynched on street corners. ABC activists, students and even soldiers rampaged through Havana settling old scores. What Roa calls the 'reprimidos rencores' (1969: 227) that had embittered daily lives for a lustrum or more were exorcised in a wave of violence that seemed to match the brutality of the *machadato*, eye for eye and tooth for tooth:

> En las aceras del Prado [...] donde estuvo el *Diario de la Marina*, órgano centenario de la reacción, vimos matar a un hombre a palos, pedradas y adoquinazos. No le dieron ni un tiro, ni siquiera una puñalada. Fue macerado. Desde los balcones de los entresuelos del hotel Pasaje, su esposa

y su hijo vieron la macabra secuencia de una multitud enfebrecida que corría al "amok". (Kuchilán 1970: 59)

The truly savage and *insensible* spirit that had overcome police superintendents and terrorists now seems to drive the entire *pueblo* to 'run amok'. After a week of complete chaos, however, the bloodlust began to be analysed as writers sought to bring some sense to the *dérèglement* on the streets. The first post-Machado edition of *Bohemia* is particularly noteworthy. From the front cover (which depicts a diabolical Machado devouring helpless and naked victims) to the editorial that classified the ex-president as a 'troglodita vestido de hombre civilizado', it is clear that *Bohemia* intends to demonise Machado and his most aberrant acolytes (1933a: 5). The article 'Servidores de la Tiranía', for example, offers a grotesque gallery of *machadista* politicians with all their perversities exposed: the mayor of Havana 'Pepito' Izquierdo is pilloried 'por sus diligencias de proxeneta para ofrecerle al Amo las refocilaciones orgíacas y lascivas que reclamaba su grosería de sátiro decrepto'; police chief Antonio Aínciart is portrayed as a monstrous figure whose immorality was manifest in the 'degeneración física de su cuerpo' (1933b: 33). This focus on extremes can be read as an editorial outpouring of 'reprimidos rencores' but also, and more fundamentally, as a recognition of the potentially catastrophic consequences of Roa and the ABC's suggestion that the passive observation of *machadato* crimes was just as heinous as their perpetration, that anything short of ardent *activismo* was tantamount to treachery. Without unambiguous enemies upon whom to unleash 'la cólera unánime del pueblo', this popular ire could easily lead to bloody internecine strife that would tear Cuba apart (del Valle 1933: 26). With the malevolence of the Machado years concentrated (and therefore contained) within the most noxious representatives of the regime, however, the possibility of a cathartic exteriorisation of previously suppressed rancour seemed real, the chance to exonerate the more passive observers of the *machadato*, extirpate the *machadista* canker, and carry collective *sensibilidad* towards gradual recuperation, seemed achievable. This metaphor of disease and radical recovery appears throughout the 20 August edition of *Bohemia*, but comes particularly to the fore in Gerardo del Valle's article 'La revolución comienza ahora'. For del Valle, the flight of Machado and his cronies and the subsequent unfettering of the Cuban people's 'mano dura' that 'supo castigar' was gratifying, but not sufficient to guarantee a return to collective psychosocial health: 'Los bacilos hambrientos han fenecido momentáneamente, pero la llaga purulenta sigue en toda su repugnancia fisiológica invitándoles a tornar en sus danzas macabras' (del Valle 1933: 26). What was needed was a potent prophylactic (in Turner's terms), an invasive remedy that would prevent any recurrence of the virulent maladies that had plagued the Republic for thirty years: 'Se precisan inmediatamente cirujanos sociales que arranquen de un golpe de bisturí los tumores ancestrales e inyecten, contra la misma voluntad del enfermo, sangre nueva a las arterias y fosfórica fuerza a las células adormecidas' (ibid.). Although visceral in tone, this can be read as a plea as much for textual as for corporeal social surgeons; can be seen as the first tentative steps towards re-valorising the analysis of the national story as well as its active inscription, of re-establishing the link between life and *letras* and reasserting the equilibrium that the liminalists of this study had defended and embodied.

As August turned into September, and September into October, however, clarity remained elusive, a sense of collective culpability persisted and convincing catharsis and the reintegration that comes after was still distant. After Machado's flight, the ABC capitalised on the influence they had won during US ambassador Sumner Welles's *mediación* between Machado and the opposition to claim key posts in the new government, presided over by the almost unknown diplomat Carlos Manuel de Céspedes (whose blood link to his grandfather, 'el padre de la patria', was practically his only credential for high office): Martínez Sáenz took charge of the Ministry of Finance and Saládrigas of the Ministry of Justice. Despite immediate US recognition, however, the new government enjoyed little stability, and by the end of August even the habitually optimistic Ambassador Welles (prone to drastically understate the unrest in a post-Machado Cuba in which he clearly felt he had played a major and positive part) admitted the rule of chaos in many parts of the island: 'Students and radicals of every shade are breaking into houses, promoting lynchings, forcing resignations from ex-senators' (in Thomas 2001: 388). But the fatal blow to Céspedes's government came from an unexpected quarter. On 4 September 1933, an uprising of NCOs and rank-and-file soldiers disgruntled about unpaid wages and rumours of cuts to come made its appearance on the island's socio-political stage. With the crimes of the *machadato* as yet incompletely atoned for, a group whom many believed had failed to 'limpiarse el uniforme [...] cubierto de sangre y lodo', suddenly found itself, with a thirty-two year old stenographer sergeant called Fulgencio Batista at its head, taking control of the post-Machado physical and moral reconstruction of Cuba (de Almagro 1933: 16). As in the Presidio, the dividing line between order and disorder was blurred and uniforms were no guarantee of rectitude. At the outset, the so-called 'sergeants' revolt' was content to support the DEU-dominated civil junta (known as the *Pentarquía* and formed by Grau San Martín, José María Irisarri, Sergio Carbó, Guillermo Portela and Porfirio Franca), which came forward in this situation of great uncertainty and accepted President Céspedes's resignation on 5 September. But from that date forwards, contradiction and confusion reigned. Many of the commissioned officers refused to have terms dictated to them by their former subordinates and ensconced themselves in the cliff-top stronghold of the recently opened Hotel Nacional.[13] On 8 September, Carbó authorised Batista's promotion to colonel without consulting his fellow *Pentarquistas* and two days later, in anger at this unilateral decision and compelled to drastic steps by the ongoing civil unrest, lack of official international recognition and ring of US warships tightening around the island, the DEU dissolved the *Pentarquía* and designated Grau San Martín as president of the Gobierno Provisional Revolucionario. Nevertheless, the US embassy recalcitrantly withheld its blessing, the warships remained in sight off the coast and the officers were joined in the Hotel Nacional by scores of disgruntled ABC activists.

During the autumn of 1933, therefore, the 'acumulación de tánatos' that had invaded Cuban *sensibilidad* during the brutal *machadato* proved difficult to dispel (Cabrera Infante 1992: 182). When Machado fled, some hoped that a 'golpe de bisturí' against the most notorious culprits of the past would serve as a prophylactic, allowing Cuba to cathartically channel its 'reprimidos rencores' and amputate infected parts of the socio-political *corpus* in order to spare the rest (even if it had been previously passive) for future salubrity. In *Bohemia*'s editorial of 1 October 1933, however, this post-traumatic seren-dipity seems distant indeed:

> Lo cierto es que los ánimos están en perpetua efervescencia, que la intran-quilidad se entroniza en todos los espíritus e invade todos los rincones [...]. Impera un estado de anarquía que siembra la intranquilidad y hasta el terror en los espíritus. (1933d: 33)

Whereas some analyst-authors had perceived and projected previous turning points as temporary, whilst others had seen the essence of Cuban identity as limen-type flux, here this effervescence is more corrosive than creative, and leads backwards to dissolution rather than onwards to reaggregation. Despite *Bohemia*'s best efforts to focus popular ire on the departed demon, the disturbing sense of collective culpability for the crimes of Cuba hung in the air, provoking an atmosphere of mutual recrimination and mistrust. As in Montenegro's account of the Presidio Modelo and Hernández Catá's stories from the mainland, 'se había borrado la senda que separa lo inverosímil de lo real. Ningún hombre osaba mirar a otro cara a cara, por pudor y por pavura' (Hernández Catá 1933: 209). At dawn on 2 October, this rumbling

---

[13] *Bohemia* claimed that the officers were provoked by an insolent Batista who arrived at a meeting of truce 'rodeado por veinticuatro de sus hombres armados de ametralladoras' (1933c: 30).

unrest exploded into internecine strife when Batista attempted to dislodge the entrenched officers from their cliff-top hotel redoubt.

The siege of the Hotel Nacional offers thought-provoking evidence of the cycle of bloody violence that remained unbroken in Cuba after Machado's departure. Throughout the morning of 2 October, the well-armed and well-trained officers harried the attacking soldiers with accurate sniper fire from the hotel roof. By the afternoon, however, the sergeants had brought in their artillery and casualties within the hotel began to mount. The most notorious casualties, however, occurred after the battle was over. As the surrendering officers filed from the building, unidentified assassins opened fire and scores more men fell dead or gravely wounded.[14] In *Bohemia*'s coverage of the siege, the prevalent sentiment was frustration at the malignant continuity between the *machadato* and the *revolución*. Although the editors had attempted to attribute all evils to the demonic ex-president, what they called 'la herencia del Diablo' was proving difficult to exorcise, no matter how much sacrificial blood was shed:

> Bien está que la sangre de los hombres corra cuando con ella se va a robustecer la savia de los más altos ideales [...]; muy bien también que para exterminar de raíz una tiranía bestial, el pueblo brinde su sangre a los instintos asesinos de Machado; pero está muy mal que la falta de entendimiento, las vanidades y las pasiones sectarias, hagan que se derrame sangre viril y necesaria a más altos fines. Tal parece que la tragedia se empeña en ensombrecer la alegría de la liberación cubana, tal parece que desde las sombras sigue palpitando la maléfica influencia del machadato sediento siempre de sangre cubana. (1933e: 42)

The second convulsion of the autumn came on 8 November, when ABC militants joined armed-forces malcontents and rogue colonel Juan Blas Hernández in a bombing raid on the Columbia military base and the occupation of several Havana police stations. Tipped off by a traitor amongst the rebels, Batista's response was swift and decisive. As the bombers were repelled and the police stations fell to government forces once again, more and more conspirators took refuge in the Atarés fortress by the harbour. The thick limestone walls of the eighteenth-century castle gave a deceptive sense of security that was shattered when the first mortar fell amongst the rebels; 250 were killed (many after the raising of the flag of truce) and 150 more were injured. With this blood on its hands, Grau's government limped on until

---

[14] Kapcia offers careful examination of the evidence of the post-siege shooting in his article 'The Siege of the Hotel Nacional, Cuba, 1933: A Reassessment'.

mid-January 1934 when Batista crowned his meteoric rise from stenographer to all-powerful king-maker by removing the president in a coup and replacing him with the first in a series of puppet premiers.[15] As Cuba entered the first New Year since 1925 without the pernicious presence of Gerardo Machado, the fate of the unfortunate island had passed, if indirectly, into the hands of a new ruler: Fulgencio Batista.[16] Cuba was caught in an insalubrious interstice and seemed in danger of suffocating in 'una atmósfera de inquietud e incertidumbre [...], como la que precede a los grandes cataclismos' (*Bohemia* 1933g: 3). For Roa, the liquidation of the past in the revolutionary crucible of August 1933 had failed and the 'herencia del Diablo' was here to stay: 'se había ido Machado; pero subsistía el machadato [...], se convalidaba el bestiario y la selva' (1969: 226).

The revolution that deposed Machado, whether seen to commence in 1930 or 1933, is often portrayed as a noble endeavour undermined by debilitating frustration, as raising hopes of 'una etapa histórica brillante [...] que respondería a los vivos afanes y sublimes sacrificios del país', but ultimately succumbing to 'un maremagnum de personalismos y recelos, entre una atmósfera envenada por el encono y la ambición' (*Bohemia* 1933f: 31). 'La revolución se fue a bolina', declared an uncompromising Roa (1969); 'El 4 de septiembre no era un parto, sino un aborto', claimed Mario Kuchilán, with the kind of dogmatism that came to characterise many reflections on 1933 from beyond Cuba's other twentieth-century revolutionary watershed (1970: 112).

Although partially agreeing with these portrayals of 1933 as a historical turning point overcome by a stultifying sense of frustration, we have proposed alternative readings of the intranscendence of Cuba's first twentieth-century revolution. Following Turner's assessment of the potential *dérèglement* during the rite of passage, this chapter has explored the notion that the aberrant liminality of the complete degradation of structure in an extreme margin like the Presidio Modelo was unbound during the *machadato* and became prevalent across the island. Far from a cathartic temporary exposure to extremes in order to acquire the self-discipline and equanimity required for integral life in the post-liminal real world, it has been suggested that the *dérèglement de tous les sens* became a key trope within the Cuban national narrative, that an

---

[15] Carlos Hevia (16–18 Jan. 1934); Manuel Márquez Sterling (18 Jan. 1934); Carlos Mendieta (18 Jan. 1934–11 Dec. 1935); José Agripino Barnet (11 Dec. 1935–20 May 1936); Miguel Mariano Gómez (20 May–24 Dec. 1936); Federico Laredo Brú (24 Dec. 1936–10 Oct. 1940).

[16] For Kapcia, the successful smashing of the Hotel Nacional siege ensured that Batista's star continued to rise, thus entrenching heavy-handed militarism at the heart of post-1934 politics (Kapcia 2002: 302–9).

acceptance of, and even relish for, sanguinary acts of brutality was as evident in Havana as it was on the Isla de Pinos.

When the dicator finally fled in August 1933, the explosion of sanguinary recriminations that followed did not 'cleanse the Doors of Perception', as Turner (citing Blake) suggested of the prophylactic violence of the limen, but rather demonstrated that the morbid 'acumulación de tánatos' during Machado's rule had survived his flight and propelled post-dictatorship Cuba from one internecine catastrophe to another (1974: 253). In this, our indication of an aberrant and inescapable limen of vengeful violence and counter-violence can be usefully compared with Hannah Arendt's understanding of revenge as 'the form of re-acting against an original trespassing, whereby far from putting an end to the consequences of the first misdeed, everybody remains bound to the process, permitting the chain reaction contained in every action to take its unhindered course' (1958: 240–1). By condoning even localised acts of brutal retribution in the first days after the fall of Machado, the national narrative became trapped, in Arendt's terms, within a bitter and unbreakable cycle of mutual mutilation in which the misdeeds of the past hung 'like Damocles' sword' over every new generation' (ibid: 237). The *porrista* lynched from a lamppost became the unarmed officer shot in the back in the gardens of the Hotel Nacional, became the airman blown up by mortar fire in the sinister Atarés fort. Despite *Bohemia*'s best efforts to contain the malevo-lence of the *machadato* by demonising the ex-president and his coterie and thus exonerate the long-suffering *pueblo* and permit some post-revolutionary (and post-liminal) reintegration, collective culpability and the vicious mutual recriminations it inspired continued to haunt the national narrative.

The revolution of 1933 'se fue a bolina', we have argued here, not because of the 'personalismos y recelos' of some of the principal actors, or the malfea-sance and thuggery of the military elite alone (*Bohemia* 1933e: 31), but because of a *dérèglement* of the senses that extended beyond the physical and metaphysical limen of prison colony or torture cell; which was aggravated, not ameliorated, by the violent August exorcism of 'reprimidos rencores', and which went on to fuel the internecine enmity of the macabre post-Machado panorama. The *revolución del '33* did not operate successfully on the malig-nancy of the *machadato*, the self-sacrificial bloodshed did not invigorate the health of the whole; instead, the collective *sensibilidad* seemed to succumb to a gradual yet implacable metastasis,[17] the blood that was shed pooled inside the collective corpus in a virulent and durable bruise. With Castells

---

[17] The term also deployed by Pérez Firmat to describe the invasion of the core by the periphery in Luis Martín-Santos's *Tiempo de silencio* (and some of the Hispanic texts he analyses in *Literature and Liminality*).

and Santiesteban gone from the Isla de Pinos, the *porristas* purged and 'Él' removed from his diabolic throne in Havana, the beast-in-the-making that was Batista stepped into the limelight that illuminated Cuba's persistently unsettled socio-cultural panorama.

Nevertheless, where analysts like Roa and Tabares, Soto and Le Riverend see the revolution of 1933 'yendo a bolina', never to recover until the late 1950s and the triumph of the true Revolution, one need not go so far to see initial, and then undeniable signs of civic recovery in Cuba. Within just a few years, evidence began to appear of a much longer-lasting legacy of the 1933 turning point, the beginnings of a return to collective health and the purge of shared sins.

The first sin to be expunged was the Platt Amendment, the original sin itself. Almost thirty-two years to the day on which it had become a stain on the new Republic's conscience, the Amendment was finally abrogated from the Constitution.[18] In some senses, and certainly in the terms proposed here in which the primary socio-cultural struggle in independent Cuba was with itself and over its selfhood, this externally imposed blemish was relatively easy to erase. A more potentially deadly sin that had come to the surface of *sensibilidad* during the *machadato* was a deep distrust and even latent hatred for one's neighbours, made even more acute by the sense that, despite attempts to lay all the blame at the feet of psychopathic prison governors or cynical and self-interested bourgeoisie, there was always a Gregorio Santiesteban or an illiterate *porrista* to trouble this Manichean examination of the collective *conciencia*. A particularly important dimension for this study is that the pact between *activismo* and *escritura*, whether in Homeric acts of derring-do followed by less bellicose analysis (as in Mella), or in the mundane but sublime heroism of the wetnurse archetype (as in Luján) was jeopardised by a mutual recrimination in 1933 that sent tectonic tremors under the *ciudad letrada cubana* and its contribution to collective *sensibilidad*. Although this strife would not easily be soothed (and will return as a major characteristic in future readings and writings of the national narrative), Cuba did ultimately free itself from the self-destructive spirit of the aberrant limen and did eventually make 1926–33 a meaningful turning point through two interrelated and mutually reinforcing psychological and civic traits.

First came the kind of Augustinian confession in which candid admission of personal guilt becomes a collective first person narrative of shared responsibility. By as early as the end of 1933, analyst-authors were already encouraging self-confession as a step towards collective pardon, with the

[18] The Plattist terms that had been incorporated into the Cuban consitution of 1901 were all abolished, except those clauses concerning Guantánamo Bay (see Thomas 1971: 694–5).

November *Bohemia* editorial, for example, 'Cuba pide sacrificios', calling not for the sacrifice of blood, but for the catharsis of collective contrition and mutual forgiveness: 'Todos tenemos que arrepentirnos de algo; porque todos somos culpables' (1933h: 27). Despite the grisly reminder offered by the shattered silhouette of the Atarés fortress overlooking the city, *Bohemia* pointed optimistically towards a cautious return to civic harmony: 'En los actuales momentos, corazones y semblantes ceden al dulce influjo de la esperanza [que] como un bálsamo de alivio, logra que se atenuen en el espíritu público los recelos y la inquietud' (ibid.). The sublime liberation of true forgiveness, which for Arendt frees 'both the one who forgives and the one who is forgiven' (1958: 241) seemed to draw significantly closer.

The second trait begins in the first. St Augustine's confession only becomes truly meaningful and effective when enunciated in text: 'in stilo autem meo coram multis testibus' (*Confessions* book 10, in Derrida 1995: 39). The reconciling dialogue that *Bohemia* proposes to stimulate the renascent *espíritu público* was to be conducted in texts of quasi-biblical authority: the 'Tablas Nuevas de la Ley desde un modern Sinaí' (1933h: 27). In this, the aberrant disorder of the senses of the previous seven years was countered with a return to *civitas*, both with law and as lexis at the core of its restored *sensibilidad*. And if this recovery (which in some sense does represent something of a reaggregation after the cathartic trials of the 1933 turning point) began with the righting (and writing) of a perceived legal wrong with the abrogation of the Platt Amendment from Cuba's first constitution, it fully coalesced in the drafting of its second. Only six years after the bloody strife of 1933, representatives from all credible Cuban political parties came together in a Constituent Assembly to draft a magna carta for a post-Machado, post-Platt Amendment Cuba. After the spite-filled recriminations exchanged between them, this Assembly notably brought together seventy-six delegates from nine different political parties in relatively non-partisan cooperation.[19] The new Constitution that resulted was widely praised at the time and continues to be the object of admiration off and on the island,[20] with Raúl Capote claiming that it was 'una de las más avanzadas y progresistas del mundo' (2006: under 'Mitos y

---

19 Old *avance* editorial partners Mañach and Marinello were both delegates, although representing different political parties (the former for the ABC, the latter for the Partido Socialista Popular).

20 Although the 1940 consitution was replaced in 1976 by a document inspired by the ideological tenets of Marxism-Leninism, and thus often portrayed in Revolutionary Cuba as a superseded bourgeois legacy, critical attention on the island has brought the document back into focus over the last decade, with the Secretary of the Council of State, Homero Acosta, acknowledging in October 2010 that the 1940 constitution was 'un hito trascendental en la historia constitucional cubana' (in Pérez Navarro, *Granma digital*, 8/10/10, online edition).

realidades'). The 1940 Constitution is a testament to Cuban intellectuals as *letrados activistas* for whom the self-serving self-defensiveness pointed to by Graña couldn't have been further from their minds (in Miller 1999: 2). Perhaps most noteworthy for this study are the new Constitution's specific measures to address aberrant practices that had so plagued the island, its attempts to install both the ethics and legal mechanics to bring peace to fracticidal Cuba and finally dispel the 'acumulación de tánatos' that had blighted the 1933 revolution: presidential terms were limited to four years (with no re-election in the subsequent eight years), the right of *habeas corpus* was enshrined, and the aberrant brutality of the Presidio Modelo and urban torture cell was tacitly acknowledged and explicitly outlawed: 'no se ejercerá violencia ni coacción de ninguna clase sobre las personas para forzarlas a declarar' (Article 28). In this the Assembly took constitutional steps to enshrine the freely offered and fruitful confession of Augustine into law and give sensible (and *sensible*) Cuban *civitas* full legal and lexical force.

Had Arnold van Gennep turned his attention to Cuba in 1940, he might well have heralded a successful transition from the unsatisfactory and contested structures of the early Republic, through the horrific but cathartic crucible of the early 1930s, to the maturity and integrity of the 1940 legislative exercise. The impression was consolidated in the summer of 1940 when, with the new Constitution ratified, the country turned its attention to the election of a new president. Although still remembered by some as the military man behind the Hotel Nacional siege or the bombardment of the Atarés fortress, General Batista swapped his martial uniform for a civilian suit, made improbable strategic deals with the communists (and others) and won the election at the head of the popular Coalición Socialista Democrática.[21] In due adherence to the new constitution, Batista made way for Grau San Martín in 1944, who was in turn succeeded by former DEU activist Carlos Prío Socarrás in 1948. Although thuggery, chronic cronyism and graft were by no means eliminated from the Cuban political panorama, 1940–52 mark a relatively peaceful semi-parliamentarian period after the despotism and bloodshed of the late 1920s and early 1930s. The pen seemed to have triumphed over the sword. In the words of Mañach,

Hicimos una nueva Constitución, y a su amparo reanudamos, y creíamos haber preservado ya de todo peligro, el hábito de la transmisión pacífica y

---

[21] Although some were suspicious of Batista, others perceived him as one of the saviours of the 1933 revolution. The Cuban communists entered into the 1940 pact not so much out of ideological affiliation, but because of COMINTERN encouragement to ally themselves to strong nationalist currents in their countries (see Caballero 1986).

legal del poder. Ese progreso político y social se vió todavía maculado de abusos, desórdenes funcionales y, sobre todo, de graves violaciones éticas. Pero representó sin duda alguna, un incremento extraordinario de vitalidad nacional, un aseguramiento de conquistas externas y concretas que iban dejando reducido cada vez más el problema de la Nación a un problema de edificación moral y de cultura. (Mañach 1953b: 59)

But *dérèglement* refused to relinquish its hold on the island. On 10 March 1952, citing palace whispers of a disgruntled President Prío's intention to 'establish himself unconstitutionally as a dictator', Batista inaugurated his second presidential term with a *blitzkrieg* coup (Thomas 2001: 492). Overnight, the auspicious signs of stability and post-crisis reintegration were swept away and Cuba was pitched once more into insecurity and self-doubt.

PART II

1953–1965

4

1953: José Martí and Cuba's centennial *conciencia*

At the beginning of 1952, under the auspices of the third successive democratically elected (if increasingly unpopular) president, Cuba celebrated its fiftieth independent year with a largely positive taking of stock. This blossoming sense of optimism was given a further fillip by the prospect of upcoming elections (to be held in July 1952) in which it was widely believed that the Partido del Pueblo Cubano, or Ortodoxos, led by the cousins Eduardo Chibás and Roberto Agramonte, would ride to victory on an anti-corruption platform. But disorder came to the fore once more with the return of coup-monger Batista, still in his civilian suit but bearing a striking resemblance to the cocksure colonel of a previous and unsavoury age, and the stock-taking began to be much less positive. How had Cuba managed to come so far from the malfeasance of the early 1920s and the violent and vengeful excesses of the early 1930s, only to fall prey once more (and seemingly without much of a fight) to the despotic designs of a brutish *caudillo*? Significantly, although declaring loyalty to the 1940 Constitution, Batista immediately suspended some constitutional guarantees (including the right to strike) and would go on (in April 1952) to introduce a new 275-article constitutional code that gave the executive the ability to suspend the rights of free speech, assembly and press without parliamentary consultation (Thomas 1971: 790). When the fiftieth independent year waned and 1953, the centenary of José Martí's birth, began, the psycho-social stage was once again set for an intense re-examination of selfhood. This second period of study opens, therefore, with another liminal moment in Cuba's collective rite of passage.

Although his writings and persona were largely unknown on the island until the Wars of Independence ended (due mostly to effective Spanish censorship), the exiled Cuban cigar workers of southern Florida had already baptised Martí 'el Apóstol'. His apostolic example of political activism, poetic genius and self-sacrifice survived his premature death at Dos Ríos in 1895 and became intrinsic to Cuba's most cherished aspirations for itself in independence. For many, Martí was simply 'lo mejor y lo más limpio que tenemos', the very incarnation of the country's *conciencia*, 'el corazón de nuestra patria' (Sáenz 1953: 7–8). In many senses, Martí was a totem of the kind of pure patriotism and unrelenting abnegation that had been sorely lacking amongst post-independence Cuban leaders. The commemoration, bordering on deification, of Martí after his death was at least partly due to the absence of unequivocal heroes amongst those *independentistas* who had survived the war. To commemorate Martí's centenary was inevitably to re-examine the Republic in the light of his luminous example, was an assessment of the historical, ideological and spiritual continuity between contemporary Cuba and the martyr who fell at the outset of the campaign that would finally see Cuba free. In 1953, to appreciate Martí's intellectual and ideological legacy was seen as the lodestone of authentic and vital Republicanism, the key to ensuring Cuba lived up to its own high historical expectations, honoured the sacrifices made in its name and transformed merely formal autonomy into the conscious and conscientious possession of 'soberanía congénita y con plena personalidad' (Ortiz 1955b: 37–8). In short, to be a committed *martiano* was to be a good Cuban, to take the Apostle's name in vain was tantamount to treachery: 'en lo que seguimos a Martí, hemos adelantado a la República; en lo que nos apartamos de él, hemos retrocedido' (Mañach 1953b: 80).

Batista's tightening grip on executive power and the re-emergence of the dismally familiar signs of civic and moral decadence on the island was a bitter blow to the dream of congenital sovereignty, and seemed to demonstrate a flagrant disrespect for Martí's memory.[1] In these circumstances, the centenary commemorations took on more profound implications and the latent introspection turned more viscerally intense. As in the previous turning points, self-critical introspection became an oblique method of resisting the malfeasance of Republic structures. To reflect on the direction of the national narrative became a *letrado* but very active way to challenge the momentum that seemed always to lead to a conclusion in despotism, avarice and violence. To expose the narrative to critical interrogation was to challenge its frustrating inevitability and seize the possibility of 'standing aside not only from one's own social position but from all social positions and of formulating a potentially unlimited series of alternative social arrangements' (Turner 1974: 13–14). The commemoration of Martí's centenary, therefore, became the fulcrum of a liminal reconsideration of Cuba's *sensibilidad* and its socio-cultural manifestations in the island's daily life. Examining Martí's ideological legacy in his article 'La República ante el legado de Martí' (*Bohemia*, 15 Feb. 1953), Mañach concluded that

---

[1] Batista populated the Senate and House of Representatives with his allies, the armed forces became an ultra-privileged class and Havana became US mobsters' favourite and most lucrative safe-house, with 'Lucky' Luciano, Meyer Lansky and Santos Traficante Jr all owning hotels or casinos in the Cuban capital.

> Estamos en condiciones de preguntarnos si los cubanos hemos sabido serle
> fieles a ese ideario, que es el de nuestra propia entraña y voluntad histórica.
> Esta es la cuestión fundamental que en el Centenario nos plantea. ¿Ha sido
> la República un éxito? (1953b: 59)

For a melancholic Ortiz addressing President Batista and the country's most
notable dignitaries at the official event to mark the centenary, 'será su mejor
homenaje si, en este natalicio del Apóstol, todos los cubanos hacemos, en el
sagrario de nuestra mente libre, un riguroso examen de conciencia y un sincero
acto de contrición' (1955b: 248).[2] As in previous turning points, both Ortiz
and Mañach oscillate between analysis of and self-recriminatory acceptance of
their authorship of some of the errors of the Republic.

This chapter reads across several analytical-authorial 'exámenes de
conciencia' during the liminal year of 1953. It will bring forward alternative interpretations of Martí's ideological legacy and its application in the
Cuba of the time. It will also reveal a critical recasting of the debate on the
island between activism and authorship (between the *venceremos* and *luchita*
approaches to Cuban history and identity) in very different readings of the
Apostle Martí. From one ideological flank comes Fidel Castro's defence
speech before the Sala del Tribunal de Urgencia, convened to try Castro and
his ninety-four co-defendants for their participation in the 26 July 1953 attack
on the Moncada barracks in Santiago de Cuba. In his speech (later published
[Castro 1953] as *La historia me absolverá*), Castro named Martí as the 'autor
intelectual del 26 de Julio', and called on that intellectual legacy to propose
an uncompromising historiography of the Republican period and advocate
single-minded and radical action. (Castro 1953: 15). In counterpoint, other
analyst-authors (including Ortiz and Mañach, Félix Lizaso, Juan Marinello,
Francisco Ichaso and María Zambrano) offer an alternative reading of the
Apostle and his *ideario*, within which a more ambivalent hero emerges to
inspire the beleaguered people of Cuba.

Fidel Castro and *la historia*

A first reading of the historiography of *La historia me absolverá* reveals a
certain concordance with Mañach's assessment of the Republic's tenacious
progress by the early 1950s, thwarted by Batista's coup de état:

---

[2]   Rojas points to this 'melancolía, zozobra y escepticismo' as one of the key Cuban intellectual traits of the first half of the twentieth century (2006: 51). My reading of certain 1953
contributions to the *ideario martiano* will show that this melancholy was certainly not inherent.

> Había una vez una república. Tenía su constitución, sus leyes, sus libertades; presidente, Congreso, tribunales; todo el mundo podía reunirse, asociarse, hablar y escribir con entera libertad. (Castro 1953: 84)

The fairy-tale tone of this paean to pre-coup Cuba is charged with rhetorical intent. Although seeming to agree with Mañach about the state of the nation in the early 1950s, Castro is rather determined to demonstrate that any superficial signs of Republican well-being obscured a nightmare reality of violence and vice out of which the latest '*Monstrum horrendum*' had emerged to devour Cuba and the Cubans (14). In immediate answer, therefore, to Mañach's survey of the health of the Republic and the vitality of Martí's creed on his hundredth anniversary, Castro offers an uncompromising reply: 'Parecía que el Apóstol iba a morir en el año de su centenario, que su memoria se extinguiría para siempre, ¡tanta era la afrenta!' (110). For Castro, the Batista dictatorship, or *batistato*, is the pernicious polar opposite of everything the Apostle had aspired towards in an independent Cuba: its ruler was a bloodthirsty despot whose avarice and ill-governance had brought about chronic political and economic impotence unimaginable even in colonial Cuba, and whose disregard for *el pueblo* had brought it to the brink of disaster. This is familiar discursive terrain, of course, with an ideological topography similar to that charted in the 1920s and 1930s. In echo of Martínez Villena and Roig de Leuchsenring's idealisation of *el pueblo puro*, Castro's initial assessment of the culpability for this catastrophe shares some of the narrative over-simplicity displayed in his fairy-tale description of Cuba before 10 March 1952. For Castro the population is divided into 'la gran masa irredenta, a la que todos ofrecen y a la que todos engañan y traicionan' and 'los sectores acomodados y conservadores', so utterly devoid of integrity that they bowed down 'ante el amo de turno hasta romperse la frente contra el suelo' (1953: 38–9). In contrast to Ortiz and Mañach (but in direct agreement with Roig and Martínez Villena), Castro displays no sense of first-person collective responsibility for the Republic's troubles, instead displacing all blame away from *el pueblo* and towards a conservative and self-serving elite. In both his active and this corollary narrative contribution to 1953, Castro clearly gives little credence to an Arendt-type sense of forgiveness and seeks instead to re-chart clear frontiers between innocence and guilt, to better punish the latter. Although perhaps inevitable in a self-defensive and ideologically charged speech that was to become a bellicose manifesto for forthcoming social struggle, this binary exposition of Cuban society also indicates that Castro's interpretation of the Republic's half-century and Martí's legacy therein would have little truck with the indefinition and flux so typical of the limen. In essence, *La historia me absolverá* posits chronic *frustración* as the key trope of the troubled Republic: the diligent and heroic Cuban people had been unable to make the most of their inherited talents because of brutish rulers who at best paid them little heed and at worst extracted perverse profit from the *pueblo*'s precipitous decline.

Even for those analyst-authors we have seen advocating a betwixt-and-between ethos, the retrospective of 1953 was far from comfortable. Mañach is as scornful as Castro of the Republic's recent record, and lambasts Batista's self-styled 'revolution' of 10 March as 'un golpe militar artero, maquinado por conciertos nefandos de la experiencia y del oportunismo, de la ambición y del soborno' (1953b: 59). Mañach undoubtedly has Batista in mind when he chides José Vasconcelos for eulogising the 'unidad de espíritu' the Mexican claimed to have witnessed in a 1953 trip to Cuba:

> Sería ya mucho dejar entender que las virtudes martianas hablaron por igual en unos y en otros, y que al espíritu de Martí [...] le hubieran sido igualmente gratas las honras nostálgicas de los cubanos fieles a su credo y las de aquellos otros que, con su conducta de hoy, violaron y traicionaron todo lo que Martí quiso para nuestra República. (1953a: 48)

Unlike Castro, however, Mañach does not perceive any group or social class in Cuba as mere victims of the malice of others, nor does he exonerate anyone from blame for the Republic's inability to live up to the expectations of independence. Instead, Mañach advocates an honest exploration of the flaws within the collective Cuban character to explain the spiritual degeneration into which Martí's Republic had slumped. His own diagnosis is not promising:

> Cada día es mayor el número de cubanos que se rigen por los instintos, y no por la conciencia: los dispuestos a vender su patrimonio más sagrado por un plato de lentejas; los claudicantes, los faltos de carácter, los débiles ante las tentaciones de la vanidad o del medro [...]. Todos exigimos; nadie se exige nada a sí mismo. (Mañach 1953b: 59)

Both Castro and Mañach make much of solidarity and self-discipline, but the ends to which these means were directed by each were very different, as we shall see.

Beyond the *batistato*'s immediate detrimental effects on Cuba's vital civic organs, Castro accuses the dictator of a crime which for the defendant was many times more grave: his forked words and foul deeds had violated the sacred memory of Cuba's heroic history: 'No podréis negarme que el régimen de gobierno que se le ha impuesto a la nación es indigno de su tradición y de su historia' (1953: 43). Of course, Castro was not the only Cuban for whom *historia* was sanctified. As Kapcia suggests, the meta-myth of Cuban history was a national obsession, even if the interpretations of the characters and characteristics making up that myth differed (2000: 170). The protagonism of *historia* in Castro's defence speech is clear from the title alone. His reading of this history is somewhat idiosyncratic, however. At first, and in common with others' interpretations, fealty to historical precedence becomes the lodestone of citizenship for Castro. Although the speech lauded Cuba's pre-coup democratic structures and practices and referred to the 1940 Constitution as 'la verdadera ley suprema del Estado' (1953: 96), the key to truly authentic Cuban identity, the essence of the island's 'plena personalidad' and blueprint for a patriotic archetype was not the *magna carta* at all, but something much more nebulous:

> Hay una razón que nos asiste más poderosa que todas las demás: somos cubanos, y ser cubano implica un deber, no cumplirlo es un crimen y es traición. Vivimos orgullosos de la historia de nuestra patria; la aprendimos en la escuela y hemos crecido oyendo hablar de libertad, de justicia y de derechos. (108–9)

For Castro, therefore, the duty of every Cuban, above and beyond observance of the civic code, is loyalty to a consensual historical capital, an accurate exegesis and faithful emulation of the most epic events of yesterday, combined with a determination to purge the national narrative of indignities, misinterpretations and historical wrong turns. Those who fulfilled this duty could boast direct and legitimate descendance from the patriots of the national pantheon and stake a claim to true Cuban *sensibilidad*; those who betrayed Cuba's history were to be excised from the national narrative. *La historia me absolverá* is Castro's opening bid for historiographic hegemony in a moment of collective disorientation. At this stage, *historia* isn't yet charged with the pejorative sense of being 'what took place before the revolution, or *antes*' that Miller indicates (2003: 149). Instead, Castro's defence speech presents a new interpretation of the 'historia de nuestra patria' in which a new genealogy between distant forebears and current acolytes is imagined. Although speaking just after the Republic's fiftieth anniversary and cross-examining the parlous socio-political state of the Cuba of the day, it is striking that Castro's historical reference points, illustrative anecdotes and even the very descriptive milieu of his speech are all drawn from half a century before. The most telling example of this is his failure to explore in detail the parallels between the *batistato* and the *machadato*, which ended just twenty years previously and was hence still present in popular consciousness. Despite the fact that he calls Batista a '*Monstrum horrendum*' (in an unmistakeable echo of the popular

1933 vilification of Machado as 'el monstruo'), and despite the fact that some of the brutal tactics of the *batistato* were exact copies of those used by Machado's thugs in the early 1930s, Castro almost completely overlooks the resemblance between the two regimes. Hence, he compares the assassination of the *Moncadistas* after the barracks assault was over, not to the murders of the Presidio Modelo or Atarés fortress of twenty years before, but to 'el crimen del 27 de noviembre de 1871', when the colonial authorities executed eight Havana medical students accused of defacing a Spanish journalist's grave (Castro 1953: 78). While Castro predictably accuses the *batistato* of being 'un régimen de terror y de sangre' (36), he binds the current president in a genealogy of perversion, not with the notorious butcher of Camajuaní, but with the embodiment of ignobility from Cuba's pre-1898 past:

> Matar prisioneros indefensos y después decir que fueron muertos en combate, ésa es toda la capacidad militar de los generales del 10 de marzo. Así actuaban en los años más crueles de nuestra Guerra de Independencia los peores matones de Valeriano Weyler. (78–9)[3]

The sharpest barbs of Castro's invective ignore the Republic entirely and leapt backwards sixty years to associate Batista and his government with the worst of Cuba's distant history: Batista becomes 'Barriguilla', a murderous sergeant in Weyler's army, whilst his military cronies in the *cuartelazo* 'no habrían servido ni para arrear las mulas que cargaban la impedimenta del ejército de Antonio Maceo' (78). This oversight might seem historiographically strategic. By 1953, interpretations of the *revolución del '33* were still inconclusive and many remained reluctant to attribute wholesale blame or give absolution to any of the many sides of the civil conflict (the success of post-crisis plurality in the 1940 Asamblea Constituyente having made the absolute marking of frontiers between benign and malign actors even more problematic, as we have seen). In *La historia me absolverá*, Castro can be read as opting for prudent laconicism and dogmatic over-simplification on the topic of 1933 in order to avoid disagreements that would dilute the rhetorical force of his address. Whilst not ruling out this possibility, an alternative is to explain Castro's historiographic long-sightedness and over-simplicity through reference to his ideological intent as the primary figure of a youthful revolutionary movement.

---

[3]   Valeriano Weyler y Nicolau was the colonial Governor of Cuba from January 1896 to October 1897. He became infamous for his policy of *reconcentración* through which hundreds of thousands of civilians were forcibly relocated in the far west of the island in an attempt to rob the Cuban troops in the east of human and logistical support (conditions in the 're-concentration' camps were appalling and many thousands died of disease and starvation).

Firstly, he is obviously inspired by a remarkable empathy with pre-Republican history which causes the more proximate past to pale in comparison. This is not unexpected, given that he admits that his admiration for the era of the *Guerras de Independencia* was inculcated from an early age: 'Se nos enseñó a venerar desde temprano el ejemplo glorioso de nuestros héroes y de nuestros mártires. Céspedes, Agramonte, Maceo, Gómez y Martí fueron los primeros nombres que se grabaron en nuestro cerebro' (109). As has already been seen, however, admiration for past sacrifices was no mere pastime for Castro; the correct interpretation of Cuba's history (with heroism and self-sacrifice at its core)[4] was at the heart of his conception of authentic Cuban identity. Thus, drawing on a vivid historical imagination, in *Historia* he elaborates a strategy to arrest the degeneration of contemporary Cuba: 'Los problemas de la República sólo tienen solución si nos dedicamos a luchar por ella con la misma energía, honradez y patriotismo que invirtieron nuestros libertadores en crearla' (55). From this perspective, fifty years of complex human ebb and flow become a historical cul-de-sac, an irremediable deformation of the legacy of Martí, an aberrant aside from which Cuba has to be saved; Castro and his 26 July Movement are those saviours:

> Este movimiento [...] salvó a la joven generación de cubanos de 1953 de sucumbir prostituida en la sentina de la politiquería, la subordinación a mezquinos intereses nacionales y foráneos, el vicio y otras lacras que habían caracterizado la vida política de la isla durante medio siglo de pseudo república. (Haydee Santamaría and Melba Hernández, in Rojas 1966: 23)

The Republican past with its heroisms and betrayals, advances and undeniable defeats is simply erased from the national narrative by this angry young man and his acolytes. But this is no nihilistic whim of a radical few, Castro claims however, but the heartfelt desire of the entire Cuban *pueblo* who 'miraba el pasado con verdadero terror' (1953: 57). The obvious antidote to this fear is to draw an impermeable frontier between past and present, to deploy the heroic legacy of distant history against the vicissitudes of a more contiguous past, to start Cuba's independent history afresh from the original and originary foundations laid down by Martí, thus enabling *el pueblo* finally to take control of its own 'personalidad plena'. In a historiographic pirouette reminiscent of Eduardo Abela (although without the arcadian rural inflections), Castro seeks inspiration for *hoy* and *mañana* in a very distant *ayer*. And he portrays his own movement as the genealogical link between Cuba's authentic origins

---

4   Of the five *independentista* heroes Castro mentions, only one survived the wars.

and the present day, claiming that it was this message of transcendence that Batista feared the most: 'Querían desvirtuar el hecho más grave para ellos: que nuestro movimiento no tenía relación alguna con el pasado, que era una nueva generación cubana con sus propias ideas, la que se erguía contra la tiranía' (55–6).

At the heart of this youthful epiphany was Martí. Just as it seemed his moribund memory would finally succumb, a group of heroic young people calling themselves 'la generación del centenario' came to the rescue and resuscitated the Apostle's creed with words and deeds. Castro takes observance of Martí's ideological legacy to a new level. Beyond offering inspiration as the *autor intelectual* of the Moncada attack, he suggests a more visceral affinity between himself and the Apostle: 'Traigo en el corazón las doctrinas del Maestro' (ibid.: 15). Complementing his conviction that Batista's regime was a direct descendant of the despotic colonial era, and that pre-1898 ideological and political solutions thus remained the most valid for the Republican malaise, Castro advocates the regeneration (almost a reincarnation) of Martí and his *ideario* amongst the young men and women for whom he was the mercurial leader: 'Que hable por mí el Apóstol' (61).

Much like his interpretation of fifty years of Republican history, Castro's exegesis of this *ideario* is inspired by fierce convictions, an unrepentant rejection of ambiguity and an almost messianic faith in the veracity of his own creed. For Castro, and for many others before and since 1953, Martí offers an archetypal example of perfect *cubanía*, 'lo mejor y lo más limpio que tenemos' (Sáenz 1953: 7–8). In many senses, Castro's 1953 contribution to the *ideario martiano* resembles Mella's of 1927: for both, decisive (even bombastic) action is at the heart of true homage to *el Apóstol*. But Castro's hermeneutic in *Historia* is particular. Mella read Martí as a philosopher and sought retrospectively to convert the Apostle to the socialist creed, but he made it clear that he would set all reflection aside to dedicate himself fully to action, returning only when the fight was finished. For Castro, the most important aspect of the Apostle's legacy to the Republic he helped forge but never knew was the ability of the man of letters to transform himself into a resolute man of war, thus making him an essential comrade-in-arms, not a catalyst for post-war reflection. This interpretative turn is presented gradually. At the beginning of his defence speech, Castro pays tribute to Martí the patriotic philosopher who is seen to pit intellect and integrity against martial brute force: 'para dar a entender que estaba resuelto a luchar contra tanta bajeza, añadí a mi escrito aquel pensamiento del Maestro: "Un principio justo desde el fondo de una cueva puede más que un ejército" ' (1953: 17).

In this, Castro could perhaps be seen to concur with Ortiz, whose 'La fama póstuma de Martí' attempts to synthesise the most salient *martiano* message for 1953 into the maxim 'libertad sin ira' (1973c: 307). Castro also seems to swap ire for carefully considered invectives against his adversaries: 'no quiero que la ira me ciegue, porque necesito toda la claridad de mi mente y la serenidad del corazón destrozado para exponer los hechos tal como ocurrieron' (1953: 21). Both Ortiz and Castro, at this stage, seem to seek an escape from under the Damoclean sword of cyclical violence and vengeance that Arendt describes. As Castro's speech progresses, however, this willingness to counter violence with 'principios justos' alone is displaced by increasing bellicosity and the exaltation of the warrior over the philosopher-poet. Although beaten on the field of battle, Castro was convinced that 'en igualdad de condiciones' the *Moncadistas* would have meted out 'una soberana paliza a todos los generales del 10 de marzo juntos, que no son ni militares ni patriotas' (20). Cataloguing the crimes committed against those who were captured after the failed attack, the young revolutionary is full of menace: '¡O Cuba no es Cuba, o los responsables de estos hechos tendrán que sufrir un escarmiento terrible!' (72). Likewise, the *martiano* maxims and poems with which Castro peppers his speech become increasingly martial or, one could argue, increasingly infused with the 'acumulación de tánatos' that influenced Cuban *sensibilidad* so profoundly during the aberrant *machadato* (Cabrera Infante 1992: 182). From fighting armies with ideas, Castro shifts to portraying the Apostle undergoing an almost supernatural transformation, displacing poet with pugilist through the absorption of the restless and vengeful spirits of past victims of tyranny:

> Cadáveres amados los que un día
> ensueños fuisteis de la patria mía
> ¡arrojad, arrojad sobre mi frente
> polvo de vuestros huesos carcomidos!
> ¡Tocad mi corazón con vuestras manos!
> ¡Gemid a mis oídos!
> ¡Cada uno ha de ser de mis gemidos
> lágrimas de uno más de los tiranos!
> ¡Andad a mi redor; vagad en tanto
> que mi ser vuestro espíritu recibe! (Martí, in Castro 1953: 57–8)

For Castro, therefore, Martí was an archetypal man of uncompromising convictions who never wavered from his patriotic purpose. In this interpretation, the Apostle undergoes his own brutal, but necessary, rite of passage (complete with symbolic gestures and markings) from a precocious poet to a more coherent and integrated man of unambiguous action (as his fate at Dos Ríos allegedly demonstrated). This is the essence of the *martiano* legacy over which Castro and the *generación del centenario* claim hermeneutic hegemony, portraying themselves as the only ones to marry words and deeds in true commemoration of the Apostle's creed. And this activism is at the core of Castro's attitude towards the 1953 watershed: it is not a moment for dilated national reflection, but a time to transform words into dynamic deeds and move relentlessly forwards towards collective conclusion. So while ideologues squabbled about the best way to deal with the swaggering coup-imposed president, Castro emulated the Martyr of Dos Ríos and took armed struggle right to the dictatorship's doorstep. While Ortodoxo leader Manuel Bisbé insited that 'en momentos como estos se peca tanto a más por el mucho hablar como por el poco hacer' and yet did nothing (Bisbé 1953: 49), and Grau San Martín negotiated his political position ahead of the widely discredited elections, Castro and his comrades united the intellectual and the bellicose legacies of the Apostle and attacked the second largest barracks in Cuba.

For Castro, it is this setting aside of the pen to take up the sword that confirms his credentials as the Apostle's authentic heir: just like Martí, seventy-one Moncada assailants enacted the sanguinary sentiments of the national anthem and embraced 'una muerte gloriosa' without fear and thus, in Castro's eyes, warrant the same honours as those rendered to the Apostle: 'algún día serán desenterrados y llevados en hombros del pueblo hasta el monumento que, junto a la tumba de Martí, la patria libre habrá de levantarles a los "Mártires del Centenario" ' (1953: 74). From this reading, the relationship between analysis and activism is fractured (as it was in 1933). Here the national narrative is not to be inscribed but acted out. What could be read as a speech of immediate and limited intentions (to defend himself before the Santiago court) becomes a landmark contribution to Cuba's story of selfhood. By presenting a new hermeneutic, both of Republican history and of Martí's *ideario*, this speech becomes a bi-focal nihilistic attack: fifty years of Republican history will be erased as an infected appendix to the national narrative, and the responsibility for inscribing all new pages will pass to those authors prepared to write in their own self-sacrificial blood. This utter militancy may be novel, but its ideological roots link it to Martínez Villena, Mella, Roa and others. Like them, Castro posits resolution, heroism and a strident rejection of the ambiguous 'nadar entre dos aguas' (for which Roa lambasted Mañach) as the key to authentic *cubanía* and the lodestar which Cuba's *sensibilidad* had to follow towards true liberation (Roa 1969: 27).

An alternative *Apóstol*

Mañach seems initially to agree with Castro's exegesis of Martí and the state of the Cuban nation in 1953. In 'La República ante el legado de Martí', for example, he seems to echo Castro's cry for heroism: 'Lo que nos hace falta para la vida futura [...], es sobre todo una tensión constante de heroísmo' (1953b: 80). But their hermeneutics of heroism couldn't be more different. Mañach calls not for the bloody sacrifice of Moncada, nor the valiant dash of Dos Ríos, but instead exhorts a daily combination of humble acts and attitudes, a heroism, 'no en el sentido espectacular, sino en el silencioso, continuo y fecundo de cada día: la decisión positiva de ser útiles, creadores, cumplidores de nuestro deber, servidores generosos de nuestro pueblo' (ibid.). Hence, between Castro and Mañach (and between the *sensibilidades* they propose) a fundamental difference of opinion emerges over the definition of 'heroism' and therefore over the role to be played by the *letrados activos* alongside the *activistas letrados*. The unspectacular valour that Mañach perceives as a key doctrine of the *legado martiano* links the Apostle not with Mella or Roa nor even with the *generación del centenario*, but rather with Luján 'el procurador', the archetype of temporal and ideological ambivalence. Against Castro's portrayal of the steely warrior-poet, therefore, Mañach juxtaposes the generous wetnurse of the Republic, 'el que más da de sí, el más saturado de aquella "leche de la bondad humana" ' (1926: 11). And far from a pell-mell dash into bombastic action, Luján's contribution comes from perspicacious observation from 'el arroyo' at the side of the road; his activism is inherently analytical (Mañach 1926: 12).

Mañach was not alone in this unorthodox reinterpretation of *el ideario martiano* that set aside the facile hagiography or ideological reincarnation proposed by others. 'La República ante el legado de Martí' is part of a sophisticated exegetical tradition that began (according to leading *martiano* scholar Félix Lizaso) at the end of the 1920s and reached its zenith in the centenary year. Intellectuals in this tradition challenged not only the fundamental coordinates of heroism and its alleged application throughout Martí's life (and particularly at his death), but actually deconstructed the entire apostolic icon in an attempt to interrogate facets of the *ideario* overlooked in the panegyric assertions of his secular sainthood that had become so common in the early Republic. By doing so, these intellectuals portrayed a less resolute, less bellicose and infinitely more ambiguous Apostle and reassessed the Republic's fealty to (or wilful ignorance of) Martí's example throughout what many of the *generación del centenario* had begun (and would continue) to call the 'pseudo-República'.

As we have seen, Castro believed that Martí's moribund ideological legacy was only saved from certain death by the bloody immolation of the young 'Mártires del Centenario':

> Parecía que el Apóstol iba a morir en el año de su centenario, que su memoria se extinguiría para siempre, ¡tanta era la afrenta! Pero vive, no ha muerto,

su pueblo es rebelde, su pueblo es digno, su pueblo es fiel a su recuerdo; hay cubanos que han caído defendiendo sus doctrinas, hay jóvenes que en magnífico desagravio vinieron a morir junto a su tumba, a darle su sangre y su vida para que él siga viviendo en el alma de su patria. (1953: 110)

For Castro, therefore, doctrine and death are inseparable, and only self-sacri-ficial blood can revive Martí's legacy. Whilst many observers agreed that the Republic had not fully lived up to Martí's aspirations for an independent Cuba, some roundly disputed the idea that the Apostle's example was on the brink of extinction in his hundredth year. To some it seemed that Marti's luminous example of 'libertad sin ira' (Ortiz 1973c: 307), as well as his more terrestrial recommendations for the practicalities of self-rule, had actually been carefully preserved and faithfully transmitted throughout the independent half century: 'Me conmueve esta labor cubana constante de mantener vivo a Martí, de convi-virlo', said Cubanophile Gabriela Mistral (in Mañach 1953b: 74). Although, as Castro claimed, this intimate co-habitation with Martí's *ideario* seemed not to have produced an elixir of word and deed to safeguard Cuba's sovereignty and democratic development, it could by no means be dismissed as mere hollow commemoration of a once-great *patriota*. From others' perspectives, the approximation to and appreciation of Martí's intellectual legacy during the Republic appeared concerted, impassioned and carefully analytical. According to Lizaso's meticulous 1953 catalogue of the development of *el culto martiano* ('Medio siglo de culto a Martí'[5]), the Apostle's legacy was present from the very first days of independence, imported onto the island by those who had known the man and his work in exile: 'era el momento de dar salida al torrente de devociones, y puede decirse que cuantos lo habían conocido, cuantos sabían de su obra y de su ejemplo, trataban de volcar sus recuerdos' (Lizaso 1953: 299).

This devotion translated into the dissemination of the *ideario martiano* through the publication of Martí's writings. Gonzalo de Quesada y Aróstegui began on 19 May 1900 (five years to the day after Martí's death) with the first in a series of *Escrituras Martianas* (the fourteenth and final volume was published in 1919); in 1918, Néstor Carbonell began his own collation (which ran to eight volumes); between 1925 and 1928 the Argentinian Alberto Ghiraldo published another eight volumes of Martí's work. The first anthology appeared in 1910 (Américo Lugo's *Flor y lava*); followed by the first edition of Rafael Argilagos's *Granos de oro* in 1918 (further editions appeared in 1928, 1936, 1937 and 1942); Max Henríquez Ureña's *Páginas escogidas*

---

5   One of the essays in Lizaso's two-volume collection *José Martí: Recuento de Centenario* (1953).

were published in 1919; Mañach's memorable biography *Martí, el Apóstol* appeared in 1933; 1934 saw the publication of Emeterio Santovenia's *Bolívar y Martí* and Emilio Roig de Leuchsenring's *Martí en España*. Finally, in 1936, the first attempt at a definitive edition of Martí's complete works appeared to great acclaim:

> Pocas empresas literarias han logrado en Cuba el fervor público que alcanzó la edición de Martí realizada por la "Editorial Trópico". Y la mejor prueba de lo que decimos es el hecho de que a fines de 1948 se habían completado 74 volúmenes. (Lizaso 1953: 318)

This interaction with Martí's thought was not a simple act of selective reproduction. Contrary to Castro's claim that the *generación del centenario* was the first in fifty years to engage fully with the Apostle and rescue him from empty hagiography, mention could be made of Mella's *Glosando los pensamientos de José Martí* (1926) that, as we have seen, sought to expose the *ideario* to a rigorous if ideologically inspired dialectic that situated him within 'el momento histórico en que actuó' (Mella 1975: 269). For Lizaso, the exegetical epiphany to which Castro laid claim actually began in the late 1920s: 'entre 1928 y 1930 ocurren cambios que nosotros consideramos decisivos en lo que toca al culto martiano' (1953: 318). At that time, as subsequently, socio-political frustrations (the *machadato* had begun to show its truly aberrant colours) provoked a reappraisal of Martí as the cardinal point to which the Republic needed to steer. From the pages of *revista de avance* (whose February 1929 editorial contained an article entitled 'Nuevo Martí'), Mañach, Marinello and Lizaso (all *avance* editors at the time) lamented the fact that, despite multifarious publications of his work, Martí remained 'un ilustre desconocido' in Cuba (*revista de avance* 1929: 36). Pre-empting Castro by twenty-five years, all three claimed theirs as the first independent generation with sufficient percipience to undertake an authentic re-reading and regeneration of the Apostle's creed: 'A nuestra generación parece tocarle el duro privilegio de comenzar a comprenderle en su grandeza histórica y humana' (ibid.). Just as Castro sought deliberately to erase fifty years of Republican history, therefore, he similarly sought to overlook his predecessors' contributions to the *ideario martiano*. In both cases, details ceded to dogma as the young revolutionary attempted to inscribe an indelible frontier between the present and the near past. At least in terms of reflection on the ideological legacy of Martí, and the part it could play within contemporary Cuban *sensibilidad*, this schismatic frontier was fallacious.

And where Castro pointed to ardent heroism and willing self-sacrifice as the indisputable ideological axes joining the Apostle and his *centenario* acolytes (the former at Dos Ríos, the latter at Moncada), by 1953 some thinkers had begun to interrogate the more monochromatic accounts of Martí's 1895 martyrdom. Although his melodramatic death in battle seemed to leave little space for ambiguity or interpretative nuance, Manuel Bisbé suggested that after many years defending the *Cuba Libre* dream in speeches, articles and manifestoes from overseas, Martí's return to his country to fight the Spanish face to face (and thus become something more than an *autor intelectual* of the island's independence) was stimulated as much by external pressures as internal convictions. Bisbé recounts Martí replying angrily in August 1892 to a Cuban correspondent who had criticised his inactivity in New York: 'Poco haríamos y mal si pudiese yo decir a Ud. todo lo que hacemos' (Bisbé 1953: 49). But the criticism, or what Mella had called 'la envidia de los roedores del genio' (1975: 272), seems to have pricked the Apostle's pride and spurred him to match his uncompromising words with pugilistic deeds: 'Para mí la patria no será nunca triunfo, sino agonía y deber [...]. Mi único deseo sería pegarme al último tronco, al último peleador: morir callado. Para mí, ya es hora' (in Lizaso 1933: 13).

It is this suggestion of almost suicidal fatalism that is at the heart of María Zambrano's article 'Martí camino de su muerte' (*Bohemia*, 1 Feb. 1953). Zambrano initially appears to concur with Castro in perceiving Martí's heroic self-sacrifice as the oracle by which to interpret his legacy and the necessary antidote to debilitating indecision in an archetypal man of action: 'El sacrificio es la acción que vence a la ambigüedad en que se debate siempre la vida de todo hombre' (1953: 45). But this article is in fact no paean to martyrdom; Zambrano goes on to suggest that this victory over ambiguity was an unfortunate necessity of war, not an eternal blueprint for proto-Cuban identity: 'Se había vencido a sí mismo, que tal cosa es sacrificarse. Nacido poeta tuvo que ser hombre de acción [...]. Se hizo a sí mismo en contra de sí' (ibid.). The most salient lesson to be drawn from Martí's death, according to Zambrano, is that whilst *civitas* could sometimes cede to *bellum*, this is a painful (even lamentable) necessity in times of crisis, not the basis of an entire *ideario* and its application in everyday life. Moreover, for Zambrano, Martí's martial spirit is undercut by critical, humble, almost self-deprecating self-perception. In Zambrano's reading, self-sacrifice is only authentic if made with a disregard for transcendence; those who flaunt their heroism (in Homeric profile or finger-wagging self-defence) and approach self-sacrifice with ambition actually undermine their own epiphany and are contaminated with the ambiguity they want so desperately to overcome: 'El que sabe que se sacrifica de modo consciente, torna ambigua, dudosa esa acción que necesita, para ser cumplida, ser inocente' (Zambrano 1953: 45).

In contrast to Castro's portrayal of the 'ejemplo glorioso' of Martí and his fellow *libertadores*, some thinkers in 1953 undertook the seemingly iconoclastic task of exploring the *ideario martiano* for less idyllic qualities. Despite the ideological impetus of his political affiliations (he had been a member of the Cuban Communist Party from its inception), Marinello's 'El caso literario de Martí' (first given as a speech on 27 January 1953) resists all temptation to score partisan points and criticises all religious and political (including Marxist) attempts to recruit Martí's creed to their particular causes (unlike revisionist Mella in the previous period): '[Martí] discrepó – y discrepó mucho – directa e indirectamente, de las concepciones primordiales de Carlos Marx' (Marinello 1954: 26). Whilst insisting that the reification of any historical period or deification of any of the social actors therein is sterile, Marinello nevertheless suggests that Martí was embedded so deeply within the Cuban *sentir de la nación* as to make objective analysis almost impossible. Martí, for Marinello, is an enigma and as such all attempts to shepherd his legacy beneath any one ideological banner were erroneous and would inevitably lead to an absolutism that had no resonance with the fluidity, multiplicity and interconnectivity of the Apostle's infinitely inclusive *ideario*: 'La verdad es que todo análisis de Martí intentado por un cubano de nuestro tiempo es como una pelea en que se entrecruzan la historia y el presente, lo lejano y lo íntimo, la responsabilidad enjuiciadora y la identificación cordial' (ibid.: 11–12). Far from as an intransigent anti-colonial warrior, Marinello portrays Martí as an apostle of flux, as a pragmatic advocate of confluence, concession and inevitable continuity.

Francisco Ichaso's 'El sentido político de Martí' (in *Bohemia*, 1 Feb. 1953) agrees. For Ichaso, Martí's most lasting legacy was not inscribed by a vainglorious cavalry charge against enemy lines, but rather by his untiring labours as a 'zurcidor de voluntades', as the man who consolidated the disparate elements of anti-Spanish sentiment into the coherent Partido Revolucionario Cubano (Ichaso 1953: 55). None of this, Ichaso suggests, was achieved without a measure of political pragmatism that the *culto martiano* had often been reluctant to recognise: 'se equivocan los que pintan a Martí como un idealista encandilado' (81). From this perspective, Martí's fight for an independent Republic becomes not the all-or-nothing dogmatic quest for transcendence and a bellicose march towards future victory (as in Castro's portrayal and embodiment), but a more ongoing, oblique, present-tense *luchita*: 'no vacilamos en calificar de realista la política de Martí'; for Ichaso, the Apostle was fully aware that in politics, as in life, 'la virtud triunfa de lado' (55 & 81).

Building on this betwixt-and-between interpretation of Martí, and in echo of discursive confrontrations from the 1920s and 1930s, some analyst-authors in 1953 offered a radical counterpoint to Castro's extirpation of the Republic as a historical dead-end, and argued instead that it was actually not necessary to eliminate all errors from the much maligned Republic in order to pay fitting

homage to the Apostle's memory, that frailty and fallibility were not tantamount to treachery, that Cuba in Martí's centenary was not compelled to write
off a half-century of independence as a historical cul-de-sac and seek a return
to the 'authentic' source that the Apostle supposedly embodied. The most
significant advocates of this radical reinterpretation were Ortiz and Mañach,
who took the oft-cited *martianismo* 'la revolución no es la que vamos a iniciar
en las maniguas sino la que vamos a desarrollar en la República' and fully
interrogated its implications for Cuba's *sensibilidad* in its fifty-first year (in
Mella 1975: 269).

In 'La República ante el legado de Martí', Mañach suggests that to truly
honour Martí's legacy it is perhaps necessary to accept frustration as an inevitable element of the Cuban condition. Whereas Castro looked to the Apostle
for ideological momentum with which to move beyond the frustrations of
the present towards a perfect future in which the purely heroic past would be
reincarnate, Mañach is less persuaded by paradise: 'Rara vez en la vida de un
indivíduo o de un pueblo marchan las cosas tan bien que no dejen margen a la
preocupación y a la superación, ni tan mal que no quede hueco para el esfuerzo
y para la esperanza' (1953b: 59). As in 1927, Mañach becomes an advocate
(a *procurador*, even) of the *márgenes* and the *huecos*, of the insight of a
sideways glance. Although stung into action by the events of the early 1930s
(and barbed attacks from people like Roa), here Mañach reasserts the right to
be both ardent author and critical analyst, here he can be seen swimming with
some determination 'entre dos aguas'.

For Mañach, Martí was not an archangel sent to save Cuba in life or even
after his death, but rather an admirable proto-patriot who made an undeniable
contribution to Cuba's search for selfhood which every subsequent generation
was called to build upon: 'Recordemos que la salvación de Cuba es más
larga y profunda tarea' (ibid.: 80). In response to his own centenary question,
therefore, Mañach once again advocates the strategic equilibrium that Luján, his
young-old, traditional-progressive archetype encapsulated so well. Mañach's
answer is a non-answer; the question, he argues, 'es demasiado importante
para que nos la contestemos precipitadamente', whether by succumbing to
'conclusiones pesimistas' or the 'optimismo oficioso que tanto se parece al
turbio conformismo' (59). Liberated from the imperative to condemn every
Republican shortcoming as a deviation from the pure and patriotic path
illuminated unambiguously by Martí and other distant heroes, Mañach's (and
others') *examen de conciencia* begin to reveal new facets of a half-century of
history, start to overcome collective shame and anguish and bring tentative
appreciation alongside rightful condemnation. Unlike Rafael Rojas, therefore,
who sees Republican thinkers like Ortiz and Mañach as labouring under an
all-pervasive 'melancholy', we rather see Mañach recognising that Martí

would be far from satisfied by the Republic, but celebrating the not-insignif-
icant achievements of the first fifty years of independence (during which his
own generation had added their contributions under the banner of the 'Nuevo
Martí'):

> Hoy día, en efecto, Cuba es mucho más rica y más dueña de su hacienda
> que cuando estrenó su independencia; la riqueza está mejor distribuida;
> el nivel de vida es más uniforme y más alto. Por otra parte, la soberanía
> se ha afianzado gracias a la perserverancia con que luchamos contra el
> bochorno de la enmienda Platt. En la vida política del país, logramos rebasar
> los conceptos caudillísticos, las formas de primitivismo polémico de los
> partidos, la inercia sectaria en los movimientos del electorado [...]. Todo
> esto se alcanzó, en buena parte, a través de la revolución que nos vimos
> obligados a hacer – no sin realizar una profecía de Martí – para vindicar
> los derechos del ciudadano en general. Tras mucho esfuerzo y sangre de
> cubanos, dejamos reafirmado que en los asuntos públicos, como enseñó el
> Apóstol, el sentir de la nación, es lo que cuenta, y no la voluntad de hombre
> alguno que en nombre de ella se alce. (ibid.: 80)

Unlike Castro, Mañach's historiography of the Republic is not Manichean,
but measured, and seeks dialogue with the highs and lows of the past rather
than a dogmatic erasure of a whole period. Importantly, Mañach also offers a
positive appraisal in which collective endeavour has safeguarded the 'derechos
del ciudadano en general', in contrast to the unmitigated collective suffering
for which Castro sees the sanguinary self-sacrifice of a heroic few as the only
remedy.

    Ortiz is equally pragmatic in his assessment of the Republican ebb and
flow and Martí's intellectual role therein. Whereas Castro portrayed Martí
purified by his own traumatic rite of passage and forged into an unambiguous
archangel, Ortiz doubts whether this integration (or post-liminal reaggregation) would ever come. In his article 'Más y más fé en la ciencia', Ortiz
rather sees his fellow Cubans (and fellow humans) trapped in an endless interstice, neither wholly pure nor completely putrid: 'en todas partes una misma
humanidad; ni bestial ni angelical, sucia o limpia, soliente o dichosa, de varie-
dades infinitas pero todas ellas capaces de odios y de amores, de arrastrarse y
de trepar, de subir y de caer' (1955a: 45). For Ortiz, therefore, the Apostle's
gift of percipience did not reveal a future Cuba triumphing over frustration
and strife and 'living up to' the supposed idealism of antecedent examples, but
rather an island content just to live, to engage in the endless and universally
human *luchita* without any guarantee of ultimate victory. Ortiz is adamant that
Martí condemned 'el empeño pueril de realizar en una agrupación humana

el ideal candoroso de un espíritu celeste, ciego, graduado de la universidad bamboleante de las nubes'; the Apostle of the Cuban people fully recognised that 'no por ser cubano se liberta el hombre de las flaquezas propias de la humanidad' (1955b: 245–6).

For Ortiz and Mañach, therefore, what Martí would have expected from the heirs to his legacy was nothing more heroic than an intelligent and honest approach to the frustrations of self-rule, a willingness to learn from the inevitable mistakes of a young society, a determination not to turn away from the past in terror, no matter how disastrous, but rather to use the salutary lessons of hard times to consolidate and safeguard the *sentir de la nación*: 'Nos ha llevado medio siglo de posteridad advertir que Martí tenía razón, que no era un hilvanador de monsergas ni un sorbedor de nubes: que no era un visionario, sino un vidente' (Mañach 1953b: 80).

After thirty years of anguished introspection, the resolution of Cuba's collective rite of passage seemed as far off as ever and the Republic found itself, in 1953 as in 1923, in 'un paréntesis institucional de la vida cubana' (Mañach 1953b: 80). What was called for once more was a candid examination of the *conciencia colectiva*, guided by the luminous creed of a truly human hero all Cubans could rally behind. '¿Ha sido la República un éxito?', Mañach asked (59), and for Fidel Castro, the answer was obvious: fifty disastrous years of pseudo-Republic had left Cuba in a worse plight than ever and had desecrated the legacy of the heroic Apostle. For the *generación del centenario*, Martí was ideal *cubanía* incarnate, his resolute thoughts, but more importantly his metamorphosis into a man of decisive deeds, made his an eternal example of the *sensibilidad* befitting a Republic for which so much had been sacrificed. Castro was convinced that he and his Moncada comrades could live up to these high historical expectations and honour the unambiguous legacy of the archangel of Cuban independence. To do so, however, the *martiano* creed had to be approached with faith and applied with historiographic fundamentalism; the point was not to squabble over exegetics, but simply to allow a reincarnated Apostle to speak again and, more importantly, to fight again. Given that the Republican half-century had been a historical wrong turn that had tarnished Martí's memory, betrayed his legacy and contributed little to Cuba's *libertad*, it had to accept obsolescence and make way for a youthful epiphany that would take up the Apostle's torch and rebuild the Republic from the unambiguously heroic foundations laid down in the Wars of Independence, which were read, as was the turning point of 1953, as a Manichean battle between utter evil and apostolic (and angelic) good. In his 1953 defence speech, Castro asked not that history offer him and the *generación del centenario* absolution (the sins, after all, were of others), but that it recognise these young rebels as those chosen to bring Martí's message to *las masas*, to faithfully re-inscribe, but more importantly to heroically re-enact, the most glorious passages of the national narrative, locating the poets turned warriors as the unambiguous protagonists of the tale once again, to live up to the vertiginously high expectations they imagined Martí would have had for his longed-for *Cuba Libre*.

For analyst-authors such as Ortiz, Mañach, Marinello, Ichaso and Zambrano, the answer was other. Whilst accepting and celebrating Martí at the marrow of the Cuban sense of self, 1953 saw them begin to question whether he sought to establish a creed at all, or ever saw himself as an Apostle of the Cuba to come. These thinkers challenged the idealised portrayal of a bellicose and almost untouchable icon whom only the most exulted could hope faithfully to emulate, leaving many others with an unsettling perennial sense of inferiority and the debilitating conviction that 'somos muy pequeños todavía para comprender a José Martí' (Cruz Cobos 1953: 12). Instead, these thinkers asked whether Martí did not rather fight to secure Cuba's fundamental *derecho* to make sovereign mistakes, to assert the *pueblo*'s capacity to get things wrong on their own terms and willingly accept all the consequences. Importantly, these analyst-authors saw Martí's most salient lessons in his writing, not his fighting, saw his ink, not his blood, coursing along the historical veins between the past and the present day. In this they read his immolation at Dos Ríos, not as a blueprint for all future action, but as somewhat incongruous with his creed, as a momentary *dérèglement* of his senses in response to external jibes. What would independent Cuban have been, they mused, if Martí had rather insisted on swimming against the bellicose tide, had saved himself for the revolution 'que vamos a desarrollar en la República', rather than dying prematurely in the 'manigua' (in Mella 1975: 269). And far from spurring a nihilistic erasure of the proximate past, did Martí not actually advocate an acceptance of some historical continuity, some colonial residue in the Republic? Did Martí, in luminous example and written legacy, not embody the sublime and irremediable ambiguity of the human condition in which poet and politician, visionary and nostalgist, hero and pragmatist combine? Did the perspicacious Apostle of Cuban independence not predict the frustrations against which Castro and others raged? Did he not preach a doctrine of sanguine acceptance of anguish and an assimilation of frustration in a quest for true 'libertad sin ira'? Did Martí not recognise that 'Libre' was just the beginning for 'Cuba' and that independence was only the first step in the national rite of passage within which many ill-fated beginnings would necessarily precede Cuba's ultimate conclusion?

"No nos obfusquemos con nombres de *independencia* y otros nombres meramente políticos." Martí ansiaba algo mejor, más esencial y sustantivo, la realidad de su patria como nación en plena capacidad y ejercicio de sus funciones, nacida por ansiedad, autogénesis, esfuerzo y derecho propio de su pueblo. (Ortiz 1955b: 237–8)

For some of the Cuban Republic's most percipient thinkers, the zealous determination to honour Martí's legacy had imprudently deified the man and ossified his example. Far from a saintly hero single-handedly and single-mindedly purging fear, indecision and ambiguity from within Cuba's collective *sensibilidad*, they perceived a heroically human Cuban whose conviction of his compatriots' abilities to fend for themselves was matched by his wry acceptance of inevitable future frustrations against which *la luchita* would go ever on. Perhaps, unlike Castro, Martí asked history not for absolution, but for a constant reminder of the ineluctability of guilt.

On the centenary of Martí's birth and at the initiation of a renewed mood of self-cognisance, Cuba remained poised between a definitive answer to and a quizzical re-reading of the question of national identity, between historiographic fundamentalism and an anoriginal epistemology of perennial flux. Our analysis will now move to the often overlooked turning point of 1957 and the confrontation within Cuban *sensibilidad* between the stimulating sense of historical transcendence emanating from the violent events in the eastern mountains and the cities' streets, and the sneaking suspicion that nothing would ever change on an island always and forever condemned to an unbearable lightness of historical being.

5

1957: A moment in and out of time

In a 1953 speech, on the centenary of Martí's birth, Ortiz had called for 'un riguroso examen de conciencia y un sincero acto de contrición' (1955b: 248). While intense introspection was evident, as we have seen, there had been no agreement on the kind of collective contrition that was called for or, indeed, whether fallibility and 'sin' could and should be expunged. Beyond analysis, Castro and the *generación del centenario*'s authoritative attempt to take the national narrative by storm in July 1953 had ended in a bloody catastrophe which seemed to prove that the aberrant legacy of the *machadato* had merely lain dormant during the relatively pacific and democratic interlude of the 1940s. As state-sponsored brutality joined corruption and graft after March 1952, the socio-psychological cycle in Cuba seemed to have come full circle, from Zayas the crook to Machado the butcher to Batista the coup-monger. Arendt's most pessimistic predictions about eternally frustrated and eternally vengeful humankind seemed to be coming dismally true in Cuba. But in May 1955, in an almost inexplicable display of apparent compassion (stimulated perhaps by a sense of unassailability), Batista announced an amnesty and Castro and the other Moncada survivors suddenly found themselves free. But neither side was prepared to seek the kind of oblique, side-of-the road compromise that Martí (and Luján) had seemed to point to. Although pardoned by the amnesty, Castro was far from forgiven, with rumours that 'a car riddled with bullets already existed – ready for his body to be found within (killed "fighting the police")' (Thomas 2001: 563–4). Castro himself showed little willingness to forget (or forgive) the extra-judicial assassination of his comrades. Whereas other analyst-authors moved on from their reflections on Martí's legacy to constantly berate Batista with their pens, Castro seemed unwilling to relinquish the sword he had taken up in 1953: 'The general atmosphere in Havana in mid-1955 was antipathetic to him. Having staked all on the politics of action and, if need be, violence, the amnesty itself and the mood of compromise which it had created played against him' (ibid.: 563). Flight to Mexico and the conglomeration of a new band of derring-do youngsters followed until, on 25 November 1956, harried by the Mexican police and perhaps goaded by his own audacious proclamation that he would either be back in Cuba or dead by the end of 1956, Castro and eighty-one others set sail from Tuxpan in the yacht *Granma*. Instead of the landing planned for the town of Niquero, designed to coincide with a series of diversionary guerrilla strikes in Santiago de Cuba, *Granma* arrived a day late, missed its target, was spotted by a navy reconnaissance plane and eventually ran aground in the mangrove swamps near Playa de los Colorados, ten kilometres down the coast. The disembarkation was laborious and maddeningly slow, much of the arsenal had to be left on board and the disoriented invaders were soon under concerted attack in the cane fields near Alegría de Pío. Within just a few days, only around twelve of the eighty-two original *Granma* passengers remained. The rest had been killed in (or after) combat with Batista's army or had fled the fighting to seek refuge in the cities.[1] Once again, Castro found himself at the head of a disastrous attempt to oust Batista by force. Despite the hyperbole of *La historia me absolverá*, at the beginning of 1957 the young rebel leader was an emblem not of heroism but of pathos, with Fundora Núñez (in the 13 January 1957 edition of *Bohemia*) referring to him with heavy irony as the ' "redentor" de la Patria' who 'nunca lograría organizar en Cuba más que otro Moncada' (57).

The *fisonomía* of the age, therefore, was best captured not by Arendt's conception of perpetual vengeance, but by Cintio Vitier's notion of an unbreakable cycle of 'tiranía-sacrificio, sacrificio-tiranía', or what he called the 'callejón sin salida de nuestra historia' (Vitier 1958: 489). By 1957, Cuban history seemed to have developed the habit of repeating itself, the national narrative stuck on the same frustratingly painful page; the animation in Cuba's account of itself seemed suspended in a taut and inconclusive inter-stice that sapped strength and infused *sensibilidad* with cynicism and apathy: 'observando la cohesión del ejército, la acción tácitamente saboteadora y refrenadora de la oposición moderada y la escasa conciencia revolucionaria de las masas, era fácil darse cuenta de que cualquier movimiento armado fracasaría' (Fundora Núñez 1957: 82). If the mood four years previously had been of repentant but energetic introspection, by 1957 Cuba was overcome by what Vitier called a 'sensación del estupor ontológico' (1958: 484). If all four previous periods examined in this study witnessed an often anguished historical stock-taking, in 1957 Cuba seemed to contemplate the end of its history altogether. Once again, therefore, this pause in the collective rite of

---

1   The actual number of *Granma* combatants who went on to constitute the initial guerrilla fighting force in the mountains is disputed, but the number twelve, with its connotations of biblical disciples and messianic miracles, has become the standard in revolutionary folklore, with Carlos Franqui entitling his testimony of the early years of the revolutionary campaign *El libro de los doce*, for example.

passage appears neither as a productive margin from where to restructure society and *sensibilidad* towards future reaggregation, nor as a perennial interstice which accepts the ongoing *luchita* with no expectation of ultimate victory. Instead, in 1957 as in 1933, the limen is negative, although its aberrance is more surreptitious here and is marked, not by vicious internecine violence, but by a sense of direction lost. Rojas's reading of 'melancolía, zozobra y escepticismo' once again seems accurate (2006: 51). Once more, however, we will uncover evidence of resilient optimism in the midst of ennui and despair. Some analyst-authors will be seen who sought to break the cyclical history of tyranny and sacrifice and reinvigorate the nation and its *sensibilidad* through the kinds of heroic acts of derring-do that Martínez Villena, Mella, Roa and Castro had advocated previously. Others will come to light who sought to locate Cuba's experiences within the inescapably (even absurdly) frustrating human (not just Cuban) condition. And others, more radically, will be shown here neither to have sought to renew socio-civic dynamism nor resigned themselves to the pointlessness of life, but instead to have embraced Cuba's 1957 stasis as invigorating, put forward a paean to *intrascendencia* and *ingravidez* and elaborated a very alternative mythography of Cuban identity.

Absurdity and amorality in the atemporal limen

In the short story 'El viaje', Virgilio Piñera offers his own analysis of Cuba's perceived lack of momentum in 1957. The protagonist in the story is a wealthy middle-aged man who, after forty years of contemplation, has experienced 'una revelación' on the road through his semi-idle life. This turning point is hardly momentous, however. Although the *viajero*'s travels are surely intended to provoke association with an existential epiphany on a road elsewhere and elsewhen,[2] Piñera's protagonist's revelation has led him to a peculiar conclusion: he will travel 'sin descanso' seated in a child's pram and pushed by a team of indefatigable *niñeras* (Piñera 1999: 107). Here conversion becomes clownesque, the awakening of the epiphany becomes an inescapable nightmare in which the link between maturity and knowledge has been severed and all cardinal and moral direction has been lost: 'He decidido viajar hasta que la muerte me llame' (ibid.).

There is possibly a redolent morality in the socio-economic panorama on display in this tale, which could even be seen to bring Piñera alongside Castro: to the latter's merciless description of the 'sectores acomodados

---

[2] In the New Testament, the pharisee Saul became the Christian Paul (later Paul the Apostle) after meeting the risen Christ on the road to Damascus (Acts of the Apostles 9: 3–9).

y conservadores' who were utterly devoid of integrity, Piñera brings this boastful and self-satisfied traveller who is convinced that 'como tengo mucho dinero, todo marchará sobre ruedas' (ibid.: 107). For Piñera, the toiling masses (the thousand *niñeras* who push the traveller and, later, the hundreds of *cocineras* who push another mid-life traveller, the 'famoso banquero Pepe' who is making his absurd journey 'sentado sobre una cazuela') are subjected to the petulance of the inactive few and treated as impassive objects to be disposed of according to the master's plan (108). The *niñeras* are not even permitted the dignity of familiarity behind an ascribed and uniform identity: they will not actually be dressed as nannies at all, 'sino de choferes' (107). But on closer inspection, perhaps Piñera rescues the traveller's morality with an oblique suggestion of residual compassion for his chattels. Far from enslaving one nanny and forcing her to push the pram until collapse, he employs sufficient staff such that each shift would be no more exhausting than a nanny's habitual daily labours: 'calculando que una niñera pasea a su crío por el parque unas veinte cuadras sin mostrar señales de agotamiento' (107). Or perhaps not. Perhaps this stage-posting of the *niñeras* is not benevolence, but merely logistical precision to ensure the journey 'marchará sobre ruedas'. Perhaps in this story (as in many others) both morality and immorality give way to Piñera's characteristic amorality. In the introduction to the 1956 edition of *Cuentos fríos*, Piñera offered an unequivocal expression of this ardent amorality:

> El autor estima que la vida no premia ni castiga, no condena ni salva, o, para ser más exacto, no alcanza a discernir esas complicadas categorías. Sólo puede decir que vive; que no se le exija que califique sus actos, que les dé un valor cualquiera o que espere una justificación al final de sus días. (Piñera 1956: 7)

Herein lies the essence of Piñera's understanding of the possible empathy between *viajero* and *niñeras*. Like Turner, Piñera saw all his protagonists bound together in inescapable communitas. Unlike in Turner's ritual limens, however, this solidarity leads not to recognition of 'a generalized social bond that has [...] yet to be fragmented into a multiplicity of structural ties', but to collective acceptance of an utterly absurd fate: the masses, like the masters they serve, have been lulled into a physical and mental stupor by the tedious cycle of life which seems determined not to disturb their slumber with anything approaching vitality (Turner 1974: 96).

   In many ways, 'El viaje' can be read, not as an account of escape from inconsequence or *ingravidez* through the privilege of wealth, but rather as a tale of the irremediable levity of life, regardless of the socio-economic circumstances that sustain it. In Piñera's story, existential *intrascendencia* and liminality combine. The notion that travel broadens the mind and affirms the identity is debunked, as the physical locomotion of the traveller offers no relief from metaphysical inertia: 'No saldré del país, ésto no tendría objeto' (Piñera 1999: 107). The traveller's immobility is virtually a disability; not only will he never deviate from the tiresome road that stretches monotonously towards the horizon, but the pram pushed by the relay team of nannies renders him almost totally immobile. Even amongst fellow *iluminati*, the opportunities for meaningful contact to ameliorate alienation are absent. The traveller's constant companions on the journey through the rest of life (*las niñeras*) never speak to him, and Pepe the banker, who presumably embarked upon his own pointless peregrination after a revelation not dissimilar to the traveller's, is equally isolated in fatuous ceremony and impenetrable incommunication: 'El azar ha querido que siempre, en el momento de pasar yo en mi cochecito, Pepe, girando en su cazuela, me dé la cara, lo cual nos obliga a un saludo ceremonioso' (108). Definitive demarcation of space and determined forward momentum across it are frustrated. Even after 'sus buenos cinco años que ruedo por el camino' (107), the traveller makes no mention of the end of the road, a change in direction or any spatial variation to challenge the limbo of constant movement without progression. The few landmarks alluded to draw the eye neither forwards nor backwards to future or past horizons but only to the immobile sides of the road, where 'necesidades humanas' are satisfied, where impassive *niñeras* await their turn and from where the mysterious 'salvajes' observe the *cochecito* go by. This liminal edge is the location of real life in 'El viaje'. Unlike in other analyst-author's accounts, however, this space at the side of the road is sterile. Luján, for example, gladly occupied the *arroyo* as a privileged viewpoint, a place where his acutely sensitive *sensibilidad* (which would bring tears to his eyes at the sight of others' suffering) was tempered by objective distance into a liminal perspicacity. In 'El viaje' the same space at the side of the road is either the locus of ignorant savagery stuck in physical and metaphysical stasis (the *salvajes* never move and never communicate) or a scatological site where the traveller pauses in his journey for motions of a different kind.

In this story, therefore, although the journey was originally portrayed as a prelude to death, there is nothing to suggest even the physical deterioration of the traveller. The first sentence traps him in the liminal middle of life: 'Tengo cuarenta años', an age Piñera described elsewhere as 'esa pálida edad del hombre en que uno está situado entre la deslumbrante luz de la vida y el negror de la tumba' (in 'El Enemigo', Piñera 1964: 191). Trapped on a temporal hyphen, he is neither wholly alive nor descending gratefully to death, but rather moving across a liminal purgatory without hope of either absolution or damnation. In life, as well as in this allegorical journey, to reach maturity is only to dally in a lifeless limbo between womb and tomb. But from Piñera's radically amoral perspective, this is neither a salvation nor a condemnation: life simply doesn't 'alcanza a discernir esas complicadas categorías' (1999: 7). In this, Piñera's depiction of this point-less existence does seem to strike a chord with Ortiz's and Mañach's analyses and authorship of the national narrative, and particularly their readings of Martí. For all, the *modus* is simply to live, not to 'live up to' anything. In Piñera's reading, however, there is no redolent optimism at all (no matter how subjunctive and susceptible to the inconclusive *luchita*). And yet, in the *viajero*'s resignation to existential ennui with apparent felicity, his paradoxical inclination 'to have done with the world and yet redeem it' (Schopenhauer, in Glicksberg: 39), there is perhaps a tentative hope: salvation from the torpid journey towards unremarkable death should be sought in a regression towards birth. The traveller, at forty, can learn little more of the ways of the world and has decided, after careful contemplation, to spend the rest of his life in a pram. The regression is physical, metaphysical and grammatical, as the author retreats from the future tense, making of the suspended chronology a maxim for terrestrial bliss: 'Lo empujará una niñera [...]. Cada una de estas niñeras empuja el cochecito a una velocidad moderada [...]. Hace ya sus buenos cinco años que ruedo por el camino' (Piñera 1999: 107). In the regressive and anti-didactic dogmatism of the traveller there perhaps lies a search for solace from grown-up frustrations in callow candour, or what Friedrich Schlegel called the *reelle Sprache* of the child. For Schlegel, the infant's intuitive understanding of the bitter paradoxes of the human condition was expressed in the 'strange, the absurd, childlike yet sophisticated naiveté of "authentic language"', which sought not to eviscerate myth with reason nor vanquish all that is incomprehensible (or *unverständlichkeit*) with absolute explanation, but rather to 'suspend the notions and the laws of rational thought and to replace them within a beautiful confusion of fantasy in the original chaos of human nature' (Schlegel, in de Man 1996: 181). Although arriving at their epiphanies down different roads, therefore, perhaps there is some discursive harmony, rather than discord, between Piñera and the liminal analyst-authors of this study. For all, future-focused knowledge is acquired at the expense of true percipience and teleological progression through life's journey can lead us away from the source of our most insightful epistemology. In this Piñera's *viajero*, like Mañach's Luján, perhaps walks alongside the mythical Sisyphus on an endless and seemingly pointless quest with no guarantees of a predestined *destino*; perhaps all are similarly resigned to life being defined by 'algún vago dolor disimulado', and yet subtly redeemed by 'alguna alegría limpia y humilde' (Mañach 1926: 11 & 12) which will see all enjoying a paradoxical yet 'evidente felicidad' (Piñera 1999: 108).[3] In this story then, as in Camus's reading of the Greek myth, perhaps 'the struggle itself towards the heights is enough to fill a man's heart' and 'one must imagine Sisyphus happy' (Camus 2000: 111). Ennui as ontology and anomie as myth come even further to the fore in the next text.

Timeless *cubanía*

Cintio Vitier's *Lo cubano en la poesía* is a noteworthy reflection on Cuba's collective *sensibilidad* and the perceived hiatus of 1957. Although ostensibly a work of literary criticism, Vitier's epistemological intent is clearly more comprehensive: 'siempre será provechoso el intento de ceñir y valorar lo que más genuinamente nos expresa en cada instante del devenir histórico' (1958: 11).[4] Like many of his antecedent analyst-authors, Vitier laments the parlous state into which Cuba's *sensibilidad* had slumped and advocates earnest introspection as an essential prerequisite to any collective 'cura': 'la necesidad profunda de conocer nuestra alma, cuando parece que sus mejores esencias se prostituyen y evaporan' (484). But for all its apparent orthodoxy within this intellectual tradition, *Lo cubano en la poesía* actually proposes a radical re-calibration of the ontological foundations of Cuban national identity and displays an epistemological audacity that sets it apart from many of its textual predecessors. Vitier's text does not suggest, for example, that the Republic's stubborn infirmity was due to the misinterpretation or outright betrayal of distant history, nor does it advocate the predominance of a perspicacious generation of Benjamins able to tutor their errant elders and thus save the nation, nor does it condone the selective excision of awkward episodes from the past to render the national narrative more fluent and more instructive. For Vitier, the problem is not that history had been misread and misapplied, in the Republic or beforehand, but that history as a 'meta-myth' (and hence unifying force) had simply never coalesced in Cuba: 'Fundar algo sobre esta arena movediza, en medio de esta difusa y terrible hambre de frustración que nos rodea, es en verdad improbable faena' (489). Hence, although recognising the half-century obsession with the historical foundations of the new nation, Vitier is sceptical of the supposed pre-1898 Golden Age of anti-colonial statesmanship whose subsequent betrayal condemned Cuba's civic foundations to

---

3   In Greek mythology, Sisyphus was condemned for his hubristic defiance of Zeus and deception of Thanatos to push a stone up a mountain only to see it endlessly roll back down to the bottom.

4   Although it was published in 1958, Vitier wrote '12 de julio 1957' on the final page of *Lo cubano en la poesía*.

ideological erosion and the Republic to ever-imminent ruin. If the founding fathers' legacy was so pre-eminent, Vitier asks, where is it now? 'Volvemos continuamente los ojos a las generaciones de "fundadores" de nuestro siglo XIX [...], pero lo que ellos fundaron, ¿dónde está?' (488). History in this reading is neither truth nor myth, but rather *historia* in the other Spanish-language sense: story, make-believe, history as *puro invento*.

This scepticism was not Vitier's alone. *Lo cubano en la poesía* is part of an intellectual paradigm that came to prominence in the 1940s amidst a group of poets and on the pages of their landmark literary magazine, *Orígenes*.[5] With *Orígenes*, and particularly with its chief editor José Lezama Lima, Cuban (and Hispanic) letters discovered writers whom Chiampi describes as unrivalled 'guardians of arcane poetic secrets' in the modern tradition that includes Rimbaud, Mallarmé, Pound, Darío and Joyce (in Solé & Abreu 1989: 1125). Lezama Lima, and other *Orígenes* poets, have been read as purveyors of complex, ornate or even wilfully obscurantist literary expression (as in Souza[6]), as heterodox heroes rescuing Cuban letters from stagnation with a radically new 'sistema poético' (as in Rowlandson[7]), or interrogated for what Emilio Bejel calls the literary 'rhythm of desire' that reconciles writer, language and the wider world in 'the vacuum produced by the loss of natural order' (1990: 72). They are introduced here both to illustrate the creative context with which Cuban writers of the late 1940s onwards were almost obliged to engage (whether in supportive contribution or bitter contestation[8]), and to demonstrate the particular influence of the group's scepticism of historical meta-narratives on Vitier's *Lo cubano en la poesía*. What Chiampi called the *Origenistas*' 'desconfianza de la historia' is palpable in many editions of the magazine (in Lezama Lima 1993b: 13). In the inaugural edition of the magazine, which appeared in the spring of 1944, for example, the editors declared (in tones reminiscent of *revista de avance*'s claim to be absolutely independent, 'hasta del tiempo' [1:1, 1]) that the mutability of the magazine had nothing to do with the passage of time: 'Como no cambiamos con las estaciones, no tenemos que justificar en extensos alegatos una piel de camaleón' (*Orígenes* 1:1, 5). In 1944, a year seemingly charged with historical significance in which the chronic spasms of war continued to afflict much of

---

5   The principal contributors to *Orígenes* were Vitier himself, José Lezama Lima, Virgilio Piñera, Gastón Baquero, Justo Rodríguez Santos, Ángel Gaztelu, Eliseo Diego, Fina García-Marruz, Octavio Smith and Lorenzo García Vega. Roberto Fernández Retamar and the exiled Spanish writer María Zambrano also published frequently in the journal.

6   See 'The Sensorial World of Lezama Lima', in Souza 1976 (53–79).

7   See Rowlandson 2007.

8   The polemic with the *Orígenes* project was particularly visceral after 1959, as illustrated in Chapter 6 below.

the world and in which Cuba experienced its first truly democratic transition of presidential power, *Orígenes* was completely unmoved by any sense of historical gravitas, opting instead for a defiant *reductio ad nihilum*, regardless of the painful implications for Cuba's self-perception and projection:

> Hoy nos encontramos ante la dilatada vastedad de un mundo cuantitativo sucesivo, donde las revoluciones y los peces impresionistas, las glorificaciones y la lepra, las más herméticas formas de la clausura y las más dionisíacas descargas populares, ofrecen una violenta riqueza sucesiva que es necesario reducir, en la dolorosa reducción del yo a la nada. (1:1, 7)

For the *Orígenes* poets, and for *Lo cubano en la poesía*, therefore, history just couldn't be trusted. Such is Vitier's conviction of Cuba's ahistorical antiessence that he iconoclastically chose Enrique José Varona (who for many was one of the few examples of past Republican rectitude and hope for continuity into a traumatic present) as his archetype of *intrascendencia*: although Varona was once a paragon of civic and moral edification, Vitier claimed that he ended his life bitterly disillusioned with the Republic for which he had fought so hard, and so 'minado ya de escepticismo' that he had his headed paper printed with the slogan 'En la arena fundo y escribo en el viento' (Vitier 1958: 488).

Nevertheless, the poets associated with *Orígenes* were not of the same nihilistic pedigree as Eduardo Abela and the more historiographically radical *vanguardistas* who had contributed to *revista de avance* in 1927. Instead of a romantic retreat to the unsullied legacy of a mythical past, the *Origenistas* sought to counteract the ennui felt in the face of the decrepit foundations of the nation, to escape the compulsion to circumscribe present actions and inaction within inherited socio-cultural frameworks, and to free Cuban culture and *sensibilidad* from the tyranny of legacies through a momentous imaginative coup: the solution to the Republic's problems was not history, but poetry. In his July 1945 article 'Después de lo raro, la extrañeza', Lezama Lima described Cuban culture (with *Orígenes* in its vanguard) undertaking nothing less than a hermeneutic revolution in the collective comprehension of past, present and future experiences on the island:

> Lejos de poder utilizar la delicia de un recuerdo potenciado, se ha visto obligado a utilizar la profecía [...]. Quizás la profecía aparezca entre nosotros como el más candoroso empeño por romper la mecánica de la historia, el curso de su fatalidad. En realidad un joven profeta desea dar un tajo en la historia cuando un antecedente invariable va a entregarnos una sucesión decrecida [...]. Si no había tradición entre nosotros, lo mejor

era que la poesía ocupara ese sitio y así había la posibilidad de que en lo
sucesivo mostráramos un estilo de vida. (*Orígenes* 2:6, 51–2)

Although written more than a decade after *Orígenes*'s initial celebration of
what the magazine saw as the demise of history and its replacement with
poetry, *Lo cubano en la poesía* insists on the same shift in the philosophical
roots of Cuban *letras* and life: 'Tenemos la sensación del estupor ontológico,
de la situación vital en el vacío, por eso volvemos los ojos al testimonio
poético, donde ese mismo vacío puede adquirir sentido como síntoma del ser o
del destino' (Vitier 1958: 484). In this, Vitier's book is not so much a survey of
how archetypal identity has been articulated in, or ornamented by, poetry, but a
declaration that poetry, not history, is the oracle through which to examine the
Cuban soul: 'la poesía se convierte en el vehículo de conocimiento absoluto,
a través del cual se intenta llegar a las esencias de la vida' (373). Vitier's
critical study of one hundred years of Cuban poetry therefore becomes what
Rojas calls a 'poetic archaeology' of the quiddities of Cuban identity (2008a:
66). For Rojas, the *Origenistas* simply turned their backs on more than fifty
years of introspective re-cognisance of Cuban identity and sought to draw a
clear frontier between their own poetic epiphany and the 'discourse of national
civic renovation' of the 1920s, the *vanguardismo* of *revista de avance*, and 'the
revolutionary movement crystallised in the 1940 Constitution' (67).

The *Origenistas* found their prophet of this poetic liberation of identity in
Lezama Lima. For Vitier, Lezama was an instinctive inhabitant of the historical
hiatus, at once offspring and overlord of the timeless interstice of which 1957
was an apotheosis: 'no había en él la menor continuidad con lo inmediato
anterior [...]; su tiempo no parecía ser histórico ni ahistórico, sino, literal-
mente, fabuloso' (1958: 370). Lezama was the nemesis of all those thinkers
(like Castro) who had sought sustenance for idealised Cuban identity in more
accurate interpretations of past legacies or extirpations of historical anomalies,
of all those who had cast their hopes backwards to a distant prelapsarian past
(like Abela), and even for those who sought a pragmatic balance between
youthful zeal and age-old cynicism (like Mañach). For Lezama Lima, the cure
for the ailing collective *corpus* was neither selective surgery nor the prophylactic assimilation of all ills, but rather resignation to the death of all previous
articulations of *cubanía* to allow a radical reincarnation, not in chronological
narrative, but in an isolated and hence liberated poetic 'imagen': 'la imagen
como un absoluto, la imagen que se sabe imagen, la imagen como la última de
las historias posibles' (ibid.: 393). In response to the unsatisfactory saga of the
Republic so far, Rojas sees Vitier (and other *Origenistas*) using the hiatus in
Cuba's temporal progression to enact a poetic epiphany and bring about 'the
beginning of another history' (2008a: 67). This reading of the *Origenistas*'

condemnation of the often oppressive impetus of historicism in Cuba and scorn for attempts to locate (or invent) a pure past upon which to found an equally pure present is suggestive. Nevertheless, Rojas's portrayal of the *Origenistas*' pursuit of 'another history' is perhaps hasty in the specific case of Vitier and *Lo cubano en la poesía*. There seems rather to be some evidence of much less certainty and much more ambivalence than a determined genesis of a poetic tradition could permit. Even though Vitier's express intention was to survey a hundred years of this poetic tradition, he arrives at no clear conclusions, either about the expressive contours of insular *poeisis*, or about the quiddity of the Cuban *sensibilidad* that inspired it. I rather read Vitier in much closer creative symbiosis with the sense of temporal stasis that circumstances had engendered in 1957. From this perspective, *Lo cubano en la poesía* is not a frontal assault on the hegemony of history, as Rojas suggests, but a liminal critique, forever 'venturosamente al margen', of the 'siniestro curso central de la Historia' (Vitier 1958: 492). I rather read Vitier joining the intellectual tradition of Ortiz, Mañach-Luján, and (to a certain extent) Piñera in seeing marginality (and liminality) as the *locus amoenus* of Cuban national identity.

In Vitier's exploration of what he called Cuban poetry's 'desideratum normal de nuestra alma' (ibid.: 485), five of the ten characteristics identified are more in keeping with the assertion that identity is 'betwixt and between all fixed points of classification' than with any notion of a resolute archetype, whether rooted in history *or* poetry (Turner 1974: 232). Thus, Vitier's taxonomy points to Cuban sensibility's 'ingravidez' (or what he calls the 'fuerza de lo suave', 'flexibilidad, vaguedad', 'anticasticismo, antifanatismo, no teluricidad'); its 'intrascendencia' (displayed in an 'ausencia de dogmatismo', 'inconsecuencia' 'choteo' 'irresponsabilidad'); its 'lejanía' (involving a 'nostalgia desde adentro', 'intuición de lo otro, lejanización radical del mundo, historia y cultura como sueño'); and its 'despego' (or 'falta de arraigo último, disponibilidad para ir siempre a otra cosa, escaso sentimiento nacionalista, soledad') (Vitier 1958: 485–6). This description of a Cuban persona (up)rooted in *ingravidez* and ambiguity provoked ire in some quarters, with an anonymous author in the sole 1959 edition of *Ciclón* magazine lambasting Vitier's book as tragic testimony to the 'flojedad de nuestras convicciones nacionales [...], la perpetua autodenigración de nuestros mejores valores' ('Refutación a Vitier'). From within our theoretical framework, however, Vitier's 1957 enunciation of the *desideratum* of Cuban *sensibilidad* has a clear resemblance to the well-established tradition in which the *imago* of national identity was not to be found in future cohesion, integration and conclusion, but in a present-tense, not-*ever*-yet complex of perennial flux.

There is ample evidence of this. In *Un catauro de cubanismos*, Ortiz had eschewed attempts to isolate the Cuban language community behind borders of impenetrable insular peculiarity, positioning himself instead between origin and invention, endogenous immobility and exogenous flux, from where to best appreciate (and give authority to) the multivalent voices he heard articulating Cuban *sensibilidad*. Just as Ortiz turned his lexicographer's ear to the 'expresiones náuticas' and 'acepciones marítimas' (Ortiz 1923d: 21 & 23) with which the Cuban vernacular voice was seasoned, Vitier the poet insists that the quintessence of Cuba's physical and metaphysical terrain is not land-bound but 'marina y aérea [...]; es decir, esencialmente comunicante' (1958: 491). Both countered the telluric rootedness of origins with the fluid anti-essence of oceanic subjectivity, with an 'anoriginal ontology' that 'erodes the sedentary *habitus* of the modern subject' (Dubow 2004: 219). Both spurned the fantasy of *homo cubensis* for the 'flexibilidad', 'vaguedad' and 'ingravidez' of *homo maritimus*.

Similarly, Vitier's taxonomy sidelines the Homeric heroism of people like Mella, whose melodramatic pledges to open his veins 'para que se reorganice la Patria Cubana', or Castro, whose martial instincts made the sword of Damocles his weapon of choice; both are anathema to the 'anticasticismo' and 'antifanatismo' Vitier perceives at the core of the Cuban spirit (Mella 1975: 43). *Lo cubano en la poesía* rather privileges the anti-heroics of an archetype such as the Luján-Mañach twin in *Estampas*, who as 'el último criollo' displayed many of the psycho-cultural contours of Cuban *sensibilidad* as described by Vitier (Lavié 1927: 34). From the 'arcadismo' of Luján's passion for tradition, to Mañach's 'nostalgia desde adentro' for his now unrecognisable 'cuadra niña', to the *procurador*'s 'intuición' for the *el 'otro' habanero* whose 'dolor disimulado' brought him almost to tears, Mañach-Luján appears to be the embodiment of Vitier's understanding of *lo cubano* (Mañach 1926: 11–12 & 36).

Vitier's charting of the 'ingravidez' and 'intrascendencia' of *cubanía* also resonates with the less hagiographic interpretations of Martí, his legacy, and Cuba's politico-cultural panorama after a half-century of independence. The kind of 'anticasticismo' that Vitier celebrates adequately describes the heroism that Mañach advocated to reinvigorate the Republic in the centenary year: 'no en el sentido espectacular, sino en el silencioso, continuo y fecundo de cada día' (Mañach 1953b: 80). Similarly, Vitier's 'flexibilidad, vaguedad, ausencia de dogmatism' (1958: 485–6) in many ways synthesises the pragmatism that Ichaso portrayed in his assertion that 'se equivocan los que pintan a Martí como un idealista encandilado' (1953: 81).

Through this ideological resonance with Ortiz, Mañach and Ichaso, Vitier's assessment of *lo cubano* also draws alongside Turner's logic of liminality. What for Vitier is archetypal *ingravidez* and *intrascendencia*, for Turner is the subjunctive mood 'of may-be, might-be, as-if' so typical of liminal transitions (in Alexander 1991: 30). Despite his detailed taxonomy of *lo cubano*, therefore, Vitier makes his reluctance to be categorical about *cubanía* clear from early in his analysis: 'Desde ahora anuncio que yo no aspiro a sacar conclusiones absolutas ni a decir: lo cubano es ésto o aquello, sino a que seamos capaces de sentirlo' (1958: 14). For Vitier as for Turner (and the other Cuban identity liminalists), 'the cognitive schemata that give sense to everyday life no longer apply, but are, as it were, suspended' (Turner 1982: 84). Despite the apparent clarity suggested in the title of the book, all uncomplicated definitions are eschewed and the essence of identity evaporates: 'no hay una esencia inmóvil y preestablecida, nombrada *lo cubano*, que podamos definir con independencia de sus manifestaciones sucesivas y generalmente problemáticas' (Vitier 1958: 12). A preliminary reading of *Lo cubano en la poesía*, therefore, locates it amidst the canon that grow melancholy over what Rojas calls the 'ucronía' (2008a: 65) of the inconclusive Cuban Republic in which the shifting sands of *ingravidez* and the 'frustración que nos rodea' had made the founding of a national tradition and archetypal identity a truly 'improbable faena' (Vitier 1958: 489). A further re-reading in the 'subjunctive mood' of liminality, however, reveals an alternative, more ambiguous, less conclusive thesis within Vitier's text. While he certainly draws attention to the ever-frustrated task of laying down firm foundations for a politically and psychologically independent Cuba, he does not seem to rush from an unsatisfactory historical beginning to a teleological poetic end, but rather lingers in an interstice charged with the 'ambivalence and unset definition' of the limen (Dening 1997: 2). Rojas does not completely overlook this 'edginess' in Vitier's analysis. For him, all the *Origenistas* purposefully occupied the physical margins in 'a space that might be called *secret*' (2008a: 84), and thrived on the metaphysical edge in their hermetic poetic experiments that sought to move through 'la dolorosa reducción del yo' towards 'la nada' (*Orígenes*, 1:1, 7). But for Rojas this absence is a prelude to an inevitable presence.[9] For him, the liminal hiatus in which history was overcome would ultimately be filled by a post-liminal ascendancy of poetry; hollowness was lauded not as end in itself, but as 'a margin wherein the substantial form is established' (Rojas 2008a: 66). The reading here is other. Whilst concurring that *Lo cubano en la poesía* is a manifesto for marginality, there is, it seems to me, a reluctance to gravitate towards the core and a stubborn determination to celebrate incompletion, partiality and inconclusive emptiness:

> Ahora bien, ¿por qué no aceptar esa imposibilidad como una esencia, y en lugar de ser vencido por su aspecto más superficial, convertirla en lo que

---

[9]   Understandable, perhaps, given that the maxim goes on to say: 'la dolorosa reducción del yo a la nada y de ésta a un nacimiento' (*Orígenes* 1:1, 7).

realmente es: la inspiración misma de nuestra alma? Entonces empezamos a ver todo el esplendor de lo discontinuo, de lo fragmentario y *lo imposible* en el reino del espíritu. (Vitier 1958: 493, emphasis in the original)

It is no mere coincidence that the very last paragraph of Vitier's nearly six-hundred page text should include this final poetic pirouette: 'La poesía nos cura de la historia y nos permite acercarnos a la sombra del umbral' (585). Whilst poetry may be administered as an antidote to history in Vitier's text, the final destination for a Cuban *sensibilidad* so 'cured' is the shadowy world of the perennial threshold.

In contrast to this inconclusive conclusion, however, and returning to the absences of *Lo cubano en la poesía* from another perspective, Vitier is surprisingly silent on the violence inherent in Cuba's bellicose birth as a nation and never far from the surface ever since. Although born in 1921 and so a young witness to the worst excesses of the *machadato*, Vitier's *sensibilidad colectiva* is strangely pacific. Although his book was an assessment of identity in poetry, not a socio-political history, his inclusion within the 'desideratum del alma cubana' of 'anticasticismo', 'antifanatismo', 'inocencia' and 'cariño' seems idealistic if not wholly myopic (ibid.: 485). Whilst undoubtedly aligning himself with what we have described as the liminal sense and sensibility of Cuban identity, Vitier can be accused of making a myth of the margin and overlooking the 'surreptitiously aberrant quality' of the limen (Giles 2000: 43). In his poetry-inspired taxonomy of identity, Vitier perhaps over-abstracted Cuban *letras* from the daily vicissitudes of Cuban life, making his *intranscendente* ethos increasingly unpalatable to some Cubans at the time. In 1957, the confrontation between poetry and history within the Cuban national narrative was certainly far from over and, as the year progressed, the levity so celebrated by Vitier came under concerted attack from the historical gravity building in the eastern mountains and spilling out onto the streets of Cuban cities.

Chronology makes a comeback

Despite the frustration and apparently endemic despotism on the island, some Cubans in 1957 retained their faith in further acts of audacious sacrifice as the only effective prophylactic for the ailing Republic. Although Castro's eighty-two-strong invading force had been reduced to an out-gunned twelve, these stalwart *venceremos* prophets did not relent, even achieving an almost biblical resurrection in the foothills of the Sierra Maestra mountains, described by *Bohemia* as 'un pedazo de historia' (6 Jan. 1957: 78), where the disciples gathered around their indomitable leader Fidel. Tenuous but irrepressible historical promise and momentum seemed to condense in those mountains, and its beacon could be seen all across Cuba. On 13 March 1957, at the opposite end of the island to the historical mountains, youthful courage and a disposition to immolation once more made their presence felt when a handful of urban fighters stormed the presidential palace in Havana in an attempt to assassinate Fulgencio Batista. Despite its amazing audacity, the so-called Directorio Revolucionario[10] attack came to nought (fading away when its reserve forces failed to materialise) and most of the rebels were slaughtered trying to fight their way back out of the palace. From one angle, the *asalto* was just another grisly turn of the tyranny–sacrifice cycle, a failed frontal assault that took its place alongside Dos Ríos and Moncada as courageous, but lamentable, chapters of the national narrative. But the attack can be read in another, more suggestive, way. Alongside their intention to kill the dictator, the men of the Directorio can actually be seen as making a determined assault on the perceived temporal stasis of the time, a desperate bid to reinvigorate Cuba's forward momentum, a discursive raid on Cuba's 'moment in and out of time' (Turner 1974: 238). From this perspective, whilst the attack can be classified as a tactical disaster, it warrants new examination as a discursive triumph, a 'fecha heroica incrustada con letras de sangre en las páginas de la historia de Cuba' (Directorio Revolucionario 1957: 2). Such is the proposal here, in reading Faure Chomón's account of the *asalto*.[11]

Although Chomón provides many details about his co-conspirators 'Carbó, Machadito, Wangüemert, Abelardo, Osvaldito, Leoncito, Briñas, Tony y yo', the prime protagonist in his account is time itself:

> A cada rato [...]
> En pocos minutos [...]
> Por varias horas [...]
> Desde horas tempranas [...]
> En las próximas horas [...]
> Alrededor de las dos de la tarde [...]
> Con la llegada de los primeros claros del día [...]
> Sin perder un minuto de tiempo, dimos la orden de estar listos para iniciar la marcha sobre el Palacio en cualquier de las próximas horas. (Chomón, in Franqui 1969: 126–9)

[10] The Directorio Revolucionario was a FEU scion, formed by student leader José Antonio Echevarría at the end of 1956 to include both students and workers in the anti-Batista fight.

[11] Published in Carlos Franqui's *El libro de los doce* (1969). Chomón was wounded in the doorway of the presidential palace and thus survived the attack, going on to become one of the principal leaders of the Directorio Revolucionario and overseeing its anti-Batista pact with Castro's Movimiento del 26 de Julio in December 1958.

The actions narrated are always carefully situated in and surrounded by time; although the attackers were resigned to the sacrifice of lives, the idea of wasting any time was an unbearable torment: 'Batista se nos pudiera escapar durante las horas que faltaban para que llegara el día en que teníamos concertada aquella cita con la historia' (ibid.: 123). Far from turning their backs on history, therefore, a punctilious observance of time became the key to success and collective salvation. In stark contrast to the *Orígenes*-sponsored idea that what was called for was the 'dolorosa reducción del yo a la nada' (*Orígenes* 1:1, 7), for Chomón each moment of the twenty-four hour epic he relates seems overloaded with historical gravity and each detail requires meticulous recording for posterity: 'constantemente había un compañero de turno con los audífonos pegados a las orejas [que] apuntaba cuidadosamente todo cuanto escuchaba, en una libreta, haciendo constar la hora' (in Franqui 1969: 123). This urge to 'make time count' is evident both in the direct narrative insistence on chronological accountability, and in coincidental conceits within the story that assert time's dominion over the realms of fact and fiction: the truck in which most of the *asaltantes* approached the palace was painted with the slogan *Fast Delivery*; Chomón recounted that the convoy almost got split up on the way but was able to regroup in front of the offices of the *batistiano* newspaper *Tiempo*; and the auxiliary action to the storming of the palace was José Antonio Echevarría's seizure of *Radio Reloj* (from where he had intended to broadcast the news of the dictator's demise). There is nevertheless some oblique agreement here with Vitier's assessment of the 'intrascendencia', 'provisionalidad' and 'inconsecuencia' of Cuban *sensibilidad*: when describing the rebels' reconnoitring of the palace, Chomón records their amazement at the guards' inability to appreciate the consequence of events unfolding before them, their blindness to the clear indications of imminent change:

> Comentábamos lo estúpidos que eran los agentes que [...] cuidaban a Batista, sin llamarles la atención nuestro automóvil, de un color escandaloso rojo mamey, que a una hora en que hay muy poco tráfico de vehículos, daba vueltas continuas alrededor de Palacio, teniendo que pasarles varias veces por el lado. (126)[12]

Similarly, as he drove towards the palace, Chomón was suddenly startled by the innocent ignorance of the people he saw in the streets: '¡Qué ajenas estaban

---

[12] Their own 'estupidez' in choosing such an eye-catching car and awkward hour goes uncommented, of course. This disdain for the protection of invisibility could perhaps be read as a further manifestation of the self-destructive tendencies we have pointed to in Martí, Mella and Castro, all of who charged the enemy head-on in one way or another.

al acontecimiento que iba a producirse dentro de unos minutos, conmoviendo a toda la nación!' (ibid.: 131). Unlike Vitier (and others), however, the *asaltantes* were enraged by this levity and were determined to storm both the palace and the stultifying atmosphere of *ingravidez* that had overtaken the Cuban people: 'sabíamos que nuestro ataque al Palacio era una empresa de trascendental dimensión histórica, que haría libre a nuestro pueblo' (133). Far from spurning time for an atemporal hiatus or embracing what Vitier described as the 'flexibilidad' and 'vaguedad' of Cuban *sensibilidad*, the rebels rather replicate the implacable rhythm of the 'mecánica de la historia' so criticised by *Orígenes* and become wholly obsessed with synchrony in the final preparations for the attack:

> Cuando comprobaba que no había nadie, le daba una señal a otro compañero, que, situado en el pasillo lateral donde empieza la escalera, transmitía la señal a otros compañeros, situados en los pisos de arriba que nos la comunicaban, siendo entonces cuando bajaban, primero los bultos de armas, y despúes los hombres en parejas. (130)

Whereas the *Origenistas* and Vitier celebrated temporal stasis as either an opportunity for a turning of the ontological tide or as a demonstration of the atemporal and ateleological quintessence of Cuban identity, Chomón's account of the 13 March assault seeks to re-centre time and implacable progression within the national narrative, to move from the static temporal logic of the limen to the accelerated time of revolution, to mark the dawn of a hyper-history of transcendental change in which the present rushed towards the future: '¿Cuántos días le quedan de vida a la dictadura batistiana?', asked the July 1957 editorial of the clandestine paper *Barricada*:

> ¿Cuántas semanas? ¿cuántos meses? ¿o será simplemente cuestión de horas? Los momentos que vive Cuba son sumamente trascendentales. Hasta un ciego puede ver que los días del batistato están contados. (*Barricada*, July 1957: 1)

In uncompromising contrast with the 1957 sense of stasis and with those who welcomed this as an opportunity to re-calibrate collective *sensibilidad* away from its obsessive historicity, a growing number of young rebels in the cities and in the mountains once more pinned their hopes on history, backed themselves to break the cycle of tyranny–sacrifice–tyranny and attacked the alleged 'ausencia de destino' within the Cuban *alma* with zealous belief in a future heavy with promise: 'Es que en realidad en aquella tarde éramos el Destino para nuestro pueblo' (Chomón, in Franqui 1969: 132).

In his analysis of rites of passage, Turner often points to a liminal state in which relentless reiteration makes chronological progress hard to calibrate, a moment in which the 'structural view of time is not applicable' and 'every day is, in a sense, the same day, writ large or repeated' (1974: 238 & 239). In Cuba in 1957 (as in the Presidio Modelo of 1933), a similar sense of cyclical repetition and temporal hiatus reigned. Personalities and pernicious practices from the past had returned to haunt the island and there seemed to be little that the exhausted *pueblo* could do about it. Although audacious attempts to wrest Cuban history from the hands of the nefarious president and his coterie were made, the cycle of tyranny–sacrifice–tyranny that had arrested Cuba's civic impetus, and historical momentum seemed impervious and perpetual. Fidel Castro embodied the derring-do of the moment that, despite its evocation and application of (a martial version of) the founding fathers' legacy, was repeatedly condemned to pathos and pain. Thus, only three years after the disastrous July 1953 attack on the Moncada barracks, Castro was once more at the head of what seemed to be an equally catastrophic attempt to kick-start the country's forward momentum. Cuban history seemed suspended in liminal inanimation.

Some responded with lamentation and lassitude, but Cintio Vitier took up *Orígenes*'s expression of deep distrust, not only of the principal actors in the country's historical-political drama, but of the role played by history itself. He advocated instead a fundamental shift in collective consciousness away from the tyranny of hegemonic histories towards the liberation of poetry, thus to enunciate with greater fluency the *ingravidez* and *intrascendencia* which his fellow *Origenistas* had posited as an integral part of the authentic Cuban condition. For some analysts, this poetic renaissance was designed to generate its own momentum and carry *cubanía* beyond ethical and imaginative stagnation towards 'the beginning of another history' (Rojas 2008a: 67). But Vitier was reluctant simply to swap the *ucronía* of fifty frustrating years in the Republic for a poetic utopia in which 'la imagen' would become the exclusive cardinal point of Cuban identity. This chapter has examined evidence of Vitier's advocacy instead of what could be called a liminal *imago* of Cuban identity in which 'lo discontinuo' and '*lo imposible*' [*sic*] became the keystones of Cuban *sensibilidad*. Vitier, like Ortiz and Mañach before him, posited a malleable Cuban archetype amalgamating around congenital *flexibilidad*, *vaguedad* and inescapable *ingravidez*. Setting himself at a critical distance from those analyst-authors of the national narrative who sought to cure the Republic's maladies with a prophylactic dose of pure and proper history, but also from his co-*Origenistas* who welcomed the historical hiatus of 1957 as a teleological opportunity to reshape the Cuban *alma* in a poetic 'nacimiento', Vitier lingered in the liminal middle, eschewing peremptory conclusions and condemning stubborn attempts to resist the lightness of Cuba's historical being and the suspended collective animation of 1957: '¿Por qué no aceptar esa imposibilidad como una esencia, y en lugar de ser vencido por su aspecto más superficial, convertirla en lo que realmente es: la inspiración misma de nuestra alma?' (Vitier 1958: 493). But this clarion call for a much more bearable *ingravidez* coincided with an accumulation of transcendental intent in the cities and enigmatic mountains of the island. From east to west, opposition to the static and cyclical status quo was gathering amongst those willing to risk all to see Batista brought down. The storming of the Palacio Presidencial on 13 March 1957 can be read both as an attempt to remove a president and as a bid to restore executive authority to temporal momentum and the future tense. By the end of 1957, the writing was on the wall for Batista's regime and, to some extent, for an adherence to archetypal *ingravidez*. Within a year, the embattled *doce* had become a dauntless multitude that marched down the mountains to join their urban co-conspirators on the cusp of another transcendental turning point in Cuba's twentieth-century trajectory. For many, New Year's Eve 1958 saw not only the flight of a dictator, but also the birth of a new and revolutionary chronology.

6

1959–60: The turning of all tides

Although the transcendentalism that infuses the historiography of January 1959 is to some extent a subsequent and retrospective projection, even immediate observations of the events of that New Year and their inchoate effects on Cuban *sensibilidad* transmit a potent sense of epiphany, with Emma Pérez claiming as early as 11 January in *Bohemia*, for example, that 'como en la recomendación de San Pablo, "han llegado los tiempos"' (Pérez 1959: 14–15). As in 1927, and particularly as in 1953, some expressions of this epiphany portrayed it not as a genesis *ad nihil*, but as the long-awaited vindication of the legacy of Cuba's founding fathers, with the warrior-poet Martí at their head. As Fidel Castro marched jubilantly across the island in early January 1959, leaving behind the mountain redoubt where catastrophic defeat had seemed a near certainty only two years before, he increasingly acquired political but also mythological momentum. During the week-long procession from Santiago de Cuba to Havana (known as the *caravana de la libertad*), Castro seemed to enter the final phase of a miraculous metamorphosis from brave but pathetic figure of failure to all-conquering and super-human hero, the embodiment of the hopes of most of the nation: 'In the euphoria of victory, the new Revolution was seen as the culmination of the betrayed and frustrated *martiano* project, the fulfilment of his hopes and the justification of his death' (Kapcia 2000: 176). This sense of culmination is at the core of this chapter. From the leader of a few hundred urban activists, Castro had become the commander-in-chief of a three-thousand-strong army reminiscent of the ragged ranks of indomitable *mambises* of almost a hundred years before. From being an electoral hopeful in the mêlée of early 1952, he had put himself beyond mundane politics to reconnect in strategy and spiritual purity with the original *padres de la Patria*. As he had predicted in 1953, every aspect of the *triunfo* of the Revolution seemed to fulfil an all but forgotten prophecy from the fight for independence: the *rebeldes*' abnegation and self-sacrifice, their hit-and-run tactics against a numerically superior force, the physical and spiritual succour they drew from the rural hinterland, the audacious late 1958 march across the island following the legendary footsteps of Antonio Maceo, the Bronze Titan of his time. When the entire Cuban army capitulated to the band of *barbudos* from the east, acolytes and sceptics alike became increasingly convinced that these were legitimate sons and daughters of the Apostle Martí who would finally make the *Cuba Libre* dream come true.

Whilst examining evidence of this transcendence written into the national narrative during the initial revolutionary crucible of 1959–60, our reading of this period will nevertheless remain analytically consistent with what has come before. Having traced the debates around archetypal national identity since the early 1920s and having pointed to a fundamental discursive clash between those thinkers we have called the reaggregationists, for whom teleological momentum would carry Cuba ultimately towards victory and the consolidation of a perfect collective *sensibilidad*, and those we have called liminalists, for whom this pursuit of perfection was quixotic and should be swapped for a more pragmatic, but not pessimistic, acceptance of cyclical *luchita*, we will now examine the evidence of a stubborn persistence of the liminalist perspective well into the Revolutionary era, despite the very best efforts of their ideological adversaries. Hence, in 1959–60, analyst-authors once again argued about the clear frontiers between the 'angels' and 'devils' of the national narrative (as in 1923), again confronted each other in a recalcitrant clash across the generational divide (as in 1927), again advocated or condemned violence as a cathartic cure for the country's congenital ills (as in 1933), brought José Martí to the moral forefront once more in antithetical readings of his ideological legacy (as in 1953), and again turned their attention to the ontological struggle between poetry and history within Cuba's collective *sensibilidad* (as in 1957). On the basis of our investigative experience so far, however, we will show that this was no simple and balanced retrospective on more than half a century of identity debate. In 1959–60 (and subsequently), as Rojas suggests, the intellectual 'pacto republicano y democrático' was broken (2006: 103). In our reading of this rupture, however, the key fight for hermeneutic hegemony was not between 'una corriente liberal o republicana […], otra marxista […], y otra católica o cristiana', as Rojas suggests (107), but between liminalists and future-focused reaggregationists, in which the latter had a clear upper hand. Hence we will examine evidence that the prevailing appetite was for a radical re-calibration of the archetype to better reflect the cataclysmic changes occurring in almost every socio-political sphere; the desire was conclusively to resolve the enigma of *cubanía* that had perplexed analyst-authors since the earliest days of the Republic; the intention was not simply to amend previous inscriptions, but to carry the national narrative irreversibly beyond an impermeable Revolutionary frontier. The aspiration, therefore, was not simply to instigate another episode of introspection, but to propel Cuba and Cubans towards the 'post-liminal' self (van Gennep 1965: 210). In short, 1959–60 can be read as an attempt to mark the beginning of the end of Cuba's fifty-year rite of national passage.

Despite this widespread appetite for, belief in, and even evidence of a transcendental turning point as the decadent 1950s became the rebellious 1960s, some analyst-authors remained stubbornly unconvinced by the sense of culmination or persuaded by the *Cuba Libre* dream come true. This chapter will read across the frontier of 1959–60 by revisiting the key themes from previous chapters to reveal continuity where others see only schism. Hence, from a reappraisal of the *ingravidez* so fêted in 1957, we will move to a reading of Castro as Martí reincarnate, to an examination of the cathartic violence of the early months of revolutionary rule, to the orchestrated *falta de respeto* against the old guard from the pages of landmark cultural supplement *Lunes de Revolución*, to conclude with a critical reading of the *guajiro* archetype proposed early in the Revolutionary project. In each case, the allegedly reaggregated identity will be shown to be under determined attack by stubbornly ambivalent counterpoints, the future-perfect's conquest of the Revolutionary present challenged by the persistence of the subjunctive mood of the limen.

La sombra del umbral illuminated

In 1957, Cintio Vitier had claimed that the essence of Cuban *sensibilidad* lay in atemporal effervescence, and that Cuba's nation-building project had always been based on the ephemeral foundations of 'lo discontinuo', 'lo fragmentario' and '*lo imposible*' (1958: 493, emphasis in the original). In the place of historical gravitas, Vitier had celebrated an infinitely bearable lightness of being and exhorted his fellow Cubans to explore the psycho-cultural possibilities of a young nation with no debts to pay or scores to settle. In 1959, however, as prophecy after prophecy from the past seemed to be coming true before the *pueblo*'s bedazzled eyes, an advocacy of *ingravidez* suddenly appeared at best short-sighted and at worst just another example of the kind of feckless lack of faith that had marred Cuba's *sensibilidad* since independence. Alongside their economic and political reforms, the *rebeldes* seemed to revolutionise chronology itself and turn the hopeful *venceremos* of previous years into a much more contiguous and continuous *estamos venciendo*, with Roig de Leuchsenring marvelling that 'la historia, en esta Cuba de hoy, ha marchado tan de prisa que nos parece haber vivido lustros en meses, meses en instantes, cual si cada día nuestro presente se adueñase de un ancho trozo de porvenir' (1961b: 348). Written in 1958 but first published only in early 1959 (allowing the author to retrieve the manuscript and illuminate his chronicle of Republican ill-health with 'unos destellos de esperanza' [ibid.]), Roig's *Males y vicios de Cuba republicana sus causas y sus remedios* stood on the threshold of a new revolutionary age. And despite the habit of frustration, picked up over thirty years of socio-cultural setbacks, this analyst-author had no doubt that 1959 would finally witness Cuba's liberation from the cyclical suffering, tyranny and futile sacrifice that had marked collective sensibility from the 1920s and whose 'dolores forman el mas vívido y sorprendente contraste con la esplendorosa realidad que hoy vive Cuba' (ibid.). For Roig, at least, Cuba's rite of passage was practically complete.

Just as Vitier's conception of a historical hiatus in which Cuba could reconnect with stimulating *intrascendencia* was challenged by an experienced observer such as Roig, so his proposition of the ascendancy of poetry over history was attacked with equal vehemence by more callow analyst-authors. For young poets such as Heberto Padilla, Antón Arrufat and José Baragaño, the condemnation of history was intolerable in an age of historical promises come true. What Cuba required, they claimed, was not a 'testimonio poético' in which *inconsecuencia* 'puede adquirir sentido como síntoma del ser o del destino' (Vitier 1958: 484), but empirical *imágenes* that would once again turn to the muse of transcendental events for inspiration:

> Una poesía de sustancia humana, una poesía que se realice en la historia, en el tiempo histórico humano … el momento que vive la Isla es de tal manera estelar, que nuestra toma de conciencia del destino hacia el que apuntamos es tan profunda, luminosa que, la poesía en su dimensión más auténtica, nos sorprende con un gesto invasor. (unnamed author, 'Refutación a Vitier', *Ciclón* 1959: 67)

From this perspective of social hyper-consciousness and militant commitment, Vitier's and the *Origenistas*' 'desconfianza de la historia' was execrable (Chiampi, in Lezama Lima 1993b: 13). In a late 1959 edition of *Lunes de Revolución*, Padilla, the poetic Robespierre of the period, described the imaginative reign of *Orígenes*, not as the harbinger of a collective rebirth 'en la dolorosa reducción del yo a la nada y de ésta a un nacimiento', as Lezama Lima had envisaged (*Orígenes* 1:1, 7), but as a terrible 'zona de penumbras, de confusión, de gratuidad donde quedó estancada nuestra poesía' (Padilla 1959a: 5). Turning their own *intrascendencia* against them, Padilla claimed that a poetic tradition posited as the antithesis of history could make no indelible mark on Cuban self-cognition and would thus disappear (along with its authors) without a trace:

> ¿Qué queda, pues, de *Orígenes*? ¿Dónde está el gran libro de esa generación? […]. No hay nada […]. Sin clarividencia para entender su realidad,

víctimas de un drama nacional que los rebasaba, impotentes para establecer
profundas resistencias, diez poetas se reunieron para edificar y modelar una
muerte sin grandeza. (1959a: 5)

After concluding his six-hundred page examination of *Lo cubano en la
poesía* with the assertion that 'la poesía nos cura de la historia y nos permite
acercarnos a la sombra del umbral' (1958: 585), Vitier soon underwent his own
Revolutionary epiphany. What was an inconclusive and shadowy threshold
in 1957, that led neither onwards nor back but rather suspended animation
in a liminal *umbral*, became for Vitier (as for his antagonists) a landmark to
be left behind, a betwixt-and-between hiatus dissolved and resolved by the
revelation of Revolution. His ficto-autobiographical *De Peña Pobre* finds alter
ego Kuntius gathering with old friends to usher 1958 out.[1] Although from
the pen of the former champion of the 'tiempo ahistórico' (Vitier 1958: 485),
Kuntius is irked by the threshold in which time 'le pareció como detenido,
fuera del tiempo, exactamente en el punto que no era ya el año viejo ni todavía
el año nuevo' (Vitier 1990: 129). Far from an innervating arrest of momentum
to allow Cuba's *sensibilidad* to contemplate its own *ingravidez*, Vitier now
portrays the indeterminate moments of *el fin de año* in terms not dissimilar to
those of the most ardent historicist poets (such as Padilla):

> Despedirse para volverse a recibir y a despedir eternamente […]. Sensación
> de estar todos muertos en el tránsito astronómico del año […]. La tristeza,
> aquella noche, de un horror que empezaba a girar sobre sí mismo como una
> tuerca desgastada, ya inservible. (128–9)

In this new and revolutionary reflection, however, the *sombra* of this *umbral* is
soon to be dispelled and the levity of Cuban identity infilled with the gravity
of 1 January's epiphanic dawn:

> Le parecía asistir, por fin, al cumplimiento de las profecías poéticas y
> heroicas de la patria, tantas veces frustradas; a la encarnación de la justicia
> […]. Sentía la próxima entrada de Fidel y su columna invasora, precedida ya
> por las columnas del Che y de Camilo, como la entrada de todos los héroes y
> mártires que no habían podido ver el triunfo de su causa: la causa de Cuba,
> de Martí, de "los pobres de la tierra" en la isla ensangrentada, deformada y
> explotada. (145)

---

[1] Although transporting the readers to the 1958/1959 *umbral*, *De Peña Pobre* was not
published until 1978 and is clearly influenced by the intervening two decades of Revolutionary
(and reaggregationist) discourse.

Once the spokesman for *lo fragmentario* at the core of *cubanía*, Vitier had been persuaded by the condensation of historical substance around Castro and the *rebeldes*. Far from rejecting suggestions that he and his fellow *Origenistas* had been smothered by their own *intrascendencia*, Vitier rather seemed retrospectively to accept the acerbic criticism and embark upon a painful individual *examen de conciencia* leading to a self-critical contrition: 'pero él, ¿qué había hecho por su patria? Sentir, pensar, sufrir. Poemas, ensayos, estudios, libros, libros' (ibid.). This one-time liminalist seems even to go beyond a mere act of contrition and move towards an unflinching exorcism of his *letrado* soul. But as we shall see, not all those who had celebrated the inherent *intrascendencia* of the Cuban condition were prepared to adopt this repentant tone of self-chastisement.

Angelic Fidel

An undoubtable influence on those former sceptics who made a leap of revolutionary faith was Fidel. Although his (mis)adventures at Moncada and on *Granma* were retrospectively portrayed as visionary acts of calculated heroism, in 1953 and 1957 (as we have seen), Castro's derring-do seemed condemned to catastrophe; his closest resonance with Martí seemed to be an inability to convert rhetorical zeal into tactical success. But when the cars converging on Moncada and the overloaded boat stuck in the mud of Niqueros became the victory march sweeping euphorically across the island from Santiago, Fidel's transition from tragedy to triumph seemed complete. Commentary on the rebel leader in those early days ranged from sober admiration to outright adulation. Ángel del Cerro, for example, began his article on the July 1959 gathering of farmers in Havana in support of agrarian reform by comparing the *guajiros* to 'ovejas que no tenían pastor' and Fidel to the dependable shepherd who 'los recibió y comenzó a enseñarles muchas cosas' (1959: 56). From the sale of the first lock cut from Fidel's hair after he came down from the mountains (reminiscent of the trade in religious relics), to the apocryphal alighting of the doves of peace on his shoulder during a speech in Havana's main military barracks, 1959 witnessed the transmogrification of Castro the man into the Fidel the demigod: 'Todos querían verlo, todos querían llevar en sus pupilas la visión del hombre que había dejado de ser figura humana para entrar en la leyenda, para convertirse en cíclope, en gigante, en mito' (*Bohemia* 1959b: 92). This secular sanctification has been extensively examined,[2] but the interest for this study is specific. If Castro was indeed a Messiah for the new Cuba, his was

---

2   See Rojas's study of the messianism of this period (and of earlier and subsequent periods) in *Tumbas sin sosiego* (2006: 51–92).

a second coming; from paying homage to the ideological and moral legacy of Martí in 1953, Castro had now donned the apostolic mantle himself:

> Occasionally after years of struggle and disappointment, and for many reasons, peoples decide to place their collective willpower in the hands of a single man. Ever since the death of Martí, the Cubans had been searching for such an individual. Now they believed they had found one. (Thomas 2001: 697)

In effect, Castro's entrance into Havana marked both the victory of his military campaign against Batista and his triumph in the *ideario martiano* debate. Whereas in 1953 analyst-authors such as Ortiz, Mañach and Ichaso had been able to read across the panegyrics and posit an alternative, more nuanced, less strident Martí, victory had charged Castro's exegesis with a seemingly indisputable authority: history had not only 'absolved' the rebel leader, but had elevated his reading of Martí and his interpretation of Cuba's ideal *sensibilidad* to the almost unassailable hermeneutic high ground. As Kapcia suggests, this *cubanía revolucionaria* began to condense around the ideals of agrarianism, culturalism, heroism in the face of seemingly insurmountable odds (embodied in the idea of Cuba as a plucky David squaring up to antagonistic offshore Goliaths), and the notion of a 'new man' (Kapcia 2000: 125). Most suggestive for this study is the underlying emphasis on an unwavering faith in human perfectibility and the ability of the *rebeldes* to lead Cubans towards it. Hence, the apostolic archetype that Castro embodied offered both an earthly salvation from palpable enemies and a psychological liberation of the *conciencia colectiva* from the devil of indecisiveness and the perennial 'nadar entre dos aguas' (Roa 1969: 27) that had so enraged previous disciples of radical creeds:

> Aquí hay un hombre que ha tenido fe en sí mismo y en su idea, que contagió primero de esa fe a sus más cercanos colaboradores, que la imprimió al movimiento histórico que fundara, que la irradió progresivamente a los demás grupos y tendencias que luchaban en la Revolución […] que ha terminado incorporando a todo el pueblo de Cuba, por un proceso de contagio masivo. (del Cerro 1959: 57)

In this sense, Fidel has become a vaccine against the betwixt-and-between flux that others had perceived as vital to *cubanía*. Drawing inspiration from the prelapsarian past of the independence wars and with his gaze fixed firmly on the future, Castro now demanded that history absolve itself by purifying itself, by fulfilling his genealogical prophesy of 1953 and uniting the *padres de la patria* with *la generación del centenario* to thus extirpate Republican deviations from Cuba's story of selfhood. From this perspective, Fidel appears as a prophet of historical gravity, collective resolve and teleological momentum away from an unsatisfactory past and towards a truly transcendental future. Where Ortiz and Mañach had seen an acceptance of frustration and fallibility and a lingering in an inexorable margin between 'preocupación' and 'esperanza' as the lodestone of Martí's 'libertad sin ira', Castro rather resembled a post-liminal man, immunised against ambiguity, far beyond flux, tempered by the trials of the rite of passage and determined never to return (Mañach 1953b: 59). In the events, attitudes and appetites of 1959–60, therefore, can be read a concerted assault on the kind of 'ambivalence and unset definition' so typical of the limen (Dening 1997: 2).

Despite admiration for, and public adulation of, *el comandante*'s revolutionary project and the promise of a truly transcendental step forward in the island's history, not all analyst-authors saw the conclusion to Cuba's story of selfhood as so imminent. Whilst Vitier may have seen the latest acts of super-human heroism as finally breaking the cycle of 'sacrificio–tiranía–sacrificio' (1958: 489), others were not convinced. One of the Republic's leading historians, Herminio Portell Vilá (in a February 1959 *Bohemia* article entitled 'Tesis sobre el suicidio en la historia política de Cuba'), acknowledges the ideological empathy between the most outstanding *independentistas* and Castro, but sees in this the potential for great tragedy. Spurning facile hagiography of past heroes, and in echo of Zambrano's *martiano* article of 1953, Portell Vilá rather complains of the triumph of imprudence over long-term vision during the nineteenth century and beyond, claiming that the deaths in battle of Carlos Manuel de Céspedes, Ignacio Agramonte and Antonio Maceo 'no tienen otra explicación sino una especie de resignación fatalista con lo peor que pudiera ocurrirle, equivalente a un suicidio' (1959b: 69). And far from an example of infallible faith to be enshrined within archetypal *sensibilidad*, Portell Vilá portrays Martí's immolation at Dos Ríos (at a critical moment of the independence campaign) as a lamentable faltering of faith: 'Hay motivos para pensar que Martí había perdido el entusiasmo por vivir, que se arriesgó más de lo que debía y que así perdió la vida' (ibid.). Thus refusing to idealise even pre-independence history, Portell Vilá imagines an island in which the *padres de la patria* had lived on to become the *abuelos* of a truly different kind of Cuba. But this was no idle hypothetical daydream. Portell Vilá agrees that 1959 marked a historical schism, but argues this would not lead to the emergence of more integral collective identity until the suicidal bravery that had cost Cuba so many sons and daughters was added to the nihilistic pyre. Far from commending Castro's emulation of (or reincarnation as) Martí, the historian warns that this rebirth could be a tragic stillbirth:

Hay abundantes señales de que el doctor Fidel Castro está al borde de vivir el complejo nacional del suicidio en la evolución histórica del pueblo cubano [...]. Ya hasta habla de la posibilidad de que él pueda desaparecer por causas naturales o por el crimen político, y dice que se han tomado las disposiciones adecuadas para que su obra revolucionaria no se pierda, cosa esta que también pensaron Céspedes, Agramonte, Martí, Maceo, Guiteras y Chibás; pero sin que el éxito les acompañase en sus planes. (113)

In uncompromising counterpoint with one of the most sanctified codes of Castro's brand of self-sacrificial *sensibilidad*, and in unmediated condemnation of the derring-do of this, and previous, rebellious ages, Portell Vilá posits moderation and self-restraint as the true secrets of transcendentalism:

La letra del Himno Nacional, al proclamar que **morir por la Patria es vivir**, [...] estaba dando la consigna de que éso es, precisamente, lo que debe hacer todo cubano para serlo a plenitud. VIVIR PARA ELLA es lo verdaderamente trascendental del dirigente. (69; emphasis in the original)

Although Mañach praises Castro's audacity, like Portell Vilá he nevertheless reserves the right to stand at a critical distance from the Revolutionary creed and remain on the ideological frontier between conviction and scepticism that he had occupied since the 1920s. His April 1959 article in *Diario de la Marina*, 'El ángel de Fidel', is a paradigmatic contribution to the disputed national narrative at the time. The article recounts a late-night discussion with 'el más conservador' of Mañach's acquaintances about the revolutionary changes taking place on the island. After attempting to preserve the amicability of the exchange, Mañach finally feels forced to declare his adamant support for Castro and the new government, despite the heavy-handedness of some of their initial proclamations and acts:

Ya no tengo más remedio que ser explícito. Te diré. Nos hemos pasado la vida (al menos me la he pasado yo, como escritor público) pidiendo una honda y total rectificación de la vida cubana. Más de una vez escribí que ésto necesitaba "una cura de caballo", "una cura de sal y vinagre". Y ahora que éso ha llegado, me parece de canijos asustarse [...]. Una revolución democrática como ésta no es cosa que pueda hacerse sin desquiciamientos, sin desajustes, sin tanteos, sin riesgos más o menos graves. (1959c: unpaginated proof)

In this, arch-liminalist Mañach seems to have made a determined conversion to the reaggregationist cause, to have purged (like Vitier) his former ambivalence about the perfectibility of the Cuban condition with his very own 'cura de caballo'. But he then lets the 'amigo' speak. Or could it in fact be Mañach himself placing his contrapuntal opinions in the mouth of a convenient third-person, an alter ego on the epistemological margin, just as he had done in 1927 with his friend Luján? The similarities between the two are notable: Luján is a law clerk, the 'amigo' 'un abogado de grandes empresas'; Luján's percipience is matched by the lawyer's 'factura mental muy sólida'; Luján, 'el último criollo', is met and matched by this new companion whose 'espíritu cubano sobrio' is never in doubt (Mañach 1959c: unpaginated proof). Alter ego or not, this article gives voice to those Cubans neither wholly hostile nor completely convinced by the beatification of the Revolution and its leader:

> Este muchacho me tiene consternado. Hay momentos, muchos momentos, como esta noche, en que le escucho con algo mas que simpatía: con una profunda emoción. Se le ve tan sincero, tan férvido, tan entregado a su causa, tan manifiestamente animado de un anhelo de justicia, de dignidad y de bienestar para todos, que parece realmente un milagro humano ... Sí, un milagro ... cubano. Algo como Martí. Pero ... (ibid.)

The final word encapsulates the sense of suspension and uneasy reserve that runs through the entire article. Although impressed by Castro's heroic assault on corrupt executive authority, the *abogado* doubts his administrative skills in the 'orden económico'; although admiring the *rebeldes'* aspirations, Mañach's 'friend' asks himself whether they were not in fact 'construyendo peligrosa-mente una utopía sobre premisas hijas de su deseo más que de la realidad'; although inspired by Fidel's zeal, the *abogado* was deeply suspicious of the 'trance casi hipnótico en que sus palabras lo ponen a uno' (ibid.). Even when reclaiming the authorial voice once more, Mañach's opinions are suddenly riddled with ambiguity. The 'ángel de Fidel' of the title could refer either to an extraordinary mission or an unearthly ability to seduce. And although Mañach certainly portrays Castro with phantasmagorical images befitting a celestial being, an 'ángel dialéctica y hasta de espada flamígera, como los del paraíso', what that archangel's flaming sword has been unable to dispel is ambivalence and deep-seated doubt: 'Se está, a lo peor, lleno de aprensiones. Que si los fusilamientos; que si las pobres viudas afectadas por la rebaja de los alquileres; que si el comunismo; que si una tendencia a calificar de reaccionarios a cuantos disientan' (ibid.). Mañach's rhetoric makes every opinion inconclusive. And so, unlike Vitier, this analyst-author doesn't seek to exorcise his lettered self or swap his pen for the 'espada flamígera' of Revolutionary zeal, but rather deploys all his rhetorical abilities to leave an interstice of ambivalence open and show that analysts are as important as authors of the national narrative.

Even amidst his most ardent call for a purge of Cuban *sensibilidad* with 'sal y vinagre', Mañach obliquely defends the *activismo–letrado* pact. As an 'escritor público' Mañach suggests that the *letrados* are just as 'compenetrados' with *el pueblo* as the *guerrilleros*, that the *lex* and text of their interpretation of *civitas* is wholly *publicus* and that out of this dialogue between utter determination and lingering doubt a true *res publica* or common good can emerge. In 'El ángel de Fidel', therefore, Mañach's lexis actually remains in the subjunctive 'may-be, might-be, as-if' mood of the limen (Turner, in Alexander 1991: 30). Thus, what initially seemed an adamant celebration of Castro's gift becomes an expression of irresolvable apprehension; the teleological progression away from the rite of passage and toward an integral *Cuba Libre* is suddenly arrested by doubt, the island's future frozen in a rhetorical 'What if …?' Although initially seeming to join the adulation of Castro in this 'new' Cuba he had helped engender, Mañach suddenly retreats to stand alongside his ambivalent friend in determined indecision.

Theatrical Piñera

In 1957, the Piñera of 'El viaje' had scorned the idea of teleological progress towards the rewards (or the punishments) of life. But by November 1959, this analyst-author seemed to have undergone the kind of epiphany he had denied his *viajero* (and similar to Vitier's) and wrote of gazing up at the island's Rimbaudian 'cielos delirantes' to proclaim (seemingly without irony) that: 'estamos viviendo una etapa de sagrado delirio […]. La Revolución ha apartado de nuestros ojos la imagen atroz de una Cuba despedazada, fragmentada, reemplazándola con un organismo revolucionario intacto' (1959b: 2). Like Mañach, however, Piñera's reaggregationist epiphany was incomplete and by 1960 (and the prologue to his *Teatro completo*) he had drawn back from any sense of absolute enlightenment to suggest an alternative reading of the *triunfo* of the year before. Despite continuing to refer to Castro as Cuba's 'mesías político', Piñera's evocation of the rebel leader's entry into Havana seems peculiar, if not outright iconoclastic:

> Envidio al hombre que salió desnudo por la calle, envidio a ese otro que asombró a La Habana con sus bigotes de gato, envidio al que se hizo el muerto para burlar al sacerdote, y por supuesto, a Fidel Castro entrando en La Habana. (1960: 7)

For the playwright, therefore, the victory march seems as absurd as the most clownesque figures to grace the urban stage at the end of the 1950s, making Castro not a Messiah or re-born Apostle, but the principal jester or head fool.

But this is no slur on Cuba's epic and charismatic acts and actors. Piñera joins others in welcoming the Revolution's attack on the 'frustración del ser en toda línea', but insists that transcendentalism was not to be approached with zealous faith, but rather through a revelation of its paradoxical mundanity and infinite potential for farce: 'nada como mostrar a tiempo la parte clownesca para que la parte seria quede bien a la vista' (ibid.: 8). In this Piñera joins Ortiz, Mañach, the pre-1959 Vitier and even (as we have previously suggested) the pragmatic Martí in insisting on the congenital fallibility of human (and Cuban) kind, on exposing the everymen within supposed supermen. From a liminal perspective, the epiphany that Piñera perceives did not conclude the rite of passage nor elevate the extraordinary rebels above the vicissitudes of decidedly ordinary Cuban life at the time. Rather, much like the ritual rulers in Turner's description, Cuban 'headmen' had to be prepared to receive the slights, slanders and abuse of their subordinates: 'entre nosotros un Hitler, con sus teatralerías y su wagnerismo, sería desinflado al minuto' with a well-timed 'trompetilla' (10). Just like the *viajero* sat atop the child's pram and the *banquero* in the pan, Castro should embrace absurdity and prepare to be mocked. Because for Piñera this *falta de respeto* was at the very core of Cuban *sensibilidad*: 'a mi entender un cubano se define por la sistemática ruptura con la seriedad' (ibid.). This was to be stimulated, not stymied, as it had been pivotal in preserving *sensibilidad* from total submission during the long years of frustration: 'esta resistencia hizo posible que Fidel Castro encontrara intacto a su pueblo para la gran empresa de la Revolución' (11). Here again we see a possible Sisyphean reading of Piñera's ethos: it was the stoicism of *el puebo*, as much as super-human heroism of its *líderes*, that had kept the *Cuba Libre* dream alive. The solution for Piñera, and his contribution to the reading of the *rebeldes* so elevated above the Cuban crowd, was to counterbalance heroism with self-deprecation, hagiography with mockery, and to insist that even Messiahs recognise and respect 'el clown que lleva dentro' (8).

A purge of the *conciencia colectiva*?

In 1959, as in 1933, many of the worst perpetrators of crimes against Cuba were able to flee the island, but many lesser *batistianos* were rounded up. Despite the feeling of temporal and ethical rupture and the sense that the most lamentable episodes of Cuba's collective history would finally be left behind, the similarities between the *machadato* and the *batistato*, and the popular reaction to the demise of both, are striking. Under Batista's regime (as under Machado's) violence reached aberrant extremes, with around 20,000 Cubans killed between 1952 and 1959. Despite Castro's 1953 attempt to erase the *machadato* from the national narrative (in *La historia me absolverá*), the

Damoclean sword of cyclical violence seemed to swing over the island again, and an 'acumulación de tánatos' seemed about to be released in 1959 as it had in 1933 (Cabrera Infante 1992: 182). *Bohemia*'s early January edition, for example, recounted how six members of Batista's secret police were lynched on the outskirts of Santa Clara, and how an enraged mob gathered outside a Pinar del Río police station to demand the blood of the *batistianos* held within.

There are critical differences between the two periods, however. In 1933, Havana (and other cities) witnessed several days of bloodshed in which anyone with a grudge and a gun (or a machete, or even a paving slab, as we have seen) could administer their own brand of justice on the city's anarchic streets. In 1959, the *rebeldes* stepped into a remarkably similar scenario and immediately monopolised the administration of justice. When *Bohemia* described popular anger in Pinar del Río and elsewhere, it was clear that this would be channelled and hence controlled by the new authorities:

> Las voces se alzan, se crispan los puños, se llenan de ira los ojos [...]. Pero allá dentro, los esbirros pueden estar seguros, nadie les golpeará, nadie les torturará, ni siquiera les escupirán al rostro tanto odio y tanto desprecio como ellos hicieron nacer en el pecho de cien, de mil, de varios millares de ciudadanos. (Cabrera 1959b: 28)

The sense of schism with a pernicious past was therefore restored; 1959 promised to quell the violence of the *batistato* and finally sheathe the sword of Damocles:

> A pesar de los muchos atropellos y vejámenes que han sufrido los revolucionarios en su carne y en su espíritu, no les anima un propósito revanchista. No quieren ellos castigar el crimen con el crimen, sino con la ley [...]. Fidel Castro ha dicho [...] que la revolución podrá permitirse el lujo de ser generosa porque hará justicia y la justicia, por muy rigurosa que sea, es incompatible con la venganza. (*Bohemia* 1959b: 29)

This did not mean that the implementation of Revolutionary justice would be bloodless, with approximately two hundred ex-officials being executed by 20 January 1959 (Thomas 2001: 726). But this apparent purge can be read liminally. By claiming authority over the prosecution and punishment of all criminals from the previous regime, the new government effectively imposed order on a situation that could have collapsed into chaos and violent excess. By regulating revenge, the Revolution sought to dissipate aberration by increasing organisation. In effect, revolutionary justice became an antidote to the *dérèglement de tous les sens* whose persistence beyond the fall of Machado in 1933 we examined in Chapter 3:

> El tránsito de una situación de oprobio a una situación de decoro se ha realizado en la mínima trepidación posible gracias al orden impuesto desde los primeros instantes por las milicias revolucionarias y a la cálida exhortación de todos los jefes para que nadie se entregue a la venganza o al desbordamiento de sus pasiones. (*Bohemia* 1959b: 29)

Thus, the trial and execution of *batistiano* criminals can be read as another example of the quest for the kind of catharsis that stimulates progression through the rite of passage. And in 1959, to a much greater degree than in 1933, this catharsis was charged with the kind of didactic exposure to extremes that Aristotle had advocated. So whilst the notorious trials carried out in a Havana sports stadium 'filled with a furious and yelling crowd' and described by one of the defendants as a 'Roman circus' produced disquiet overseas, they can be read as a liminal rite, as the extirpation of execrable individuals and the collective memories associated with them to prepare Cuba and its *sensibilidad* for post-rite of passage reaggregation (Thomas 2001: 738). This in part explains the vitriolic reaction by the Cuban public and press to any external criticism of their intimate and introspective affairs, with *Bohemia* asserting in January 1959 that the Cuban people had 'crecido demasiado en conciencia y en responsabilidad para que puedan oír sin recelo ciertas reprehensiones y advertencias sobre el modo de conducir sus asuntos y sentenciar sus procesos internos' (1959b: 29).

For Mañach, an increasingly vocal (and increasingly isolated) critic of aspects of the Revolutionary re-inscription of the national narrative, the physical purge of pernicious individuals as a kind of 'profilaxis social' could have short-term strategic merit in satisfying 'el resentimiento, la indignación, la furia' of a *pueblo* on the cusp of a new beginning, but early in 1959 he had begun to dispute the idea that the protracted punishment of *batistato* criminals could lead to ever-increasing integrity and psycho-social well-being:

> ¿No ha llegado el momento de considerar que esa necesidad ha sido suficientemente satisfecha […]? ¿No sería prudente, elevado, sano para la conciencia pública cubana y deferente a la opinión extranjera – que no por extranjera ha de desdeñarse – que las sanciones pendientes se encauzasen por vías penales menos extremas? (1959a: unpaginated proof)

Although earlier jibes about his 'posición contemplativa y cauta' had seemed to goad Mañach into radical action (Roa 1969: 27), in 1959 he stoutly defended his call for balance and painted a foreboding picture of continuity beyond the schism of 1 January 1959 if such measure were lacking:

> La sanción excesiva es siempre generadora de nuevos estragos […]. No vacilo en pedir – aunque muchos se lo tengan por pusilanimidad – que se acabe con la sangre, para que la sangre, que es siempre un maligno bebidizo, no acabe con nuestra conciencia. (1959b: unpaginated proof)

By the early 1960s, therefore, one of the most prominent and influential analyst-authors of the Cuban national narrative since the early 1920s began to distance himself from the theory and practice of Revolutionary *cubanía*. He was not to be the only one.

The *rebeldes* ultimately seemed to agree, although perhaps due more to external rather than Mañach-type internal pressure. From the guerrilla campaign in the Sierra Maestra, Castro and his commanders had demonstrated an acute awareness of the importance of international public opinion,[3] and so by February 1959 Fidel drew back from the administration of justice in the public arena, informing foreign correspondents at a news conference that the need for, and use of, the death penalty was waning: 'a los culpables se les aplicarán otras penas mediante un procedimiento cuidadoso' (*Bohemia* 1959d: 103). This is not to say that catharsis was curtailed. After the initial extirpation of aberrant individuals, there was a turn towards what could be described as a purge of ideas. And an illuminating example of this is to be found in the 1960 demise of Cuba's oldest newspaper, *Diario de la Marina*.

The death of *Diario*

Founded on 1 April 1844, *Diario de la Marina* always seemed to side with Goliath in Cuba's long fight for freedom. The first owner, Isidoro Araújo Alcalde, not only vilified Narciso López's filibustering from the pages of his paper, but also enlisted in the *voluntario* brigade that fought the *independentistas* with greater viciousness than the Spanish regulars.[4] During the 1895–98 war, *Diario* welcomed the death of General Antonio Maceo and even lambasted the Apostle Martí as 'el fanático incurable tenazmente adherido a sus absurdos ideales' (in Ortega 1959: 6). Despite these slurs on the island's

---

[3] 'Che' Guevara allegedly admitted that the presence of a friendly US journalist in the Sierra 'was more important for us than a military victory' (Thomas 2001: 698).

[4] Narciso López was a general in the Spanish army who had fought against Bolívar in Venezuela before being posted to Cuba *siempre fiel*. In the mid-nineteenth century López led several attempts to instigate a rebellion in Cuba as a pretext for annexation by the United States. He was eventually captured by the Spanish and garroted in 1851.

most heroic Davids, the paper survived the end of empire and flourished into the Republic. For some commentators, however, independence for the island had done nothing to alter *Diario*'s anti-Cuban ways: 'José I. Rivero se puso a las órdenes de Batista en plena huelga de marzo 1935, como su padre se había puesto a las órdenes de Weyler, y su hijo se pone hoy a las órdenes de la contrarrevolución' (Ortega 1959: 7).

By early 1960, the paper's discrepancies with the Revolution and its supporters (particularly among its own staff) produced an inevitable collision. Initially, the printers had taken to including inserts, or *coletillas*, within the newspaper criticising the editorial line.[5] In response, *Diario* attempted to marshal support for proprietor 'Pepín' Rivero in a badly handled petition that developed into a lock-out of the *coletilla* writers, which in turn provoked the occupation of the paper's offices by many of the backroom staff. In just a few spring days of 1960, *Diario de la Marina*'s 128-year trajectory was brought to an abrupt end.

The most interesting aspect of the fate of *Diario de la Marina* for this study is not its alleged crimes, but the ritual that marked its passing. The paper was not simply closed; it was theatrically mourned and buried at the foot of Havana University's *escalinata* accompanied by funereal dirges from the Rebel Army band and *choteo*-fuelled 'elegies' by some of its most vehement foes: 'Se procedió al entierro del órgano de anti-cubanismo, encerrado simbólicamente dentro de un féretro negro, mientras la multitud procedía a entonar cánticos alegóricos y pronunciaba frases de subido sentido patriótico' (*La Calle* 1960c: 3). As in the Revolutionary trials in the sports arena, this was Aristotelian catharsis at its most potent. Although the paper's own workers filled the ranks of the funeral procession, the event was depicted as a sudden upsurge of anti-*Diario* sentiment from the whole *pueblo* with 'estudiantes de todos los centros docentes, obreros, campesinos cercanos a la capital, profesionales, pequeños comerciantes, todo lo que constituye el nervio vital de la nación' joining in (ibid.). Despite this heterogeneous participation, all were united in the euphoria of what *La Calle* called a 'Carnaval Revolucionario', or what Turner would describe as a *dérèglement* of the senses, an outpouring of riotous emotion to liberate pent-up energy and previously suppressed frustration: 'Como enfermo a que le han extirpado un tumor maligno, el pueblo de Cuba sonrió, jubiloso, descansado. No se publicaría más el *Diario de la Marina*' (ibid.).

But this was not the kind of solemn socio-cultural surgery advocated at previous turning points or put into practice in the *fusilamientos*; the death and burial of *Diario* was a very ludic kind of catharsis indeed. So unlike

---

5   For an insightful study of these rebellious editorial additions, see Ortega 1989.

in other notable examples of mass participation during this initial phase of Revolutionary rule (such as the Milicias Nacionales Revolucionarias and the literacy campaign[6]), and in contrast to the new government's monopolisation of post-war justice, this joyous dance through the streets of Havana bearing an effigy of a vilified past was anything but ordered or structured. In contrast to more martial *brigadas* marching through the city in 1959–60, in *Diario*'s funeral procession liminal theatre and prophylactic play were paramount, with *La Calle* taking obvious delight in describing one of the highlights of the burial:

> Un espectáculo simpático se produjo cuando varios jóvenes realizaron una hipotética invasión al frente de la cual aparecía el capitán Aureliano Sánchez Arango. En este grupo de supuestos invasores iban personas disfrazadas de Trujillo, Pedraza, Lojendio, Ugalde Carrillo y otros. (1960c: 3.)

For Turner, this kind of rambunctious role-play is actually typical in the rite of passage in which 'we have an overdose of order, and want to let off steam […], or because we have something to learn through being disorderly' (1982: 28). Whereas order had neutralised excess in the physical purging of criminal elements from the *ancien régime*, the extirpation of the ideology represented by *Diario* could not help succumbing to jubilant disarray, to what Piñera had described as 'la parte clownesca' of transcendental change, to the spirit of what Carlos Franqui called 'Fiesta. Pachanga. Libertad […]. Una forma cubana de cambiar la vida' (1981: 130). Although an act of cultural extirpation, therefore, this march still bears the hallmarks of ludic liminality. This playfulness would not always be so welcomed.

Despite its spontaneity and fun, the burial of *Diario de la Marina* had a clear and clearly teleological intent: to channel liminal exuberance towards a sense of solidarity behind a common cause: 'Con motivo del entierro de 'la decrépita' se han producido incontables adhesiones de instituciones profesionales, cívicas, estudiantiles y obreras, que muestran su absoluta identificación con el Gobierno Revolucionario' (*La Calle* 1960c: 3). From the ambiguous introspection of previous rites of passage, in which collective *sensibilidad* was pulled between the disparate poles of elusive purity and unabashed fallibility, elderly circumspection and youthful revolt, hagiography and pragmatism, the turning point of 1959–60 seemed intent on instilling 'absolute identification' with an all-encompassing and universally appealing

---

6   The Milicias were established in October 1959 (participation would eventually become compulsory). The literacy campaign ran from 1959 to late 1961 (principally in rural areas) and saw literacy rates rise by around 20% (to *c*. 95% of the adult population).

motif: *Revolución*. Hence, although riotous and impromptu, the burial of *Diario de la Marina* was presented in subsequent analysis as elucidating an unquestionable resolve amongst participants and spectators alike: 'A lo largo de las aceras, en los portales y balcones por donde marchó el entierro, los habaneros exteriorizaban su alegría por la desaparición del periódico de los Riveros, con vivas continuados a la Revolución' (ibid.).

Even as the *Diario* was being ushered out of existence with an exuberance that was read as consolidating Revolutionary *sensibilidad*, some commentators raised quiet but firm voices of dissent. Was this cathartic purging of ideas (alongside the extirpation of bad blood) actually necessary, some asked? Must the Revolution seek to expel any and all dissenting voices beyond the walls of the *ciudad letrada* and *revolucionaria*? Although by May 1960 *La Calle* was describing the demise of the *Diario* as 'un acto de justicia, largamente esperado' (ibid.: 3), only four months earlier it had wondered whether 'la prensa reaccionaria' should not in fact be tolerated within a new and self-confident Revolutionary reality wherein to limit the liberty of the press was 'reconocerlos a nuestros enemigos una vigencia y una influencia que no tienen' (1960a: 4). Although not doubting the malicious past and present intent of the *Diario*, at the beginning of 1960 *La Calle* had been completely confident of the *pueblo*'s ability for fend for itself without the need for an ideological clean sweep: 'No puede ser la tarea del Gobierno Revolucionario la de "proteger" al pueblo contra "ideas peligrosas" ' (ibid.). In contrast to its subsequent resolve, this early edition of *La Calle* worried that ideological 'absolutismo' would be a Trojan horse within the Revolutionary *ciudad*: 'Nunca debemos olvidar que una revolución lo mismo se puede destrozar desde adentro que llegar a aplastar desde afuera. ¡Generalmente la destrucción que se hace desde adentro surge bajo el pretexto de salvar al revolución de sus enemigos exteriores!' (ibid.).

Nihil admirari ... again

In 1959, as in 1927, some Cuban thinkers inspired by the radical turning of the socio-political tide envisioned a similar schism within the national narrative and thus called for a prophylactic dose of youthful nihilism to 'get rid of the weight of dead men's thoughts' (Lewis 1965: 13 & 5). In the sole 1959 edition of *Ciclón*, for example, José Rodríguez Feo drew up a blacklist of writers worthy of collective contempt that included some of the leading intellectuals of the previous generation such as Ichaso, Salvador Bueno, Miguel Chacón y Calvo, Medardo Vitier, Emeterio Santovenia and even Mr Cuba himself, Fernando Ortiz. For many amongst the cultural vanguard of 1959, these analyst-authors were incongruous because they were old. For Kapcia, youth was one of a triumvirate of pivotal myths underpinning the Revolutionary project from the time of the Moncada disaster:

> The image of the Revolution as an essentially youth-led and youth-oriented process was integral from the outset – from the inherent generationalism of the 1950s, and from the evident youthfulness of the guerrillas, together with the underlying and explicit references to renewal and a 'new Cuba'. (2000: 202)

To insist on youth as a congenital characteristic of *cubanía* was to exclude paragon intellectuals from ongoing authorship of the national narrative. Even when some of the *viejos* demonstrated critical distance from past generations and the *fisonomía* of a decadent age, there could be no guaranteed crossing to the other side of the frontier between *antes* and *ahora*. In 1959, however (as at turning points from 1923 to 1957), there was a crime more capital than age alone. At a time when the extraordinary deeds of a group of 'supermen' had eliminated ennui with dynamism, kick-started historical momentum, and transformed the effervescence of Cuban identity into a palpable essence, the deadliest sin was not the unerasable blemish of age, but indecision, passivity and flux, the 'nadar entre dos aguas' of liminality (Roa 1969: 27). Rodríguez Feo did not vilify those on his blacklist simply because of their age, but because of their lack of activism against (or at least their neutrality before) the recently removed regime and concomitant 'falta de apoyo a la causa revolucionaria' (1959: unpaginated insert). What he proposed was in effect the exorcism of the most most 'passive' (and hence the most 'sinful') analyst-authors in order to save Cuba's cultural soul in these new and Revolutionary times: 'Todos estamos en el deber ineludible de señalar a los culpables para que no se nos vengan a tildar de "neutrales" de la cultura' (ibid.).

And no one, it seemed, was above criticism. In *Bohemia*'s 12 July 1959 edition, Agustín Tamargo compared unfavourably Ortiz's political participation in crisis times with that of Varona during the *machadato*, seeing only reprehensible indifference from so-called Mr Cuba:

> En 1933, casi en los umbrales de la muerte, el Maestro Enrique José Varona se reunía con los estudiantes universitarios. Los escuchaba. Los alentaba. ¡Qué diferencia con este buen señor Fernando Ortiz, encerrado en una concha de indiferencia durante los siete años en que el batistato desangró a la juventud cubana! Ortiz no recibe a nadie. No quiere ver a nadie. La vieja cultura deserta. (1959a: 61)

Mañach fared little better. The feud between this analyst-author and the Revolution was by no means inevitable. From the early 1950s, Mañach had consistently praised Castro, despite the ire of the *batistato* authorities. One biographer claims that the 26 of July Movement had such confidence in Mañach that they entrusted him with the edition of their 'manifesto' (and the echoes of his 'active' 1933 participation with the ABC are undeniable): 'La confianza de los revolucionarios en Mañach los llevó a depositar en sus manos el documento de Fidel Castro 'La historia me absolverá'. Casi nadie sabe que fue Mañach quien revisó las pruebas de imprenta y corrigió el estilo' (Baeza Flores: undated and unpaginated). 1 January 1959 found Mañach in Madrid, but he returned to Cuba in February to take up his post as Professor of Philosophy at the University of Havana. He had hardly arrived when the attacks from the new generation of *vanguardistas* began. Despite his demonstrable and active support for the Revolution, Padilla rounded on what he saw as Mañach's congenital moderation: 'el pensamiento del antaño revolucionario de la *revista de avance* ha carecido, durante largos años, de violencia revolucionaria' (1959b: 15). For Padilla (pre-empting Castro, as we shall see), the choice facing politicians, writers and the entire Cuban *pueblo* was clear: 'o se está con la Revolución – es decir, con todo lo que existe de genuinamente cubano y por ende, muy universal – o se está contra la Revolución' (ibid.). For Padilla, Mañach's early 1960 televised defence of *Diario de la Marina* definitively demonstrated that he was either *contra* or, what was perhaps even worse, *ambivalente*:

> Cuando en nuestras adolescencias queríamos designar esa zona intermedia de opinión que nuestro pueblo ha definido como "estar en la cerca", nos gritábamos "eres un Mañach". Y lo tomábamos a la diabla, sin otorgarle crédito sustancial, como una diatriba que las generaciones literarias inventan para mixtificar o enardecerse; pero Mañach ha hecho suyo el estigma. El rostro enjuto, pálido que vimos en las pantallas de televisión volvíendose hacia Fidel para intentar su defensa del Diario, entregó esa noche sus últimas armas. Y fue un Mañach inmemorable. ¡Su tribuna es la cerca! (ibid.)

The anti-ambivalent (or in our terms, anti-liminal) sentiment couldn't be clearer here. Analyst-authors would no longer be allowed to revel in their hyphenated contributions to Cuban *sensibilidad*; the balanced, pragmatic, oblique and liminal inscriptions of the national narrative were to be replaced 'absolutely' by the kind of 'violencia revolucionaria' that Padilla so praised.

The Old Guard's defence

Despite this violent attack on their alleged accommodation 'on the fence' of Cuban civic and cultural life, the ossification of the frontier between *antes* and *ahora*, and the seemingly implacable march towards a Revolutionary conclusion to Cuba's story of selfhood, some Rip van Winkles of the 1959–60 watershed didn't succumb to obsolescence without a fight and, like Irving's hero, belied the perceived need for 'an exclusive attachment to one historical period', rather encouraging their compatriots to 'remember the conditions, cultural attitudes, and characters' from pre-Revolutionary times and thus restore chronological continuity to the national narrative (Pease 1987: 15). In 'Dos Épocas' (*Bohemia*, 19 July 1959) Portell Vilá rounds on *enfant terrible* Tamargo and his criticism of Ortiz with a stern warning of the latent dangers of the myth of youth. Recognising his belligerent and self-righteous *vanguardismo*, Portell Vilá assures Tamargo that he too would soon have to defend himself against the next generation who 'no han pasado por todo lo que él ha tenido que arrancarle a la vida con lecturas y observaciones' (1959a: 88). For Portell Vilá, there is nothing novel in the Revolution's glorification of youth. From the Movimiento de Veteranos y Patriotas of 1923 to the student-appointed (and student-dethroned) *Pentarquía* of 1933, the youth of Cuba had often been credited, Portell Vilá claims, with a nobility of purpose and assuredness of action they had not always earned. For the historian, for example, one of Grau San Martín's critical mistakes in 1933 was to pay scant heed to the advice of experienced politician and lucid social analyst Fernando Ortiz: 'los "jóvenes" de entonces […] no hicieron caso y así prepararon el terreno ellos mismos para todo lo que ocurrió en los años sucesivos hasta nuestros días' (ibid.). If there was any alienation between Ortiz and the militant youth of the moment, Portell Vilá claims, '¡culpa es de la nueva actitud de los jóvenes que no tiene otra cosa que éso, la juventud que dura escaso tiempo!' (90). The ailing Ortiz agreed. In an open letter to *Bohemia*, he accepts his *años* but denies the anachronistic spirit that Tamargo ascribed him: 'Pero si soy un bisabuelo, viejo de años y de arterias, no soy **reviejío**. Estoy desde hace tiempo plantado en la juventud definitiva […] aspiro a "morir joven, pero lo más tarde posible" ' (1959b: 3). In contrast to the sanctimoniousness of Tamargo, it is rather Ortiz's linguistic playfulness and ludic *sensibilidad* that appears most youthful.

Mañach was also determined to resist the enforced obsolence of his *cubanía* ethos and the Revolutionary erasure of his forty-year contribution to the national narrative. In 'De cómo vivir en revolución' (*Bohemia*, 29 May 1960), the Mañach of the ABC and of *La historia me absolverá* offers perhaps his most pithy manifesto yet. Observing the single-minded concentration on irreversible and fast-paced change that seemed to possess collective *sensibilidad* in 1959–60, Mañach warns of what he called an 'embriaguez de carretera' that could overtake and obfuscate teleologically inspired analyst-authors:

> Resulta siempre peligroso no mirar más que de frente [...]. Se trata de una
> forma dinámica de cerrazón pre-expuesto a lo cerril. Da de sí el fanatismo,
> que se parece mucho a la ceguera. Está bien el entusiasmo; pero abierto y
> generoso. (1960a: 61)

In memory of generous Luján, but equally in communion with Vitier's (and
to extent with Piñera's) location of clear-sightedness not in the middle but at
the sides of the endless road through life, Mañach adds his own praise for
marginality and his own advocacy of liminal suspension as 'an allegory for the
possibilities of narrative itself to fashion a gap in the order of things – a gap in
which there is "room for maneuver" ' (Stewart 1996: 3). Where the youthful
Revolutionaries and their journalist acolytes rushed forwards pell-mell towards
a brighter and more conclusive future beyond the vicissitudes of a sixty-year
rite of collective passage, Mañach is content to linger in the 'arroyo', to look
forwards, but also to the side: 'Uno, con perdón sea dicho, ha querido ser
siempre hombre de camino y de paisaje' (1960a: 61). Thus, after forty years
of meditation on, and contribution to, the Cuban national narrative, Mañach's
conclusion remains inconclusive. Claiming an equally authentic ideological
lineage from Martí, Mañach sees revolution not as a sloughing off of all affin-
ities with the past, nor as an invasive socio-cultural surgery of any allegedly
passive parts of the collective corpus, but rather as what Martí had called an
'evolución constante' (ibid.). From this perspective, the secular sanctification
of Revolutionary individuals or the process they had brought into being was
not progress at all, the Revolutionary violence unleashed on those *letrados*
who had inhabited Cuba's cultural city *antes* was misguided, and the attempt
to engender a *pueblo puro* to populate a new (and irredeemably post-liminal)
period of Cuban history was shortsighted folly:

> Si por señalarlo me llaman reaccionario o contrarrevolucionario (aunque me
> duelen los dedos de escribir pidiendo para Cuba rectificaciones profundas),
> ello no me quitará el sueño. Lo sentiría sólo por Cuba y por la suerte de
> la gran oportunidad histórica que le ha agenciado el valor de los hombres
> que hicieron con el brazo lo que antes muchos preparamos con la palabra.
> (1959d: unpaginated proof)

Vilified in the press and marginalised in the public arena, Mañach retreated
into the university. But in August 1960, Article 3 of Revolutionary Law No.
859 made even that redoubt uncomfortable. As part of university reforms,
designed to ensure that 'el progreso y transformación que ha emprendido Cuba
desde el triunfo de la Revolución, encuentren en esa Universidad la cooper-
ación indispensable', the law gave the new university authorities the ability to

disponer, en los casos en que lo estime conveniente, la jubilación [...] de aquellos profesores, funcionarios, empleados y técnicos de esa Universidad que tengan más de cincuenta y cinco años de edad y hayan prestado en ella más de veinte años de servicios o tengan más de sesenta años de edad y mas de quince años de servicios. (Folleto de Divulgación Legislativa 1960: 8)

The law effectively enabled the university to replicate the uncompromising temporal and ideological frontiers being charted elsewhere and exclude any professors thought too old or too identified with the past. Revolutionary *lex* joined in the concerted campaign to radically alter Cuban *civitas* and Mañach was duly invited to retire. Although once able simultaneously to defend and attack tradition through his bi-focal anti-hero Luján, by 1959 the margin for this kind of duality had narrowed. The ubiquitous analyst-author at every turning point from the 1920s saw his determined decision never to decide about definitive Cuban *sensibilidad* turned into a cardinal crime:

> Me están poniendo en el trance de tener que reorientar una vida que ya tenía hecha, hoy, precisamente, he recibido la noticia de que me han "jubilado" a la trágala, es decir, sin yo solicitarlo [...]. Y como no soy sino profesor y escritor, y ninguna de estas actividades las puedo desenvolver hoy aquí, me veo en el caso de buscarme nuevos horizontes. (undated letter to José Ortega Spottorno; emphasis in the original)

In a last-ditch act of defiance, Mañach emulated Rip van Winkle and sought simply to survive and thus offer testimony of life before the Revolutionary episode: 'Como en la revolución francesa y en la frase de Sieyes [...] la única consigna posible parece ser DURAR' (letter of 28 April 1961 to Miguel Chacón y Calvo). Thus harried at home, Mañach left for Puerto Rico in November 1960. Not far from home yet increasingly distant from the new Cuba, Mañach's energy for assaults on the nihilistic frontier and his determination to demonstrate the survival of previous, alternative and fiercely ambivalent articulations of Cuban *sensibilidad* failed him: 'Entre mi enfermedad y estas pesadumbres espirituales, yo siento que me estoy despidiendo de mi propia vida. Le confieso que no siento interés alguno por "durar" [...]. Con melancólica serenidad, espero ya mi hora' (undated letter to M. Hernández). By June 1961 Mañach was dead.

Cubanía campesina

Whereas Mañach warned against the teleological pursuit of perfection and an ardently conclusive Cuban *sensibilidad*, others lauded the success of

the cathartic purge of Republican 'males y vicios' in every sphere. Roig de
Leuchsenring's faith in the Cuban people's resilient purity had never faltered.
Although he had witnessed the frustration of great promise from the early
1920s, by 1959 he believed that the 'diseases' of the Republic had finally been
cured:

> No hay uno solo ¡uno solo! de los males y vicios cuyos orígenes y estragos
> en las páginas anteriores se describen, al que la Revolución no haya aplicado
> remedio tan enérgico y radical que en la mayoría de los casos ya han sido
> extirpados por completo. (1959: 348)

The result, for Roig, was a change to the very physiology of Cuba's collective
sensibilidad. One of the most significant manifestations of this, in his opinion,
was the sudden sense of unity and integrity that had taken hold of Cuban
society. Where Vitier was amazed by the sudden shift from taciturnity and
mutual suspicion at the end of 1958 to the 'comunicabilidad absoluta, fluida,
rayana a veces en la incoherencia' on New Year's Day 1959 (1990: 134), Roig
de Leuchsenring talked of a tidal wave of solidarity lifting Cuba onto its crest:
'hoy vemos fundirse en esa unidad que convierte al país en verdadera nación'
(1959: 348).

One of the most potent symbols of this new unity (and an important
milestone in the shifting discourses of Cuban *sensibilidad*) was the arrival in
Havana in July 1959 of half a million peasant farmers, or *guajiros*, responding
to an invitation from then Prime Minister Castro.[7] The stated purpose of the
gathering was to allow direct participation in the discussions on agricultural
reform by some of those most affected by proposed structural change in the
countryside: 'para que los guajiros lo digan con sus propias palabras', said
Tamargo in *Bohemia*, 'para que lo griten aquí en la capital' (1959b: 61).
This participation took the form of a mass meeting on 26 July 1959 in the
Plaza Cívica (soon to be renamed as the 'Plaza del la Revolución') at which
the crowd not only had the opportunity to demonstrate their support for *la
reforma agraria* with a multitudinous brandishing of their machetes, but were
also called upon in an act of dramatic direct democracy to restore Fidel to
the prime-ministerial role he had resigned after clashing with then President
Urrutia about the reforms: 'El plebiscito estalló incontenible; alzándose
hacia la altura. Ovaciones, agitar de sombreros, brillar de machetes al sol, un
enorme "sí" haciendo estremecer el ambiente, fueron la respuesta' (*Bohemia*

---

7   Manuel Urrutia was the first president of the Revolutionary government, but resigned in
July 1959 after clashes with Castro. He was succeeded by Osvaldo Dorticós, who was succeeded
by Fidel in 1976.

1959e: 85). Fidel was reinstated, agrarian reform was approved and the mass gathering of peasants in Havana provided potent visual testament to the enormous popularity of the Revolutionary regime.[8]

This *guajiro* 'invasion' of Havana can also be read within the discursive framework of the rite of passage. Many observers have commented on the importance of the *rebeldes'* two-year isolation in the depths of the Oriente countryside for the distillation of their increasingly radical ideology. For the mainly urban (and often middle-class) guerrilla leaders who fought with Castro in the Sierra Maestra mountains, the contact with the poverty and injustice of rural Cuba was what Kapcia describes as 'a cultural shock of deep personal and long-term significance' (2000: 103). For Jean-Paul Sartre, it was not Fidel and his men who brought ideological enlightenment to the hinterland, but rather 'it was the peasants who "radicalised" the rebels' (in Torres Cuevas 2005: 119). The presence of 500,000 peasant farmers in the Cuban capital in 1959 can be interpreted as an attempt to replicate that instructive contact between *campo* and *ciudad* on a massive scale. *Bohemia* reported some success, claiming that initial urban trepidations and prejudices fell away in the face of the exemplary behaviour of their guests: 'Muchos habaneros descubrían con asombro la caballerosidad campesina. Los grupos errantes cosechaban sensaciones imborrables en los ascensores, fuentes de soda, cinematográficos, escaleras automáticas y otros artefactos emocionantes para ellos' (1959e: 69).

But the peasants' presence provoked more than simple delight at *campesino* ingenuousness. Suggestively for this study, after fifty years of intense examination of the *conciencia colectiva*, the convocation of peasants to the capital brought urban Cubans' cardinal sins of ignorance about, or disdain for, the most socially marginal (although spatially central) citizens to the fore. In the *capitalinos'* new-found compassion for the *campesinos*, *Bohemia* saw not a rediscovery of selflessness, but rather a recognition of past errors and a desperate act of contrition: 'No creas que La Habana que te acogió fue demasiado generosa contigo. Más bien estaba siendo desesperadamente generosa con ella misma' (ibid.). For Tamargo, this penance was effective and country and city could finally come together as a united Cuba, ready for the tasks ahead: 'Y cuando todo haya pasado, La Habana quedará quizás un poco más desordenada. Se habrán acabado quizás algunas existencias de víveres. Pero la conciencia de la ciudadanía resplandecerá de satisfacción por el deber cumplido. ¡Cubanos: estamos haciendo historia!' (1959b: 61). With a newly cleansed collective conscience, the perfect future was now not far away. The

---

8   There is a striking rhetorical echo, of course, between Castro's appeal to the peasants and Castells's appeal to the prisoners that we saw in Chapter 3.

guajiro presence in Havana, however, was not a simple salve to the urban conscience, nor a straightforward reconciliation across the rural–urban divide; *la ciudad*, it could be argued, was being asked to do much more: not only to cleanse itself through contact with the peasantry but actually to re-orient its socio-cultural compass away from the coastal margins and in towards the rural core, to 'peasantise' its *sensibilidad*. Hence, the concentration of countryfolk in Havana in the summer of 1959 was a striking physical manifestation of a decisive discursive turn towards what could be called *cubanía campesina*. Agrarianism was not a new trope within the national narrative. From the *cimarrón* slaves of colonialism to the *mambises* of the Wars of Independence, the countryside had often been perceived as the natural habitat of the suffering and self-sacrifice so central to certain interpretations of Cuban identity. Despite the overwhelming primacy of Havana in Cuba's self-perception, Kapcia claims that by the 1950s there was a sense that *el campo* 'held an almost sanctified connection with the past heroism and the future glory of the 'real' Cuba, as opposed to the 'unreal', often corrupt, distorted urbanism in which most Cubans lived and worked' (2000: 86). In 1959 this subliminal appreciation became an overt encouragement to emulate the archetypal Cuban identity incarnate in the visiting *guajiro*. Pérez's report of the peasants hosted in the University of Havana, for example, presents their sojourn in the city as a revolution in the long-established pedagogical direction: 'Allí estaban, humildes maestros de la más trágica y más amarga de la lecciones [...]. Ellos – y no los profesores por sabios que fuesen – eran los llamados a impartir la más necesaria de las enseñanzas a todos los cubanos' (1959a: 46).

Further and persuasive evidence of this 'peasantisation' of Cuban identity can be found in a seemingly conventional piece of correspondence entitled 'Carta de un guajiro a su esposa desde La Habana' published in *Bohemia* in August 1959. Although purportedly written by a *guajiro* 'everyman' encountered amongst the half-million gathered in Havana, this simple letter back home condenses all the critical coordinates of *cubanía campesina*. The *guajiro* begins by describing the typical daily difficulties faced by rural Cubans (and often unknown by the comfortable *capitalinos*):

> ¡Qué bien dormirías tú aquí, aunque todas las noches, según tu costumbre, tuvieras que ponerte un taco de guayacol para calmarte el dolor de muelas! Aunque el reuma te atacara las rodillas y la neuralgia te pusiera gacha la sonrisa. (Miranda 1959: 54)

But this peasant has been touched by more than mundane and domestic distress; the rural tradition of super-human sacrifice has not left this family untouched: 'Quisiera hablarte del pobre Fabián Alberto, el mayor de nuestros hijos, que murió en la batalla de Güisa, pero no sigo porque sé que los ojitos se te van a llenar de llanto' (ibid.). Despite the tragedy, this indomitable man has always been willing (if not always able) to risk his life for the *Cuba Libre* dream: 'Durante la Guerra, mis años y mis achaques [...] no me dejaron subir al lomerío de la Sierra Maestra donde él estaba peleando por la libertad de nuestra patria' (55). Despite the hardships and ingrained grief, this *guajiro* is no sceptic and has travelled to the capital to evaluate the promises of the new government. He is not disappointed. Although far away from home and under an unfamiliar roof, he is completely at ease in a new Cuba in which 'se puede dormir a pierna suelta sabiendo que nadie nos engaña [...], que ningún semejante abusará de nuestro sudor' (54). Because, above all, this *guajiro* (and the archetypal identity he embodied) is fervently faithful to his gods, his new leaders, and the teleological progress of his beloved homeland:

> Nuestro pobre Fabián Alberto está en el cielo viendo lo que hacen Fidel y la Revolución por nosotros [...]. Déjame decirte que debes tener fe en Fidel y en la Revolución. La Reforma Agraria nos hará felices a todos [...]. La Reforma Agraria, Fredes, es nuestra salvación. Para nostros ha llegado la hora de comenzar a ver la dicha que antes estaba tan lejos de nuestra exist-encia. (55)

In the space of a sentence or two the promise of future victory that had inspired some analyst-authors at every turning point studied so far has been transformed into present-tense satisfaction. For this man (and the *sensibilidad* he embodies), 'ha llegado la hora'. And his most emphatic faith is reserved for Fidel. Although one in half a million, this *guajiro* recounts an intimate encounter with the rebel leader which has left an indelible impression. Castro is portrayed as the quintessential Great Man poised on the brink of transcendence. He is physically imposing: 'el mismito hombrazo de que nos hablaba Fabián Alberto en los días en que batallaba con él' (ibid.). Moreover, he is infinitely accessible to and empathetic with the common man, the perfect fusion of familiarity and self-assured authority:

> Fidel me dijo muchas cosas. Me habló de la Reforma Agraria y me aseguró que cuanto él ha dicho de esa Ley es ya un hecho, por lo que muy pronto todos nosotros vamos a estar bien. Fidel es nuestro jefe y también nuestro hermano. (ibid.)

In this reading, Castro's word becomes law, his lexis becomes the *lex* of the new Cuban *civitas*. Most importantly, Castro is portrayed as the embodiment of chronological and ideological schism, a revolutionary leader confounding all the practices and characteristics of a long line of scurrilous Republican politicians who had betrayed the countryside (and thus betrayed Cuba): 'Solamente hay que verle los ojos para saber que es distinto a los otros, a aquellos que iban por allá a buscar el voto y cuando salían representantes o senadores, no les veíamos el pelo por ninguna parte' (ibid.).

This simple letter from a peasant in Havana to his wife back home thus makes a dual contribution to the nascent Revolutionary mythography of 1959–60. First, although the tone is more telluric than some urban journalists' paeans to Castro, the *guajiro* adds his voice to the secular sanctification of the rebel leader which, for Beaupied, guaranteed that although seeking to emulate Martí at every step, Castro attained ideological immortality earlier than did the Apostle (2010: 10). Second, the letter condenses in one place, and in the *vox populi* in which the new Cuban *sensibilidad* was to be enunciated, all the key codes of archetypal identity in the contemporary context. With his combination of candour and ingenuousness, his dedication to family and blissful ignorance of the decadent urban world, with his ability to face great suffering with forbearance and his unshakeable faith in Cuba's luminous future under an extraordinarily enlightened leader, this *guajiro* is a source of inspiration to all Cubans during a critical turning of the ideological tide.

But how authentic is this archetype? The *carta* is clearly a synthesis of a particular understanding of Cuban identity, forged during a guerrilla fight against tyranny and drawing on a combination of the ideological and mythological capital of a distant past and an idealisation of the qualities of the Cuban *campesino*. It is perhaps equally clear, however, that this is a stage-managed amalgamation of impossibly ideal characteristics translated into a faux peasant style for propagandistic effect. The evidence of this stage-management is manifold. In the photograph accompanying the article we see the *guajiro* writing the letter himself and, although complaining of his children's illiteracy, his own handwriting is elegant and flawless. Although the letter is allegedly a glimpse into the private world of this peasant, the photograph shows him writing on a broad desk in a very public office space, suggesting that this was an encouraged and facilitated epistolary. Although the transcription of the letter includes the date, the photo shows no date. Although presumably intending to actually post this letter to his wife, the only address given is 'Sra Fredesvinda Quesada, Sierra Maestra, Oriente'; whilst the symbolic portent of this address is clear, such lack of detail would probably have made the Cuban postman's job practically impossible. In asking about his children, the peasant names them all in full – 'Amancia de la Caridad, Isidrito, José Orfilio' – which, in an intimate letter to their mother, seems almost incongruous, although it does afford opportunity to infuse the letter with the kind of telluric colour so common in folklore of the Cuban countryside (or at least in preconceived urban perceptions of it). Also, there is a stark contradiction between the educational levels of the peasant's children: although one has never been to school and dreams only of being able to read and write, another has had sufficient preparation to enable him to hatch bold professional ambitions: 'antes quería ser procurador y ahora desea estudiar para ingeniero' (Miranda 1959: 55), the shifting aspirations fortuitously reflecting the strategic re-focusing of the Cuban economy towards industrial productivity. Unlike in Pérez's account of the overcrowding of *guajiros* in the makeshift university dorms, this letter-writer enjoys a hotel suite all to himself in which he sleeps

> sobre una gran cama, donde uno se hunde como en un charco, frente a un aparato que echa frío como aire echan esos remolinos que se presentan antes de los nortes o que anuncian las mangas de viento que en ocasiones tumban maizales y platanales. (ibid.: 54)

Whilst the ethnographic detail perfectly paints an image of a bucolic lifestyle in the mind of the urban reader, it seems superfluous in a letter to a *sierramaestrense* wife. Throughout the letter, there is a fundamental contradiction between the desire to describe the inhuman conditions *campesinos* have been forced to tolerate since time immemorial, and the desire to portray a timeless, telluric and blissful rural way of life that had preserved the *guajiro*'s moral purity intact.

This 'Carta de un guajiro', therefore, offers the most contrived representation of Cuban *sensibilidad* examined thus far. The determined discursive shift within the national narrative away from urban epistemological sophistication towards a more elemental gnosis is not presented by analyst-authors like Ortiz or Mañach, but by the candid protagonist himself, infusing it with credibility whilst at the same time displacing exegetic authority from the lettered city towards the soon-to-be-lettered countryside. Mirroring Castro's direct democracy in the Plaza, in which all votes and parliamentary procedures were dispensed with, this direct and visceral contribution to the national narrative seems to make all mediation unnecessary. The walls of the *ciudad letrada* are beginning to crumble.

And foremost in the *guajiro*'s comprehension and articulation of Cuban *sensibilidad* is his admiration and respect for the enlightened example of Fidel. This *carta* thus became part of a Revolutionary parable in which a Messiah-shepherd guided the Cuban flock from the wilderness and towards integrity, unity and the satisfaction of their most noble desires: 'estaban como ovejas que no tenían pastor, y los recibió y comenzó a enseñarles muchas cosas, hablandoles del Reino de Dios y sanando a los que tenían necesidad de salud' (del Cerro 1959: 56).

For every guardian angel there is a devil close by, however, and Fidel and the Cuban *pueblo* were no exception. In 1959–60 some of these devils were apparent to all and had been exposed to Revolutionary justice. For Roig de Leuchsenring, the campaign against 'males y vicios' had been so effective that evil had practically been eradicated from the collective consciousness and Cubans made immune to the *pecados* of the past. For the letter-writing *guajiro*, the perils of the malfeasant (if repentant) capital were plain to see and easy to exorcise:

> Por desgracia, en la capital no han faltado algunos majases, de esos que Fidel llama contrarrevolucionarios. Pero la verdad es que esos majases no pueden con nostros los guajiros. Ellos no sabían que si nosotros traíamos nuestros machetes no era para adorno, sino para defender a Fidel y a lo que Fidel dice. (Miranda 1959: 55)

Other enemies, although more concealed and difficult to discern, were no less antithetical to the *campesino* archetype elaborated in the *carta* and elsewhere. From a criticism of urban ignorance of the rural plight and a call for an act of contrition through hospitality and generosity, *Bohemia* began to move towards a more unforgiving assault on urban Cubans, assigning them a more pejorative role within the parable of Revolutionary identity:

> Abel era sencillo y justo, y sembraba la tierra y recogía sus frutos, y su corazón amaba a Dios y no conocía la maldad. Caín lo envidiaba porque Abel era bueno y el señor lo veía con complacencia. Así tú en la familia cubana, ha sido como Abel: bueno, sencillo, trabajador, piadoso y sufrido. Y nosotros te hemos envidiado lo único que no hemos podido quitarte: el espíritu libre y el corazón sencillo. (1959e: 61)

From simple egotists, urban Cubans have become proto-sinners forever excluded from the bucolic paradise of Cuba to come. In this condemnation, and in the contours of *cubanía* charted in the 'Carta de un guajiro' and elsewhere, can be read a decisive blow in the ideological battle over Cuban identity that sees the 'reaggregationists' claim ascendancy over their 'liminalist' opponents. In the rootedness of archetypal life in an imagined landscape of 'maizales' and 'platanales', any resonance with Ortiz's uprooted and anoriginal ontology of identity is negated. In the swing of the moral-imaginative compass away from the capital and towards the *campo*, the influence of the quintessentially urban anti-hero Luján was reduced (it is, probably, coincidental that the *guajiro*'s ambitious son had rejected the life of a *procurador* for the utilitarian merit of engineering). In an insistence on the importance of moral fortitude and a disposition to constant, active and bloody self-sacrifice, both the aberrant world of the 1930s' violent margins and the legal and lexical triumph of the conciliatory and pragmatic Constitution of 1940 were left behind.[9] In the panegyrics for an apostle reborn and transformed into a demi-deity dispensing absolute truths and miraculous cures, the 1953 alternative understanding of a pragmatic Martí who had accepted that 'virtud triunfa de lado' was overruled (Ichaso 1953: 81). In the plain-speaking heroism of the countryfolk and the unadorned historical gravity that brought them down from the Sierra Maestra and impelled them into the very core of the *cubanía* discourse, the 1957 celebration of Cuba's collective *ingravidez* was relegated to a footnote in the national narrative. In short, the betwixt-and-between anti-heroes of the previous forty years were confronted in 1959–60 by the apparent answer to the riddle of the Cuban condition, by the resolution of the not-*ever*-yet complex, by *cubanía* concluded. In this latest turning point in Cuba's cultural-historical trajectory, the Revolutionary angel had apparently stripped the liminal 'devil' of all psycho-social force and cast it out into the wilderness, and condemned the anti-heroic other Cubas and their *sensibilidades* to a fast-fading past. Predictably, perhaps, these devils refused to give in without a fight.

In Defence of the Devil

Despite Roig de Leuchsenring's confident charting of an impenetrable frontier in the new Cuba between the devilish 'directores' and the angelic *pueblo*, evidence can be uncovered of subversive breaches and subtle but significant erosions of this Manichean frontier (Roig de Leuchsenring 1961b: 350). Nine months after the initial cathartic excision of *batistato* evil, for example, *Bohemia* reported the appearance of a disguised devil amongst the honest citizens of the eastern city of Holguin. Marcelino Vidal had been one of 'los más destacados componentes de la gavilla de malvados que [...] puso crespones de luto en muchos hogares holguineros', but had shed his identity to save his skin as the rebels marched into town: 'Vidal se quitó el bigote, se cambió el peinado, alteró su apariencia personal' (Cabrera 1959a: 36). Significantly, this fugitive did not choose subterfuge in the capital city, nor attempt to flee the island altogether, instead opting to conceal himself in the rebel heartland behind the most morally impeccable facade: 'Compró ropa de guajiro, le metió en una jaba junto a un machete viejo' (ibid.). This worm

---

[9] In both *La historia me absolverá* and the so-called 'Manifiesto de la Sierra Maestra', Castro and the 26 of July Movement had pledged to reinstate the 1940 Constitution partially suspended by Batista in 1952. In reality, the constitutional situation remained essentially the same until the new (and very different) Constitution of 1976.

at the heart of the *cubanía campesina* apple was disconcerting, this ability to disguise past crimes and criminals cast a disturbing shadow across the illuminated purity of the half-million *guajiros* gathered in Havana to usher in a new age with a wave of their own 'machetes viejos'. Furthermore, this devil was not one of the (often urban) 'directores' upon whom Roig de Leuchsenring had heaped all blame for past sins, but an anonymous rural everyman: 'un nativo de Tunas que, como mucha otra gente del campo, soñaba con ser Guardia Rural o policía. Tener un uniforme, un revolver, una representación, sentirse alguien' (ibid.). This retrograde desire for personal glory at any expense obviously clashes with the *guajiro* ideal enunciated in the 'Carta'. But Marcelino Vidal was not the only everyman to belie this ideal. For Mañach, the subjugation of the armed forces to Batista was also due to the shortsighted self-interest of an officer class largely elevated from the ranks in the Sergeants' Revolt of 1933 (and subsequently) without ever losing what Mañach called 'la suspicacia y el cerrado espíritu conservador de los campos' (1959e: 168). As for the dichotomy between evil before and purity after the Revolutionary epiphany of 1959, other voices raised subtle critique. Although defending the resilient moral integrity of the Cuban people, *Bohemia* nevertheless admitted that 'haría falta [...] una edición entera de la revista' to present even the most notorious criminals of the *batistato*, all of whom were aided and abetted by 'una legión de subalternos duchos en torturas, expertos en inventar martirios' (1959c: 152). Even Castro, the shepherd of the revitalised Cuban flock, seemed indirectly to admit that a complete exorcism of past evils was neither possible nor practical: 'si aquí hubiéramos hecho presos por batistianos [...] haría falta un provincia casi para meter a todo el que se retrató, recibió un favor, y le hizo un homenaje y fue allí al Palacio Presidencial' (in *La Calle* 1960b: B-15).

Just as Unamuno spoke up for the innervation of illness, so others explored the psycho-social merit of being bad. For Schopenhauer, malignance was unavoidable and there could be no meaningful exorcism of humans' inner fiends: 'The chief source of the most serious evils affecting man is man himself; *homo homini lupus* (man is a wolf for man)' (1969: 577). As some of the analyst-authors of the national narrative turned on others in a bitter witch hunt of the ideologically uncommitted, Virgilio Piñera once again took to the public intellectual's stage to welcome willingly the role of the defender of the old guard – a devil's advocate, if not the devil himself: 'En nuestra incipiente literatura [...] este rol de lobo feroz ha sido muy beneficioso. ¿A qué cumbres de estupidez no llegaríamos si, de vez en cuando, estos animales temibles no hicieran su aparición en el campo literario cubano?' (1960: 11). Of all Turner's liminars, he speaks with particular relish of those betwixt-and-between artists (like Piñera) who shuttle between respectable expression of infrastructural mores and uninhibited assaults on the whole socio-cultural edifice, 'for each society requires of its mature members not only adherence to rules and patterns, but at least a certain level of scepticism' (Turner 1974: 256). For Turner, these artists and writers are the jesters of the liminal landscape, availing themselves of sinuous and disguised language to strike at the very heart of august authority.

And so we return to Fernando Ortiz. After pitting Cuba's foul mouth and 'mala vida' of 1923 against the Royal Academy's sworn aim to clean, fix and make the Spanish language splendid, and after spurning all attempts in 1953 to elevate *el pueblo* to 'el ideal candoroso de un espíritu celeste, ciego, graduado de la universidad bamboleante de las nubes' (1955b: 245–6), Ortiz's final substantial publication was his 1959 *Historia de una pelea cubana contra los demonios*, a four hundred-page history of demonic possession on the island. Although the bulk of the book is concerned with an infamous seventeenth-century case of collective possession and a local priest's attempts to exorcise the Beast from Bayamo, Ortiz's text is peppered with more abstract reflections on Cuba's historical contact with the forces of darkness. Turning from the pages of the foreign press in November 1959, with their reports of summary executions, bearded revolutionary wildmen and ever-encroaching communism, for example, Ortiz can only conclude that the whole world believed Cuba and the Cubans to be 'entregados a todos los demonios' (Ortiz 1973a: xiii). Far from leaping to the defence of *el pueblo*'s impeccable purity, Ortiz admits that the newspapers might have a point: 'Los teólogos aseguran que todavía los demonios siguen metidos entre cubanos, persistiendo en sus fechorías. Sea de ello como fuere, parece peligroso dar por suprimidos a los diablos' (xv–xvi). In an almost wilfully archaic turn of a subjunctive phrase Ortiz seems to resist the forward thrust of the future's (and future tense's) conquest of the present with a much more speculative and uncertain mood. Moreover, the devils that Ortiz has in mind are not the pernicious 'directores' nor the 'gavilla de asesinos', nor even the lumpen *batistianos* of the past. Adding yet more fruit to his lexicographic *catauro*, Ortiz rather believes that the most beastly black arts were not practised by the soul, but by the tongue, that real devilishness was in the detail of language. For Ortiz, therefore, hell is inhabited by 'santimoniosos y falsos sermoneros, como propagandistas [...] de toda clase de añagazas' (xiv). At a time when Cuba was enthralled by the public and often verbose speeches of Castro and other leaders of the Revolution, Ortiz's displacement of cardinal sins from actions to words is significant. Whilst the 'Carta de un guajiro' advocated unwavering faith in the omnipotent figure of the popular prime minister who had performed almost miraculous acts and whose word was as good as his deed, Ortiz calls for a re-calibration of the unquestioning respect afforded figures in positions of power, particularly those for whom rhetoric was an important weapon in their arsenal: 'Un cura, por solo serlo, no es un ángel ni un demonio. No es un numen; es un hombre. Ni más ni menos que un hombre. Todo un hombre, pero sólo un hombre' (559). As the Revolution sought to purge physical and ideological mistakes through uncompromising catharsis, and as the *fisonomía* of the age turned from ambivalence and *ingravidez* to the necessary and 'absoluta' identification between *el pueblo* and its super-heroic leaders, Ortiz puts absolutism amongst his own list of deadly secular sins: 'pese a estos siglos de creciente racionalismo y demás respetos humanos entre las gentes, la política sacerdotalista de algunos no ha cesado de propagar la "absolutización" de su incondicionada autoridad' (560). As *Bohemia* published articles in which Fidel before the *guajiros* was compared to Christ on the Mount, and as the image of the young and self-sacrificing rebel leader touched by the divinity of white doves was becoming indelibly imprinted upon the national imagination, Ortiz's scorn for false prophets of the past seems close to revolutionary sacrilege: 'Esta envanecida denominación de "Hombre-Dios" ha sido a veces título que en Cuba [...] se han arrojado algunos charlatanes curanderos [...] con la misma parodia (gran barba, grandes mantos talares, mirada desviada a lo alto, austeridad fingida)' (ibid.). For Ortiz, therefore, the demons which Cuba had to engage in mortal moral *pelea* were not those underworld enemies determined to assail the purity of *el pueblo*, but rather the notion of purity itself; the arch enemies of a hale and wholesome *conciencia colectiva* were not *demonios* at all, but rather those individuals who felt themselves touched by a transcendence that elevated them above 'todos los pecados de la tan admirable como flaca naturaleza humana' (559). Ortiz claims that this elevation (whether of priests or propagandists) to a super-human plane merely set the idols and the people that emulated them up for an apocalyptic fall: 'El prejuicio que los exalta hasta la sublimidad sobrenatural es el más peligroso, porque trata ilusivamente de excluir a los eclesiásticos de las limitaciones racionales que la conciencia social impone a todo ejercicio humano' (ibid.). The ongoing *pelea* was not against dangerous devils, therefore, but against the pernicious belief in infallibility. Hence, as individuals and ideas from a purportedly malignant age were marginalised from the national narrative, as an archetype of telluric integrity came forcibly to the fore and as paeans were sung to the rebel messiah-shepherds and their pure flock, Ortiz emerged from his almost constant cloak of self-deprecation to offer the highs and lows of his own life as the outline of an alternative, less resolute and infinitely ambiguous archetype:

> Os confieso que he cultivado sin gran esfuerzo los pecados necesarios para poder sentirme ser humano, pleno y cabal, sin petulancias de santidad; y que también he practicado sin desviaciones ascéticas, un número de virtudes suficientes para firmar mi hombría, llana pero libre de ignominias y vilezas (48).

Amidst the triumphant euphoria of 1959–60, Ortiz quietly suggested that the fight against the devil went on.

In the euphoria and chaos of 1959–60 the sense of triumph was palpable. Fidel Castro's entry into Havana in January 1959 also marked the arrival into the very core of Cuban identity of an individual of extraordinary influence and resolve. Shaped by the frustrations of past attempts to lift Cuba out of lethargy and ill-governance, and by the more intimate failures of his own acts of derring-do, Castro and the *rebeldes* were determined to turn the chronological end of the decade into an epistemological frontier beyond which the Cuban national narrative could be radically re-written with a truly free hand. Their prime (and perhaps fictitious) protagonist was an almost impossibly virtuous peasant, marked by suffering without respite, valiant to the core and fiercely faithful to the perfectible future of his beloved Cuba and the enlightened leaders who had sworn to lead it ever onwards to purity and the end of all troubles.

Confronting this messianism across the chronological and ideological frontiers stood some of the most influential analyst-authors of the Cuban national narrative. Whilst welcoming the obvious transcendence of the Revolutionary 'triunfo', these sage observers of, and contributors to, a half-century of Cuban *civitas* found their own leaps of Revolutionary faith fall short. Ortiz, Mañach and Piñera were the kinds of intellectual Turner described elsewhere as 'threshold people', convinced that a teleological and dogmatic dash towards telluric and perfect *cubanía* was pernicious for Cuba's long-suffering *sensibilidad* (Turner 1969: 95). For these betwixt-and-between analyst-authors Cuba's suffering had perhaps been so long and unrelenting not because of any peculiar ill fortune hanging over the island, but simply because pain, doubt and frustration were integral aspects of the human and Cuban conditions. For these, an otherworldly messiah and his flock of elevated angels offered a paradoxically malicious model for the inexorably terrestrial *pueblo* always striving for and never achieving post-crisis and post-liminal conclusion. Instead, they argued, let the archetype be a didactic devil, a fundamentally flawed and yet sublimely virtuous everyman standing on the limen between past and present, good and evil, looking optimistically forwards towards Cuba's collective future but never losing sight of the more mundane but no less instructive space at the side of the road. In 1959–60, therefore, these 'threshold people' confronted the inflamed messiah with sulphurous daily devils, counterpointed the exalted end of Cuba's rite of collective passage with a stubborn lingering in an inconclusive interstice.

Although at the peak of their analytical powers, however, Ortiz and Mañach were on the cusp of their own rites of final passage: the latter did not survive to see 1962 and the former retreated into increasingly infirm seclusion in his Havana house.[10] With this internal recalcitrance fading, and with both internal and external factors propelling Revolutionary Cuba towards ever more radical postures in almost every socio-political and cultural sphere, what had been an inchoate *campesino* archetype became distilled into the notion of a 'new man', galvanised by collective moral incentives, liberated from the vicissitudes of daily life and seemingly closer than ever to definitive conclusion. With the absence of Ortiz, Mañach and others, an ambivalent, open-ended and devilish counterpoint to the new man seemed unlikely. But some Rip van Winkles remained. In the following chapter we will examine how in 1965 'el lobo feroz' of Cuban letters, Virgilio Piñera, and a new arrival in the Cuban *ciudad letrada*, Edmundo Desnoes, sought to punctuate the newest ardent archetype of conclusive collective *sensibilidad* with elusive and fractured identities and a stubborn adherence to the liminal principle that 'no existe nada verdadera-mente doloroso o absolutamente placentero' (Piñera 1960: 9).

---

[10] Other liminal intellectuals such as Ichaso, Lizaso and Montenegro had exiled themselves from the island and thus distanced themselves from the insular narrative.

7

1965: Post-liminal Cuba?

In this examination of pivotal periods in Cuba's twentieth century, in which the *fisonomía* of the age was marked by an acute and often anguished re-cognisance of collective identity, 1965 may seem like an unusual conclusion: in the first mercurial years of the 1960s, other dates seem to stake stronger claims for obligatory exploration as peaks of transcendental activity and self-analysis. In March 1960, for example, the merchant ship *La Coubre*, that was bringing armaments from Belgium, was torn apart by a catastrophic on-board explosion that killed seventy-five. Just as the sinking of the *USS Maine* in 1898 (only a few hundred yards across Havana harbour) had heralded the beginning of the end of Spanish colonialism, so the destruction of *La Coubre* provoked a significant swing in collective sensibility away from the improvisation and contingency of the early years towards a more steely mood of mute resolve, with Sartre (who was in Havana at the time) reporting the cancellation of the annual carnival and the channelling of all organisational energies towards 'una colecta nacional para comprar armas y aviones' (1960: 243). In terms of transcendence, however, 1960 was but a prelude to the events of 1961, in which Roig de Leuchsenring's prediction of chronological acceleration seemed to come true as Cuba lived 'lustros en meses, meses en instantes' (1961: 348). Although the cause of the explosion on *La Coubre* was never irrefutably proved (in a further eerie echo of the *Maine*), suspicious eyes turned towards the increasingly hostile northern neighbour. Since Castro's tense April 1959 visit, relations between the United States and Cuba had descended quickly towards non-diplomacy. Loath to tolerate a radical nationalist revolution just ninety miles from its southern shores, the US sought to make its hemispheric hegemony felt by drawing a mercantile noose around Cuba to throttle the island's attempts at self-determination: in May 1960 US-owned refineries on the island refused to process recently-arrived Soviet crude oil, Cuba responded by taking them over, the US retaliated by limiting Cuba's all-important preferential access to the US sugar market, Cuba replied by nationalising foreign-owned sugar mills. In a matter of months, the special relationship at the core of Cuba's foreign policy for more than half a century had turned sour. Consequences came almost immediately. On 15 April 1961 bomber planes piloted by recently exiled Cubans killed seven and disabled part of the rebel air force in brazen daylight raids into Cuban airspace. At the funeral of the victims next day, Fidel alluded to a collective rite of passage since January 1959 through which the Revolution had come to comprehend its new (and potentially perilous) place in the geopolitical world:

> Todavía nosotros no habíamos podido adquirir la dura experiencia que hemos ido adquiriendo durante estos dos años y medio; todavía no conocíamos bien a nuestros enemigos; todavía no conocíamos bien sus procedimientos; todavía no sabíamos lo que era la Agencia Central de Inteligencia del gobierno de Estados Unidos [...]. ¡Cómo sirven estos hechos para comprender!, ¡cómo sirven estos hechos para enseñarnos las realidades del mundo!, ¡cómo sirven estos hechos para educar a nuestro pueblo! (1961a: para. 7)

Castro saw the solution in the physical fortification of the island's frontiers and the ideological consolidation of its *sensibilidad* beneath the pole star of socialism: 'Éso es lo que no pueden perdonarnos, que estemos ahí en sus narices ¡y que hayamos hecho una Revolución socialista en las propias narices de Estados Unidos! (Aplausos y exclamaciones de: "¡Pa'lante y pa'lante, y al que no le guste que tome purgante!")' (para. 100).[1] The purge of the collective corpus advocated by analyst-authors of the past was now being clamoured for by the entire *pueblo*. On 17 January the expected invasion came, and was beaten back from the beaches of Bahía de los Cochinos (or the Bay of Pigs) in less than seventy-two hours. The victory snuffed out the large-scale military ambitions of Cuba's external enemies, significantly stifled internal resistance to the new regime,[2] and provided the Revolution with a priceless ideological fillip, enabling it to portray itself as the tried and tested leader of the Latin American (and more broadly Third World) fight against US imperialism.

After a springtime of military conflict came a summer of cultural collision. When *Lunes de Revolución* funded a seemingly innocuous 1961 'free cinema' experiment (entitled *P.M.*) that followed a one-man and rum-soaked odyssey across Havana, the vitriol it inspired in some cultural sectors indicated a new and uncompromising determination to maintain an inviolably united front, with Alfredo Guevara, the influential president of the Instituto Cubano del

---

[1]   Although the Revolution was only declared socialist in this April 1961 speech, by late 1960, 'había comenzado la institucionalización de los estudios del marxismo' through the creation of Escuelas de Instrucción Revolucionaria and university reforms 'que comprendía de manera obligatoria asignaturas de marxismo-leninismo' (Torres-Cuevas 2005: 238).

[2]   Many alleged collaborators were arrested during the Playa Girón campaign; others were encircled in the Escambray mountains and defeated over the next few years in the so-called *lucha contra los bandidos*.

Arte e Industria Cinematográficos (ICAIC), accusing *P.M.* and its backers of attempting to 'dividir la Revolución desde el interior; de ser enemigos de la Unión Soviética; de revisionismo y confusionismo ideológicos' (in Franqui 1981: 265). Although a seemingly histrionic over-reaction, Guevara's venom can be explained through reference to earlier purges of anti-Revolutionary (or even a-Revolutionary) ideas. Whereas in the ludic 1959 funeral march for the *Diario de la Marina* a kind of parodic lightness and liminal fun was tolerable, by 1961 the same sentiment enraged Cuba's new cultural elite (ever conscious of the need to prove their activism, as we saw in the previous chapter), who saw it as completely incongruous with the tenebrous events and the heroic *sensibilidad* of the day. To draw a line under the *P.M.* polemic, Castro called Cuban intellectuals to a series of meetings at the National Library, brought to a close with his famous 'Palabras' (of which we heard an earlier version from Padilla): 'dentro de la Revolución, todo; contra la Revolución, nada' (Castro 1961b: para. 49). For many observers, this was the first draft of an uncompromising 'topography of the Revolution' upon which all intellectuals were obliged to position themselves, or risk banishment from the cultural space (Quintero Herencia, in Serra 2007: 60). And this was not the only tectonic shift under the foundations of the lettered city in the early 1960s. From 1 January 1961 one hundred thousand volunteers (many of whom were only adolescents) went with their books and their iconic oil lamps to bring the illumination of learning to the rural hinterland in a year-long literacy campaign. With literacy rates soaring, public intellectuals were exposed to, and obliged to cater for, a much larger *pueblo*. Then just as breathless 1961 drew to a close, Cuba's historical trajectory almost ended in cataclysmic tragedy in 1962 as spy planes, launch sites and superpower brinkmanship brought the storm of nuclear war to Cuba's (and the whole world's) horizon (as we will see later in this chapter).

With all these events in mind, it's clear why 1961–62 could be considered a transcendental turning point in Cuba's twentieth-century history. But whilst not seeking to deny the import of those first two years of Revolutionary rule, I rather agree with Kapcia that the transformations experienced therein were inchoate and lacked decisive direction.[3] Although undoubtedly striving towards a uncompromising framework for Revolutionary cultural policy which would replicate the Manichean simplicity of the angels/devils debate we saw in the previous chapter, the cultural topography charted in 'Palabras' actually left an ideological threshold open for those who 'sin ser contrarrevolucionarios no se sientan tampoco revolucionarios' (Castro 1961b: para. 35). Far from a

3   See Kapcia 2008: 46–63.

dogmatic charting of inflexible frontiers between Revolutionary loyalty and counter-Revolutionary betrayal, Castro actually celebrated the candour and clarity of undecided intellectuals whose lack of 'espíritu revolucionario' was not necessarily cause for censure (para. 38). Similarly, even though the setting up of schools for Marxist instruction and public declarations of socialist affiliation suggested a determined turn towards ideological orthodoxy, Cuba at the beginning of the 1960s was not, and seemed determined not to become, a scion of the Soviet Union, with 1962 witnessing virulent attacks on the so-called *sectarismo* of Moscow-oriented socialists such as former Partido Socialista Popular senior cadre Aníbal Escalante.[4] Moreover, despite the apparent clarification of Cuba's place on the geopolitical world map, 1962 to 1964 saw the very public and high-level re-examination of the key ideological tenets of the new Revolutionary government in the so-called Great Debate.[5] Thus, like all the apparent turning points examined thus far, the transcendence of 1960 to 1962 was at least partially hollowed out by inconclusion and flux. The focus of this chapter moves forward, therefore, to 1965, a year on the leeside of the early geopolitical drama. Whereas the *fisonomías* of 1923, 1933, 1953, 1957 and 1959 were all marked by intense and sometimes antagonistic dialogue about the *sensibilidad colectiva*, 1965 saw a determined assertion of socio-cultural and ideological structures to match the transformed times, an uncompromising consolidation of a radically new Cuban *civitas*, a resolute move from the liminal indecision of previous periods to a once-and-for-all reaggregation of Revolutionary Cuban selfhood.

If the ambivalence of 'Palabras' and the oscillations of the Great Debate had left some ideological questions pending, the founding of the Partido Comunista de Cuba on 3 October 1965 seemed to offer the final answer. The transition to this unified political force occurred in several stages from 1959. What had initially been disparate anti-Batista political movements (including Castro's Movimiento 26 de Julio, the Partido Socialista Popular led by Blas Roca, and the Directorio Revolucionario led by Faure Chomón) were consolidated in July 1961 as the Organizaciones Revolucionarias Integradas (ORI) under the leadership of Aníbal Escalante. When ORI was blighted by the sectarianism of its chief, it was replaced (in 1962) by the Partido Unido de la Revolución Socialista. But in 1965, this organisational flux took a turn towards definition. Speaking before a meeting of the most senior government officials, Castro described the emergence of a unified revolutionary consciousness to be consolidated by a political party of the same stripe:

---

4   For a detailed account of this anti-sectarianism campaign, see Kapcia 2000: 130–2.
5   For further reading see Fitzgerald 1994: 51–9 and Kapcia 2000: 132–7.

Partido Unido de la Revolución Socialista de Cuba dice mucho, pero no dice todo […]; da todavía la idea de algo que fue necesario unir, que recuerda todavía un poco los orígenes de cada cual. Y como entendemos que ya hemos llegado al grado tal en que de una vez por todas y para siempre ha de desaparecer todo tipo de matiz y todo tipo de origen que distinga a unos revolucionarios de otros, y hemos llegado ya al punto afortunado de la historia de nuestro proceso revolucionario en que podamos decir que sólo hay un tipo de revolucionario, y puesto que es necesario que el nombre de nuestro Partido diga no lo que fuimos ayer, sino lo que somos hoy y lo que seremos mañana, ¿cuál es, a juicio de ustedes, el nombre que debe tener nuestro Partido? (aplausos y exclamaciones de: "¡Comunista!") […] ¡Partido Comunista de Cuba! (exclamaciones de: "¡Comunista, Comunista!") (1965: para. 36)

This extract makes several noteworthy contributions to the discursive affray we have been following throughout our analysis. The insistence on a single ideological origin seeks to eliminate the possibilities of future discrepancies, but also closes the door on the heterogeneous cultural contributions from the *homo maritimus* archetype posited during an earlier turning point. Similarly, the purported schism between *antes* and *ahora* is here writ large in the suggestion that remembering one's origins (or even remembering at all) is unnecessary when the present and future have come to have such predominance that *venceremos* has been transformed into *hemos vencido*. The unequivocal intention, therefore, is to 'decirlo todo', to move inexorably away from origins, to elaborate a unique and exclusive paradigm of revolutionary identity for today and for the collective tomorrow and thus close the ideological space left open in 1961 for the betwixt-and-between, a-Revolutionary Cubans and their heterogeneous, ambivalent and what we have described as liminal contributions to the national narrative. Thus, whereas Sartre had marvelled in 1960 at a revolution in which the normal articulation of theory and practice had been inverted, and in which the heuristic daily experience of revolution had made doctrine secondary and brought intuitive action to the fore, by 1965 this elasticity had ossified and theoretical orthodoxy was back on top: 'Y no habrá un sólo problema que no sea objeto de estudio y de análisis profundo por parte del Partido, para que de cada análisis salga la orientación, la orientación correcta y la mejor orientación' (Castro 1965: para. 17). In a further, and somewhat surprising, inflection of the analysis-authorship complex, activity is now subsumed under analysis of a very particular ideological tenor. The crumbling walls of the *ciudad letrada* are shored up, although its ideological map is more reminiscent of the earlier city that Rama describes in which the bureaucrats' exclusive ability to decipher the lexis of colonial order and offer 'la orientación correcta y la mejor orientación' had yet to be challenged by education, immigration and the vernacularisation of literature.

Unity, cohesion and the eradication of 'todo tipo de matiz' from Cuba's *sensibilidad* made 1965 a decisive year, a year José Antonio Portuondo described as the 'etapa final de la integración de una conciencia socialista en nuestra patria' (1965a: 7). And this sense of swapping perplexing questions for uncompromising prescriptions for archetypal identity in the Revolutionary age is confidently inscribed in Ernesto 'Che' Guevara's *El socialismo y el hombre en Cuba* (1966), a text that offers a blueprint for the morally superior new men and women Che believed would overcome any objective shortcomings and lead the island towards conclusion in 'la sociedad del hombre comunista' (Guevara 1966: 13). Although often read primarily as a critical contribution to twentieth-century socialist thought, here we will suggest that Guevara's text draws on and contributes to the discursive paradigms and cognitive codes present in every critical turning point explored herein and thus takes its place within the Cuban identity canon. Hence, this chapter will bring *El socialismo y el hombre en Cuba* alongside other analyst-authors' (often subversive) 1965 reflections on Cuban *sensibilidad*, their challenges to the full-stop that was being proffered as the definitive end, *de una vez por todas y para siempre*, of the island's national narrative.

El hombre nuevo

There can be no doubting the socialist and internationalist import of *El socialismo y el hombre en Cuba* or Guevara's role as an influential twentieth-century Marxist theorist. He wrote the essay (originally sent as a letter to Carlos Quijano, editor of the Uruguayan periodical *Marcha*) at the beginning of 1965 whilst on a three-month diplomatic tour that took in China, North Korea, Tanzania, Congo, Ghana, Egypt, Algeria and Czechoslovakia. After returning, he would spend only one more month in Cuba before leaving for good, first back to the Congo and then on to Bolivia, where he would be killed in October 1967. Guevara is not an automatic candidate for inclusion amongst the pantheon of analyst-authors who had contributed to 'the cosmology of Cuban' since the mid-nineteenth century (Pérez Jr 2005: 5). The Argentinian only arrived in Cuba in 1956, was given honorary Cuban citizenship in 1959, but renounced it (and hence any claim he could have on official Cuban assistance) before leaving in April 1965. Although neither the man nor his *oeuvre* have automatic entry to the *cubanía* canon, a close reading of *El socialismo y el hombre* reveals an unmistakably Cuban discursive skeleton beneath its much-commented internationalist flesh, and demonstrates that *el hombre nuevo* described by Guevara would have been intimately familiar to the likes of Martí, Mella and Mañach. This distinctively Cuban framework is apparent in Guevara's attitude to heroism, in his analysis of the sins and sinners that had hindered Cuba's attempts to be free, in his prescriptions for a conclusive contrition to ensure future absolution and in his future-oriented and profoundly teleological approach to social and psychological progress (which he drew principally from Marxism, but which was equally prevalent in the underlying ideologies of other 'reaggregationist' analyst-authors, as we have seen).

Guevara points early in his thesis to the primary importance of heroism in Cuba. For a nation-building project engendered in an audacious *grito* against the status quo and perpetuated by extraordinary acts of valour, from Martí's fatal cavalry charge to the collective resolve in the face of the nuclear menace of October 1962, Guevara recognises that heroism was woven into the very fabric of Cuban citizenship. Whilst acts of bravery in response to extraordinary events were admirable, however, the great goal for Guevara was that this inherent 'actitud heroica' spill over into everyday life, that isolated acts of derring-do become a constant moral disposition to perform acts of more mundane, but more constructive, heroism such as the mass labour mobilisations that rapidly became a part of Cuba's productive panorama (Guevara 1966: 6). 'Mass' and 'massive' are important epithets: the valour posited by Guevara was no longer a trait limited to the individual *héroes* who had populated the national narrative previously; the 'new man' was actually 'new men': 'Todos y cada uno su cuota de sacrificio, conscientes de recibir el premio en la satisfacción del deber cumplido, conscientes de avanzar con todos hacia el hombre nuevo que se vislumbra en el horizonte' (23). In this, Guevara approaches the dialectic of the psycho-cultural encounter between the individual and the collective with some subtlety. Individualism in which alienanted competitors clawed their way through 'una carrera de lobos' towards the goal of egotistical victory 'sobre el fracaso de otros' was socially destructive and at the very core of what Guevara calls the nefarious 'leyes del capitalismo' (9). What was needed was the re-orientation of ambition towards collective endeavour, from the protagonism of the individual towards the predominance of 'las masas' (13). Guevara does not offer this as an abstract aspiration, nor suggests that the birth of these new men and women would be an act of miraculous collective epiphany: 'El cambio no se produce automáticamente en la conciencia' (16). In this, Guevara's conceptualisation of the new man reveals the influence of early Soviet elaborations of a novel communist archetype who would 'master his own feelings, raise his instincts to the heights of consciousness [...] to create a higher social biologic type, or, if you please, a superman' (Trotsky 1991: 283). This Marxist overtone within Guevara's new man is in a sense not new at all in Cuba, but rather finds resonance in the insular ideologies of thinkers such as Varona, whose positivism-inspired reform of the post-independence education system can be traced both in the Universidad Popular José Martí's efforts (under the leadership of Mella and Martínez Villena) to extend high-level learning well beyond the university and in the philosophical foundations of the 1961 literacy campaign. For all and at all times, the new man would be the result of a heroic effort of self-improvement towards the goal of both personal and collective progress. Guevara describes the realisation of this effort coming about through a combination of external and internal influences. Externally, the revolutionary authorities must lead by good example, but must also not shy away from more intrusive pedagogy, or what Guevara calls 'educación indirecta' under the auspices of 'organismos tales como el Ministerio de Educación y el aparato de divulgación del Partido' (1966: 12). More important still, however, was the 'direct' counterpart through which citizens feel compelled to temper their individualism from within:

> El individuo recibe continuamente el impacto del nuevo poder social y percibe que no está completamente adecuado a él. Bajo el influjo de la presión que supone la educación indirecta, trata de acomodarse a una situación que siente justa y cuya propia falta de desarrollo le ha impedido hacerlo hasta ahora. Se autoeduca. (ibid.)

This suggestion of perfectibility and concentration on the 'compulsión moral' within psycho-social development was, of course, no novel contribution to the Cuban national narrative (15). The 'impacto' from rapidly changing circumstances and the almost frantic attempt 'acomodarse' to these – motivated by a sense of latent inadequacy surmountable through a faith in perfectibility – could describe any of the periods of anguished introspection we have examined in which Cuban society took 'cognizance of itself' (Turner 1974: 239–40). And in 1965, as in every other limen, Guevara demonstrates an inveterate intolerance of the subjunctive, a-teleological, anti-structural mood of 'may-be, might-be, as-if', posited not as a temporary pause in the implacable progress towards perfection, but as the *imago* of obstinately unfinished identity (Turner, in Alexander 1991: 30). Like Martínez Villena, Mella, Roa and Castro, Guevara could not conceive of half measures and had no patience with the conjunction of the angels and devils of Cuban *sensibilidad* that Mañach, Ortiz and others had championed. Now that redemption from past iniquities was possible, lingering in an irresolute limbo was unthinkable; now that the Cuban *pueblo* had been given the right to rule itself and improve itself, every necessary measure, including those that would bring a degree of prophylactic pain, must be deployed to eradicate doubt and division *de una vez por todas*: 'las masas sólo ven a medias y deben ser sometidos [*sic*] a estímulos y presiones de cierta intensidad; es la dictadura del proletariado ejerciéndose no sólo sobre la clase derrotada, sino también, individualmente, sobre la clase vencedora' (Guevara 1966: 13). We will return to these 'estímulos y presiones' soon.

Further approximations between Guevara and anthropological reflections on rites of passage are illuminating. From the anthropological perspective, the combination of external and internal pressures that Guevara advocated to attenuate egotism and forge collective cohesion can be brought alongside Turner's notion of liminal 'communitas' in which stratified individual identities are forcibly (even violently) levelled to give rise to 'an unstructured or rudimentarily structured and relatively undifferentiated comitatus' bound by strong bonds of empathy and solidarity (Turner 1969: 96). The examples of Cuban communitas in the early years of revolutionary rule are manifold, from the effusive *habanero* welcome given the *guajiro* visitors in July 1959, to what Guevara called the 'actos de valor y sacrificio' seen after the devastating passage of Hurricane Flora in October 1963 (1966: 6), to the enthusiasm for acts of mass mobilisation, such as the Milicias Nacionales Revolucionarias, described by Sartre as 'un agente decisivo [...] de interiorización de nuevas conductas e ideas' (in Torres-Cuevas 2005: 216). But the focus here is rather on those hierarchies that withstood the levelling force of communitas, on the vertical nexus between the increasingly cohesive masses and the revolutionary *vanguardia*. Just as Turner accepts that not all hierarchy is dissolved in communitas, and that neophytes infused with a strong sense of liminal egalitarianism will nevertheless 'submit together to the general authority of the ritual elders' (1969: 96), so Guevara points to the directory role in Cuba's rite of Revolutionary passage played by the political vanguard, 'constituida por el Partido, por los obreros de avanzada, por los hombres de avanzada' (1966: 13). For Turner the elders are beyond the trials and torments of liminal transition and can thus expedite the neophytes' reintegration into society. Guevara's vanguard fulfils a similar function, being described as the 'motor impulsor de la movilización, generador de conciencia revolucionaria y de entusiasmo combativo', all of which would lead *el pueblo*, 'masa todavía dormida', towards liberty and human plenitude (5–6). Hence, although the trajectory from opprobrious past to bright future and from alienated old men to integrated new men remained a work in progress in Guevara's thesis, his characterisation of the vanguard gives a strong sense of momentum. Members of this vanguard are further along in their own individual rites of passage: they have condensed the undifferentiated and effusive social connections of communitas into more selective and more structured alliances of reaggregated men in which 'el marco de los amigos responde estrictamente al marco de los compañeros de la revolución'; the heroism common in extraordinary moments has spilt over into their everyday actions, stimulated not by the promise of 'retribución material' or individual glory, but by the profound satisfaction of collective duty well done; they have fused 'un espíritu apasionado' with 'una mente fría' within integrated individuals able and willing 'tomar decisiones dolorosas sin que se contraiga un músculo' (21–2). In many respects (as in Fidel's October 1965 address to senior government officials), this vanguard usurps the analyst-authors by adopting their narratological role and even reproducing their ability to oscillate between passionate proximity and objective distance from where their passionate *sensibilidad* will not prevent them from taking the hard decisions called for at times of transcendental transition. Outstanding amongst this analyst-author supplanting vanguard is Fidel, a true 'superman' in Trotskyist terms:

> En las grandes concentraciones públicas se observa algo así como el diálogo de los diapasones cuyas vibraciones provocan otras nuevas en el interlocutor. Fidel y la masa comienzan a vibrar en un diálogo de intensidad creciente hasta alcanzar el clímax en un final abrupto, coronado por nuestro grito de lucha y de victoria. (8)

This turgid hyperbole in the midst of a mostly sober manifesto is striking (almost Wagnerian, Piñera might suggest). But Guevara's vibrations have a point. Fidel is presented as the apotheosis of the integration evident amongst the vanguard, an extraordinary man who nevertheless retains an umbilical link with the masses, is able simultaneously to direct, and be guided by, *el pueblo*. Castro's rite of passage (from pre-Batista political ambition to tragiheroic attacks on tyranny, from the hostile school of guerrilla survival to confirmation as the undisputed 'dirigente máximo') is populated by the kind of liminal trials to which Turner's ritual king was also exposed (Guevara 1966: 21). For both, their gradual and painful 'becomings' guarded against unworldliness, their exposure to the vicissitudes of more mundane lives ensured that these supermen never forgot what made everymen tick. Critically, Guevara suggests that Fidel's proximity to *el pueblo* means that the archetype he and the Revolutionary vanguard embodied is wholly accessible to anyone in Cuba with the desire needed to undertake self-progression towards plenitude, with the discipline called for to achieve full 'reaggregation' (Turner 1969: 94).

Despite this proximity and accessibility, not everyone in Cuba in 1965, Guevara claims, could hope to emulate the hero. In *El socialismo y el hombre*, Guevara, like Roig de Leuchsenring, Martínez Villena, Padilla, Tamargo and others before him, develops his own taxonomy of unforgivable sins and irredeemable sinners. And for Guevara (as for his forebears) the combination of advanced age and what is seen as underdeveloped ideology is a particularly deadly sin, era and ethos are inextricably linked and no act of contrition could overcome this. So just as some earlier analyst-authors had sought to draw a schismatic frontier between the unsatisfactory past and the hope-filled future, so Guevara advocates his own brand of historical nihilism to safeguard the purity of the present: 'Las taras del pasado se trasladan al presente en la conciencia individual y hay que hacer un trabajo continuo para erradicarlas' (1966: 9). And whilst the 'trabajo continuo' of Revolutionary education could assist some to make the transition from the *ancien* to the new regime, Guevara is particularly scornful of the possible redemption of intellectual sinners from the past. Much critical attention has focused on his condemnation of 'las formas congeladas del realismo socialista' (19). The somewhat hastily extrapolated conclusion is that, whilst drawing back from absolute expressive 'libertad' (arguing that the true metaphysic of liberty would not exist 'hasta el completo desarrollo de la sociedad nueva'), Guevara warned against entangling culture in the 'camisa de fuerza' of slavish representation of socialist reality, instead (like Castro in our reading of 'Palabras') advocating reasonable freedom to all 'expresión artística' that was not counter-revolutionary (ibid.). The first counterpoint to make to this reading is that Guevara's understanding of artistic endeavour is as a 'mecanismo ideológico-cultural' whose prime objective is 'educar al pueblo', to teach them the practical skills and cognitive codes for socialist citizenship and future progress towards 'la total conciencia de su ser social, lo que equivale a su realización plena como criatura humana' (18 & 15).[6] But for Guevara, not all Cubans are eligible for, or capable of, this education. For him, Cuba's current artists and intellectuals are fatally doomed by the congenital limitation of being born before the Revolutionary epiphany, by their past and malignant habits that would spoil any contribution they could make to the creation of new Cubans: 'La culpabilidad de muchos de nuestros intelectuales y artistas reside en su pecado original; no son auténticamente revolucionarios' (20). Far from relying on implacable progress towards a socialist future to rectify these original sinners, they had to be isolated and ostracised, cut off from the new-men-in-the-making, pushed to the margins of collective consciousness there to live out their ideological obsolescence: 'Nuestra tarea consiste en impedir que la generación actual, dislocada por sus conflictos, se pervierta y pervierta a las nuevas […]. Las nuevas generaciones vendrán libres del pecado original' (20). Thus, although adhering to a linear and heuristic history (like St Augustine), Guevara did not expect all to be ultimately saved. His imperative is actually one that we have come

6   In an unmistakeable echo of Eduardo Abela's claim we came across in Chapter 2 in which 'el futuro artista será el hombre que después de ganar su sustento, regresará por la tarde a su hogar, y para satisfacer una necesidad de su espíritu, se recreará pintado las emociones del día' (1927: 105).

across before: his primary concern in seeking to extirpate certain characters from the ongoing national narrative is that forward momentum should not be arrested by the 'sins' of the past, that the transition from egotistical isolation to seamless cohesion should be fully stimulated, the incorporation of new cognitive codes and moral compulsion placed at the centre of new Cuba's sense of self, the 'national discourse of the teleology of progress allowed to reign (Bhabha 2010: 216).

In our analysis of articulations of identity as elements of a collective rite of passage, one aspect of Guevara's text (mirroring aspects of political life on the island that we have already pointed to) comes immediately into relief. After the euphoria and reactive ideological praxis of 1959–60 came determined 1965 attempts by the new 'directores' of Cuban socio-political life (in response to external threats and the internal radicalisation of the Revolutionary creed) to reassert structure. As we have already seen, the newly founded Partido Comunista de Cuba was charged with consolidating out of earlier ideological flux and steering Cuba away from chaos. Castro's speech inaugurating the new party was a hymn to seamless integrity in which 'todo tipo de matiz' had been erased and in which the trials of the previous six years had brought Cuba and its sense of self to the 'punto afortunado de la historia' in which all difference and disparity were eliminated and it could be declared that 'sólo hay un tipo de revolucionario' (Castro 1965: para. 36). Although Guevara was not as conclusive as Castro, accepting that 'el camino es largo y lleno de dificultades', like Fidel (and like all advocates of post-liminal reaggregation), he was unequivocal in his assessment of the need for structure along the way:

> En la imagen de las multitudes marchando hacia el futuro, encaja el concepto de institucionalización como [...] aparatos bien aceitados que permitan esa marcha, que permitan la selección natural de los destinados a caminar en la vanguardia y que adjudiquen el premio y el castigo a los que cumplan o atenten contra la sociedad en construcción. (1966: 14)

Hence this text by an Argentinian Marxist finds its natural ideological home within the reaggregationist canon of Cuban identity debates. And as we have seen, its declared goal of engendering citizens immune to the maladies of the past and moving steadfastly towards a perfect future through a combination of structural-prophylactic pressures and diligent self-instruction is actually not that novel at all. Where Guevara points to the new man and describes 'la nueva sociedad donde los hombres tendrán características distintas' (13), others had preached of the future vindication of Cuba's *pueblo puro*, of the resurrection of a prelapsarian innocence, of a genealogical and ideological unification of past and present heroes, or of the exorcism of socio-cultural devils to finally allow the righteous angels to reign. When Guevara talks of 'la sociedad del hombre comunista', we can read a well-rehearsed Cuban desire for life beyond the limen.

This uncompromising manifesto did not go without answer. Some of the analyst-authors from previous turning points who remained on the island and alive refused to accept Guevara's instruction that they be condemned as mere footnotes within the national narrative, and continued to analyse the life they saw around them and articulate it into their own contributions to the public debate. Perhaps more surprising, and certainly less commented upon, is the fact that despite the combined force of direct and indirect Revolutionary education, the re-assertion of structure and the deployment of 'estímulos' to extirpate original ideological sins and allow a new *conciencia* to emerge, some of the new generation of Cuban creators, interpreted by many critics as joining the ranks of the 'multitudes marchando hacia el futuro' (ibid.: 14), can on closer reading be seen to offer rather more ambivalent, less decisive and more liminal contributions to the still contested national narrative.

The sinners rebel

Some analyst-authors certainly did concur with Guevara's diagnosis of Cuba's (and particularly Cuban intellectuals') past errors and with his prescriptions for a new moral epoch, even though the resultant *imago* of collective identity would involve at best an anguished *mea culpa* and painful contrition, at worst their absolute exclusion from the national narrative. There is a remarkable ideological resonance, for example, between *El socialismo y el hombre en Cuba* and Roberto Fernández Retamar's 1966 essay 'Hacia una intelectualidad revolucionaria en Cuba', in which the author bemoaned 'el desaliento e incluso el despego' that had stultified Cuban culture for many years (and particularly after Batista's 1952 coup). Retamar joined Guevara in calling for a sincere act of contrition, neatly synthesising the external and internal pressures that should be brought to bear on intellectual sinners: 'es lo cierto que, a los ojos de la revolución, como lo han expresado Fidel y el Che, los intelectuales teníamos que recuperar el tiempo perdido, recuperarnos a nosotros mismos, hacernos intelectuales *de* la revolución *en* la revolución' (1967a: 172). This is the mood of abject culpability which Rojas sees as leading writers such as Retamar to always approach their creative contributions to the Revolution as a 'penitencia o un sacrificio', which in turn preconditioned artists on the threshold between the old world and the new 'soportar cualquier castigo a cambio de la equívoca gloria de ser considerado un "buen revolucionario"' (Rojas 2006: 166). Although guilt, fear and a desperate desire to conform do undoubtedly permeate the story to which we now turn, its author is only an ambivalent penitent and a dubitable 'buen Revolucionario'.

The first six years of revolution were turbulent for Virgilio Piñera. In mid-1959 he joined the writers at *Revolución* and *Lunes de Revolución*, marvelling at the changes sweeping the country and at the sudden explosion of publishing possibilities. In his 5 November *Revolución* article 'El arte hecho revolución, la revolución hecha arte' (Piñera 1959b), he exultantly joined other *venceremos* prophets of the future conquest of the present and proclaimed (without irony), 'estamos viviendo una etapa de sagrado delirio' (2). In October 1960, however, this delirium turned feverish when Piñera was arrested during the infamous 'Operación *P*', which saw alleged prostitutes, pimps, pederasts and other *antisociales* interned without charge by the Revolutionary police. Although quickly released after high-level pressure was applied by his friends,[7] the incident obviously brought Piñera's gaze down from the Revolutionary heavens to the more mundane and potentially painful realities of a radical socio-cultural transformation. Despite this sobering contact with the heavy-handed kind of 'educación indirecta' Guevara had spoken of, Piñera remained in Cuba and steadfast as the iconoclastic *lobo feroz* of Cuban *letras*. When Castro (in the meetings brought to a close by his 'Palabras') pugilistically demanded that intellectuals state their concerns about cultural freedoms under Revolutionary rule, Piñera was the only one to rise to his feet in a demonstration of paradoxical fearlessness, declaring: 'tengo miedo, tengo mucho miedo' (in Ponce de León 1999: para. 1). This fear did not translate into a desire for penitence and self-sacrifice, however; any anxiety Piñera may have felt did nothing to impede his audacious creative endeavours. If not a direct response to *El socialismo y el hombre*, Piñera's 1965 story 'La rebelión de los enfermos'[8] certainly sustains a dialogue with the moral imperatives of the new man, the taut dichotomy between the individual and 'las masas', the potential pains of direct and indirect Revolutionary pedagogy and the shifting sands of heroism, sickness and original sin.

'La rebelión de los enfermos', like 'El viaje' before it, is a liminal tale in which any sense of forward momentum is arrested and all confidence that 'las nuevas generaciones vendrán libres del pecado original' (Guevara 1966: 20) is smothered in a tense, painful, even desperate present The story begins in a hospital ward. Carlos (the first-person narrator) has broken his collar bone but has complete faith in the doctors and confidence in a swift recovery. José, the patient in the neighbouring bed, is less jovial: 'Ayer me

---

7   Carlos Franqui reports his defence of Piñera's case before Ramiro Valdés (then head of the police force) and Castro (in Franqui 1981: 280–6).
8   Written in 1965 but only published in Piñera 1999.

operaron, por duodécima vez, esta pierna [...]. Y no crea que aquí acabarán mis sufrimientos. Es muy posible que las operaciones continuen' (Piñera 1999: 572). Their antithetical attitudes to illness and good health are not due simply to different degrees of optimism: José is fomenting rebellion against the endless (and seemingly ineffective) sanitary routine, against the very frontier between sickness and health: 'Haga que una persona, en perfecto estado de salud, se acueste, digamos, un año y lo verá contraer esa dolencia que recibe el nombre de "desesperación" ' (574). Carlos (a maths teacher and staunch supporter of order) attempts to reinstate certainty and emphasise proper authority: 'Se deja el hospital cuando el médico ordena el alta; no antes. Además, la voluntad del enfermo no cuenta' (573). Within our reading, Carlos and José are diametrical opposites in the *venceremos/luchita* debate. Carlos is convinced that the rite of passage from illness to health (all played out in the liminal space of the hospital) is necessary but temporary. José, on the other hand, thinks illness is here to stay. In this, Piñera distances himself both from Guevara's reaggregationist imperative, and from the liminalist perspective of Ortiz and Mañach who (in echo of Martí and Unamuno) saw turning points as moments when the re-cognisance of identity can also involve the re-cognition of illness as innervating, in which the patient is best left 'sudar su propia calentura' (Martí, in *Denuncia*, 1 Feb. 1933: 1). For Piñera (through José), there **is** momentum through this moment of flux, but it leads only towards disaggregation and death; for José, the present is painful, but the future will only make things worse. The exchange between the two patients ends and Carlos, convinced of his neighbour's insanity, is duly returned to his normal life away from the hospital and back to the city-centre core. The madman is soon proved a prophet, however: within a few days Carlos receives an enigmatic telegram instructing him to present himself 'con carácter urgente, en el Hospital Nacional. Hora: doce meridiano día de la fecha. Favor llevar consigo *smoking* y cepillo de dientes' (Piñera 1999: 574). Thus begins Carlos's descent into a lunatic world in which all diagnostic and logical borders are erased, all sense turned on its head, all structures made chaotic, all order overcome by its disordered opposites: the hale are to be confined to hospital whilst the infirm are to be sent onto the streets. Although Piñera's narrative is notoriously abstract and rarely contains circumstantial evidence that would enable the reader to anchor it in specific times or places, this 1965 story can at least be read with the Cuban political and ethical context at the time in mind, can be brought alongside *El socialismo y el hombre* as an imaginative exploration of moments of radical change in which, as Sartre said during his 1960 visit to the island, 'una sociedad se quiebra los huesos a martillazos; demuele sus estructuras; trastorna sus instituciones' (1960: 68).

Despite his avowed obedience to medical authority, Carlos vacillates before the strange telegram's instructions and is unable immediately 'acomodarse' (as Guevara would say) to the new reality. A call to the Director of the hospital resolves all doubt:

> Perdone, doctor – dije con voz entrecortada –. Se trata de un telegrama que acabo de recibir … En efecto – me contestó con voz placentera –. He cursado dos mil telegramas, y también estoy recibiendo otras tantas llamadas. (Piñera 1999: 578)

Caught between external authority (the subliminal incentive to obey the biblical and patriarchal-sounding Dr Isaac Morales is clear) and 'el impacto' of a new social order to which a significant portion of *el pueblo* seem exposed, Carlos somewhat reluctantly puts Guevara's instructions into practice, relinquishes his inclination to individual resistance, accepts his 'cuota de sacrificio' and succumbs to a collective fate with a rather anxious sense of 'satisfacción del deber cumplido' (Guevara 1966: 23): 'Me resigné y puse la cabeza en el tajo. Una orden es una orden, y más cuando, como acababa de enterarme, esa orden concernía a dos mil ciudadanos de esta ciudad' (Piñera 1999: 578). In this, his decision to conform is hardly indicative of clear resolve and what Guevara might have referred to as Carlos's 'autoeducación' remains incomplete: whilst outwardly preparing to swap city-centre life for the margin of the hospital, his *sensibilidad* remains in unresolved torment and his fear produces a paradoxical valour: 'Mientras me ponía las medias pensé en el suicidio' (ibid.). But the impetus of the absurd moment carries Carlos into the crowded streets around the hospital where, despite his reservations, he is impressed by the demonstration of collective intent amongst the disciplined mass of 'pacientes' marching towards their new home: 'no se podía negar que todo aquello presentaba un golpe de vista magnífico' (579). The synchrony and cohesion of the masses in action, what for Guevara was a 'marcha hacia el futuro' through the medium of institutional 'aparatos bien aceitados' (1966: 14), finds an aberrant echo in the scene before the hospital gates: 'Pensé en un hormiguero, y esta sobada imagen de la vida humana como diligentes hormigas nunca tuvo mejor explicación. Hormiga yo también, me uní a las hormigas' (Piñera 1999: 579). What for Guevara had been a hope-filled vision of a utopian near-future becomes for Piñera a nightmarish scene of of 'deber' degraded into mindless and conformist instinct, of *sensibilidad* robbed of all sense, of humanity brought low. Thus, as a healthy man confined to hospital, Carlos's new life in this absurd and aberrant limen begins.

As a literary exploration of psycho-social experience during (and after) schismatic change, three further points of dialogue between Piñera's story and Guevara's manifesto suggest themselves. After some days of confinement Carlos begins to reflect upon the implications of his new situation: '¿Adónde habían ido a parar los cientos y miles de enfermos [...]? ¿es que todos habían fallecido repentinamente [...]? O contrariamente, ¿todos habían sanado de golpe ... ?' (ibid.: 581). Charged with the mood of uncanny speculation, these reflections resonate with the debate on human perfectibility and the role of psycho-social sickness and sin that had preoccupied Cuban analyst-authors since at least 1923. At that time, intellectuals such as Martínez Villena and Roig de Leuchsenring saw Cuban society split fundamentally beween the *pueblo puro* (whose only sin was an excess of good faith) and a rogues' gallery of ethical devils. Even these *maleantes* were not without hope, however; through a contrite turn to the 'rosario de rectificación', even the most inveterate sinners could hope to extirpate their 'malos mayores' and join the *pueblo* in the pursuit of collective perfection (Martínez Villena 1923: 19). By 1959, as we have seen, the prophylactic attack against 'sickness' (embodied in emblems of the malignant past such as *Diario de la Marina* and Mañach) had moved determinedly towards a definitive cure. In 1965, Guevara claimed that not all were apt for salvation, but that efforts to isolate the perversions of the past were beginning to give conclusive results, with new Cubans finally coming into being 'libres del pecado original' (Guevara 1966: 20). Hence, for all these thinkers, the definitive eradication of psycho-social sickness would bring about a future-perfect Cuban *sensibilidad*; for all, the *conciencia colectiva* would be complete when it was cleansed. Piñera, through José, challenges this ideology outright. But he also disputes the converse approach to sickness, as both congenital and ultimately necessary. Without the stimulation of illness, said Unamuno, the organism would become addled; without pedagogical devils, said Ortiz, humans would simply become expert in the cardinal sin of self-aggrandisement and would fatally forget their own imperfections. Piñera's reading is more hopeless. 'La rebelión' rejects the idea that 'illnesses' will be cured as Cuba moves towards socio-physiological perfection (as in Guevara), but also rejects the notion that the collective corpus will actually be healthier, more self-aware and more wholesome with illness incorporated. For Piñera, the masses are trapped in a psychological double bind: they are fundamentally optimistic and credulous and refuse to reconcile themselves to the perfect imperfection pointed to by Ortiz and company, but neither are they able to make the complete leap of faith that Guevara exhorts; instead they fall into a psychotic in-between reality in this story, in which the 'recovery' of the infirm has actually opened a disturbing hole in society's sense of self that has to be filled with new pathologies in order to avoid disaster: 'Todos habían sanado de golpe y ésto podía despertar sospechas y hasta que la gente se acostumbrara al milagro, se nos retenía como enfermos en éste y demás hospitales' (Piñera 1999: 581). Getting under the skin of earlier readings of the 'miracle' of Revolutionary victory led by the omnipotent shepherd Fidel, 'Rebelión de los enfermos' suggests *el pueblo*'s innate suspicion of miracles that will not be overcome through self-instruction or through the more direct ideological shepherding of the Revolutionary *pastor*, but through the sacrifice of the story's obedient hospitalised lambs. This narrative reality can perhaps be extrapolated outwards to events of the early 1960s and Guevara's (and the Revolution's) fixation with original sin. As the virulent illness of the *batistato* was eradicated through the imprisonment, execution or exile of its principal vectors, there was a sense that Cuban society was being 'sanado de golpe'. Whereas Roig de Leuchsenring, for example, began writing his *Males y vicios de Cuba republicana* in 1958 with a lament about the all too common moral transgressions of the decadent Republic, by the 1961 Revolutionary re-edition he had been convinced that 'en la mayoría de los casos ya han sido extirpados por completo' (1961b: 348). As in Piñera's story, it could be argued that when facing the possibility of a miraculous cure, Cuba's collective faith faltered, and instead of complete perfection it beheld a disturbing ethical lacuna that had to be filled with new ills, new diagnoses and new prescriptions for an ever-more radical 'cura'. Thus, when the *batistianos* were all dealt with, Cuba turned to more subtle social 'sinners' and their misdemeanours: to the three Ps of prostitutes, pimps and pederasts (of which Piñera was considered an infectious element), to the 'revisionismo y confusionismo ideológicos' and the rest of a long litany of counter-revolutionary sins of which Alfredo Guevara accused *Lunes de Revolución*, to perverse a-revolutionary intellectuals damned on the wrong side of a chronological and ideological divide (Franqui 1981: 265). From this stubbornly infirm world, Piñera elaborates an absurd narrative reality in which even the normal physiological order is revolutionised: whereas Carlos is suddenly found to be pregnant, confined to a labour ward and told 'será preciso practicar la cesárea y muy probablemente perderá la vida', his friend Alicia is diagnosed with prostate cancer (Piñera 1999: 580). For neither could there be any cure, of course, but that was not the point: the sickbed had been filled, the lacuna closed, the new world order preserved.

The second point of dialogue between *El socialismo y el hombre* and 'Rebelión' (and between Piñera and some of the more optimistic liminalists we have seen so far) is around the characteristics of transcendental change. Although Guevara accepted that the new man was an as yet unfinished project, the trials of the rite of Revolutionary passage from dictatorship to guerrilla struggle to absolute autonomy, and from capitalist scion to socialist neophyte, had nevertheless brought the rewards of greater integrity, collective coherence and a sense of irreversible progress:

Así vamos marchando. A la cabeza de la inmensa columna – no nos avergüenza ni nos intimida el decirlo – va Fidel, después los mejores cuadros del Partido e, inmediatamente, tan cerca que se siente su enorme fuerza, va el pueblo en su conjunto; sólida armazón de individuos que caminan hacia un fin común. (Guevara 1966: 22)

In Piñera's story, the healthy in hospital and the infirm outside are similarly exposed to the terrible trials of a radical transition, but the result is not a Guevara-type implacable march towards the common and certain cure that Carlos had previously been so sure of, nor is it the lingering in wholesome liminal illness that Unamuno and Ortiz had advocated. Without the care administered in hospital, the sick on the streets are deteriorating rapidly: Carlos is to be visited by a 'healthy' man whose brain tumour has left him 'a dos dedos de la muerte' (Piñera 1999: 581); for the new 'patients' there can be only two kinds of progress: infection by their visitors and discharge into the outside world of perverse health, or a descent into the 'desesperación' and panic that José thought the most virulent ill of all. For Piñera, therefore, the revolution that has seen the healthy and the sick swap places has stimulated no forward momentum at all: both remain suspended on an awful and endless frontier between infirmity and health. Although Carlos's visitor is on the brink of death, his shuffling visits continue; although his physical appearance and laboured breathing are 'anunciadores de un fin inminente', he clings stubbornly to life, even making plans for the distant future: 'pienso hacer un largo viaje' (582). Similarly, as we have already seen, although Carlos has succumbed to external instructions and the self-stimulated pressure 'unirse al hormiguero', these provide no release from his doubts nor word miracles of reintegration, leading him instead to desperate anomie: 'No sé si los locos cuando están a punto de volverse locos se preguntan por la inminente pérdida de su razón, pero yo, que ahora me encontraba en esa postura de ni cuerdo ni loco, empecé a preguntarme por la mía' (579).

One of the starkest contrasts between Guevara's and Piñera's texts is to be seen in their representations of the genesis of the next generation. For Guevara, Cuba's new men and women were actually new boys and girls, 'la arcilla maleable con que se puede construir al hombre nuevo', born beyond the Revolutionary schism and in instinctive symbiosis with a socio-cultural reality to which their elders came hamstrung by 'taras anteriores' (Guevara 1966: 20). In Guevara's thesis, regeneration would only occur when the perversions of current Cubans (and particularly those of sinful intellectuals) were excised. In contrast, birth in 'La rebelión' is perversion personified: the next generation will be born of a man on the brink of madness (and not expected to survive) before being taken into the stewardship of his terminally ill visitor, one of this revolution's 'miracle cures': 'En caso de que usted fallezca de resultas del parto, le prometo hacerme cargo de su hijo. No vaya a creer, tengo mis ahorros' (Piñera 1999: 582). This future is not perfect but rather infected by a terrifying subjunctive mood of uncertainty. In such a future, only monstrous new men would be born.

The final counterpoint between these two texts also points to some reconciliation between Piñera's bleak world vision and that of more optimistic, but nonetheless liminalist, analyst-authors such as Mañach and Ortiz. This final counterpoint is around understandings of heroism. For Guevara, the achievements of great men and women had to be perpetuated in the everyday heroism of the masses, inspired still by clarity of purpose and disposition to great sacrifice, but turned from extraordinary individual acts towards collective endeavours 'realizados por todo un pueblo' and 'conscientes de recibir el premio en la satisfacción del deber cumplido' (1966: 6 & 23). In 'La rebelión', this sense of heroism through collective conformity and sense of duty is presented in a very different light. Determined individualism, in Carlos's new world, is certainly censured. When fellow patient and friend Alicia refuses to put on the standard-issue pyjamas of the prostate cancer ward to which she has been sent the consequences are immediate: 'el enfermero se vió en la necesidad de amarrarla a la cama' (Piñera 1999: 580). Alicia refuses to learn this lesson in uniformity (in every sense), however, and at the monthly soirée, in which 'toman parte tanto sanos como enfermos aunque […] a la altura en que estamos no puede decirse en rigor quién es el sano o quién es el enfermo' (582), she sets aside the theatre of ascribed illness to consume large amounts of food 'con grandes signos de alegría y gula' and boldly declare her health: 'Carlos, ¿qué es de tu vida? Chico, yo aquí, encantada. Sana, sanísima. Como de todo, a mi no me duelen ni los callos' (583). In Piñera's world, standing out from the conformist crowd will not be tolerated, and as in previous turning points, a partial and half-hearted epiphany is as unacceptable as outright rebellion: 'Y mientras me lo decía rodaba muerta a mis pies' (ibid.). Carlos survives, but neither through absolute conformity or complete assimilation of the internal and external pressures to which Guevara referred, nor through the mass heroism of the 'sólida armazón de individuos que caminan hacia un fin común' (Guevara 1966: 22). Between Alicia's uncompromising rebellion and his own earlier proclamations of the need to conform, Carlos finally charts a paradoxically brave middle way between obedience and resistance where heroism is not rooted in duty fulfilled, but in subterfuge; where individualism is not exorcised, but merely obscured. Whilst contemplating suicide, he ultimately opts for ironic survival accompanied by a 'sonora carcajada'; although driven almost mad by the absurd theatre of his new life, Carlos puts courageous prudence before derring-do and when consoled about his chances

of survival by his terminally ill visitor, he chooses to protect his inner ambivalence behind a crust of external obedience:

> Casi estuve por protestar y decirle que él estaba a dos dedos de la muerte.
> Pero conservé mi serenidad, y moviendo la cabeza lancé un suspiro y
> balbuceé:
> – ¡Muy grave! (Piñera 1999: 582)

Here Carlos makes surreptitious use of the subject-neutral collective spirit
by leaving the conjugated verb out altogether. By saying neither 'estoy' nor
'estás', Carlos both is and is not, conforms and yet subtly rebels. Whilst in his
pre-revolutionary life he had insisted on the clear frontier between sickness
and health, he now realises that crazy José was right all along and that life lies
in the liminal middle:

> Siempre le pondrán al enfermo la muerte por delante como al niño le ponen
> el coco … – expresó con sorna y amargura a la vez –. O te curas o te mueres
> … Pero éso no deja de ser un simplismo, y de los más idiotas que la falsa
> piedad haya discurrido. Ninguno de esos tontos se ha detenido a pensar
> un poco en el hiato inscrito entre la enfermedad y la muerte, he aquí la
> verdadera dolencia. (573).

Carlos thus belongs neither amongst Guevara's communitas of the faithful
masses inspired to self-chastisement by a false sense of piety, nor with the
almost-integrated vanguard at the head of the Revolutionary column. Whereas
Guevara (and others) perceived heroism as imparting the fortitude required to
face any foe, whether a potentially cataclysmic military strike, a more natural
catastrophe, or the assaults of the bitter inner enemies of doubt, duality and
flux, for Piñera, as for Martí, Ortiz, Mañach, Ichaso and many other analyst-
authors of Cuba's twentieth-century national narrative, 'la virtud triunfa de
lado' (in Ichaso 1953: 55 & 81). In Carlos's passive yet paradoxically valiant
resistance, Piñera brings this mundane anti-hero alongside Luján and his
'esfuerzo de lo pedestre hacia lo ideal' (Mañach 1926: 11). Carlos's outward
acceptance of radical transformations and stubborn inner defence of doubt,
despair and the unheroic determination to get by bring him great serenity,
not in the kind of inevitable integration that Guevara perceived on the leeside
of Cuba's rite of passage, but in the perennial dislocation of assured self by
Cuban sensibility's *intransigencia* (as Vitier would say); not in submission
to the dauntless dictatorship of the collective, but in the embodiment of a
heterodox declaration that 'blind, straight courage is all right for individual
piety and immortality, not for ensuring collective survival' (Nandy 2009: 108);

not by following an absolutist vanguard towards teleological perfection, but by following a hopeless Sisyphus in ironic resignation. Facing the incursion of the absurd into the very core of his sense of self, Carlos has emerged purged of all attachment to reason and purpose and exorcised of any urge to resist. His epiphany has not been towards the integration of the human spirit on the moral high ground of communism, 'lo que equivale a su realización plena como criatura humana, rotas las cadenas de la enajenación' (Guevara 1966: 14–15), but rather in an acceptance of incomprehensibility that Sisyphus (and his analysts) would recognise: 'It was previously a question of finding out whether or not life had to have a meaning to be lived. It now becomes clear on the contrary that it will be lived all the better if it has no meaning' (Camus 2000: 51). When neither serendipity nor salvation are realistic dreams in a nightmare world, tranquillity must suffice; Carlos's rebellion is a tragic stoicism of which Sisyphus himself would be proud: 'He terminado por adaptarme a mi nueva vida. En el momento en que escribo estas páginas mi tranquilidad de espíritu es perfecta' (Piñera 1999: 583).

In 'La rebelión de los enfermos' Piñera offered Sisyphus to Cuba as the manifestation of the ironically hopeful maxim that had saved the island until then: 'ese saludable principio de que no existe nada verdaderamente doloroso o absolutamente placentero' (Piñera 1960: 9). With this epiphany, Sisyphus lingered in the limen. After depositing his stone at the top of the mountain, only to see it cascade past him into darkness, he sighed and began his own descent in a moment 'like the breathing-space which returns as surely as his suffering' and is 'the hour of consciousness' (Camus 2000: 109). Unconvinced by the paradise to come and uncowed by the paradox of here and now, Piñera and his ironic anti-hero find their spirits at peace in the landscape of the liminal middle: 'The struggle itself towards the heights is enough to fill a man's heart. One must imagine Sisyphus happy' (Camus 2000: 111). This schismatic identity and heterodox anti-heroism is at the core of our final text.

Cryptic confessions and subversive sin

Edmundo Desnoes's *Memorias del subdesarrollo*[9] is in many ways the perfect (or rather imperfect) text with which to conclude this exploration of the ideological confrontations within the Cuban identity debate at critical twentieth-century turning points. In many senses it synthesises, and is usually read as, a thoughtful contribution to the *venceremos* ethos in which ambivalence and doubt are overcome and the collective story of selfhood reaches

---

9 First published by Casa de las Américas in 1965 and subsequently re-written as a screenplay for Tomás Gutierrez Alea's 1968 film of the same name.

a Revolutionary and final full-stop. Our reading will instead illuminate the ongoing *luchita* within this purportedly post-liminal text.

For many readers *Memorias del subdesarrollo* is what Ana Serra calls a 'confessional narrative', an attempt by the author to emulate the example and follow the instructions of the Revolutionary vanguard and seek an encounter with his ambivalent pre-revolutionary self, not as an act of reconciliation across the epistemological frontier, but as an imaginative extirpation of sinful traits and tendencies from the past (Serra 2007: 60).[10] In this sense, the protagonist Malabre becomes, in Imeldo Álvarez's term, 'el gran antihéroe', the embodiment of the *sensibilidad* from which Revolutionary society, and its exemplary analyst-authors, sought to distance themselves: 'está muy claro el rompimiento que la obra plantea' (Álvarez 1980: 67). In this, the text can be read as satisfying an 'obligation to repent' or a 'wish to commit' to thus expedite authorial integration (or reaggregation) whilst simultaneously making a cathartic contribution to a post-crisis archetype around which the Cuban people could rally in collective accord (Serra 2007: 60). Neither Serra nor *Memorias* suggest that this exorcism of the aberrant self will be easy or conclusive: whilst claiming that the book bears witness to the determined articulation of a wholly new *sensibilidad*, for example, Serra also points to the space left open for 'shadowy Others', although for her these marginal men and women are wracked by 'self-loathing, guilt and duplicity' (85–6). Our reading of *Memorias* is different. Whilst examining the reaggregated narrative new man, we will turn to focus more fully on his shadowlike alterity: on Malabre as a Rip van Winkle of Cuba's memory war, as 'un muerto entre los vivos' who resists resurrection but refuses to resign himself to death (Desnoes 1968: 48); on a betwixt-and-between Malabre, not a subversive (or indeed subliminal) corollary to conclusive *cubanía revolucionaria* (Kapcia 2000: 125), nor a stubborn residue on the edges of a narrative exorcism, but the prime protagonist in what I apprehend as Desnoes's subtle condemnation of the whole notion of confession; on Malabre as the principal spokesman for his author's steadfast manifesto for life in the liminal middle.[11]

Beyond the central schism between the pre- and post-Revolutionary identities of the protagonist, Malabre in fact demonstrates several personalities that split and splinter into often contradictory shards of subjectivity within this text. The archetypal bourgeois *malo* faces the extra-textual and contrite author

[10] To support her exploration of this text as an exorcism, Serra cites Desnoes, in interview with William Luis, describing Malabre as a part of his personality that he was attempting to 'get rid of, to understand, to exorcise, like catharsis' (Luis & Desnoes 1982).

[11] Enrico Mario Santí suggests that Desnoes's introspective in *Memorias* is splintered by the inter-textual confusion between author and protagonists, manifest most clearly in the inclusion of three short stories at the end of the novel supposedly written by Malabre (Santí 1981).

Desnoes, but Malabre also turns to face his childhood friend Eddy, the talented and adventurous writer whom he had so admired 'porque hacía todo lo que yo no podía por miedo' (Desnoes 1968: 46). After his own rite of passage in New York, however, Eddy has returned as a ficto-autobiographical Edmundo Desnoes, a budding cultural commissar keen to demonstrate his fidelity to the Revolutionary creed. Within each confrontation, oscillations between the ideal and aberrant selves make contrition complex and exorcism almost impossible. We'll take the personalities in turn.

A first reading identifies Malabre as bourgeois *maldad* incarnate: he opted for the solitary 'carrera de lobos' of a lucrative business career over his childhood sweetheart and cultivated an indulgent and wasteful life between cocktail bars and high-class travel, whose broad horizons have left him with an entrenched prejudice against what he sees as the provincial post-revolutionary Cuban *pueblo* and their *subdesarrollado* sensibilities. Despite this ill fit in the new Cuba, however, when his entire family departs for exile in the US, Malabre stays behind in Havana to undertake the kind of existential self-dissection which Serra and others describe as a vicarious confession on the part of the author: 'No quiero huir más del hueco que llevo adentro. Quiero sentirme solo y ver hasta donde puedo llegar, si llego al fondo de mi vacío' (ibid.: 26). This earnest introspection soon appears suspect, however, as Malabre's words and deeds rather reveal him to be an obdurate cynic, a recalcitrant adherent of the *ancien régime* unable 'acomodarse' to the new. Although initially impressed by the frenetic urban activity he encounters on the streets of the 'new' Havana, he soon launches a rancid attack on the urban *muchedumbre* and the crass city they now inhabit:

> La Habana parece ya una ciudad del interior, Pinar del Río, Artemisa o Matanzas. Ya no parece el París del Caribe, como decían los turistas y las putas. Ahora parece más un capital de Centro América, una de esas ciudades muertas y subdesarrolladas, como Tegucigalpa o San Salvador o Managua [...]. Es la gente también; ahora, toda la gente que se ve por las calles es humilde, viste mal [...]. Todas las mujeres parecen criadas y todos los hombres obreros. (15)

In riposte to Guevara's assertion that the new men and women of Revolutionary reality would be increasingly liberated from 'las relaciones mercantiles' (Guevara 1966: 10), Malabre rather paints a dismal picture of the common *habaneros*' ignorance and avarice: 'Ahora tienen un poco de dinero y lo gastan en cualquier cosa; pagan, por mi madre, hasta veinte pesos por un orinal si se lo ponen en una vidriera' (Desnoes 1968: 15). Amidst these less than ideal everymen with no inkling of the super-heroics of social(ist) reaggregation, Malabre histrionically describes the cohesion of community to be an unbearable calvary: 'No aguanto estar mucho tiempo cerca de nadie. No hay nada más asqueroso que muchos hombres hacinados […]. Un hombre solo es algo impresionante y muchos hombres juntos es algo deprimente' (76). Unlike Guevara's spirited model citizens of the new age, Malabre is a disconnected, non-participative and unapologetically idle *flâneur* who spends most of his time sleeping or flirting. In further contrast to the new man, Malabre is insidious physical degeneration incarnate, the antithesis both of the vigorous youthism so central to Revolutionary conceptions of *cubanía* and of the sense of teleological progression, improvement and illumination enunciated by Guevara and a long tradition of optimistic analyst-authors: 'Tengo treinte y nueve años y yo soy un viejo. No me siento más sabio como esperaría un filósofo oriental, ni más maduro. Me siento más estúpido. Más podrido que maduro' (65). Finally, the calibration of Malabre's cultural compass is also chronically anachronistic. Whereas Revolutionary Cuba increasingly turned towards its own endemic cultural traditions, or began to explore modes and models of creative expression from other parts of the Third World,[12] Malabre values only the cosmopolitan creations of the Old World:

> Cada vez que leía una novela francesa me daba cuenta de nuestro atraso social y psicológico […]. Ahora no tengo punto de referencia para nada: no vienen libros ni productos de los países capitalistas. Todo ha cambiado aquí y los periódicos sólo traen consignas políticas. (42)

This is Malabre the arch-bourgeois 'bad guy', stereotyped, perhaps, in order to make his exorcism from the ideal self more clear-cut, the confession more strident and hence more conclusive. But within Malabre, and confronting the unsavoury otherness, is a more ambiguous self who boasts of his superiority over the lumpen, but at the same time admits that loneliness has hollowed him out: 'como si la soledad fuera un cáncer que me estuviera comiendo' (11). Although sneering at others' gratification in simple pleasures, he also understands with painful clarity that such guilelessness reveals his own anguish as 'estúpida' (12). His condemnation of the ill-dressed Havana passers-by is undercut in the end by last-minute qualification: 'todas las mujeres parecen criadas y todos los hombres obreros. No todas y todos, casi todas y todos' (15). What's more, his scorn for the masses is matched by his disgust for his bourgeois ex-best friend whose reactionary attitudes actually spur Malabre

---

[12] In 1966, for example, Cuba opened its borders to eight hundred delegates from more than eighty countries as the Tricontinental Conference infused Havana with a very different conception of cosmopolitanism.

to the Revolution's defence: 'Es tan cretino que dice que todo el mundo está contra el gobierno [...]. Le dí *To the Finland Station* de Edmond Wilson [*sic*], para que tuviera aunque sea una idea del desarrollo de las ideas sociales, del socialismo' (24 & 6). In Serra's reading, this is the *bildungsroman* of *Memorias*, its central rite of passage from cynicism to embryonic faith, the psycho-narrative therapy through which Malabre (and his author) 'achieves greater harmony within him [...] and the society' (2007: 14). Whilst this interpretation is certainly plausible, an alternative, and liminal, reading of *Memorias* is also possible. Whilst perceiving the potential for confession, there is also evidence to suggest that this text is actually a subtle condemnation of the whole notion of ideological original sin, a rejection of the belief in socio-cultural perfectibility and the psychological acts of contrition necessary to bring this about. In fact, *Memorias del subdesarrollo* can actually be read as a manifesto for irrevocably ambiguous and constantly oscillating identity in which the shadowy other is not the tidy distillation of retrograde tendencies but the betwixt-and-between threshold-dwelling amalgamation of Malabre, Eddy, Edmundo and the author-progenitor behind them all. Thus, Malabre can be read, not as an archetypal *malo*, but as an imaginative *malabarista*, juggling identities, playing tricks with ideological perspectives and constantly refusing to confirm who he is or what he thinks. From this angle, Desnoes is not a contrite analyst-author driven by 'estímulos y presiones' towards an 'obligation to repent' and 'a wish to commit' in an age of Revolutionary piety, but rather the most recent arrival in the pantheon of the unrepentant and the uncommitted, the 1965 spokesman for those Cubans and that Cuban *sensibilidad* that we have called liminal (Guevara 1966: 13; Serra 2007: 60).

Thus, where Malabre confronts his own author, he also turns to face his old friend (and contrapuntal other) Eddy (Desnoes). Initially we are led to believe that their sensibilities are opposed. Whereas Malabre describes the film *Hiroshima Mon Amour* as 'una bomba de profundidad',[13] Eddy is reported as writing 'mierda' about it in *Lunes de Revolución* (Desnoes 1968: 30). In what is the clearest indication of split personalities in the whole text, Eddy is everything that Malabre once wanted to be. He is a spontaneous adventurer who left the more timid businessman behind: 'Era bohemio, vivía en una casa vieja y abandonada que le dejó Lam. No trabajaba y sólo escribía y pintaba mientras yo me pasaba el día en la oficina ganando dinero para vivir sabroso' (46). He is man of uncompromising principles who left Cuba when continued island inhabitance carried the stigma of inevitable (if indirect) collaboration with

---

[13] A 1959 film by Alain Resnais in which memory and forgetfulness are pitted against each other in a fight for exclusive predominance.

all the abuses of the *batistato*. Now pre-revolutionary Eddy has returned as Revolutionary Edmundo Desnoes, a fêted man of Cuban letters and poet who will finally intone 'el canto del hombre nuevo con la auténtica voz del pueblo', as Che would say (Guevara 1966: 20). He has made the return journey both because of Cuba's revolutionary transformation, but also because he could no longer stomach the northern neighbour's ideological aggression against his homeland. In the literary symposium where they meet, Eddy is on the podium while Malabre is down below amongst the anonymous (and ill-dressed) masses; as a member of the cultural vanguard, Eddy is a figure 'con nombre y apellido' (ibid.: 5), but also remains in intimate empathy with the common man (and with the superman) through the iconic cigar he rolls between his fingers as he gives his speech. Nevertheless, far from representing the ideal self in clear opposition to the shadowy other, Edmundo as model man and committed intellectual is exposed as a fake, as insubstantial, inconsistent and assailed by the same oscillations of identity as his supposed antagonist Malabre. His former adherence to Bohemian spontaneity has mutated into an appetite for supercilious preaching from the revolutionary cultural pulpit: 'parecía un juez sentado en la tarima' (Desnoes 1968: 45); the ideological commitment that drove him from dictatorship and brought him back to Revolution is simply a sham: '¡Qué descarado!' says Malabre, 'regresó porque en Nueva York no era nadie: para lucirse en el subdesarrollo' (ibid.). Even his cigar-smoking is an affected prop which reveals the falsity of his resonance with the Revolutionary everymen and supermen and belies the real man he once was: although years before they had argued because Eddy claimed that 'fumar era una cobardía, que la gente fumaba para huir del vacío', now Edmundo Desnoes lights his cigar 'como si fuera un fumador veterano' (45–6). At the core of both Malabre and Edmundo, therefore, is the kind of 'reducción del yo a la nada' that would have been familiar to a previous (and vilified) generation of poet-philosophers (*Orígenes* 1:1, 7).

An even closer reading reveals *Memorias* offering no simple contrasts at all between archetypes and their shadowy others; all personalities in the book are disordered, all are split and splintered, and the resultant peripatetic self oscillates endlessly between Malabre 'el malo' and Malabre the *malabarista*, between anarchic Eddy and committed Edmundo Desnoes. Even Elena, a woman barely beyond girlhood whom Malabre comes across in the street, seeks the dissolution of her adolescent identity: 'Estoy cansada de ser siempre la misma [...]. Me interesa poder desdoblar mi personalidad' (Desnoes 1968: 34–5). But even this seemingly resolute splitting of subjectivity is disturbed and inconclusive: 'Enseguida pensé que repetía algo que había oído, leído en algún libro de psicología'; the existential self-assuredness of Elena is revealed as mere pretence. In an ever more complex fragmentation of identity, however, the exposure of Elena's insincerity does not return her to a static self – even her 'unfolded' identity is inconsistent and unfounded:

> Ni se acordaba de lo que había sufrido y llorado la noche anterior [...]. Es pura alteración, como diría Ortega, lo que sentía ayer no tiene nada que ver con su estado de ánimo actual, no relaciona las cosas. Ésa es una de las señales del subdesarrollo: incapacidad para relacionar las cosas, para acumular experiencias y desarrollarse. Por éso me impresionó tanto aquella frase de *Hiroshima*: *J'ai désiré avoir una inconsolable mémoire*. (38)

Malabre (and his author), like other analyst-authors previously, assails the nihilistic frontier and points to the perils of starting a national narrative from scratch. Malabre, like Rip van Winkle before him, holds on stubbornly to his inconsolable memories of *antes* and points to the possibility of relinquishing 'the need for an exclusive attachment to one historical period [to] make it continuous with others' (Pease 1987: 15). *Memorias* is thus no neat confession of irrepressible memories of a vilified past followed by heartfelt contrition and the tidy catharsis of sin; the shadowy others from elsewhere and elsewhen come in from the edges and conquer the core of this story. Although it's possible to read Malabre's petit-bourgeois prejudices and Edmundo Desnoes's revolutionary masquerade as an attempt at what Rojas describes as typical of Cuban intellectuals' post-1959 'autopedagogía' (2006: 166), or what would later become notoriously known as 'autocrítica',[14] I rather read *Memorias* as a subversive celebration of ethical ambivalence, as a refusal to respect the binary divide between grace and malice, as an ardent defence of duality. Malabre's repeated attack on Edmundo is that he is 'un descarado' or 'shameless', but perhaps the most appropriate translation is the more literal 'faceless', or rather multi-faceted and able effortlessly to don and doff the mask most appropriate to each circumstance, able (as were Mañach's Luján, Ortiz's Martí and Piñera's 'infirm' Carlos) to infuse mere survival with enormous integrity.

This re-reading of purported confession as a determination to sin leads us necessarily to a reconsideration of *el subdesarrollo*. In placing the term at the centre of his narrative, Desnoes draws alongside an emerging intellectual school (particularly fecund in Cuba) that sought to revolutionise the epistemology of First, Second and Third Worlds and shake the philosophical foundations of development, civilisation and culture, arguing that underdevelopment should not be considered as 'algo inferior que, con esfuerzo, llegará a

---

14 In 1971 'Robespierre' Padilla faced the cultural guillotine after three years of tempestuous polemic over his 1968 poetry collection *Fuera del juego*. He was finally allowed to emigrate after delivering a pathetic *mea culpa* to his UNEAC colleagues.

ser tan desarrollado como el mundo industrializado, pero también tan desdi-
chado como él', but rather celebrated for its alterity: 'Me parece de veras, en
algunos aspectos al menos, un mundo *otro*' (Fernández Retamar 1967a: 17).[15]
Underdevelopment from this perspective becomes something not to eradicate,
but to cultivate, in so far as it signified radical alterity from established socio-
political and cultural models, in so far as it implied absolute autonomy and the
zealous defence of otherness, as long as it would lead through its own rite of
collective passage to a different kind of reaggregated development altogether.
Whilst Retamar was a key ideologue of this 'Calibanism', he claimed merely
to be articulating in text what the likes of Che Guevara embodied in his very
being: 'Cada uno de nosotros lo reconoce como suyo aunque, a la vez, hay
en él algo *de otra parte*' (Fernández Retamar 1967b: 140, emphasis in the
original). We have already examined the prime coordinates of this otherness
in *El socialismo y el hombre en Cuba*. Spurning the 'carrera de lobos' of
capitalist development, but also obliquely critical of the Soviet model in
which the psychological liberation from the tyranny of mercantilism was
far from conclusive, Guevara proposed a third way in which new men and
women would consolidate their new *sensibilidades* by amalgamating their
individuality with the collective and by replacing miserly ambition with
communist plenitude, 'su realización plena como criatura humana' (1966:
14–15). *Subdesarrollo* therefore becomes not an economic condition but an
ideological stance, the conscious choice to move towards human plenitude
along a different path.

In Desnoes's interpretation, underdevelopment is a complex and ambivalent
term. At times it appears as inconsistency, distraction and immunity to life's
lessons: it is Elena's bitter tears of the night before drying into ignorant
morning joy. But this could actually point to Desnoes's interpretation of *subdesarrollo* as 'Calibanesque', as Cuba (under)developing a new culture which is
more 'primitivo', not because of brutishness, however, but rather from honesty
of instinct and a desire to escape the artifice of more 'developed' cultures: 'Los
sentimientos del cubano son subdesarrollados: sus alegrías y sus sufrimientos
son primitivos y directos, no han sido trabajados y enredados por la cultura.'
(Desnoes 1968: 22) An alternative reading actually brings Desnoes alongside

---

[15] Retamar was a particularly influential exponent of cultural 'underdevelopment', proposing
a critical re-reading of the metaphoric archetypes offered by authoritarian Prospero, ethereal
Ariel and, particularly, cannibalesque Caliban (and hence instigating a reappraisal of Rodó's
1900 portrayal of Latin America as the spiritual *Ariel* as compared to North America as the
barbarous and greedy Caliban) to point to the liberating force of outsiderhood and the benefits of
not belonging, expressed in the geo-political arena as 'non-alignment'. See Fernández Retamar
1973.

Vitier, and what the latter called the congenital *ingravidez* of Cuban identity (1958: 485):

> Todo el talento del cubano se gasta en adaptarse al momento. En apariencias. La gente no es consistente, se conforma con poco. Abandona los proyectos a medias, interrumpe los sentimientos, no sigue las cosas hasta sus últimas consecuencias. [...]. La naturaleza del hombre es bicéfala, no puede hacer nada bueno sin meter la pata, ni puede hacer nada malo sin beneficiar a nadie. (Desnoes 1968: 80)

Identity from this perspective is a suspension of momentum, a constant and contingent adaptation and re-adaptation to shifting circumstances, a recalibration of aspirations away from teleological endpoints and towards the ambiguous everyday flux. Cuban *sensibilidad* is therefore both vigorous and sickly, malicious and blessed with grace, makes a merit out of the flexibility of *intrascendencia* and is an evocation of the 'saludable principio de que no existe nada verdaderamente doloroso o absolutamente placentero' that Piñera and others had perceived at the core of Cuba's bicephalous survival over more than half a century of frustration and pain, violence and vengeance, devils and dogmatic messiahs (Piñera 1960: 9).

And yet, the historical setting of *Memorias* will perhaps inevitably resurrect a sense of gravitas and teleological development in this narrative; will reinstate Malabre, Eddy and Edmundo as actors in a transcendental rite of passage from ambiguity to Revolutionary resolve. For although first published in 1965, the *bildungsroman* of the novel reaches its crescendo in October 1962 as the smouldering Cold War came to a point of near cataclysmic combustion and all eyes turned to Cuba in terror as the apparently insignificant island seemed about to complete its transition and become an insular bulwark of ideological conviction and geopolitical import. 'Nosotros tenemos bombas atómicas', says Malabre incredulously, 'estamos a la altura del mundo y no del subdesarrollado' (Desnoes 1968: 90–1). At this seemingly unquestionable turning point in Cuban and world history, the strident super-heroism of the new men in the making comes to the fore, with Malabre describing Fidel inflamed with faith in his own moral imperative, grabbing 'el toro por los cuernos' and rushing headlong towards ultimate conclusion in high hyperbole and glorious self-sacrifice: 'los ex-ter-mi-na-re-mos' (91). But both the historical transcendence and the archetypal derring-do to match can be suspended for a moment in re-examination from the liminal edge. In the twilight hours of 27 October, as Malabre lay trembling in his bed and the world prepared for the worst, the Cold War storm simply passed over. Through diplomatic double dealing that pushed Cuba back towards the geopolitical periphery once more (much to Castro's chagrin), the potential cataclysm ended in merciful anti-climax.[16] The apocalypse was neutralised in part by forces beyond Cuba's control, but also perhaps by what Benítez Rojo describes as the fundamental elusiveness of this 'isla que se repite', whose most instinctive psycho-cultural manifestations resonate to a syncopated rhythm that has nothing to do with the martial drums of war and everything in common with a sensual sway that soothes tempers and 'conjura la violencia'. As Benítez Rojo (like Malabre) sat on his balcony in 1962 watching for the angel of death in the sky above Havana, the mundanity of a street scene below convinced him that Cuba's destiny was different:

> Las dos negras – había un polvillo dorado y antiguo entre sus piernas nudosas, un olor a albahaca y hierbabuena en sus vestidos, una sabiduría simbólica, ritual, en sus gestos y su chachareo. Entonces supe de golpe que no ocurriría el apocalipsis. (1989: xiii)

And so whilst Castro the hero dashed out to meet his destiny and the resolution of all doubt in a heroic death to match that at Dos Ríos, Malabre 'el mediocre' held back and clung to life:

> ¿De qué me sirve agarrarme así? Y sin embargo, no quiero morir, siempre queda la estúpida esperanza de [...] ser feliz un día. Del carajo. No aprendo. Ahora, ahora es lo único que tengo. Me da lo mismo todo. Mentira, no me da lo mismo. (Desnoes 1968: 93)

But this apparent cowardice can be read as an anthem to ordinary, unheroic, inconclusive and liminal life; this mundanity can be interpreted as an act of great humanity, a humble recognition of fallibility, an acceptance of error, a forgiveness of original sin; this turning away from the strident future and future tense of *venceremos* and *exterminaremos* to instead linger on the threshold of a precious present (and present tense) is charged with its own heroism: 'being able to remain on that dizzying crest', said Camus, 'that is integrity and the rest is subterfuge' (2000: 50).

In this reading, *Memorias* is not a confession, nor attempts a cathartic exorcism of the old man from within the new. It is rather an anthem to ambiguity, a declaration of a lack of direction, a defence of the right not to decide between sickness and health, good and evil, *patria o muerte*. In this

---

[16] Bilateral diplomacy between Soviet First Secretary Khrushchev and US President Kennedy averted disaster, but Fidel (who had not taken the initial decision to station the missiles nor been consulted about their ultimate withdrawal) was reportedly furious (see Gott 2004).

Desnoes stands alongside the ambivalent everymen of 1923, 1927, 1933, 1953, 1957 and 1959 in de-scribing (or un-writing) the national narrative as a saga of inconclusion and openness, as a balancing act between implacable forward momentum and recalcitrant memory, as underdevelopment on a timeless hiatus of *ingravidez*, as a courageous cowardice that confronts life's trials not with the inflexible heroics and derring-do, but with the palliative buffer of laughter: 'el cubano no puede sufrir mucho rato sin echarse a reir' (Desnoes 1968: 39). For Desnoes, like all analyst-authors for whom the limen was their true home, the *imago* of identity is not conclusion but perennial postponement, not super-heroic archetypes around which everymen could muster, but the anti-heroic struggles of the doubtful, indecisive, devilish and cowardly characters that populated every point, and every turning point, in Cuba's independent history.

The euphoria of 1959 and early 1960 quickly congealed in the ragged wound opened in Cuban *sensibilidad* by sanguinary external attacks and the internal turn towards ferrous unity and complete cohesion. 1961 is commonly pointed to as the young Revolution's epiphany in which uncompromising topographies and paradigms were charted in more than just *palabras*, to be followed by 1962, seen as marking a near-cataclysmic turning point for an island and a world, neither of which would ever be the same again. This chapter has suggested that upon closer inspection these momentous events had only an inchoate impact on collective identity on the island; that on the leeside of all that transcendence, Cubans remained wrapped up in the same self-interrogations and unable to place the final full-stop at the end of a sixty-year great debate. This analysis of rites of passage in Cuba's twentieth century looked forwards, therefore, and in 1965 identified fundamental attempts to go beyond cyclical self-examination, diagnosis and inconclusive collective cure. In 1965, the consolidation of the initial heuristic political praxis under a single communist banner that would eliminate all discrepancy, difference and doubt 'una vez por todas y para siempre' (Castro 1965: para. 36) seemed to promise the kind of socio-ideological integration which anthropologists point to in the post-liminal phase of rites of collective passage. And whilst Castro sought to propel Cuba beyond the doctrinal pell-mell of political plurality towards a more unified new world, Guevara elaborated the archetype that would inhabit such a world. In reading the ideological topography charted in *El socialismo y el hombre en Cuba*, this chapter has argued that, although written by an Argentinian and sent to a Uruguayan from somewhere in the Far East, Guevara's text was firmly anchored in the ideological substrata of twentieth-century Cuban identity debates. The new man that took shape in 1965 was thus both an internationalist and an instinctive insularist, took his place amongst archetypes of socialist sensibility and yet was a close cousin of Martí and his most fervent disciple Fidel. In his cognisance of the moral and civic characteristics of the new man, Guevara made a convincing case for social felicity: through their susceptibility to external education, their internal compulsion to conform to noble social goals, their intolerance of incohesion and debilitating sin, the Cubans that he described were undoubtedly new men and women, enlightened citizens of a truly novel world of the near future, who would be capable of enacting a revolution in consciousness, eradicating stubborn societal frustrations and soothing all existential angst. By bringing two critical and contrapuntal 1965 texts alongside *El socialismo y el hombre*, however, we have illuminated the potential tyranny in this admirable ideal. In our examination of the pedagogical pressures, compulsion to absolute cohesion and dubious dichotomies between sickness and health, good and bad, grace and malice in Piñera's 'La rebelión de los enfermos' and Desnoes's *Memorias del subdesarrollo*, this chapter has presented evidence of Revolutionary heroism mutated into dogmatism, of the drive for moral *desarrollo* transformed into a puritanical morality that was in itself a 'sin', of unity misinterpreted as farcical conformity on the nightmarish side of the *Cuba Libre* dream. Through exploration of Piñera and Desnoes's dialogue with the moral and imaginative characteristics of the new man, this chapter has shown that Guevara and the vanguard, with their audacious ambitions for a future perfect *sensibilidad revolucionaria* that would be victorious against all internal and external foes, forgot their own good advice and moved too far ahead of 'las masas' who were left working out how to get by in a radically new Cuba (Guevara 1966: 13). Thus, whilst 'Che' and the new man made a headlong dash towards human plenitude, Carlos and Alicia, Malabre and Eddy busied themselves with the never-ending challenges of inconclusive, ambiguous and infinitely liminal life. Whilst Fidel prepared to exterminate and be exterminated in the apocalyptic October of 1962, two chattering old ladies smelling of *hierbabuena* made their oblivious way through Old Havana. As the new man appeared uncompromisingly amidst Cuba's psycho-cultural landscape he was met by a healthy man confined to hospital and seeking ironic solace in understated revolt. As a new generation of 'maleable' Cubans was born in Guevara's imagination (20), Piñera pointed to endless perverse rebirths into inescapable frustration and congenital imperfection. As the vanguard waged holy war against 'el pecado original', Desnoes demonstrated that a new *conciencia* could actually come about, not through the out-casting of the shadowy and sinful other, but by constantly folding, *desdoblando* and overlapping identities in a constant but not contrite act of self-exploration.

Heroism, for these analyst-authors therefore, was not condensed in the fortitude to fight external and internal enemies, but in the courage to face fallibility, in the humility and sagacity to ask for forgiveness whilst accepting that the conscience will never really come clean. From this perspective, the kind of absolute (and post-liminal) reaggregation that Guevara posited becomes a virulent psycho-cultural affliction; the eradication of 'todo tipo de matiz' insisted upon by Fidel becomes the real original sin of the Cuban national narrative. In 1965, as in the other 'turning points' that preceded it, implacable teleological momentum was arrested by inconsolable memories of an ever-present past, the pursuit of psycho-cultural purity was hindered by inexpungable human sin, the *conciencia colectiva* was both saintly and disgraced, the true heroes were not otherworldly future supermen, but betwixt-and-between present-day everymen who gave Cubans 'the option of choosing their futures here and now – without heroes, without high drama and without a constant search for originality, discontinuous changes and final victories' (Nandy 2009: 62). Unconvinced by the pure paradise to come (whether socialist or capitalist) and uncowed by the ambiguities of the human here and now, these anti-heroes found their spirits at peace in simple survival, in an acceptance of perennial flux, in the landscape of the liminal middle: 'He terminado', says Malabre. 'El hombre (yo) es triste, pero quiere vivir' (Desnoes 1968: 94).

Conclusion

This book has examined seven important moments in Cuba's twentieth century as points in a rite of national passage. It has shown that at each point historical circumstance, cultural and generational coincidence, a sense of ethical discomfort and the perceived need to remodel civic structures all led to an impulse to re-orient collective sensibility and begin a new chapter in Cuba's national narrative; in other words, to undertake the socio-structural 'separation' that anthropologists identify as the first phase in the rite of passage. After this initial separation came the interstitial, introspective and all-important limen, and the ideological adversaries we have followed throughout pulled on their gloves and prepared to fight, either brazenly confident that victory would ultimately be theirs, or resigned to the fact that the *luchita* could last some time. For the former, whom we have called 'the reaggregationists', a sense of forward momentum, the coalescence of a cohesive archetype and the tearing out of unsatisfactory pages from the collective narrative were all essential to move beyond such moments of existential flux and on to a near happy-ever-after future. The latter, whom we have called 'the liminalists', rather advocated a more pragmatic acceptance of flux, saw history turning in ever-repeating circles and the national narrative as an honest document of Cuba's oftentimes *mala vida*. Two fundamentally different ontologies of identity were therefore revealed and scrutinised here under the analytical light of liminality. The reaggregationists followed Arnold van Gennep through a temporal and cathartic limen in which all antecedent sins were atoned for and absolved, all maladies made better, all devils banished from the collective *alma* for ever as Cuba moved towards a post-liminal promised land in which the near perfect *pueblo* rallied around their Revolutionary shepherd. On the contrary, and contrarily, those prepared to dwell always and forever *en la luchita* saw the introspection and ambivalence of liminal turning points not as a phase at all, but as a congenital and irrevocable condition (as it is for Victor Turner). We have come across and studied moments in which the liminalists seemed to gain the hermeneutic high ground, times in which their explanation and articulation of life in *letras* seemed more in tune with the oscillations of the day, in which their blueprint for harmony within Cuba's collective sensibility and their plan for escape from under the Damoclean sword of tyranny and sacrifice seemed to make the most sense. So in 1923, when Rubén Martínez Villena and Emilio Roig de Leuchsenring beatified an embattled *pueblo* whose only sin was an excess of good faith, Fernando Ortiz illuminated and even celebrated the island's hard life, defending the Cuban people's right to speak for themselves and make their own instructional mistakes. In 1927, when Julio Antonio Mella envisaged a martial and bullish march through history in which all true Cuban heroes strove towards 'ese gran paraíso del socialismo internacional' (Mella 1975: 272), Jorge Mañach pointed to a constant oscillation between modernity and tradition in which true percipience was reserved for the interstitial 'arroyo', in which high hyperbole was replaced by the mundane pains of daily life and in which the Great Men and Women of the national narrative were joined by the humble nursemaids of collective history (Mañach 1926: 12). In 1953, stimulated by a sense of perniciously cyclical time and a crowd of coincidental anniversaries (the fiftieth of the Republic and, even more significantly, the hundredth of José Martí), the second major phase in this study began with an uncomfortable reflection on noble legacies cast aside and a *Cuba Libre* dream come to nought. For the *venceremos* brigade, the solution was to seek an antidote for the unsatisfactory present in the resurrection of the unsullied past, which they saw distilled in an ideological reading of the *ideario* of Martí as a master-plan for self-sacrificing heroism applicable without modification nearly sixty years after the Apostle's death. The liminalists read across the grain of this centenary hagiography to reveal a Martí on the margin between patriotism and pragmatism, between valour and a weary craving for death, neither setting himself up as an infallible example to follow, nor expecting the independent *pueblo* suddenly and miraculously to liberate itself from 'las flaquezas propias de la humanidad' (Ortiz 1955b: 246).

Undermining the betwixt and between as a socio-cultural ideal, however, we have also come across periods when lingering in the limen has been far from desirable, when the setting aside of social structures led only to a reign of physical and psychological terror in which *venceremos* faith in future perfection **and** *la luchita*'s optimistic resignation to the present imperfect were overcome by anomie from which even the most ardent liminalist sought escape through desperate acts of derring-do. Thus in 1933, the rite of passage went mad in a *dérèglement de tous les sens* in which the only constant was an appetite for mutual destruction across generational, political and ideological divides, in which exemplary sacrifice only released a morbid 'acumulación de tánatos' that would stain the pages of the national narrative long after despotic president Machado had fled (Cabrera Infante 1992: 182). Similarly, in 1957, as the structures and strictures of *civitas* dissolved and Fulgencio Batista's rule descended into a riot of thuggery and vice, the sense of inherent suffering and inescapable stagnation led some to see Cuba as an aberrant society populated by pointless lives that went nowhere (despite all movement), spoke to no one (despite all contact) and did nothing (despite all activity), instead remaining trapped on a meaningless margin between the womb and the tomb. At these moments, however, this *dérèglement* of sense and sensibility was ultimately worked on and worked out. After the aberrant interstice of 1933 came the constitutional pact of 1940 in which old adversaries came together to re-establish *lex* in the lexis of a magna carta that promised to put new civic structures in place to stifle any future *monstrum* before it could fully take shape, that infused *sensibilidad* with the balm of mutual forgiveness and brought it back from the brink of madness, bloodlust and chaos. From amidst the anomie of 1957 some liberation from cyclical tyranny and sacrifice was perceived, not in a headlong dash, but in the suspended animation of the historical hiatus itself. Here legacies and origins were anchored only in the shifting sands of *ingravidez* and a bearable lightness of being that invited a radical self-reinvention 'en la dolorosa reducción del yo a la nada', and shunned any subsequent *nacimiento* (*Orígenes* 1:1, 7). And to the anguish of nothing, no one, and nowhere came the surreptitious hope of Sisyphus who, although condemned to an eternal purgatory with no reward, found ironic but sublime satisfaction in the human struggle itself.

But if we have pointed to turning points that were more around-and-about turns than decisive changes of direction, the two moments examined in the final two chapters did indeed seem to indicate significant development. Here the question of the nexus between activism and commentary, *hechos* and *palabras*, blood and ink came fully to the fore as the *ciudad letrada cubana* was rocked by tectonic tremors and the fate of many of our analyst-authors took a turn for the worse. At previous points, as we have seen, the covenant between words and deeds was mostly assured and the pen had drawn as much blood as the sword. Thus, poet Martínez Villena led twelve fellow *letrados* in delivering a powerful body blow to the corrupt government of the day with a landmark *Protesta*. Thus, Fernando Ortiz threw francophone *goyaviers* back in the Academia's face in a dictionary that was really a manifesto, an ethno-linguistic exposé of Cuban culture's ebony heart, a clarion call for the inclusion of the *vox populis* in the island's autobiography to give common people authority over their own *vidas*, no matter how *malas* they might be. Thus, Jorge Mañach mixed blood and ink in his ABC manifesto, in his editorial contribution to *La historia me absolverá*, in his televised debate with Castro about the fate of the *Diario de la Marina*, and in his constant courageous call for Cuban heroism 'no en el sentido espectacular, sino en el silencioso, continuo y fecundo de cada día' (1953b: 80). By 1959, however, the ominous writing was on the wall of the lettered city, with Vitier chastising himself for all those 'poemas, ensayos, estudios, libros, libros' and a whole court of Revolutionary Robespierres calling for the extirpation, if not outright execution, of the Old Guard analyst-authors in their liminal mid-current swim that infuriated the vanguard so (1990: 145). *Activismo* seemed to be overwhelming *análisis* and the ascendant *sensibilidad revolucionaria* seemed to call constantly for blood (which they saw being generously supplied in the supposed self-sacrifice of Martí, Mella, *la generación del centenario* and the *guerrilleros* in the mountains and cities of late 1950s Cuba). In such a high-strung and hyperbolic climate, Mañach's claim that the actions of *hoy* had only been possible because of the *palabras* of *ayer* became just so much analytical ink fading slowly on the margins of the new Revolutionary pages of the national narrative. And by 1965 the topography of the *ciudad letrada* seemed to have been altered forever. The changes were made by the *letrados* who turned the sword upon themselves in a bitter *mea culpa* for all those earlier missed opportunities to demonstrate complete *compromiso* with the Revolutionary cause. But the changes were also imposed by the political vanguard who claimed that the *letrados*' original sin of defective Revolutionary spirit could only be expunged by death. The execution of the *batistianos* who didn't get away with their dictator was not this necessary death. What was called for was rather an ideological assassination, whether in the burial of the *Diario de la Marina* at the university's gate (doomed to be defiled forever by the unknowing and uncaring steps of students), or the departure of the Old Guard into bitter exile (like Mañach), or their fading away in cloistered confinement (like Ortiz).

But just as Che Guevara's prophecy seemed about to come true and the new Cuban men and women of clean *conciencias* and purely socialist *sensibilidades* seemed about to make their appearance in a reaggregated national narrative, an author and analyst like Edmundo Desnoes came along. In *Memorias del subdesarrollo*, Desnoes took tentative steps to re-unite authorship and critical analysis, to surreptitiously suggest that the new Revolutionary man could be both a cultural commissar and an idle bourgeois, could be both a callow and callous Benjamin with no memories even of his personal *ayer*, and an integral Abraham who could not, and would not, relinquish his inconsolable memories. And so at the end of our exploration, Ortiz and Mañach, Ichaso, Vitier and Piñera were joined by Desnoes and the identity-juggling Malabre. And in Desnoes's text (seen by some as a cathartic confession of pre-Revolutionary *pecados*), as in the others', we rather revealed identity split down the middle, heroic archetypes undermined by the anti-heroic enemies they railed against, bellicosity, belligerence and blood giving way to 'un consuelo, un chiste o una limosna' (Mañach 1926: 12), the high hyperbole of suicidal self-sacrifice ceding to an unapologetic desire to survive. In 1965, as in 1923, 1927,

1953, 1957 and even 1959, the *imago* of Cuban identity was not a definitive metamorphosis at all, but a perennial pupation, not a quest for a post-crisis (and post-liminal) sovereign self, but a never-ending transformation: the chrysalis cracking open to reveal another chrysalis within, already etched with the patina of future fractures.

But if in 1965 Desnoes could squeeze himself surreptitiously into the narrow limen left open to subtle ambivalence and doubt, by the late 1960s and early 1970s this margin had snapped tight shut and the fracture between liminalists and reaggregationists seemed permanent. An interesting case of suffocation in the ambivalent margin is that of Heberto Padilla. Once a committed reaggregationist who had put so many older analyst-authors to the ideological sword for their lack of what he called 'una voz de servicio' to the Revolutionary cause, Padilla's bombast soon began to stick in his own throat. In 1968 he published *Fuera del juego*, a collection of poems obliquely critical of Revolutionary reality (1959b: 6). Five of the seven judges in the Unión de Escritores y Artistas de Cuba's (UNEAC) literary competition to which the collection was presented praised Padilla's interpretation of 'revolution' as perennial rebellion, for his 'actitud que es esencial al poeta y al revolucionario: la de inconforme, la del que aspira a más porque su deseo lo lanza más allá de la realidad vigente' (in Casal 1971: 56). But the remaining judges, UNEAC and the cultural authorities amongst whose ranks Padilla had once stood interpreted his *juego* as a sinister and counter-revolutionary game that attempted to use the ideological breathing space left open in Castro's 'Palabras' to undermine collective unity. Padilla was arrested in 1971 and only released after delivering a pathetic confession of his *pecados* before his UNEAC colleagues. The so-called *quinquenio gris* of ideological orthodoxy and cultural intolerance had begun.

Once again, however, this seemingly radical turn towards a more intolerant cultural politics and a more uniform *sensibilidad* (in the obligatory olive green of Revolution) can actually be seen as another example of continuity across an alleged divide, one more surreptitous echo of Republican discourse in Revolutionary times. In 1971, in response to *el caso Padilla*, Fidel Castro radically re-charted the cultural topography of Cuba and made Revolutionary *sensibilidad* the essential passport for entry into the remodelled *ciudad letrada*: 'Para volver a recibir un premio, en concurso nacional o internacional, tiene que ser revolucionario de verdad, escritor de verdad, poeta de verdad, revolucionario de verdad (in Casal 1971: 156). Nearly fifty years before, however, Julio Antonio Mella had made the same proposition, suggesting that the island's cultural *conciencia* could and should only be entrusted to 'la nueva generacion, libre de prejuicios y compenetrada con la clase revolucionaria de hoy' (1926: 10). This final turning point towards a new future is rather a roundabout turn to face the past.

And this brings us back to the beginning, and to the two women chatting on a twenty-first century Havana street corner and to the question that has haunted this analysis throughout: what **is** Cuba's archetypal *sensibilidad*; who and what is a sensible archetype to come out of the Cuba of then to inspire the Cuba of now?

We have shown that the turning points studied here were rather moments of collective arrest in the limens of Cuba's rite of national passage. And whilst we have shown that the analyst-authors who have populated this study couldn't agree on the best next steps, they did all concur that **something** had gone wrong and **something** had to be done. And so the tropes of illness, sickness and sin, in the past, present and future tenses, all came to the fore. Hence Cuba's *conciencia colectiva* was examined, different original sins were revealed, but no agreement was reached on the most appropriate act of collective contrition. Hence Cuba's corpus was dissected, and all manner of maladies uncovered, but no common prescription for cure put forward. In a final discursive twist, however, perhaps our liminalists and reaggregationists can actually be reconciled. All could perhaps agree on an alternative diagnosis of Cuba's condition, in which the island is seen to be suffering from a chronic case of *frustración*. In Mella's text and Castro's tone, in the *venceremos* slogan always and forever pointing over the horizon to triumph and in the women's languid resignation to ever-present *luchita*, the sounds of deep-seated frustration resonate. And looking and listening back throughout this book, these same sounds are audible. So in 1923, Martínez Villena and his twelve fellow *protestantes* at the Academia de Ciencias acted on the frustrating fact that only twenty years after independence Cuba had been hamstrung by heavy-handed US anti-diplomacy and the impropriety of those entrusted with constructing a nation from the wreck of colonisation and all-out war. But *frustración* is equally audible from the alternative (and liminal) ideological flank of Ortiz's dictionary which growled against the Real Academia's lexicographic clumsiness: '¡Que no nos vengan la Academia con *guayabas*!' (1923d: 43). In 1953, Fidel was acutely frustrated that Batista's soldiers wouldn't submit to a fair fight that 26 July on which Castro was convinced they would have received a 'soberana' and Revolutionary 'paliza' (1953: 20). But in 1959, Portell Vilá is equally frustrated with Castro himself and what the historian sees as the *comandante*'s wilful inheritance of the suicidal tendency that had carried so many of Cuba's preterite patriots to a premature death. As the twentieth century progressed, these frustrations were joined by many others: between generations, between ideologies, between races and classes and creeds. Frustration soon became, not simply a feature of Cuban *sensibilidad*, but its very ontogenesis. At this stage, however, the proposed ideological reconciliation between those formerly identified as ideological foes ultimately breaks down. For the reaggregationists, *frustración* (like psycho-social sickness and sin) could actually be overcome with staunch faith in Cuba's manifestly noble destiny and the ability of the beleaguered but benign *pueblo* to fulfil this *destino*. Nevertheless, our reading across genres and times and perspectives has revealed that this belief in the subjectability of frustration actually engendered one of the most acute *frustraciones* of all: absolute faith in Cuba's destiny was frustrated by those who seemed stubbornly determined to doubt. In the terms of this study, the most serious malady for the reaggregationists was liminality itself, seen in the acceptance of an unsettled and unsettling chronological oscillation, seen in 'bloodlessness' (or at least an excess of *letrado* ink), seen in the original and cardinal sin of 'ambigüedad' (Roa 1969: 27). It was this frustration with ambiguity itself that fuelled the 1923 vilification of President Zayas, the 1953 hagiography of the monochromatic patriotism of the Apostle Martí and the 1959 ideological trial of Mañach, execrated as a symbol of everything intolerable in the so-called 'nadar entre dos aguas' approach to Cuban history and sensibility (ibid.). And as purity was proposed to exorcise all sin and a 'golpe de bisturí' the only way to cure the collective corpus, so the antidote to ambivalence was often found in extremism, the solution to liminal lingering sought in an increasingly dogmatic belief in a future-perfect Cuba. As a result, however, and critical for our search for sensible and *sensible* twentieth-century Cuban identities, the archetypes that were written into this absolutist version of the national narrative were increasingly obdurate and hard to follow: Martínez Villena proposed a perfectly pure *pueblo*, Mella set himself up as a Homeric and super-human hero, Martí was re-read as an infallible archangel, Fidel as a triumphant messiah leading a *campesino* flock immune to doubt, and the new men and women of communist Cuba to come had left the original sins of everymen far behind. In many cases, these heroes were excessively esoteric and artificially distanced from the ugly details of ordinary life. Thus, for Roig de Leuchsenring, 'no es culpable, en ningún caso, nuestro magnífico pueblo cubano' for the 'males y vicios' that had persistently plagued Cuba, even though Castro had suggested that an entire province would be needed to incarcerate all the *malos* still left on the island by the end of 1959 (Roig de Leuchsenring 1961b: 14). By the early 1960s, and despite grave warnings, the nascent Revolutionary archetype seemed to levitate above the *muchedumbre* as 'espíritus celestes […], graduados de la universidad bamboleante de las nubes' (Ortiz 1955b: 245–6). The result was not a universal rallying around the banner of national cohesion and collective well-being, therefore, but the introduction of a new and insidious form of *frustración*: frustration with the inferior self. For Piñera, for example, the 'ejemplo glorioso de nuestros héroes' that Castro saw at the core of Cuban *sensibilidad* (Castro 1953: 109) inspired only alienation and self-doubt: 'Martí is pure, Maceo is pure, Gómez is pure and on and on ... So much purity! And not a drop of slime? Not one?' (in Rojas 2008a: 69). From this perspective, even the illuminated example of the Apostle did not inspire determined acts of self-improvement, but rather instilled a sense of ignorance and inferiority: 'somos muy pequeños todavía para comprender a José Martí' (Cruz Cobos 1953: 12). Thus, the pure men and women proposed as new archetypes of Cuban identity in the mid-1960s left the not so pure everymen and women increasingly far behind and increasingly aware of their own shortcomings and sins.

Facing the lofty heroes of hyperbole and derring-do, however, we have presented a pantheon of accessible anti-heroes and everymen from the Cuba of then. For the analyst-authors we have called the liminalists, *frustración* was actually inevitable, a genetic ingredient of collective *sensibilidad* which made this particular Cuban condition incurable. Thus, a sensible and *sensible* archetype for Cubans was Luján, who empathised with but didn't attempt to eliminate every 'vago dolor disimulado' of his fellow *habaneros* (Mañach 1926: 11). From this perspective, a proto-Cuban worth emulating was a José Martí who didn't preach perfection at all, but rather the pragmatic acceptance of errors, now and for ever. From this perspective, an ancient myth to inspire modern Cuba was that of Sisyphus, whose *frustración* as the rock rolls back down the mountain is the key to his vitality and his wry and smiling decision to carry on, no matter what. From this perspective, Cubans to laud to were those who had relinquished the urge to 'live up to' anything, instead seeking only to live.

But as the sixties became the seventies in Cuba, we have seen these archetypes marginalised to the point of practically disappearing altogether, have seen their interpretations of collective *sensibilidad* confined to the much-maligned *ayer* and unable to influence the Revolutionary *ahora*, seen the Cuban Rip van Winkles put back to sleep, and permanently. But perhaps this has now begun to change. In very recent times a discreet rehabilitation of a formerly execrable intellectual has begun which offers us an opportunity for final reflection, a last example of a turning point that became an about-turn, a forward march that became an anti-teleological retracing of collective steps. Although hounded for sitting on the fence at times of great change, although retired against his will from the University of Havana and condemned to exile and textual silence for decades, arch-liminalist Jorge Mañach is now slowly reclaiming a place within the insular canon of analyst-authors of the Cuban national narrative. One of the most poignant acts of vindication was a small commemoration at the Instituto de Literatura y Lingüística in Havana in 2010 in honour of Mañach's 112th birthday. Such a commemoration could be read simply as recognition of one intellectual's assiduous contribution to the perception and expression of Cuban national identity during his lifetime. But it could also be read in a more suggestive (and more liminal) way. That small homage to Mañach could in fact be read as indication that today's analyst-authors of the national narrative, like their unapologetically ambivalent forebears, are not fully convinced that cohesion around a single, ardent archetype is imperative at all. Perhaps even the location of the commemoration is suggestive: the Instituto where the celebration was held was once the Sociedad Económica de Amigos del País presided over by Fernando Ortiz, but now named after José Antonio Portuondo, a paragon of committed, communist and *engagé* culture and one of the Revolutionary *lobos* of Cuban *letras* during the infamous *quinquenio gris*. Mañach's presence in Portuondo's Institute perhaps points to Cuban cultural history coming full circle, to Cuban identity being as irrevocably split as Ortiz, Piñera, Desnoes and Mañach himself suggested, as shadowed by others 'standing off in the cultural temporal distance' who make Cuban *sensibilidad* 'more uncertain, and more disequilibrated' and yet 'more knowing' (Geertz 1983: 48–9). And this 'knowing', this re-cognisance of Cuban identity that incorporates the lessons of the limens within the national rite of passage, is *ayer*'s truly lasting legacy to *hoy*. The descriptions and inscriptions of the national narrative written from the margins, which this book has brought forth, deserve to become cardinal reference points in current Cuban identity debates. The more nuanced cultural history of the Cuban Republic which has been charted here and in which there is actually a great deal to *admirari* (no matter what the nihilists might say) should be rescued from yesterday and brought perspicaciously to bear on understandings of the island's today and tomorrow. The about-turn turning points, which have been re-examined here in a liminal light, offer salient lessons for the analysts (and the authors) of the senses, sensibilities and collective stories of selfhood in today's post-Castro Cuba. The twenty-first century celebration of Mañach, a name that was once synonymous with utterly intolerable ambivalence, shows that at least some of Cuba's current analyst-authors accept that the conclusion of the national narrative is rather a denouement in indecision, a cliff-hanger that cedes to infinite sequels where 'The End' is displaced by the indefinite articulation of 'An End', always and forever 'to be continued'. And from this perspective, the essence of Cuban *sensibilidad* is indeed an effervescence, a not-*ever*-yet suspended state poised permanently on a socio-cultural threshold and moving constantly in and out of focus in the 'sombra del umbral'; a rite of passage in which reaggregation is perennially supplanted by an impossible discourse of self that provokes not frustration but celebration, and that once again asks Cubans to accept such an impossibility as

> una esencia, y en lugar de ser vencido por su aspecto más superficial, convertirla en lo que realmente es: la inspiración misma de nuestra alma.

Entonces empezamos a ver todo el esplendor de lo discontinuo, de lo fragmentario y *lo imposible* en el reino del espíritu. (Vitier 1958: 493)

Perhaps the twenty-first century commemoration of Mañach indicates a desire to escape teleological time and even escape the quest for identity itself. Perhaps the unrelenting inscription of a national narrative examined in this book is revealed as a tyrannical compulsion for self-cognisance, as a slavish desire 'decirlo todo' that engenders its own frustrations and sparks its own rebellions (Castro 1965: para. 36). Hence, the homage to Mañach can be read as a celebration of permanently imperfect cognition, a rejection of durable archetypes and an approach to identity and sensibility that draws quiet consolation from a man who walked alongside his anti-heroic, purely pacific and empathetic friend Luján 'en un suave y antojadizo dejarnos ir' (Mañach 1926: 12). After our own long quest for *homo cubensis* across two periods of revolutionary change and their seven collective turning points, perhaps the conclusion is that the riddles of national narrative remain unresolved, that more limens lie down the non-linear path; that each encounter with Cuba and its *sensibilidad* will also, always and for ever, be a fond farewell.

Bibliography

Primary Texts

Abela, Eduardo, 1927. 'El futuro artista', *revista de avance* (15 May), 104–5 & 107.

Aguilar, Luis E., 1972. *Cuba 1933: Prologue to Revolution* (Ithaca, NY: Cornell University Press).

Aguilar León, Luis, 1957. *Pasado y ambiente en el proceso cubano* (Havana: Ínsula).

Almagro, Luis F. de, 1933. 'El imbroglio cubano', *Bohemia* (30 July), 16.

Baeza Flores, Alberto, n.d. 'Perfil humano de Jorge Mañach' (original manuscript, Havana, Biblioteca 'Fernando Ortiz', Instituto de Literatura y Lingüística, Archivo Mañach, no. 1111).

Baquero, Gastón, 2002. *Antología poética* (Madrid: Pre-Textos).

Baragaño, José A., 1960. 'La aurora disuelve los monstruous', *Lunes de Revolución* (4 Jan.), 11.

Barnet, Miguel, 1993. *Biografía de un cimarron* (Havana: Letras Cubanas).

Barricada, 1957. 'Junta militar' (7 July), 1–2.

Beals, Carleton, 1934. *The Crime of Cuba* (Philadelphia: J. B. Lippincott).

Bisbé, Manuel, 1953. 'La Ortodoxia y la linea de la independencia política', *Bohemia* (22 Feb.), 48–9 & 83–7.

Bohemia, 1933a. 'El tirano' (20 Aug.), 5.

——, 1933b. 'Servidores de la tiranía' (20 Aug.), 23 & 38.

——, 1933c. 'Cuba – Picadillo' (17 Sept.), 30 & 52–4.

——, 1933d. 'Realidades del momento' (1 Oct.), 33.

——, 1933e. 'Sangre cubana' (8 Oct.), 42.

——, 1933f. 'Todo por Cuba' (8 Oct.), 31.

——, 1933g. 'Vivimos un momento difícil' (15 Oct.), 3.

——, 1933h. 'Cuba pide sacrificios' (26 Nov.), 27.

——, 1957. 'Sierra maestra: Un pedazo de historia' (6 Jan.), 78–9.

——, 1959a. 'Apoteosis en la capital' (11 Jan.), 92–3, 121.

——, 1959b. 'De las tinieblas a la luz' (11 Jan.), 28–9 & 162.

——, 1959c. 'Galería de asesinos' (11 Jan.), 152–8.

——, 1959d. 'Operación Verdad' (1 Feb.), 102–5.

——, 1959e. 'Más de un millón de cubanos se congregó en la Plaza Cívica el 26 de julio' (2 Aug.), 60–9 & 84–6.

Cabrera, Luis Rolando, 1959a. 'El ex-sargento Vidal, terror de Holguin, se hace aparecer como un manso cordero', *Bohemia* (18 Oct.), 36–8 & 107–8.

——, 1959b. 'Historia de horrores: La gavilla de asesinos del Comandante Menocal', *Bohemia* (11 Jan.), 28–30, 32 & 134–5.

Cabrera Infante, Guillermo, 1992. *Mea Cuba* (Barcelona: Plaza & Janés).

Capote, Raúl A., 2006. 'La Constitución del 40: Mitos y realidades de un símbolo nacional'. *Consenso*, http://desdecuba.com/07/articulos/9_01.shtml, accessed 4 Oct. 2010.

Carpentier, Alejo, 1984. *Ensayos* (Havana: Letras Cubanas).

Casanovas, Martí, 1927a. 'Arte nuevo', *revista de avance* (15 May), 156–8 & 175.

——, 1927b. 'Nuevos rumbos: La exposición de *1927*', *revista de avance* (15 May), 99–100.

Casey, Calvert, 1963. *El regreso* (Havana: Ediciones R).

Castro, Fidel. 1953 *La historia me absolverá* (Repr., Havana: Editorial de Ciencias Sociales, 1971).

——, 1961a. 'Discurso pronunciado en las honras fúnebres de las víctimas del bombardeo a distintos puntos de la República, efectuado en 23 y 12, frente al Cementerio de Colón, 16 de abril de 1961', http://www.cuba.cu/gobierno/discursos/1961/esp/f160461e.html, accessed 14 Apr. 2009.

——, 1961b. 'Discurso pronunciado como conclusión de las reuniones con los intelectuales cubanos, efectuadas en la Biblioteca Nacional el 16, 23 y 30 de junio de 1961', http://www.cuba.cu/gobierno/discursos/1961/esp/f300661e.html, accessed 24 June 2009.

——, 1965. 'Discurso pronunciado por el Comandante Fidel Castro Ruz, Primer Secretario del Partido Comunista de Cuba y Primer Ministro del Gobierno Revolucionario, en el acto de presentacion del Comité Central del Partido Comunista de Cuba, efectuado en el Teatro Chaplin, el 3 de octubre de 1965', http://www.cuba.cu/gobierno/discursos/1965/esp/f031065e.html, accessed 1 June 2010.

——, 2007. *My Life*, ed. Ignacio Ramonet, trans. Andrew Hurley (London: Allen Lane).

Cerro, Ángel del, 1959. 'Los panes y los peces', *Bohemia* (2 Aug.), 56–7 & 101.

Ciclón, 1959. 'Refutación a Vitier' (17 Mar.), 51–67.

'Código de la Familia', 1975. *Gaceta Oficial de Cuba*, https://www.gacetaoficial.gob.cu/html/codigo%20de%20lafamilia.html, under 'Del matrimonio'.

Congress of the United States of America, 1901. *The Platt Amendment*. US National Archives and Record Administration, https://www.ourdocuments.gov/doc.php?flash=true&doc=55&page=transcript.

Constitución de la República de Cuba, 1940. *Gaceta Oficial*. Vol. 2, no. 464 (Repr., Havana: Colección Legislativa Cubana, 1955).

Cosculluela, Juan Antonio, 1927. 'El territorio cubano como vínculo de unión a través de los tiempos. In *La vida de la Academia de la Historia (1926–1927)* (Havana: Academia de la Historia, El Siglo XX).

Cruz Cobos, Armando, 1953. 'Martí prometeico', *Revista Bimestre Cubana* (8 Feb.), 12.

Denuncia, 1933. 'Contra la debilidad intervencionista' (1 Feb.), 1.

Desnoes, Edmundo, 1968. *Memorias del subdesarrollo* (Buenos Aires: Galerna).

Diego, Eliseo, 1993. *Conversación con los difuntos* (Matanzas: Ediciones Vigía).

Dihigo y López-Trigo, Ernesto, 1974. *Los cubanismos en el Diccionario de la Real Academia Española* (Madrid: Comisión Permanente de la Asociación de Academias de la Lengua Española).

Directorio Revolucionario, 1957. 'Del directorio Revolucionario al pueblo de Cuba. Asalto al palacio presidencial', *Al Combate* (13 July), 1–2.

Engels, Friedrich, 1895. *The Part Played by Labour in the Transition from Ape to Man* (Repr., Moscow: Progress Publishers, 1978).

Entralgo, Elías, 1962. *Lecturas y estudios* (Havana: UNESCO).

Estenoz, Evaristo, 1909. 'Constitutional Act of the Agrupación Independiente de Color'. In Aviva Chomsky, Barry Carr & Pamela Maria Smorkaloff (eds), *The Cuba Reader: History, Culture, Politics* (Durham, NC: Duke University Press, 2003), 165–8.

Fernández Retamar, Roberto, 1962. *Papelería* (Santa Clara: Universidad Central de las Villas).

——, 1967a. 'Hacia una intelectualidad revolucionaria en Cuba'. In *Ensayo de otro Mundo* (Havana: Instituto del Libro), 158–80.

——, 1967b. 'Introducción al pensamiento del Che'. In *Ensayo de otro mundo* (Havana: Instituto del Libro), 137–57.

——, 1973. *Calibán* (Montevideo: Aquí Testimonio).

Folletos de Divulgación Legislativa, 1960. *Leyes del Gobierno Provisional de la Revolución: XXIII – 10 a 31 de Agosto de 1960* (Havana: Lex).

Franqui, Carlos, 1969. *El libro de los doce* (Havana: Instituto del Libro).

——, 1981. *Retrato de familia con Fidel* (Barcelona: Seix Barral).

Fundora Núñez, Gerardo, 1957. 'Yo estuve en Goicuria: ya está bueno de sangre derramada inútilmente', *Bohemia* (13 Jan.), 37 & 82–3.

Guevara, Ernesto 'Che', 1966. *El socialismo y el hombre en Cuba* (Montevideo: Nativa Libros).

Guillén, Nicolás, 1967. *Sóngoro Cosongo, Motivos de Son, West Indies Ltd., España: Poema en cuatro angustias y una esperanza* (Buenos Aires: Losada).

——, 1971. *El gran zoo* (Havana: UNEAC).

——, 1985. *Obra poética* (Havana: Editorial Letras Cubanas).

——, 1987, *Prosa de prisa*, ed. Ángel Augier (Havana: Letras Cubanas).

Helg, Aline, 1995. *Our Rightful Share: The Afro-Cuban Struggle for Equality, 1886–1912* (Chapel Hill: University of North Carolina Press).

Hernández Catá, Alfonso, 1933. *Un cementerio en las Antillas* (Madrid: n. pub.).

Ichaso, Francisco, 1927a. 'La crisis del respeto', *revista de avance* (15 Sep.), 275–8.

——, 1927b. 'Letras hispánicas', *revista de avance* (15 May), 113.

——, 1953. 'El sentido político de Martí', *Bohemia* (1 Feb.), 55 & 81.

Kuchilán, Mario, 1970. *Fabulario: Retrato de una época* (Havana: Instituto del Libro).

——, 1975. 'La literatura revolucionaria de los años 30', *Bohemia* (8 Aug.), 10–15.

La Calle: El Diario de la Revolución Cubana, 1960a. '¿Debe ser tolerada la prensa reaccionaria? (7 Jan.), 1 & 4.

——, 1960b. 'Fidel en el telemundo' (23 Jan.), B12–B16.

——, 1960c. 'Cien mil personas en el entierro de *La Decrépita*' (14 May), 3.

Lamar Schweyer, Alberto, 1923. *La crisis del patriotismo: Una teoría de las inmigraciones* (Havana: Editorial Martí).

Lavié, Nemesio, 1927. 'El libro de hoy', *Diario de la Marina* (26 June), 34.

Le Roy y Cassá, Jorge, 1929. *Inmigración anti-sanitaria (leído en la Academia de Ciencias Médicas, Físicas y Naturales de La Habana, sesión del 14 de diciembre de 1923)* (Havana: Dorrbecker).

Lezama Lima, José, 1945. 'Después de lo raro la extrañeza', *Orígenes*, 2:6 (Repr., in *Orígenes, la revista y las ediciones completas*, Havana: Cubarte, 2010).

——, 1953. *Analecta del reloj: Ensayos* (Havana: Orígenes).

——, 1977. *Obras completas, Tomo II, Ensayos/Cuentos* (México D.F.: Aguilar).

——, 1981. *Imagen y posibilidad*, ed. Ciro Bianchi Ross (Havana: Letras Cubanas).

——, 1988. *Confluencias: Selección de ensayos*, ed. Abel E. Prieto (Havana: Letras Cubanas).

——, 1993a. *Fascinación de la memoria: Textos inéditos de José Lezama Lima* (Havana: Letras Cubanas).

——, 1993b. *La expresión Americana*, ed. Irlemar Chiampi (Mexico D.F.: Fondo de Cultura Económica).

Lizaso, Félix, 1933. *Biografía* (Havana: Molina).

——, 1938. *Ensayistas contemporáneos – 1900–1920* (Havana: Editorial Trópico).

——, 1953. *José Martí: Recuento de centenario*, 2 vols (Havana: Úcar García).

—— & José Antonio Fernández de Castro, 1923. *La poesía moderna en Cuba (1882–1925): Antología crítica, ordenada y publicada* (Madrid: Librería y Casa Editorial Hernando).

Loynaz, Dulce María, 1955. *Obra lírica: Versos (1920–1938), Juegos de agua, Poemas sin nombre* with intro. by Federico Carlos Saínz de Robles (Madrid: Aguilar).

Manzano, Juan Francisco. 2007. *Autobiografía del escalvo poeta y otros escritos*. ed. and with intro. by William Luis (Madrid: Iberoamericana).

Mañach, Jorge, 1924. *Glosario* (Havana: Ex Libris).

——, 1926. *Estampas de San Cristóbal* (Havana: Minerva).

——, 1927a. 'Motivos del ¡Ay! y del ¡Hurra! (en el centenario del Romanticismo)', *revista de avance* (30 Nov.), 89–95.

——, 1927b. 'Vanguardismo: La fisonomía de las épocas', *revista de avance* (30 Mar.), 18–20.

——, 1927c. 'Vanguardismo III: El imperativo temporal', *revista de avance* (15 Apr.), 42–4.

——, 1939. *Pasado vigente* (Havana: Trópico).

——, 1944. *Historia y estilo* (Havana: Editorial Minerva).

——, 1951. *Para una filosofía de la vida* (Havana: Lex).

——, 1951b. *El espíritu de Martí* (Havana: Cátedra Martiana).

——, 1953a. 'Carta abierta a don José Vasconcelos', *Bohemia* (22 Feb.), 48–9 & 79.

——, 1953b. 'La República ante el legado de Martí', *Bohemia* (15 Feb.), 59 & 80.

——, 1953c. 'Martí: Legado y posterioridad'. In *Pensamiento y acción de José Martí: Conferencias y ensayos ofrecidos con motivo del primer centenario de su nacimiento* (Santiago de Cuba: Universidad de Oriente), 71–101.

——, 1955. 'Ante la prensa'. Textual version of a 14 Apr. television recording (Havana, Biblioteca 'Fernando Ortiz', Instituto de Literatura y Lingüística, Archivo Mañach, no. 1082).

——, 1959a. 'Acabar con la sangre', *Diario de la Marina* (12 Mar.), 4–A.

——, 1959b. 'De la sanción excesiva', *Diario de la Marina* (23 Apr.), 4–A.

——, 1959c. 'El ángel de Fidel', *Diario de la Marina* (4 Apr.), 4–A.

——, 1959d. 'El camino de la revolución', *Diario de la Marina* (15 Apr.), 4–A.

——, 1959e. 'El drama de Cuba', *Bohemia* (11 Jan.), 6–9, 163, 168, 172 & 174–5.

——, 1959f. Letter of 13 January to Roberto Agramonte, Madrid (Havana, Biblioteca 'Fernando Ortiz', Instituto de Literatura y Lingüística, Archivo Mañach, no. 734).

——, 1960. 'De cómo vivir en revolución', *Bohemia* (29 May), 61 & 81.

——, 1961. Letter of 28 April to Miguel Chacón y Calvo, Havana (Havana, Biblioteca 'Fernando Ortiz', Instituto de Literatura y Lingüística, Archivo Mañach, no. 11923).

——, 1999. *Ensayos*, ed. Jorge Luis Arcos (Havana: Letras Cubanas).

——, n.d. Letter to Dr M. Hernández, Havana (Havana, Biblioteca 'Fernando Ortiz', Instituto de Literatura y Lingüística, Archivo Mañach, no. 10353).

——, n.d. Letter to José Ortega Spottorno, Madrid (Havana, Biblioteca 'Fernando Ortiz', Instituto de Literatura y Lingüística, Archivo Mañach, no. 1033).

Marinello, Juan, 1928. 'Arte y política', *revista de avance* (15 Jan.), 5–7.

——, 1954. *El caso literario de Martí: Motivos de centenario* (Havana: n. pub.).

——, 1960. *Conversación con nuestros pintores abstractos* (Santiago de Cuba: Universidad de Oriente).

——, 1977. *Ensayos* (Havana: Editorial Arte y Literatura).

——, 1989. *Cuba: Cultura* (Havana: Letras Cubanas).

Marinetti, F. T., 1912. *Initial Manifesto of Futurism.* In catalogue of the 'Exhibition of Works by the Italian Futurist Painters' (London: The Sackville Gallery).

Marino Pérez, Luis, 1922. 'Las relaciones económicas entre Cuba y los Estados Unidos', *Cuba Contemporánea* 28(112): 264–70.

Marrero, Levi, 1971. *Cuba: La forja de un pueblo* (San Juan: Editorial San Juan).

Martí, José. 1895. 'Carta inconclusa a su amigo Manuel Mercado' (Repr. in *Granma*, http://www.granma.cu/granmad/secciones/26–julio–2011/de–jose–marti/articulo–14.html.)

——, 1963. *Obras completas*, vol 6: *Nuestra América* (Havana: Editorial Nacional de Cuba).

——, 1991. *Obras completas*, vol. 12. (Havana: Editorial de Ciencias Sociales).

——, 2001. *Obras completas*: vol. 4, *Cuba*; vol. 6, *Nuestra América I*; vol. 9, *Escenas norteamericanas* (Havana: Centros de Estudios Martianos, http://bibliotecavirtual. clacso.org.ar/ar/libros/marti/marti.html).

Martínez Villena, Rubén, 1923. 'La revolución del 1923: Apuntes que acaso no sean inútiles en el futuro, para la historia del presente', *El Universal* (13 Nov.), 20–31.

——, 1978. *Poesía y prosa* (Havana: Letras Cubanas).

Martínez Villena, Rubén, José Antonio Fernández de Castro, Calixto Masó, Félix Lizaso, Alberto Lamar Schweyer, Francisco Ichaso, Luis Gómez Wangüemert, Juan Marinello Vidaurreta, José Z. Tallet, José Manuel Acosta, Primitivo Cordero Leyva, Jorge Mañach & J. L. García Pedrosa, 1923. 'El Manifiesto de la Protesta de los Trece' (*Cuba Literaria*, http://www.cubaliteraria.cu/monografia/grupo_minorista/protesta13.html).

Masó Hernández, Fausto, 1959. 'Mañach y la baja cultura', *Revolución* (2 Mar.), 10.

Mella, J. A., 1926. *Glosando los pensamientos de José Martí* (Repr., with prologue by Juan Marinello, Havana: Editorial Páginas, 1941).

——, 1975. *Documentos y artículos* (Havana: Instituto de Historia del Movimiento Comunista y la Revolución Socialista de Cuba).

Miranda, Ernesto (ed.), 1959. 'Carta de un guajiro a su esposa desde La Habana', *Bohemia* (2 Aug.), 54–5.

Mistral, Gabriela, 1953. 'América tiene que agradecer esta labor cubana de mantener vivo a Martí', *Bohemia* (1 Feb.), 14.

Montenegro, Carlos, 1933 & 1934. 'Suicidados, fugados y enterrados vivo: Una serie sobre los horrores de «Cambray»', *Carteles* (17, 24 & 31 Dec. 1933 and 7, 14 & 28 Jan. 1934), multiple pages.

Novás Calvo, Lino, 2003. *El comisario ciego y otros relatos* (La Coruña: Ediciós do Castro).

Orígenes, la revista y las ediciones completas (Havana: Cubarte, 2010).

Orígenes, revista de arte y literatura, La Habana 1944–1956, dirigida por José Lezama Lima y José Rodriguez Feo, edición facsimilar, vol. VI (Mexico: El Equilibrista, n.d.).

Ortega, Gregorio, 1959. '128 años de infamia', *Lunes de Revolución* (14 Dec.), 6–7 & 10.

——, 1960. 'Segundo frente – ¡la "coletilla" va..!', *La Calle: El diario de la revolución cubana* (19 Jan.), 1–2.

——, 1989. *La coletilla: Una batalla por la libertad de expresión, 1959–62* (Havana: Editora Política).

Ortiz, Fernando, 1911. *La reconquista de América: Reflexiones sobre el panhispanismo* (Paris: Librería Paul Ollendorff).

——, 1916. *Hampa afro-cubana: Los negros esclavos. Estudio sociológico y de derecho público* (Havana: Revista Bimestre Cubana).

——, 1923a. 'El doctor de la Torre y la crisis cultural', *Revista Bimestre Cubana* (18 Jan.). 8–14.

——, 1923b. *En la Tribuna (Discursos cubanos)*, ed. Rubén Martínez Villena (Havana: El Siglo XX).

——, 1923c. *Historia de la arqueología indocubana: Publicado en "Cuba Contemporánea", septiembre y octubre de 1922. Tomo XXX, Nums. 117 y 118* (Havana: El Siglo XX).

——, 1923d. *Un catauro de cubanismos: Apuntes lexicográficos* (La Habana: Colección Cubana).

——, 1940a. 'El fenómeno social de la transculturación y su importancia en Cuba', *Revista Bimestre Cubana* 46(2): 273–8.

——, 1940b. 'Los factores humanos de la cubanidad', *Revista Bimestre Cubana* 46(2): 161–86.

——, 1943 'Por la integración cubana de blancos y negros', *Revista Bimestre Cubana* 51(2): 256–78 (Repr., *Estudios Afrocubanos* 5: 216–28, 1946).

——, 1955a. 'Más y más fé en la ciencia', *Revista Bimestre Cubana* 70: 58.

——, 1955b. Oración a Martí', *Revista Bimestre Cubana* 70: 237–48.

——, 1959a. 'La poesía en su lugar', *Lunes de Revolución* (7 Dec.), 5–6.

——, 1959b. ' "Tranquilo espero mi última partida de Cuba": Una conmovedora carta del Dr Fernando Ortiz', *Bohemia* (23 Aug.), 3 & 146.

——, 1973a. *Historia de una pelea cubana contra los demonios* (Havana: Ediciones ERRE).

——, 1973b. 'La decadencia cubana'. In *Órbita de Fernando Ortiz*, ed. Julio Le Riverend (Havana: Unión de Escritores y Artistas), 69–80.

——, 1973c. 'La fama póstuma de Martí'. In *Órbita de Fernando Ortiz*, ed. Julio Le Riverend (Havana: Unión de Escritores y Artistas de Cuba), 301–21.

——, 1975. *Los negros esclavos* (Havana: Editorial de Ciencias Sociales).

——, 1978. *Contrapunteo cubano del tabaco y el azúcar* (Caracas: Biblioteca Ayacucho).

——, 1985. *Nuevo catauro de cubanismos* (Havana: Editorial de Ciencias Sociales).

Padilla, Heberto, 1959a. 'La poesía en su lugar', *Lunes de Revolución* (7 Dec.), 5–6.

——, 1959b. 'Mañach y la Marina', *Lunes de Revolución* (2 Nov.), 14–15.

——, 1998. *Fuera del juego – Edición conmemorativa 1968–1998* (Miami: Ediciones Universal).

Pérez, Emma, 1959. 'Ocupemos de las cosas esenciales porque han llegado los tiempos', *Bohemia* (2 Aug.), 14–15 & 164–5.

Pérez Cabrera, José Manuel, 1954. *La Academia de la Historia y el centenario de Martí: Discurso leído en la sesión solemne de clausura del Año del Centenario de José Martí celebrada el día 27 de enero de 1954* (Havana: Academia de la Historia de Cuba).

Piñera, Virgilio, 1956. *Cuentos fríos* (Buenos Aires: Losada).

——, 1959a. 'Literatura y revolución', *Revolución* (18 June), 2.

——, 1959b. 'El arte hecho Revolución, la Revolución hecha arte', *Revolución* (5 Nov.), 2.

——, 1960. *Teatro completo* (Havana: Ediciones R).

——, 1964. *Cuentos* (Havana: Ediciones Unión, 1964).

——, 1968. *Dos viejos pánicos* (Havana: Casa de las Américas).

——, 1988. *Cold Tales*, trans. Mark Schafer, with intro. by Guillermo Cabrera Infante (Hygiene, CO: Eridanos Press).

——, 1999. *Cuentos completos* (Madrid: Alfaguara).

——, 2002. *Teatro complete*, with prologue by Rine Leal (Havana: Letras Cubanas).

Platt Amendment, 1901. Transcipt from US Archives Online: https://www.ourdocuments. gov/doc.php?flash=true&doc=55&page=transcript.

Portell Vilá, Herminio, 1959a. 'Dos épocas', *Bohemia* (19 July), 88–90.

——, 1959b. 'Tesis sobre el suicidio en la historia política de Cuba', *Bohemia* (1 Feb.), 112–14.

——, 1969. *Historia de Cuba en sus relaciones con los Estados Unidos y España, Vol. IV: La intervención y la República* (Miami: Mnemosyne Publishing).

Portuondo, José Antonio, 1958. *La historia y las generaciones* (Santiago de Cuba: Manigua).

——, 1965a. *Crítica de la época y otros ensayos* (Santa Clara: Universidad Central de Las Villas).

——, 1965b. 'Respuesta a Fornet', *Gaceta de Cuba* 4(42): 6–8.

revista de avance, 1927. 'Al llevar el ancla' (15 Mar.), 1.

——, 1929. 'Nuevo Martí' (27 Feb.), 36.

——, 1930. 'Editorial' (15 Sep.), 2.

Roa, Raúl, 1966. *Escaramuza en las vísperas, y otros engendros* (Havana: Editoria Universitaria).

——, 1969. *La Revolución del 30 se fue a bolina* (Havana: Instituto del Libro).

—— & Roberto Fernández Retamar, 1972. *Rubén Martínez Villena* (Havana: Instituto del Libro).

Rodríguez Feo, José, 1959. 'La neutralidad de los escritores', *Ciclón* (17 Mar.), unpaginated insert.

——, 1966. *Aquí once cubanos cuentan* (Montevideo: Arca).

Roig de Leuchsenring, Emilio, 1923. *Análisis y consecuencias de la intervención norteamericana en los asuntos interiores de Cuba* (Havana: El Siglo XX).

——, 1961a. *El Grupo Minorista de intelectuales y artistas habaneros* (Havana: Oficina del Historiador de la Ciudad de La Habana).

——, 1961b. *Males y vicios de Cuba republican: Sus causas y sus remedios* (Havana: Oficina del Historiador de la Ciudad de La Habana).

Sáenz, Vicente, 1953. 'Raíz y ala de José Martí (Biografía y vivencia hispanoamericana del prócer de la libertad de Cuba)', *Cuadernos Americanos* 68(2): 7–8 & 47–58.

Suárez, Constantino (Españolito), 1921. *Vocabulario Cubano: Suplemento a la 14a edición del Diccionario de la R. A. de la Lengua* (Havana: Librería Cervantes de Ricardo Veloso).

Tamargo, Agustín, 1959a. 'Contra ésto y aquello', *Bohemia* (12 July), 61.

——, 1959b. 'Habanero: ¡Abrele tus brazos al guajiro!', *Bohemia* (12 July), 14.

Torriente Brau, Pablo de la, 2010. *Presidio Modelo* (Havana: Centro Cultural 'Pablo de la Torriente Brau').

Treaty of Paris, 1898. http://www.msc.edu.ph/centennial/treaty1898.html, accessed 28 Sept. 2011.

Trelles y Govin, Carlos M., 1923. 'El progreso y el retroceso de la República de Cuba', *Revista Bimestre Cubana* 4: 313–19.

——, 1969. *Bibliografía social cubana* (Havana: Biblioteca Nacional 'José Martí').

Valle, Gerardo del, 1933. 'La revolución comienza ahora', *Bohemia* (30 July), 26 & 62.

Varona, Enrique José, 1922. 'La actual situación de Cuba juzgada por Varona', *Cuba Contemporánea* 28: 89–95.

——, 1938. *Obras de Enrique José Varona, vol. 3, Desde mi Belvedere* (Havana: Cultural).

——, 1999. *Enrique José Varona periodista*, ed. Salvador Bueno (Havana: Centro Cultural 'Pablo de la Torriente Brau').

Vitier, Cintio, 1948. *Diez poetas cubanos (1937–1947)* (Havana: Orígenes).

——, 1958. *Lo cubano en la poesía* (Santa Clara: Universidad Central de las Villas).
——, 1990. *De peña pobre (Memoria y novela)*, (Veracruz: Centro de Investigaciones Lingüístico-Literarias de la Universidad Veracruzana).
Zambrano, María, 1953. 'Martí, camino de su muerte', *Bohemia* (1 Feb.), 45 & 83.
——, 1987. *María Zambrano en* Orígenes (Mexico: Ediciones del Equilibrista).

Secondary Texts

Aguirre, Manuel, Roberta Quance & Philip Sutton, 2000. *Margins and Thresholds: An Enquiry into the Concept of Liminality in Text Studies*. Studies in Liminality and Literature 1 (Madrid: The Gateway Press).
Alexander, Bobby C., 1991. *Victor Turner Revisited: Ritual as Social Change* (Atlanta: Scholars Press).
Álvarez, Imeldo, 1980. *La novela cubana en el siglo XX* (Havana: Letras Cubanas).
Álvarez Borland, Isabel, 1998. *Cuban-American Literature of Exile: From Person to Persona* (Charlottesville: University Press of Virginia).
Anderson, Benedict, 1983. *Imagined Communities: Reflections on the Origins and Spread of Nationalism* (London: Verso).
Anderson, Thomas F., 2006. *Everything in Its Place: The Life and Works of Virgilio Piñera* (Lewisburg, PA: Bucknell University Press).
Arcos, Jorge Luis et al. (eds), 2008. *Historia de la literatura cubana. Tomo III: La Revolución (con un apéndice sobre la literatura de los años noventa)* (Havana: Letras Cubanas).
Arendt, Hannah, 1958. *The Human Condition* (Chicago: The University of Chicago Press).
Ashley, Kathleen M. (ed.), 1990. *Victor Turner and the Construction of Cultural Criticism: Between Literature and Anthropology* (Bloomington: Indiana University Press).
Averhoff Purón, Mario, 1972. '1923: Un año decisivo en las luchas del pueblo cubano', *Bohemia* (29 Dec.), 96–105.
Beaupied, Aída, 2010. *Libertad en cadenas: Sacrificio, aporías y perdón en las letras cubanas* (New York: Peter Lang).
Bejel, Emilio, 1990. *José Lezama Lima, Poet of the Image* (Gainesville: University of Florida Press).
——, 2001. *Gay Cuban Nation* (Chicago: The University of Chicago Press).
Benítez Rojo, Antonio, 1989. *La isla que se repite: El Caribe y la perspectiva posmoderna* (Hanover, NH: Ediciones del Norte).
Bentley, Eric, 1969. *The Cult of the Superman: A Study of the Idea of Heroism in Carlyle and Nietzsche, with Notes on other Hero-Worshippers of Modern Times* (Gloucester, MA: Peter Smith).
Berman, Marshall, 1983. *All that is Solid Melts into Air: The Experience of Modernity* (London: Verso).
Bhabha, Homi K. (ed.), 1990. *Nation and Narration* (London: Routledge).
——, 1994. *The Location of Culture* (London: Routledge).
——, 2010. *The Location of Culture*. Routledge Classics 55 (London: Routledge).
Bruster, Douglas & Robert Weimann, 2004. *Prologues to Shakespeare's Theatre: Performance and Liminality in Early Modern Drama* (London: Routledge).
Bueno, Salvador, 1953. *Antología del Cuento en Cuba, 1902–1952* (Havana: Dirección de Cultura del Ministerio de Educación).

Caballero, Manuel, 1986. *Latin America and the Comintern 1919–1943* (Cambridge: Cambridge University Press).

Cairo, Ana, 1993. *La Revolución del 30 en la narrativa y el testimonio cubanos* (Havana: Letras Cubanas).

Calderón, Damaris, 1994. 'Virgilio Piñera: antecedentes para una poética de los ochenta', *La Revista de Vigía* 5(2): 97–110.

Campuzano, Luisa, 1988. *Quirón, o del ensayo y otros eventos* (Havana: Letras Cubanas).

——, 2004. *Las muchachas de La Habana no tienen temor de Dios ... . Escritoras cubanas (S. XVII–XXI)* (Havana: Unión).

Camus, Albert, 1984. *Selected Essays and Notebooks*, ed. & trans. Philip Thody (Harmondsworth: Penguin).

——, 2000. *The Myth of Sisyphus*, trans. Justin O'Brien (London: Penguin).

Capellán de Miguel, Gonzalo, 2006. *La España armónica: El proyecto del krausismo español para una sociedad en conflicto* (Madrid: Biblioteca Nueva).

Carbonell, Walterio, 1961. *Cómo surgió la cultural nacional* (Repr., Havana: Biblioteca Nacional José Martí, 2005).

Carbonell Cortina, Néstor, 1974. *El espíritu de la Constitución cubana de 1940* (Madrid: Playor).

Casal, Lourdes, 1971. *El caso Padilla: Literatura y revolución en Cuba – Documentos* (Miami: Ediciones Universal and Nueva Atlántida).

Certeau, Michel de, 1984. *The Practice of Everyday Life*, trans. Steven Rendall (Berkeley: University of California Press).

Concise Oxford English Dictionary, Eleventh Edition, 2004, ed. Catherine Soanes & Angus Stevenson (Oxford: Oxford University Press).

Cowell F. R., 1973. *Cicero and the Roman Republic* (Harmondsworth: Penguin).

Davies, Catherine, 1997. *A Place in the Sun? Women Writers in Twentieth-Century Cuba* (London: Zed Books).

Davison, Graeme, 1995. *Australia: The First Postmodern Republic?*. Working Papers in Australian Studies 103 (London: Sir Robert Menzies Centre for Australian Studies, Institute of Commonwealth Studies, University of London).

De Man, Paul, 1996. *Aesthetic Ideology*, ed. with intro. by Andrzej Warminski. Theory and History of Literature 65 (Minneapolis: University of Minnesota Press).

——, 1996. *En torno al casticismo*, (Madrid: Biblioteca Nueva).

Dening, Greg, 1997. 'Introduction: In Search of a Metaphor'. In Ronald Hoffman, Mechal Sobel & Frederika J. Teute (eds), *Through a Glass Darkly: Reflections on Personal Identity in Early America* (Chapel Hill: University of North Carolina Press), 1–8.

——, 1998. *Readings/Writings* (Melbourne: Melbourne University Press).

——, 2004. *Beach Crossings: Voyaging Across Times, Cultures, and Self* (Philadelphia: University of Pennsylvania Press).

Derrida, Jacques, 1978. *Writing and Difference*, trans. Alan Bass (London: Routledge).

——, 1995. *On the Name*, ed. Thomas Dutiot, trans. David Wood, John P. Leavey Jr. & Ian McLeod (Stanford, CA: Stanford University Press).

Díaz, Duanel, 2007. 'El fantasma de Sartre en Cuba', *Cuadernos Hispanoamericanos* 679: 93–102

Díaz Acosta, Norma, 2001. *Universidad del Aire (conferencias y cursos)* (Havana: Editorial de Ciencias Sociales).

Domínguez, Jorge I., 1978. *Cuba: Order and Revolution* (Cambridge, MA: The Belknap Press).

———, 2007. *Cuba hoy: Analizando su pasado, imaginando su futuro* (Madrid: Colibrí).

Donald, James (ed.), 1991. *Psychoanalysis and Cultural Theory: Thresholds* (Basingstoke: Macmillan).

Dubow, Jessica, 2000. ' "From a View on the World to a Point of View in it": Rethinking Sight, Space and the Colonial Subject', *Interventions: International Journal of Postcolonial Studies* 2(1): 87–102.

———, 2004. 'The Mobility of Thought: Reflections on Blanchot and Benjamin', *Interventions: International Journal of Postcolonial Studies* 6(2): 216–28.

Enright, D. J., 1988. *The Alluring Problem: An Essay on Irony* (Oxford: Oxford University Press).

Espinosa, Carlos, 2003. *Virgilio Piñera en Persona* (Havana: Unión).

Fanon, Frantz, 1986. *Black Skin White Masks* (London: Pluto Press).

Fernández Valledor, Roberto, 1993. *Identidad nacional y sociedad en la ensayística cubana y puertorriqueña (1920–1940) (Mañach, Marinello, Pedreira y Blanco)* (Santo Domingo: Centro de Estudios Avanzados de Puerto Rico y el Caribe).

Fitzgerald, Frank T., 1994. *The Cuban Revolution in Crisis: From Managing Socialism to Managing Survival* (New York: Monthly Review Press).

Font, Mauricio A., Alfonso W. Quiroz, 205. *Cuban Counterpoints: The Legacy of Fernando Ortiz* (Oxford: Lexington Books).

Fornet, Ambrosio, 1967. *En blanco y negro* (Havana: Instituto del Libro).

———, 1970. *Cuentos de la revolución cubana* (Santiago de Chile: Editorial Universitaria).

Foucault, Michel, 1970. *The Order of Things: An Archaeology of the Human Sciences* (Repr., London: Routledge [Routledge Classics 82], 2002).

———, 1972. *Archaeology of Knowledge*, trans. A. M. Sheridan Smith (Repr., London: Routledge [Routledge Classics 3], 2002).

———, 1988. *Technologies of the Self: A Seminar with Michel Foucault*, ed. Luther H. Martin et al. (Amherst: University of Massachusetts Press).

Fowler Calzada, Victor, 1994. 'Mientras Leo a Virgilio', *La Revista de Vigía* 5(1): 91–105.

Freud, Sigmund, 2003. *The Uncanny*, trans. David McLintock (London: Penguin).

Fuente, Alejandro de la, 2001. *A Nation for All: Race, Inequality and Politics in Twentieth-Century Cuba* (Chapel Hill: The University of North Carolina Press).

García-Carranza, Araceli, 1970. *Bio-bibliografía de don Fernando Ortiz* (Havana: Biblioteca Nacional José Martí).

García Vega, Lorenzo, 1960. *Antología de la novela cubana* (Havana: Dirección General de Cultura, Ministerio de Educación).

Geertz, Clifford, 1983. *Local Knowledge: Further Essays in Interpretive Anthropology* (London: Fontana Press).

Giles, Paul, 2000. 'From Transgression to Liminality: The Thresholds of Washington Irving'. In Isabel Soto (ed.), *A Place that is not a Place: Essays in Liminality and Text*. Studies in Liminality and Literature 2 (Madrid: The Gateway Press), 31–46.

———, 2006. *Atlantic Republic: The American Tradition in English Literature* (Oxford: Oxford University Press).

Glicksberg, Charles I., 1969. *The Ironic Vision in Modern Literature* (The Hague: Matinus Nijhoff).

Gott, Richard, 2004. *Cuba: A New History* (New Haven, CT: Yale University Press)

Guerra y Sánchez, Ramiro, 1944. *Azúcar y población en las Antillas* (Havana: Cultural – Colección de Libros Cubanos).

Guiteras, Pedro José, 1927. *Historia de la Isla de Cuba, segunda edición, tomo I* (Havana: Cultural – Colección de Libros Cubanos).

Habermas, Jürgen, 1991. *Communication and the Evolution of Society*, trans. Thomas McCarthy (Cambridge: Polity Press).

Harris, Roy, 1980. *The Language-Makers* (London: Duckworth).

Harrison, Stephan, Steve Pile & Nigel Thrift (eds), 2004. *Patterned Ground: Entanglements of Nature and Culture* (London: Reaktion Books).

Howard, Dick, 1977. *The Marxian Legacy* (London: Macmillan).

Hulme, Peter, 2006. 'Travesías a Oriente: Cuba en la encrucijada' *Revista Casa de las Américas* 244, http://www.casa.cult.cu/publicaciones/revistacasa/244/hulmer.pdf.

Ibarra, Jorge, 1985. *Un análisis psicosocial del cubano: 1898–1925* (Havana: Editorial de Ciencias Sociales).

——, 1998. *Prologue to Revolution: Cuba, 1898–1958*, trans. Marjorie Moore (Boulder, CO: Lynne Rienner).

Irving, Washington, 1883. *The Sketch Book* (Edinburgh: William Paterson).

Jackson, Peter, 1989. *Maps of Meaning* (London: Unwin Hyman).

Jackson, Richard L. 1979. *Black Writers in Latin America* (Albuquerque: University of New Mexico Press).

Kapcia, Antoni, 2000. *Cuba Island of Dreams* (Oxford: Berg).

——, 2002. 'The Siege of the Hotel Nacional, Cuba, 1933: A Reassessment', *Journal of Latin American Studies* 34(2): 283–309.

——, 2005. *Havana: The Making of Cuban Culture* (Oxford: Berg).

——, 2008. *Cuba in Revolution: A History since the Fifties* (London: Reaktion Books).

Kenny, Anthony, 2006. *The Wittgenstein Reader* (Oxford: Blackwell).

Le Riverend, Julio, 1971. 'La revolución de 1933 y el nuevo giro histórico', *Bohemia* (23 July), 26–31.

——, 2001. *La República: Dependencia y revolución* (Havana: Editorial de Ciencias Sociales).

Lewis, Pericles, 2007. *The Cambridge Introduction to Modernism* (Cambridge: Cambridge University Press).

Lewis, R. W. B., 1965. *The American Adam: Innocence, Tragedy and Tradition in the Nineteenth Century* (Chicago: Phoenix Books).

Lightfoot, Claudia, 2002. *Havana: A Cultural and Literary Companion* (Oxford: Signal Books).

López, Alfredo J., 2014. *José Martí: A Revolutionary Life* (Austin: University of Texas Press).

Luis, William & Edmund Desnoes, 1982. 'America Revisited: An Interview with Edmundo Desnoes', *Latin American Literary Review 11(*21): 7–20.

Manzoni, Celina, 2001. *Un dilema cubano: Nacionalismo y vanguardia* (Havana: Fondo Editorial Casa de las Américas).

Masó, Calixto C., 1976. *Historia de Cuba (La lucha de un pueblo por cumplir su destino histórico y su vocación de libertad)*, ed. Leonel-Antonio de la Cuesta (Miami: Ediciones Universal).

Matos Arévalos, José A., 1995. 'Julio Antonio Mella. Glosando el pensamiento martiano (a manera de conclusion)', *Revista Cubana de Ciencias Sociales* 30: 83–7.

McManus, Jane, 2000. *Cuba's Island of Dreams: Voices from the Isle of Pines and Youth* (Gainesville: The University Press of Florida).

McQuade, Frank, 1993. 'Making Sense out of Non-Sense: Virgilio Piñera and the Short

Story of the Absurd'. In John Macklin (ed.), *After Cervantes: A Celebration of 75 Years of Iberian Studies at Leeds* (Leeds: Trinity and All Saints College), 203–22.

Miller, Nicola, 1999. *In the Shadow of the State: Intellectuals and the Quest for National Identity in Twentieth-Century Spanish America* (London: Verso).

——, 2003. 'The Absolution of History: Uses of the Past in Castro's Cuba', *Journal of Contemporary History* 38(1), 147–62.

Miranda, Olivia, 1995. 'Historia, Cultura y Revolución en José Martí', *Revista Cubana de Ciencias Sociales* 30: 61–9.

Molloy, Sylvia, 1991. *At Face Value: Autobiographical Writing in Spanish America* (Cambridge: Cambridge University Press).

Nandy, Ashis, 2009. *The Intimate Enemy: Loss and Recovery of Self under Colonialism* (Oxford: Oxford University Press).

Nietzsche, Friedrich, 1997. *Thus Spake Zarathustra*, with intro. by Nicholas Davey, trans. Thomas Common (Ware: Wordsworth Classics of World Literature).

——, 1998a. *Beyond Good and Evil: Prelude to a Philosophy of the Future*, ed. and trans. Marion Faber (Oxford: Oxford University Press).

——, 1998b. *Twilight of the Idols, or How to Philosophize with a Hammer*, trans. and with intro. by Duncan Large (Oxford: Oxford University Press).

Nuez, Iván de la, 1998. *La balsa perpetua: Soledad y conexiones de la cultura cubana* (Barcelona: Casiopea).

Ortega, Gregorio, 1989. *La coletilla: Una batalla por la libertad de expresión, 1959–62* (Havana: Editora Política).

Ortega y Gasset, José, 1925. *La deshumanización del arte. Ideas sobre la novela* (Madrid: Revista de Occidente).

The Oxford English Dictionary: Second Edition, 1989, prep. by J. A. Simpson and E. S. C. Weiner. Vol. 8: Interval–Looie (Oxford: Clarendon Press).

The Oxford Spanish Dictionary: Second edition, 2001, ed. Beatriz Galimberti Jarman & Roy Russell (Oxford: Oxford University Press).

Padrón Larrazábal, Roberto, 1975. *Manifiestos de Cuba* (Seville, Universidad de Sevilla).

Parkes, Graham, 1994. *Composing the Soul: Reaches of Nietzsche's Psychology* (Chicago: University of Chicago Press).

Pease, Donald E., 1987. *Visionary Compacts: American Renaissance Writings in Cultural Context* (Madison: The University of Wisconsin Press).

Pérez Jr, Louis, A., 1986. *Cuba under the Platt Amendment, 1902–1934* (Pittsburgh: University of Pittsburgh Press, 1986).

——, 1995. *Essays on Cuban History: Historiography and Research* (Gainesville: University Press of Florida).

——, 2001. *Winds of Change: Hurricanes and the Transformation of Nineteenth Century Cuba* (Chapel Hill: The University of North Carolina Press).

——, 2005. *To Die in Cuba: Suicide and Society* (Chapel Hill: The University of North Carolina Press).

——, 2006. *Cuba: Between Reform and Revolution* (Oxford: Oxford University Press).

Pérez Firmat, Gustavo, 1986. *Literature and Liminality: Festive Readings in the Hispanic Tradition* (Durham, NC: Duke University Press).

——, 1989. *The Cuban Condition: Translation and Identity in Modern Cuban Literature* (Cambridge: Cambridge University Press).

——, 1999. *My Own Private Cuba: Essays on Cuban Literature and Culture* (Boulder, CO: Society of Spanish and Spanish American Studies).

——, 2000a. *Cincuenta lecciones de exilio y desexilio* (Miami: Ediciones Universal).

——, 2000b. *Vidas en vilo: La cultura cubanoamericana* (Madrid: Editorial Colibrí).

Pérez Navarro, Lourdes, 2010. 'Destacan aportes de la Constitución del 40', *Granma* (10 Aug.), http://www.granma.cubaweb.cu/2010/10/08/nacional/artic05.html, accessed 31 Oct. 2010.

Pérez Sarduy, Pedro & Jean Stubbs, 1993. *Afrocuba: An Anthology of Cuban Writing on Race, Politics and Culture* (Melbourne: Ocean Press).

Pichardo, Esteban, 1985. *Diccionario provincial casi razonado de voces y frases cubanas* (Havana: Editorial de Ciencias Sociales).

Pogolotti, Marcelo, 1958. *La República de Cuba al través de sus escritores* (Havana: Editorial Lex).

Ponce de León, Miguel Ángel, n.d. '¿Paranoia?', *CubaNet News*, http://www.cubanet.org/CNews/y99/dec99/02a7.htm, accessed 12 Feb. 2008.

Ponte, Antonio José, 1993. *La Lengua de Virgilio* (Matanzas: Ediciones Vigía).

Potts, L. J., 1968. *Aristotle on the Art of Fiction* (Cambridge: Cambridge University Press).

Rama, Ángel, 1984. *La ciudad letrada*, with intro by Mario Vargas Llosa (Hanover, NH: Ediciones del Norte).

——, 1989. *Transculturación narrativa en América Latina* (Montevideo: Fundación Ángel Rama).

Reinstädler, Janett & Ottmar Ette (eds), 2000. *Todas las islas la isla: Nuevas y novísimas tendencias en la literatura y cultura de Cuba* (Madrid: Iberoamericana).

Ricoeur, Paul, 2007. *Evil: A Challenge to Philosophy and Theology*, trans. John Bowden (London: Continuum).

Rojas, Martha, 1966. *El juicio del Moncada* (Buenos Aires: Ambos Mundos).

Rojas, Rafael, 2006. *Tumbas sin sosiego: Revolución, disidencia y exilio del intelectual cubano* (Barcelona: Anagrama).

——, 2008a. *Essays in Cuban Intellectual History* (New York: Palgrave Macmillan).

——, 2008b. *Motivos de Anteo: Patria y nación en la historia intelectual de Cuba* (Madrid: Colibrí).

Rose, Mitch, 2006. 'Gathering 'Dreams of Presence': A Project for the Cultural Landscape', *Environment and Planning D: Society and Space* 24(4): 537–54.

—— & John Wylie, 2006. 'Guest Editorial: Animating Landscape', *Environment and Planning D: Society and Space* 24(4): 475–9.

Rosen, Lawrence, 1971. 'Language, History and the Logic of Inquiry in Lévi-Strauss and Sartre', *History and Theory* 10(3): 269–94.

Rowlandson, William, 2007. *Reading Lezama's Paradiso* (Oxford: Peter Lang).

Santí, Enrico Mario, 1981. 'The Novel from Under', *Cuban Studies* 2(1): 49–64.

——, 2002. *Bienes del siglo: Sobre cultura cubana* (Mexico D.F.: Fondo de Cultura Económica).

Sartre, Jean-Paul, 1960. *Sartre visita a Cuba: Ideología y revolución; Una entrevista con los escritores cubanos; Huracán sobre el azúcar* (Havana: Ediciones R).

——, 1988. *'What is Literature?', and other Essays*, with intro. by Steven Ungar (Cambridge, MA: Harvard University Press).

——, 2001. *Colonialism and Neocolonialism*, trans. Azzedine Haddour, Steve Brewer & Terry McWilliams (London: Routledge).

Schopenhauer, Arthur, 1958. *The World as Will and Representation*, trans. E. F. J. Payne (Repr., New York: Dover, 1969).

Schwartz, Jorge, 1991. *Las vanguardias latinoamericanas: Textos programáticos y críticos* (Madrid: Cátedra).

Schwartz-Salant, Nathan & Murray Stein (eds), 1991. *Liminality and Transitional Phenomena* (Wilmette, IL: Chiron Publications).

Serra, Ana, 2007. *The 'New Man' in Cuba: Culture and Identity in the Revolution* (Gainesville: University Press of Florida).

Solé, Carlos A & Maria Isabel Abreu (eds), 1989. *Latin American Writers*, vol. 3 (New York: Charles Scribner's Sons).

Soto, Lionel, 1977. *La Revolución del 33* (Havana: Editorial de Ciencias Sociales).

Souza, Raymond D., 1976. *Major Cuban Novelists: Innovation and Tradition* (Columbia: University of Missouri Press).

Spivak, Gayatri Chakravorty, 1999. *A Critique of Postcolonial Reason: Toward a History of the Vanishing Present* (Cambridge, MA: Harvard University Press).

Stewart, Kathleen, 1996. *A Space on the Side of the Road: Cultural Politics in an 'Other' America* (Princeton, NJ: Princeton University Press).

Suárez, Norma, 1996. *Fernando Ortiz y la cubanidad* (Havana: Ediciones Unión).

Suárez Díaz, Ana, 2004. *Cada tiempo trae una faena ... Selección de correspondencia de Juan Marinello Vidaurreta, 1923–1940*, vol. 1 (Havana: Editorial José Martí).

Sutton, Philip C., 2002. *Betwixt-and-Between: Essays in Liminal Geography*. Studies in Liminality and Literature 3 (Madrid: The Gateway Press).

Tabares del Real, José A., 1975. *La Revolución del 30: Sus dos últimos años* (Havana: Ciencias Sociales).

Terán, Óscar, 1983. *América Latina: Positivismo y nación* (Mexico D.F.: Katún).

Thomas, Hugh, 1971. *Cuba: The Pursuit of Freedom* (New York: Harper & Row).

——, 2001. *Cuba: The Pursuit of Freedom* (London: Picador).

Thrift, Nigel, 2008. 'Performance and Performativity: A Geography of Unknown Lands'. In James Duncan, Nuala C. Johnson & Richard H. Schein (eds), *A Companion to Cultural Geography* (Oxford: Blackwell).

Tilley, Christopher, 1994. *A Phenomenology of Landscape: Places, Paths and Monuments* (Oxford: Berg).

Todorov, Tzvetan, 2003. *Hope and Memory: Lessons from the Twentieth Century*, trans. David Bellos (London: Atlantic Books).

Torre, Amalia V. de la, 1978. *Jorge Mañach: Maestro del ensayo* (Miami: Ediciones Universal).

Torres, Carmen L, 1989. *La cuentística de Virgilio Piñera: Estrategias humorísticas* (Madrid: Pliegos).

Torres-Cuevas, Eduardo (ed.), 2005. *Sartre–Cuba–Sartre: Huracán, surco, semillas* (Havana: Imágen Contemporánea).

Trotsky, Leon, 1991. *Literature and Revolution*, trans. Rose Strunsky (London: RedWords).

Turner, Victor, 1957. *Schism and Continuity in an African Society: A Study of Ndembu Village Life* (Repr., Oxford: Berg, 1996).

——, 1962. 'Three Symbols of *Passage* in Ndembu Circumcision Ritual: An Interpretation'. In Daryll Forde (ed.), *Essays on the Ritual of Social Relations* (Manchester: Manchester University Press), 124–73.

——, 1969. *The Ritual Process: Structure and Anti-Structure* (London: Routledge & Kegan Paul).

——, 1970. *The Forest of Symbols: Aspects of Ndembu Ritual* (Ithaca, NY: Cornell University Press).

——, 1974. *Dramas, Fields and Metaphors: Symbolic Action in Human Society* (Ithaca, NY: Cornell University Press).

——, 1978. *Image and Pilgrimage in Christian Culture: Anthropological Perspectives* (New York: Columbia University Press).

——, 1982. *From Ritual to Theatre: The Human Seriousness of Play* (New York: Performing Arts Journal Publications).

—— & Edith Turner, 1978. *Image and Pilgrimage in Christian Culture: Anthropological Perspectives* (Oxford: Blackwell).

Unamuno, Miguel de, 1931. *Del sentimiento trágico de la vida* (Madrid: Renacimiento).

Van Gennep, Arnold, 1965. *The Rites of Passage*, trans. Monika B. Vizedom & Gabrielle L. Caffee (London: Routledge).

Viljoen, Hein & Chris N. van der Merwe (eds), 2007. *Beyond the Threshold: Explorations of Liminality in Literature* (New York: Lang).

West, Adam, 1994. 'Virgilio Piñera: Ética de redención en el fracaso', *La Revista de Vigía* 5(2): 111–19.

Williams, Colin H., 1988. *Language in Geographic Context* (Clevedon, PA: Multilingual Matters).

Williams, Raymond, 1976. *Keywords: A Vocabulary of Culture and Society* (London: Fontana/Croon Helm).

Wittgenstein, Ludwig, 1955. *Tractatus Logico-Philosophicus* (London: Routledge & Kegan Paul).

Wood, David, 1991. *On Paul Ricoeur: Narrative and Interpretation* (London: Routledge).

Wright, Ann, 1988. 'Intellectuals of an Unheroic Period of Cuban History, 1913–1923. The "Cuba Contemporánea" Group', *Bulletin of Latin American Research* 7(1): 109–22.

Wylie, John, 2007. *Landscape* (London, Routledge).

Young, Robert J. C., 2001. *Postcolonialism: An Historical Introduction* (Oxford: Blackwell).

——, 2003. *Post-Colonialism: A Very Short Introduction* (Oxford: Oxford University Press).

——, 2004. *White Mythologies: Writing History and the West* (London: Routledge).

Index